# THE COMPULSION TO CREATE

## A Psychoanalytic Study of Women Artists

# THE COMPULSION TO CREATE

## A Psychoanalytic Study of Women Artists

### SUSAN KAVALER-ADLER

**Foreword by Joyce McDougall**

ROUTLEDGE ❀ NEW YORK AND LONDON

Published in 1993 by

Routledge
29 West 35th Street
New York, NY 10001-2299

Published in Great Britain by

Routledge
11 New Fetter Lane
London EC4P 4EE

**Library of Congress Cataloging-in-Publication Data**

Kavaler-Adler, Susan.
    The compulsion to create : a psychoanalytic study of women artists
  / by Susan Kavaler-Adler
        p.   cm.
    Includes bibliographical references and index.
    ISBN 0-415-90710-1 (hb) — ISBN 0-415-90711-X (pb)
    1. Women authors—Mental health.   2. Women authors—Psychology.
  3. Creation (Literary, artistic, etc.)—Psychological aspects.
  I. Title.
  RC451.4.A96K38   1993
  153.3'5'082—dc20                                                    92-41916
                                                                        CIP

**British Library Cataloguing-in-Publication Data also available.**

*To my father, Solomon, who loved me, who cherished me, and who enabled my creativity to flourish. I'm sorry you died before your time, and when I was so young.*

*To my husband, Saul, who endured the long hours of my solitary work, and never ceased to support me.*

*To my friends and students, who kept the spirit of my work alive during my darkest hours.*

*To my analyst, Dr. Mark Grunes, who guided my spirit through its many stages of metamorphosis.*

*To my mother, who introduced me to art and dance classes.*

# Contents

Foreword                                                                    ix

Acknowledgments                                                             xi

1  Compulsion versus Reparation                                             1

2  From Mother to Father                                                    24

3  Mourning and Creative-Process Reparation                               40

4  Creative Women and the Internal Father                                 59

5  The Demon Lover Theme as Literary Myth and
   Psychodynamic Complex                                                   76

6  Portraits of Two Kinds of Creative Women                               88

7  Charlotte Brontë: Biography and *Jane Eyre*                           105

8  *Villette*                                                             121

9  Emily Brontë I: The Messenger of Hope and the
   Demon in the Nightwind                                                 154

10  Emily Brontë II: *Wuthering Heights* and the Demon Lover             168

11  Emily Dickinson: Muse and Demon                                       192

12  Emily Dickinson's Breakdown: Renunciation and Reparation             221

13  Edith Sitwell I: The Demon Lover, Poetry, and Writer's Block         249

14  Edith Sitwell II: The Aging Narcissist                               269

15  The Turn to Psychoanalytic Psychotherapy                             299

Notes                                                                     327

References                                                                339

Index                                                                     347

# Foreword

The creative self, the powerful urge to create, and the conditions which promote or inhibit this potential richness of the human spirit, are mong the many penetrating questions with which Susan Kavaler-Adler challenges the reader.

Through her eyes, six celebrated women writers: Sylvia Plath, Anaïs Nin, Charlotte and Emily Brontë, Emily Dickinson, and Edith Sitwell, come to life in a startlingly new way. Through these psychobiographies, the author enables us to follow the dynamic forces and the early psychic traumas, which illuminate the mysteries of the creative process.

Susan Kavaler-Adler's enriching insight reveals to us each artist's psychic universe, as well as the significant objects who inhabit it. "The demon-lover father," the idealized male muse, the psychically dead split-off images of unmourned parents, throng their internal worlds.

These fascinating voyages into the creative unconscious are not only tellingly narrated, but also grounded on the theoretical heritage of Freud, Klein, Guntrip, Fairbairn and Winnicott, to mention only a few of this author's sources of inspiration.

Susan Kavaler-Adler's research will stir the imagination of many an analyst, as well as all those who are possessed, at whatever cost, by "The Compulsion to Create."

*Joyce McDougall, D.Ed.*

# Acknowledgments

My gratitude extends to many people, and it is difficult to do justice to all those who helped. In needing to be brief, I hope those to whom I owe much gratitude will understand the depth of gratitude that extends beyond the echo and paucity of words.

I want to thank Art Baur for his careful reading and commentary on parts of my text. His knowledge, concern, and enthusiasm have been extremely supportive in sustaining my creative process. In the same vein, I want to thank Sheila Ronson, Dr. Roberta Schecter, Patricia Slatt, Audrey Ashendorf, Sandra Indig, Dr. Judy Moskowitz, Dr. Connie Levine-Schneidman, Thomas Cutrone, and Dr. Henry Kellerman. They all commented on aspects of the text for *The Compulsion to Create*. I want to thank Dr. Roberta Schechter for referring me to Marilyn Miller, who has helped me with some critical editing and shaping of parts of the book. I want to thank Marilyn Miller; her sensitivity as an editor is rare and is most appreciated. I also want to thank Dr. Olga Marlin, who not only commented on parts of the text, but who deeply responded to its primary premises, and who made a major contribution to my thinking in the chapter on "The Creative Woman and the Internal Father."

I also would like to thank the members of a the long-term weekly writing group, which I conduct, who have been with me in spirit throughout: Dr. Sarah Slagle, Dr. Maria Bastos, Susan McConnaughy, Karen D'Amore, and Dr. Olga Marlin.

Thank you to Dr. Paul Olsen, who introduced me to the work and life of Edith Sitwell, and who encouraged me to follow my own inspiration. Thank you to Dr. Hy Lowenheim, who made a significant contribution to my theoretical premises. Thank you to Drs. Richard and Joan Zuckerberg, who invited my presentation of my theories and studies to the Brooklyn Institute for Psychotherapy and Psychoanalysis. Thank you to Art Baur who invited my presentations at the National Institute for the Psychotherapies. Thank you to Dr. Robert Weinstein, my co-director and co-founder of the Object Relations Institute for Psychotherapy and Psychoanalysis (ORI), who has invited my presentations at our institute, and who has shared his support and enthusiasm for my work and for my ideas. Thank you to Louise De Costa, the education chairperson at ORI, who has responded deeply to later writing that is related to the themes in this work.

A special thanks to Dr. Jeffrey Seinfeld, who read, digested, and succinctly critiqued this book for Routledge Press, offering his deep appreciation of the book in highly astute theoretical terms.

In addition, I would like to thank Maureen MacGrogan at Routledge Press, who as the editor of my book has been a pleasure to work with. I would also like to thank the other Routledge staff who have been so helpful in the publishing process.

# 1

# Compulsion versus Reparation

'Tis so appalling—it exhilarates—
So over Horror, it half Captivates—
The Soul stares after it, secure—
A Sepulchre, fears first no more
To scan a Ghost, is faint—
But grappling, conquers it—

—Emily Dickinson (no. 281)

Is creativity a form of compulsive madness, driving artists by an urgent need for contact with their dark, demonic, and usually unconscious selves, or is it an effort to expel or exorcise inner ghosts? Is it perhaps a way of making friends with these ghosts, snakes, and other threatening demons? Although an essential part of the creative process involves the beauty and power of the free use of imagination, I believe that many artists simultaneously use the process to repair defects within the self and its inner world of object relations. Can creativity promote psychic self-help, even health? If it does, why do some artists appear to succeed in healing themselves, whereas others who are often equally gifted fail?

This study focuses on several distinguished creative women from a psychoanalytic object relations perspective. My interest is to examine how the creative process can or cannot be used to bring about self-reparation and/or developmental growth in terms of self-integration and self-differentiation. To explore this, I ask a number of related questions. Is the creative process freely motivated and interactive with interpersonal live? Or is it a closed system of compulsive repetition that may allow cathartic relief and even symbolic forms of emotional expression but that nevertheless defensively wards off interpersonal life? How may the power of the "creative urge" help people, especially women, achieve healthy states of psychological integration? What developmental factors prevent this from occurring? Can the creative process become captive to a pathological mourning state, with its compulsive and addictive dynamics, leading necessarily to self-

1

deterioration rather than self-development? Alternatively, can the creative endeavor promote a developmental mourning process that encourages self-development? The nature of developmental mourning and pathological mourning will be defined throughout the inquiry.

I will study women writers in particular. I choose writers rather than artists who work in other media for a simple reason: the writer's creative world is most directly accessible to us because words are a more conceptual medium than color, form, sound, or even moving images. Why have I decided to exclusively examine women writers in depth? First, relatively little has been written to shed light on the psychological dynamics of the creative process in women, in contrast to the volumes devoted to examining this issue in male authors such as D. H. Lawrence, Henry James, John Keats, George Bernard Shaw, Ernest Hemingway, and F. Scott Fitzgerald. Second, women artists present a special case. For they share, I believe, a unique element that distinguishes them from male artists: each has an internal father who is a motivational force in her creativity and creative compulsion. (Men may have a corresponding relationship with internal mothers who are oedipal objects as father figures are for women.) Third, the study of female artists allows us to ask another question that is increasingly relevant to many women today who have greater options than their ancestors: when women are not inhibited by domestic responsibility, might the compulsive urge to create be even stronger in them than in men? Also, what role does the father-daughter relationship and its incorporation within the adult female play in such compulsive creative strivings?

Examining the compulsive aspects of the creative process sharpens my focus on the significance of internalized father-daughter relationships. I hypothesize that in cases of developmental arrest, the internal father remains as a foreign object unassimilated into the respective self-structures of these women artists. The presumed split-off, malignant nature of this internal father is examined here in the creative context of its being split off from these women's loving feelings and healthy internalization of good-objects. Throughout, I call this split-off internal object the "demon lover," because it is largely colored by the father's personality. When a whole personality, as a consequence of developmental arrest, is dominated by internal fixation on the paternally colored bad object, I refer to this syndrome as the "demon lover complex." It is one particular form that a pathological mourning state may manifest, the pathological mourning state involving an addiction to a bad object based on split off primitive aggression.

In selecting writers to study in depth, I looked for women whose published work, combined with biographical and critical studies about them, offered enough data for me to probe how they employed the creative process for both defensive and developmental purposes. I also wanted to focus on artists of indisputable quality. Moreover, I felt that the women selected needed to represent various levels of psychological functioning. Books by psychoanalysts that have examined women writers by concentrating on a single subject, such as two recent biographies of Virginia Woolf by Alma Bond and Shirley Panken, have been unable to explore the differences among women artists at various developmental levels. Therefore, they cannot show how these levels may be significant in determining the degree to which creativity is dominated by pathological compulsion more than by a healthy movement toward individuation. Nor can these biographies possibly address what level of psychological development is required for creative work to have value as a reparative, healing process and a developmental-growth process, rather than just as an avenue for catharsis or for self-expression that promises only a momentary hope of connection through communication. They also cannot speculate about what happens when developmental goals have not been reached. In viewing the lives of the writers in the present books, we can see that the failure of self-repair in developmentally arrested women may have tragic personal consequences, including lifelong seclusion, continuing alienation from others, fatal illness, and suicide.

From studying these women, as well as on the basis of my own clinical practice, I believe that many creative individuals need to combine psychotherapy with the creative process to free themselves from the high probability of remaining helplessly trapped in isolated lives. In relation to such a dilemma, I speak of the "compulsion to create" as an addiction to an internal object that constitutes a pathological mourning state, in which a complex of psychologically arresting defenses and urges toward resolution of developmental mourning combine. Developmental mourning involves the capacity to process grief affects and the symbols of the object relations being grieved. Old internal world constellations of self and object relations are transformed into more differentiated and more integrated forms for higher level development. Such mourning is disrupted in pathological mourning states, where too much archaic aggression predominates, preventing integrating processes from taking place, so that internal objects cannot be modified into "good-enough" forms. The integration of the psyche through the integration of self and object internalizations requires the capacity to feel yearnings for love objects in terms of the grief affects of loving sadness. When such developmental mourning is disrupted by primitive reactions and defenses related to early trauma, the split off psychic resonance of such trauma can manifest as a compulsion towards reenactment that is revealed in the content and process of creative work. This is the "compulsion to create." This volume is a study of such a compulsion as it reveals itself in the life and work of women writers.

The well-known women authors described in this book are not alive. They have never occupied my couch, unlike the woman artist described in the closing clinical case. To study them I have used a psychobiographical approach, which I believe is essential to any substantive discussion of women who have lived in the past and whose work survives and continues to represent their lives and emotions. Such a method permits me the latitude to study not only their creative work but their entire life histories. Since Freud published his *Papers on Metapsychology* (1915–1917),[1] the inner representational world has become a lively topic of interest in psychoanalytic theory, providing the psychobiographic method with a powerful *raison d' être* for uncovering primary inner-world dialogues that might otherwise remain unexplored. Among these papers is "Mourning and Melancholia" (1917), which has been Freud's rich resource for formulations about object relations thinking and about the dynamic presence of internal objects. Having reformulated Freud's ideas about this inner representational world, object relations theorists have long emphasized its significance. Those who express these inner-world dialogues primarily through the creative process can be studied best by the psychobiographic approach since the particular creative process becomes most accessible through the context of biography. Moreover, for anyone interested in the reparative effects of the creative process, these dialogues constitute the common denominator in creative individuals who have not undergone a psychotherapeutic treatment.

## The Psychological Use of the Creative Process

When we inquire about the psychological use of the creative process, developmental issues need to be addressed. My object relations view—of child-other internalization and mourning integration—captures the essence of what we mean by "process" in creativity and in psychological life, for each evolves developmentally.

Mourning integration refers to the integration of part objects, (which can be visceral and sensory) into whole object forms, so that cognitive representations of the objects can be achieved within the internal world. Whole objects include good and bad aspects of internal object relations, with the loving affect ties to the good aspects of the objects providing sufficient containment of the internal objects for them to be fully comprehended in representational form as benign objects. When internal objects are too imbued with hostile aggression, due to critical developmental disruptions, the objects remain persecutory dynamic presences within the psyche, or "bad objects" (see Fairbairn, 1952). Then assimilation and integration of the self does not take place, since such integration requires a predominance of good object connections and of loving capacity within the self. The self splits off its experience to avoid awareness of traumatic engagements with bad objects, rather than integrating itself through the loving grief affects in developmental mourning. Developmental mourning, in contrast, allows for the gradual relinquishing of old object ties to promote progressive psychic change, and then new identification and attachments can take place. Bad aspects of the object can be relinquished in this process as well as regressive ties that inhibit development.

Before considering the developmental perspective, however, we must also look at common assumptions about creativity as a process that may distort its true nature. Only in this way can we understand the subjective motivations of women who write out of desperate desires for psychic salvation.

Consciously or unconsciously, artists pursue not only aesthetic but psychological goals. Although many psychologists and artists have alluded to the reparative potential of the creative process, a lack of understanding of the developmental criteria related to successful psychological reparation has encouraged a "creative mystique"—a belief in an image of the creative process in which the mere pursuit of creative self-expression has often been thought to be endowed with all kinds of healing powers. Such thinking can border on magical wish fulfillment.

In *The Neurotic Distortion of the Creative Process* (1958), Lawrence Kubie challenges this common and culturally reinforced idealization of the creative process, viewing it instead as a product of neurosis. The damaging effect on culture that such a defensive idealization can promote is disturbing, especially because belief in the curative nature of the creative process can cause artists, among others, to hide from their own pathology and thus perpetuate destructive patterns of living and working. An artist's notion that creativity will prosper through his or her pathology and will transform it can create a huge gap between that artist's creative potential and creative fulfillment, Kubie suggests. He believes, as I do, that both the life and the work of the artist are severely jeopardized by the singular perception that he or she will discover and use wisdom exclusively through a preoccupation with creative self-expression.

To correct this situation, Kubie has called for a study of the psychological underpinnings of the creative process and of those who use it. My own strong reactions to personal, clinical, and psychobiographical engagements with the creative process have led me to take up Kubie's challenge. But I do so with an eye toward the internal structure of self-development, which I believe extends beyond a relatively basic polarity between pathology and health. Therefore, I examine the borderline character pathology that Kubie overlooks. For it is within the peculiar nature of this pathology that we find that creativity can, for periods of time, prosper while everyday interpersonal life in the world dissipates. Such a phenomenon—which Kubie does not address because of his primary focus on neurotics (although he does mention schizophrenics)—has in itself perhaps helped nurture the myth of a ubiquitous creative cure.

## Self Psychology versus Object Relations Theory

Often it is artists themselves who ascribe to their creativity unlimited curative powers. As they strive to merge with an idealized internal object through creative work,[2] an illusion of cure may be promoted. Certain psychoanalytic theorists have followed artists in their optimistic belief in self-cure. For example, Heinz Kohut (1977; 1978), the founder of the American School of Psychoanalytic Self Psychology, has proposed that the creative process has healing powers extending beyond mere defensive compensation or temporary reparative effects.

In "Creativeness, Charisma, Group Psychology" (1978, vol. 2, 1793–844) and in *Restoration of the Self* (1977), Kohut asserts that creative work can serve psychic functions that he attributes in other instances to analysts, parents, friends, lovers, and so forth. Moreover, in discussing case examples, such as those of Mr. M. and Mr. E. (*Search for the Self,* 1978, 810–14), he claims that creative work can become the heir to the interpersonal "holding environment"[3] within psychoanalytic treatment (Kohut 1971; 1977). Such work can even substitute for interpersonal relations. Kohut does not differentiate the developmental level of object relations before and after treatment that is required for this transition from analyst to creative process to occur. Nor does he differentiate the internal object relations of creators who are able to successfully engage with the creative process therapeutically from those who are not. Instead, he speaks of cycles of hunger and satiation for creative activity ("Creativeness, Charisma, Group Psychology," 1978) that impress me as being addictive because of character pathology. Yet he does not define the developmental levels of such addicted creators according to object relations criteria. In the absence of such object relations discriminations, Kohut seems to attribute enormous reparative powers to creativity, while simultaneously (although, it would seem, unwittingly) depicting it as pathological in its vicious—and thus compulsive—mode of motivation (1978, 816). Such a contradiction can become evident only if the developmental levels of the object relations within the creative work and within the artist's life are sometimes revealed. Kohut fails to do so. By using the ambiguous term "selfobject," Kohut globally defines all levels of object relations as a primitive form of interpersonal relations, in which one person is used as an extension of the "other." The person who serves as a self object for another provides psychic functions for the other that the latter cannot provide for himself, such as soothing and mirroring (reflecting back a confirming view of the self). Providing such functions may be appropriate when the other has failed to internalize them during infancy. However, Kohut uses the word "selfobject" for the analyst and/or for the mother even when the other (patient or child) has internalized self-nurturing and narcissistically enhancing functions. He also employs the term "selfobject" to designate the functional role of the creative process. By applying his own terminology, Kohut fails to distinguish different levels of interpersonal relations and their corresponding internal object relations. He speaks of a "selfobject" as offering mirroring reflections of the other's self, "empathic understanding," and models of behavior for identification and idealization. He then employs the same term to describe the role of the creative work or the creative process of the artist.

Kohut's follower Kligerman (1980) trudges behind him through this linguistic bypass of developmental object relations issues. Like Kohut, he refers to creative work as well as its creative process as a "selfobject." Yet Kligerman appears to assign a meaning to this term, in relation to the psychological use of the creative process, that is different from that of Kohut. An artist's sense of self, Kligerman believes, can be repaired by using creative work to represent the self. This artistic representative of the self can receive applause and admiration in the form of "mirroring" from the world at large. Kligerman's conceptualization totally disregards that such narcissistic mirroring, in which a quality or product of the self is admired by others so that the artist may experience a narcissistic "glow," merely constitutes a defensive compensation for those impaired in early self-development. If preoedipal trauma has caused arrest of the primary and authentic self, the mirroring that results from talents and creative products can never heal or repair it.

Is such narcissistic mirroring what Kohut is implying when he speaks of mirroring reflections of the self? This is never clarified. In contrast, D. W. Winnicott's original use of the term "mirroring" in the essay "Mirror-Role of Mother and Family in Child Development" (1967 paper in 1971 collection) suggests that the mirroring reflection of the mother refers to her reflecting back the real self of the child in all of his or her aspects. The mother's mirroring must therefore involve her embodied and emotionally responsive awareness of the whole child, not merely her response to a particular talent that might flatter her own self-image. Perhaps Kohut's unclear use of the term mirroring reflects the confusion in his thinking concerning the "grandiose self," which he sees as a normal self in its more immature form during childhood. To reflect a child's talent without responding to every aspect of the child's self—including sadness, shame, envy, and general emotional need—could promote a pathological grandiose self as opposed to healthy self-awareness.

John Gedo, another self psychologist, makes a presumption similar to that of Kligerman and other Kohutians. In *Portraits of the Artist* (1983), Gedo suggests that Vincent van Gogh's early self-defects developed because of a lack of mirroring affirmation of his talents by his mother and other family members. I would propose, as Alice Miller does (1979, 1986), that mirroring of talents is not the necessary ingredient for integrated self-development. Instead, I believe that children need acceptance by parents of all of their feelings, traits, and self-attributes, including their most important emotional needs, as well as their narcissistic and instinctual desires. Children are extremely sensitive to rejection through parental withdrawal or attacks.[4] If parents reject a child's basic feelings (e.g., envy, love, loss, and rage) and basic needs (e.g., hunger for and autonomy from object attachment), their mirroring of talents will encourage only defensive narcissistic compensation.

If the mirroring of talent is inadequate, then Kohut's, Kligerman's, and Gedo's references to creative work as a reparative "selfobject" cannot be upheld.[5] For if artists receive merely vicarious mirroring through their work, such narcissistic admiration or even validating understanding cannot give them what they missed during critical stages of childhood self-formation. Only consistent and attuned responsiveness from a psychotherapist can accomplish this. Such attunement allows the opening up of the traumatized self through conscious experiencing of archaic affect and mourning. The idea of the creative work process serving the function of ultimate self-repair can therefore be seen as a theoretical myth.

Gedo has recently stated an even more extreme position concerning creativity. In a summary chapter of *Michelangelo's Sistine Ceiling: A Psychoanalytic Study of Creativity* (Oremland 1989, p. 151), he asserts that "Oremland . . . [emphasizes] creativity as a form of object relatedness. From my frame of reference, in creativity there may be only self-transcendence and self expansion. Even though we travel different paths, Oremland and I arrive at the same conclusion: creativity actually constitutes an alternative to loving others." Such an opinion obviously represents a major thesis of Gedo. Unlike Oremland, who seems aware that internal object relations are always involved in creativity and that self-experience is always object related, Gedo claims that creativity is a form of self-experience separate from all object-related experience and that it can actually substitute both for the object relatedness of interpersonal relations and for love. This opinion, in my view, is based on one of Kohut's basic theoretical fallacies, namely, that there is a self exclusive of interpersonal object relations. As those familiar with Kohut's work know, he has postulated two separate lines of development for the self and for object relations.[6] This thesis is stated in his *The Restoration of the Self* (1977). Gedo's most recent views reflect this premise, which denies the basic other relatedness in human nature and the core of self-development as asserted in object relations theory. Gedo's belief that people not only can function but actually can be fulfilled without love as long as they have creative work shows such a profound misunderstanding of what love, humanity, and creativity are that the publication of his opinion illustrates the profound need for studies like the present one. His view supports those who would narcissistically deny their need for others with a fantasy of "self-sufficiency" (see Modell 1975; 1976). My study suggests the tragic consequences to artists who espouse, knowingly or unknowingly, such a belief and who become so addictively engaged with creative work that they shun the interpersonal relations so desperately needed by them.[7] It also shows, in accordance with Oremland's view, that the essence of creativity is object related, although the objects to which there is relation may be infantile or pathological forms that can be seen as part objects. Whether they are whole or part objects, the creative thrust is toward relations with internal objects within the internal world and with external objects in the literary audience. Only when creative work can bring insight and resolution of psychic conflict to such internal relations do artists truly feel open to current interpersonal relations, that is, relations with external objects or others, and, more basically, to love. The capacity to relinquish bad object constellations within the internal world, through successful mourning, allows for such insight and resolution of psychic conflict. Many artists have not achieved this capacity.

Gedo's myth of self-sufficiency through creativity is predicated on Heinz Kohut's theoretical view that the self is formed without whole object internalization and continues throughout life to seek the use of other people as self-extensions. When Kohut speaks of people needing throughout their lives the ambiguous others that he labels selfobjects, he goes beyond any object relations theory of mature dependence in which we learn to accept our need for others as adults, thus relinquishing grandiose notions of self-sufficient autonomy. Instead, he implies—always through his ambiguous use of language—that we need to depend on others who are mere part objects in our minds for basic self-survival functions and that we never get beyond this point, although perhaps there are relative changes in our perception and use of others. Kohut's controversial opinions have been discussed by Martin Bergman in his historical account of psychoanalytic views on love, *The Anatomy of Loving* (1987). Bergman reexamines Kohut's idea that the symbiotic mother of early infancy can and should be rediscovered in adult relationships and that adults become "selfobjects" for each other. Although Bergman cites Kohut's ideas about love relations while I focus on internal love relations that constitute creativity, Bergman and I remain concerned that fallacies based on narcissistic fantasies—in whatever realm they are applied—can be perpetuated in the form of psychoanalytic developmental theory.

According to Bergman (1987), Kohut's belief that one can find the fantasied infantile selfobject within adult relationships contradicts Margaret Mahler's view that we always retain an unconscious yearning for the symbiotic mother that can never be realistically satisfied. This Kohutian theory also conflicts with the findings of the British object relations theorist Michael Balint. Although he precedes Mahler historically, Balint takes her reasoning one step further. According to Balint, even though the primary love sought from infancy is always longed for, the consequences would be disastrous if it were acted out in adult life (see Bergman 1987, 251; Balint 1965, 115). Such catastrophes are acted out in many marriages when one partner tries to coerce the other into being the fantasied ideal symbiotic partner and to become a mirror for self-validation. In keeping with the object relations theories of Mahler and Balint, Bergman states that Kohut's translation of infant-mother relations into adult relations as a norm rather than pathology contradicts all traditional psychoanalytic theory.

Kohut's idea could lead to the conclusion that adult artists seeking their mothers may conceivably find them through internal engagement with the creative process. However, particularly for artists who have experienced preoedipal trauma, self-disintegration and depletion must result from such a hope. For them, there follow cycles of compulsive creativity, in which hopes and strivings for primitive merger meet with renewed traumatic loss. Kohut's theoretical fantasy implies that self-deficits and self-enfeeblement can be cured without the object relations work of tolerating the anguish of mourning, since mourning is part of any recommencement of an aborted separation-individuation process. His optimism evinces an unfortunate air of naïveté in relation to the repetitive despair of the preoedipal artist.

We need only to remember the doctor who cared for van Gogh following his stay in an asylum. Irving Stone describes the belief of this physician that his patient's dedication to painting could cure his mental disturbance. In the context of van Gogh's recurrent psychosis and suicide, such biographical narration is chilling.[8] Katherine Mansfield's search for a physician to legitimize her resistance to entering a sanitorium when she became afflicted with tuberculosis is similarly distressing. According to all three of her biographers,[9] Mansfield managed to find a French doctor who told her that her salvation was in her art and that she should therefore not enter a sanitorium, since she would be required to suspend her writing. Although this advice contradicted every other medical opinion that Mansfield received, she followed it and was dead within four years.

In sum, by ignoring critical issues of development, Kohut does not consider how object relations dynamics are revealed through creative expression and their effect upon this creative expression. Consequently, he also fails to view accurately the process of self-engagement that promotes creative expression. Object relations are essential elements of the internal world of an artist and of the external world that characterizes his or her interpersonal life. To ignore object relations is to ignore reparative movements from psychopathology to mental health; yet Kohut does ignore these relations. His limited view leads him to assumptions about creativity that I believe to be fallacious.

In contrast to Kohut's views, and more closely related to those of Bergman, are the opinions of D. W. Winnicott. The prominent founder of one school of object relations theory (the British Psychoanalytic Society's "independent" or "middle group"), Winnicott is far less optimistic than Kohut when he considers the potential healing effects of creativity for the developmentally arrested adult artist:

> In a search for the self the person concerned may have produced something valuable in terms of art, but a successful artist may be universally acclaimed and yet have failed to find the self that he or she is looking for. The self is not really to be found in what is made out of products of body or mind, however valuable these constructs may be in terms of beauty, skill, and impact. If the artist (in whatever medium) is searching for the self, then it can be said that in

all probability there is already some failure for that artist in the field of general creative living. *The finished creation never heals the underlying lack of sense of self* [emphasis mine].

([1968] 1971, 64).

## The Task at Hand

Old and widespread myths about reparation through the creative process and new myths in which artists' narcissistic fantasies are taken at face value and turned into theoretical fantasies force me to take a skeptical view of the prospects for self-integration through engagement solely with the creative process. To examine to what degree the creative process—particularly without additional psychotherapeutic treatment—can be used for self-integration, I will look at important developmental and diagnostic factors. I will examine the interplay between the object relations of development and those of creativity, as well as the interpersonal relations of those whose primary employment is engagement with creativity. In order to focus on particular object relations dynamics within the internal world, as revealed through creative works and artists' lives, I will first explore early self-development from an object relations perspective.

## Self and Object Differentiation

Early development involves a separation-individuation period, as defined by Margaret Mahler (1975). This period has also been called the "transitional phase" by the British object relations theorists Ronald Fairbairn (1952) and D. W. Winnicott (1965). It is a period of transition between the states of psychological fusion in which the infant feels at once with its mother and the more mature state of self-development in which the infant becomes a separate "child," capable of experiencing autonomy and interdependence in relation to its mother and others in its world. Mutuality and interpersonal dialogue become increasingly pronounced during this transitional period, particularly during the "rapprochement phase," which follows the more autonomous "practicing phase."

Current infant research has emphasized the role of mother-infant dialogue from birth. Stern (1985), for example, minimizes the infant's fusion with the mother, emphasizing its separateness and interdependent nature. Such a view does not address the internal world of the infant, that is, the world of intrapsychic fantasy discovered by Melanie Klein in her clinical work with toddlers. Ogden (1986), a follower of both Klein and Winnicott, proposes that Stern's work depicts the more overtly observable level of differentiation of self and other, while overlooking the subtler psychological level in which psychic fantasy profoundly affects the sense of self. Ogden believes, as I do, that psychological fusion states predominate in the world of the "symbiotic-period" infant described by Mahler, despite the sensory level of self and other differentiation that is observable in empirical research. Citing Melanie Klein's theory, Hanna Segal (1985) has described states of infant-mother fusion as projective-identification modes of merger. Although Kleinians do not employ Mahler's term "symbiotic," which possibly implies a more total fusion, they refer, like Winnicott, to the mother-infant "dual unity."[10] They take seriously an early state that requires a developmental process to promote differentiation of self and other on a psychological level.[11]

## Differentiation and Self-Integration

In Margaret Mahler's developmental schema, the differentiation of self from object occurs during the separation-individuation period. It leads in turn to the formation of separate representations of self and object within the internal psychic world. With the formation of differentiated representations of self and object, these images integrate. This occurs as contrasting feelings in the mother-infant experience, such as good (pleasurable) and bad (painful), become part of a representation of the whole self. Simultaneously, the parts of the object that are perceived and felt as differentially good and bad through combined mother-infant experience are integrated into a whole object representation.

The simultaneous process of differentiation and integration of self and other is part of an overall authentic and integrative self-formation process. It continues at various levels throughout life. Yet fundamental representations of internal object relations are formed at this critical developmental stage. Without the secure differentiation and integration of the self during the preoedipal period, later self-formation will not proceed.

## The Role of the External Mothering Object

During this critical developmental stage, in which the roles of mother and child are defined, rapprochement is a significant form of negotiation of self and other, particularly for toddlers aged eighteen to thirty-six months. The toddler needs consistent and reliable object contact with a primary maternal figure—either the natural mother or another caretaker—during this time. If the mother is unavailable, the child's sense of abandonment can be traumatic and disruptive to psychic development. If the mother is too readily available, desiring contact because of her own needs, the child will feel her presence as intrusive or, more profoundly, as engulfing. Winnicott (1965) describes such a mother as "impinging," substituting her own gesture for that of the infant and forcing a kind of psychological adaptation to her role as initiator, thereby violating the infant's autonomous strivings and promoting the development of a "false self."[12] Masterson (1976) speaks similarly of the disruption of the toddler's developmentally induced striving toward autonomy. Either mode of faulty attunement—during the symbiotic phases of the "dual unity" period or later, during the separation-individuation phases of the toddler—can cumulatively traumatize (Khan 1974) a child so that a preoedipal developmental arrest results. Such arrest determines that all later psychological development is pathologically altered. Actual abuse toward the infant or toddler can also be classified as parental intrusion and engulfment, since it will definitely have traumatizing effects.

## Whole Object Internalization

Contact with an appropriately attuned mother during these early developmental stages allows the child to stay open to external emotional contact with others in the interpersonal world. If contact is pleasurable, supportive, and available when needed, the mother will be felt as a "good enough" object (Winnicott 1965) and can be internalized as a whole object. The whole object has undesirable as well as desirable features. All features—undesirable and desirable—can be tolerated as part of an interactional object representation,[13] provided that they do not annihilate the child's sense of self. However, if encounters with primary objects (mother and/or father) are traumatic because of the character of the parents themselves or constitutional or psychic vulnerabilities in the child, object experience tends to become split off from consciousness. In Fairbairn's terms, they are split off from the central ego, becoming part object components that take the form of monstrously grand and demonic internal objects.[14] Fairbairn (1952) and Ogden (1986) have described such internal objects as establishing a malevolent internal-world dynamic through their attachment to parts of the self that become split off because of relational trauma at the hands of the external mother.

## The Malevolent Internal Part Object

Klein speaks about persecutory objects, which lack the benign aspects of whole object forms. Fairbairn similarly discusses bad objects, originally calling them "internal saboteurs." The drama of these persecutory or bad objects can be described as malevolent part object scripts whose blueprint exists in the unconscious internal world as long as painful early experience has not been consciously felt and remembered. These scripts can become enactments either in the interpersonal world or in the world of creative work. The internal blueprint, based on unmourned trauma, presses for external enactment, which can be expressed through behavior but can also be expressed through creative work, i.e., work produced in that half-psychic, half-real, in-between world which Winnicott (1965) calls the "transitional world." Harry Guntrip (1976) has spoken of a psychically split-off and yet dynamic internal world in describing his patients' dreams, which display their own form of creative work. In analysis, these dreams become fantasies that can be psychically contained, just as such dreams become contained in creative work. He describes villain-victim dramas at one level[15] and dreams of voids and disintegration at a presumed earlier level.[16] When artists or writers express their internal persecutory blueprints in creative work, villains and victims rather than more ambivalent characters surface. For female writers, the demon lover theme often appears as a literary expression of an internal psychological complex.

## The Sealing off of the Self

And this is how it stiffens, my vision of that seaside childhood. My father died, we moved inland. Whereon those nine first years of my life sealed themselves off like a ship in a bottle—beautiful, inaccessible, obsolete, a fine, white, flying myth.

—Sylvia Plath (quoted in Butscher 1976, 19)

When traumatic preoedipal child-mother relations occur, the child's inner psychic self becomes sealed off, split away from external relations in the interpersonal world. The inner life is imprisoned behind a "schizoid barrier." It is far less penetrable than a repressive barrier, because affective life is not simply dissociated but is constricted and deadened. As affect is deadened, the repetitive drama of the internal world is recycled through projective and introjective mechanisms that coercively engage objects in the external world (resulting in Klein's phenomena of "projective identification"). The result is the absence of true encounter, dialogue, mutuality, or affective responsiveness to others. In their place, there exists only coercion through projective identification, which induces in another person intense archaic reactions. The other is not only perceived through projections but is effectively compelled to enact the internal drama with the subject. Through such projective identification, he or she is then perceived absolutely as the original preoedipally traumatizing object. This extreme aberration of perception is strikingly unlike neurotic levels of distortion.

Such psychic sealing off annihilates potential spontaneous expressions of the self, which require the containing of sustained processing of affect life and affective attachments.[17] The primary traumatized self remains barred from the interpersonal contact it needs. Without such contact, the individual cannot consciously feel the original trauma and thus permit reparative healing. Moreover, without an external relations dialogue, internalized blueprints that may possibly motivate intimacy, empathy, understanding, and sustained relations with others do not become formed. The inner self is increasingly debilitated over time, promoting disease, suicidal despair, and the terror of facing an inner void within the self.

## Developmental Mourning

If the mothering person adequately provides affective responsiveness and empathically attuned contact during the preoedipal stages of development, the rapprochement stage of the separation-individuation period will allow the child to tolerate aggressive and grief affects. Here, more relatively symbiotic or "dual-unity" relations are surrendered for autonomous encounters of self and other. Such surrender, however, is highly conflictual. As Gorkin (1984) has observed in response to Margaret Mahler's studies, toddlers may aggressively cling to their mothers when threatened with the shock of their own new-found autonomy. Gorkin also comments on the "low-keyedness" of Mahler's forlorn and saddened toddlers. In these repetitions of aggression and grief, we see a developmental mourning process. My own exploration of mourning within separation-individuation focuses on internal affect experience and the transformational effects of it on the internal world of representations of self and object. By grasping the affective vitality of developmental mourning, we perceive the dynamics behind the original structuralization of the internal world and the varying transformations of this world that develop with graduated levels of mourning and self-integration over time.

Normal developmental mourning occurs in relation to an external object, that is, the mothering person. Toddlers need to mourn this external mother and their earlier symbiotic relations with her in order to internalize the external mother in representational form within the nuclear self-structure of the internal world. Toddlers must let go of the closer external relations of the earlier dual-unity period to accomplish this task. They must also retain sufficient intermittent contact with the mother to tolerate letting go. A passionate dance begins, and mothers must respond to and also resist toddlers' rhythms so that separation can proceed (see Mahler et al. 1975, 77–78). Toddlers will repeatedly chase the mother and then dash away from her. They invite her to chase them in return, inciting her desire so as to reassure themselves of her exclusive interest in them as well of her ongoing presence. Simultaneously, they reign supreme with the convincing bravado of their own autonomy.

Unlike normal adults, who can mourn through an internal image of the lost object, toddlers mourn mother as she remains near yet separate. They will look for her when she is not there and for others who have recently disappeared. Toddlers will often be disinterested in mother or others when they are nearby but will become absorbed with searching for them when they are gone. A two-year-old boy never noticed my presence until I was outside the room and then asked "Where's Susan?" This boy needed to be taken again and again to see the cottage where his grandparents had recently stayed. He required repeated proof that they were gone.

Tantrums, rage, and aggressive holding on are all difficult parts of letting go of the external object; however, if mothering has been adequate and instinctual aggression is not too disruptive, the toddler will ultimately yield to a more sedate sadness. This sadness refines aggressive impulses and allows internalization to occur through intensely felt grief. In sadness there is an openness to contact both with external others and with the individual's own internal self. Such "in-touchness" allows for progressive internalization and therefore for structuralization of the internal world. Affective awareness enables each of us to accept the memory of the temporarily (but not traumatically) lost object and encourages creation of an image of the object in the form of psychic representations. To the degree that internalization occurs while the subject and the other are interactively engaged, differentiation of self and object within the internal world is promoted. Stern's (1985) description of psychic "rigs" is analogous to these internalized forms when they extend sensory introject modes to become symbols or image representations of the nuclear self. Whole object rather than part object experiences must predominate to become secure symbolic images. Only in this way can hate and aggression toward the other be contained so that psychic structuralization can occur.

Other aspects of primary developmental mourning involve toddlers relinquishing their idealized imprints of self and other from the dual-unity era.[18] The practicing stage employs the idealized form as a grandiose self, a sense of self that incorporates a perception of the whole symbiotic self-and-other unit as part of it. The "normal deflation" of the grandiose self (see Masterson 1981) is part of a relinquishment that is resisted and can be facilitated or disrupted by the maternal response during the rapprochement following the practicing period.[19] Joffe and Sandler (1965) speak of this relinquishment in terms of an anguished preoedipal mourning of the idealized self. If the idealized self is not relinquished through affective mourning, the rapprochement low-keyedness as well as the internalization of a differentiated picture of self and other cannot proceed. The mother may continue to be idealized, since the power of symbiotic feeling and fantasy is projected onto her at rapprochement. When such extreme archaic idealization is unmodified, no dialogue of sharing and mutuality between a newly perceived separate other and one's self can progress. Both aggressive affect and the "low-keyedness" that expresses the grief of mourning are affective components of the transformation process by which archaic idealization is transformed into awareness of an objectively perceived other.

I believe that this new experience of "otherness" in the mothering person, cited by Mahler as occurring during rapprochement, is based on a growing perception of the mother as having a subjective life of her own—as possessing qualities and reactions not in full harmony with the toddler's own needs. Klein speaks of children's beginning awareness that the mother on whom they depend has a life of her own (see Segal 1964).[20] When such awareness can be tolerated, despite the psychic conflict promoted, grief and mourning become critical components of differentiating growth.

If early trauma disrupts this mourning process, later levels of developmental mourning will also be arrested, often at the oedipal and adolescent periods. When early differentiation and integration of self and object are unsuccessfully structured, continuing progress in integration of self and object throughout life is blocked. A whole object internalization is necessary from this preoedipal era so that an internal dialogue of self and other can proceed during later stages of development.

## Abandonment Depression Mourning

If there is preoedipal trauma, caused either by circumstance or by parental character pathology, a sealing off of the self which prevents mourning, results. Contact between parts of the primary self and external others is disrupted, and only a false facade of the self meets the external world. For development to proceed again, the sealed-off inner self must be unsealed. This requires the external presence of an empathically attuned other. Without such a person, the internal world cannot provide an internal whole object with whom to engage in the dialogue necessary to promote mourning and self-integration, particularly since no preoedipal whole object internalization has been established in the case of early trauma.

Those who attempt self-reparation through the creative process consequently cannot heal themselves if preoedipal trauma and arrest have transpired. They need another person to be there with them when infant rage and grief open up, which occurs when early traumas are reexperienced in therapy. In other words, without the containing presence of the therapist, the affective inner world is unable to open up and growth-promoting interpersonal contact with others cannot be established.

The intense rage and grief of those traumatized within the preoedipal period have been given the name "abandonment depression" (Masterson 1976; 1981). A particularly extreme form of developmental mourning, it requires the containing presence of another, which can occur consistently only within the psychoanalytic-psychotherapy structure. The psychotherapist confronts the defenses against contact with the object that ward off the patient's experiencing of the trauma. The psychotherapist is a containing presence when a patient reexperiences the trauma within the relationship with the therapist. For example, as a patient cries, screams, or rages in response to remembering parental absence, attack, or withdrawal, the therapist is present to feel the degree of pain he or she is experiencing and gradually to understand its source. In preoedipal trauma, the acuteness of the pain and the primitiveness of the rage related to it are caused by the unavailability of the parent at a critical time. In this period, the infant or toddler is just forming a sense of self and therefore experiences the absence of communal presence or a lack of related empathy as psychic annihilation. The psychotherapist helps the patient to tolerate terror, rage, and loss so that past traumas can be "named," articulated, and connected to cognitive modes of organization.[21] Through the therapeutic process, patients consciously reexperience what they have formerly experienced only in a dissociated or unconscious way. They begin to remember what they have been perpetually reenacting. The act of remembering itself becomes a mourning process as the affects of the original experiences are felt for the first time in the context of cognitive awareness. It is the mutual engagement between therapist and patient around the patient's memories that enlarges memories in a graduated process, allowing the opening of psychic space, first to grief and loss and then to renewed love as the old wounds are felt and healed. In this transaction, the psychotherapist actually becomes the object of the rage, loss, and love that stem from the patient's original parents.[22]

I propose that the creative process can never substitute for the containing and contactful presence of the external other, which is experienced by the patient in the person of the psychotherapist. The creative process is unable to substitute for the psychotherapist's confrontation of defensive processes or for the therapeutic partnership in integrating them into a new sense of self as the therapist becomes attuned to the patient's unique vulnerability. The therapist provides an interactive other for affective contact and an interpretive function to decipher defenses and repressed or split-off object relations.[23]

## Pathological Mourning and Aborted Mourning

Without an attuned and consistently present psychotherapist, therefore, individuals afflicted with preoedipal trauma and consequent arrest will remain frozen in a state of pathological mourning. In such patients, the urge to maintain or internalize an early symbiotic state of merger with another will continually be disrupted by the archaic rage and paralyzing despair due to trauma from the separation-individuation era or earlier. Instead of tolerating mourning, they become overwhelmed with a craving to incorporate others as symbiotic self-extensions (as opposed to differentiated internalizations). They attempt to use others as prosthetic devices when psychic resources within are lacking. These patients are propelled into anguished object relations with archaically idealized others, whom they see as substitutes for the early symbiotic mother. The desired other will become, like Fairbairn's (1952) poison pie, a symbolized image for the demonic mother who is swallowed under a condition of starvation, only to be spit out again as poison. I propose that when an adequate internal dialogue with a whole object is lacking, mourning by oneself—without interpersonal modes of containment—cannot be tolerated without modes of psychic breakdown. In patients who suffer from preoedipal arrest, mourning through contact with the external object is often prevented by failures in capacities to relate to others. The other is quickly perceived as poisonous, since idealization repeatedly leads to profound disappointment. Therapists who work with preoedipally arrested creative artists can see the compulsive creative reenactment that inevitably unfolds. This reenactment opens up repetitive cycles of frustrated cravings for object incorporation, followed by or interwoven with expulsive exorcisms of the object. The object so incorporated and expelled is the idealized part object, which becomes demonic with the recurrence of abandonment and engulfment trauma. Such patients will resist taking in the realistically "good" aspects of related contact that others could provide. Borderline patients, for example, will make unrealistic demands that can never be met. They thus ensure their continued disappointment, which will be experienced as renewed abandonment. The therapist will be idealized only as long as the secret wishes for symbiotic modes of early mothering still arouse hope. These patients withhold the fantasies behind their unrealistic demands until disappointment evokes recriminations and reactions of rage that signify how the therapist has become entirely bad within their internal worlds. Their perception of the therapist is then made to "click in" with their psychic imprints[24] of the preoedipal mother of early trauma, imprints which can be referred to as bad or demonic objects. The sealing off of the affective self, combined with the harboring of fantasies that reflect early wishes, results in this closed psychic system, in which perception is transmuted through the imprints of early trauma. Such a cyclical, closed system can be characterized as bulimic. New objects are swallowed whole when interpersonal affect contact is precluded, since psychic object assimilation cannot occur without such affect experience. Thus, newly incorporated objects are spit out as soon as they click in with the bad internal objects and resonate with the unexpressed pain of preoedipal trauma.

An external empathic presence such as a therapist can provide is the only way of interceding within a self-destructive bulimic cycle. Such a presence permits mourning for the symbiotic mother and the creation of internal whole object dialogue. The psychoanalyst who provides this therapeutic function to preoedipal patients empathizes with their hidden affect states and confronts and interprets the pseudorelations that are reenactments of early mother-self, self-mother, father-self, and/or self-father experiences.[25] The therapist's penetrating way of interpreting or questioning these pseudorelations is necessary for the patient to open up to affective engagement. Only affective engagement can become sustained interpersonal engagement, and only the latter is able to provide healing through successful whole object internalization.

Adult artists suffering from preoedipal arrest usually do not have the aid of an intervening therapist to help them resolve the burden of trauma. They will therefore express their trauma in creative work. Perpetual rage, loss, and anguished bereavement will appear within it. Failing to process such affects, the preoedipally arrested artist will ultimately be unable to employ the creative process reparatively. Instead of self-integration we therefore see self-deterioration, both in the works and in the lives of such artists.

Creativity itself can become entrapping, when preoccupation with its internal relations excludes interpersonal relations. Artists who endlessly seek repair (usually unconsciously) through the creative process can become addicted to the narcissistic reflection of that process when it fails to heal them. They can also become addicted to the early relations reenacted through the creative work. Without resolution of these relations, their compulsive creative work can impede the expansion of interpersonal relations. Without reparative growth through the product of the creative process, there can be no preparation for improved external relations. Such artists are then compelled to work continually or to attempt to do so, even though the drying up of internal life through depletion of interpersonal contact blocks them creatively. The creative work can then become repetitive, as is the case with the neurotics that Kubie (1958) describes. More dramatically, however, in the case of borderline artists, the work can also be regenerated in many forms that evidence self-fragmentation or the narcissistic defenses used against it. The manic intensity that such self-fragmentation endows the creative process with can in itself become addictive for the artist, as the intensity becomes narcissistically flattering. The fear of losing such intensity can prevent many artists from entering psychotherapy, as the artists fail to differentiate this manic intensity from their creative capacities and to fear that if treatment modifies their intensity it will cause them to lose their creativity.

## Observing-Ego Development

The study of creative work, particularly of literature, can illustrate whether the artist has adequately developed the function of an observing ego as part of their psychic structure. Some artists demonstrate a capacity for the self-reflection of an observing ego, while others do not. Self-reflection is a critical component in a developmental mourning process that proceeds primarily through the use of the creative process. Mourning involves self-insight, an increasing awareness of differentiating relations between self and other.

If early preoedipal trauma disrupts development, observing-ego reflection will not be promoted and affectively alive insight into relations between self and other will not evolve. An inadequate early mother will be incorporated as a part object, remaining unassimilated into the central or nuclear self. This part object will tend to be experienced as a persecutory internal object and will often be sensed as enacting omnipotent vigilance. Such vigilance—which, if felt as persecutory, can be turned toward others or the self—differs from the way in which an adequately internalized whole object functions. The latter has observing-ego functions, permitting the observing ego to operate without promoting intense shame. In contrast, the internal part object persecutor floods the self with a sense of shame, leading to an unneutralized aggressive assault on the self, with internal persecutory judges presiding. Depersonalization, detachment, fragmentation, and suicidal despair can follow.

One defining aspect of the creator who has achieved an unarrested oedipal level is that his or her creative production can reflect a functioning and neutralized observing ego. Love and hate toward the object have been integrated. An object relations mode of neutralization of archaic affect has been affected. This observing ego possesses a capacity for self-reflection and progressive conflict resolution through the dialogue of the creative process. A reparative developmental progression within the creative process thereby becomes possible.

## The Psychic Coloring of the Parental Object

Primary internalization of the parents and of fusions and interactions of the self with the other occurs in early infancy and is followed by levels of internalization that continue throughout life. As the early parents are assimilated into the psyche of the infant, they become integrated into the nuclear self. This occurs in normal development. However, with preoedipally traumatized children, the parents become incorporated as split-off internal objects, which then function like dynamic internal presences that are repeatedly externalized in creative work and in interpersonal relations. In normal or pathological development, such objects, which are colored by psychic predispositions, can be distorted to varying degrees.

Affective and instinctual desires and impulses will color the actual parent as he or she is internalized and represented within. Love and hate, as well as their correlated erotic and aggressive impulses, will affect the experience with the other that precipitates internalization. Instinctual hungers will occasionally abate, permitting, according to Winnicott, a form of object-related play that promotes internalization.[26] Playfulness between self and other will specifically promote internalizations of mild and pleasant affect experiences that may keep the objective form of the other more intact. In contrast, instinctual cravings will color and distort the parental object, diminishing its objective form as it is perceived and then internalized.[27]

When the intensity of instinctual necessity abates, the form of the object will be more accurately perceived, although infant perspectives are still limited by immaturities in the capacities for cognitive processing. More intense affect, however, will probably turn the object into a predominantly good or bad form—sometimes with demonic overtones—even when the capacity for whole object perception is maintained. Yet the object can still be adequately assimilated and therefore need not become a split-off, demonic part object (with its counterpart, primitive fantasy formation of an archaic god ideal).

For the preoedipally traumatized infant or toddler, the distortion of the object can be much more extreme. The frustration of instinctual and developmental needs together will allow few mellow periods. This seems apparent in the kind of cumulative trauma described by Khan (1974), Masterson (1976; 1981), Balint (1979), and others, in which the parents' character pathology intrudes on development. The effects may be even more predominant during specific periods of developmental and instinctual conflict, such as during Mahler's stage of rapprochement, when an incorporative form of object usage takes place. The perpetuation of this primitive mode of incorporation[28] determines that the primary self is sealed off in an adhesive attachment to internal objects. The central self may remain open to others, as in Fairbairn's endopsychic model (1952), but the original, affectively spontaneous infant self becomes sealed off. The infant's early objects remain part object demonic forms that cannot be modified without the self opening up through the intensity of abandonment depression mourning. Guntrip's (1976) descriptions of patients' dreams—in which sadomasochistic parent-child dramas perpetuate preoedipal traumatic relations—portray this split and sealed-off inner world.

These dynamics illustrate distorting developments that influence the internalized apprehension of the parental objects and of later persons who come to be perceived through object blueprints that are imprinted early. In developmental arrest, the impact of instinctual modifications of object perception are minor in structuring character pathology, compared with the effects of pathological modes of internalization as they still exist in primitive incorporative forms. Creators who work from data gleaned through this continuing mode of pathological internalization will distort their objects in a uniform manner, since psychic object assimilation fails. Part object god-demons will haunt the internal world and become manifest in creative production. The kind of instinctual variants visible in artists with relatively high-level neuroses will have less impact on the coloration of object forms within their creative work. Thus, the demon lover is manifest both across art genres and in the particular works of individual artists or writers.[29] When an artist fails to modify the demon lover theme through the course of creative activity, due to their inability to mourn and integrate object images into more benign forms, the theme itself becomes symptomatic of pathological modes of internalization and their perpetuation. Such artists can be said to be prisoners of the creative process inasmuch as it becomes the scene of reenactment of pathological mourning.

The source of the demon lover literary theme, and its related personality complex, is the internal father. When a woman writer is profoundly engaged with this internal father, her psychic relationship with him has a dual edge to it. The internal father can be a prime source of creative motivation, but he can also become the demon lover who haunts and imprisons. In the words of Emily Brontë

> And robed in fires of Hell, or bright with heavenly shrine,
> If it but herald Death, the vision is divine . . .
> > "Julian M. and A. G. Rochelle," in *The Complete Poems of*
> > *Emily Jane Bronte*, 239, lines 91–92,

or of Sylvia Plath

> Not God but a swastika
> So black no sky could squeak through
> Every woman adores a fascist . . .
> > "Daddy," in *Ariel* (1961), 50, lines, 47–49

> You stand at the blackboard, daddy,
> In the picture I have of you,
> A cleft in your chin instead of your foot
> But no less a devil for that, no not
> Any less the black man who
> Bit my pretty red heart in two.
> > "Daddy," 50, lines 52–56.

The woman so haunted may turn to creativity to free herself. In the following chapter, I will return to early development to illustrate the interactive roles of the external mother and the external father in creating the internal father.

# 2

# From Mother to Father

## The Internal Object

The interaction of infant and mother during the preoedipal stages of development is prominently featured in empirical infant research (Mahler et al. 1975; Stern 1985; Bowlby 1969). Current research has shown the critical importance of what Winnicott told us decades ago, that an adequate intersubjective mother-infant matrix is necessary for basic self-development. Yet such observation of the external behavior of mothers and infants still leaves us with the dubious task of connecting external behavior with the internal world. It is only through such theorizing that we come to propose the nature of the internal world or psyche and to specify psychic-structure formation.

Without an adequate intersubjective matrix of self and other, the human infant cannot develop a core self. From an object relations perspective, the core self is seen in terms of an adequate integration of the mothering other as an internal object. Melanie Klein spoke specifically of the internal object. Margaret Mahler, in modifying object relations theory from the perspective of American ego psychology rejected the term internal object and its counterpart, "internal part objects." Mahler instead spoke of the integration of part object images into a whole intrapsychic representation of the other. Jacobson (1954, and 1964) also followed this vocabulary of representational internalization.

My preference is to speak of the "internal object," as did Klein and also Fairbairn (1952). As Ogden (1986) has noted, Fairbairn recognized the visceral as well as mental aliveness of the internal other.[1] Klein and her followers, such as Hanna Segal (1964), equivocated about the homunculus quality of the internal object, sometimes referring to it as an alive inner other that could be manifested as Fairbairn's dynamic "internal saboteur," and sometimes stressing that "internal objects" were only referents to psychic "phantasy"[2] (see Ogden 1986).

What can be called fantasy can also be called "representation." Yet the Kleinian notion of "phantasies" implies a dynamic and motivational component to internal object relations that Margaret Mahler's (1975) notion of "representation" does not imply. Beebe and Lachmann (1988, 310) have spoken of "prestructural representations" to differentiate symbolic cognitive conceptualizations of the object from more early presymbolic "prototypes" abstracted from individual subjective experiences of the object. I see the latter earlier prototypes as more vulnerable to infusion with primitive affect and psychic fantasies related to that affect experience. When affect is intense and aversive because of narcissistic injury, the frustration of instinctual cravings, or the loss of craved object contact, I see it as contributing to the development of split-off part objects or "bad objects." I propose that the relative success or failure of internal object integration during the critical period of rapprochement separation will determine what kind of representation (whole or prestructural) is formed. Navigation of this period involves adequate contact between mother and toddler within an intersubjective matrix before as well as during rapprochement. It also involves tolerating the feelings of mournful affect while separation is taking place. Such tolerance requires the mother's capacity to provide contact within the framework of critical development-stage functions. If the mother does so, part object incorporations, in which good and bad aspects of the object and relations with the object are divided from each other, will begin to integrate. As the good object experience outweighs the bad, the whole image of the object, including its aversive qualities, can be tolerated and thus consciously conceptualized as cognitive representations. This is a process of internalization that will be continued throughout life as the self continues to grow. It is a process of integration that distinguishes higher-level internalizations from more primitive split-off aversive, and alien incorporations, whose symbolic cognitive containment is jeopardized by the infusion of primitive affect.

## Developmental Arrest

The concept of developmental arrest has been used to define the failure of such whole object representations to form. This failure has been understood in terms both of critical failings of the mother during rapprochement (Masterson 1976) and of violations in the overall intersubjective matrix during the preoedipal years (Stolorow and Lachmann 1980). In Mahler's studies of mothers and infants, she observed that the mothers who have been adequate in relating to an infant during what she labels a symbiotic era[3] may have extreme difficulty in relating to a toddler during the separation-individuation phases, since the relatedness required pertains to alternating between engagement and letting go, between holding and sharing in a verbal mode of differentiated contact. With such mothers, she noted the development of borderline behaviors, in which splitting of the good and bad mothering objects persisted into the rapprochement period, thus interfering with the sustained relatedness that is necessary to integrate the self.

When such splitting of objects persists as a predominant intrapsychic dynamic, the split off part-objects, profoundly aggressive in nature, create the sense of bad-object persecution. There can be many degrees to which such splitting occurs. In the case of those who are preoedipally arrested, such splitting and its bad-object "phantasies" dominate affective experience. For those who suffer oedipal and postoedipal trauma, such split objects from the preoedipal years may still exist in the psyche in a repressed form, but the capacity and blueprint for overall object integration remain. Regression to early levels of object splitting can take place with aversive interpersonal experience, but the blueprint for the "good enough" integrated whole object allows mourning reparation to proceed.[4] Whether such a blueprint (or mental representation) is established within the psyche depends on the nature of early parenting. To define this parenting, I turn to the role of the preoedipal mother and then discuss the father as he interacts with the mother at various levels of development.

## Preoedipal Mothering

The British object relations theorists led the way in speaking about the early matrix of "holding," "containing," and "mirroring" that is so necessary to development of the whole self within the infant. D. W. Winnicott, in particular, addressed the nature of the early maternal matrix. He was the first to speak of the conglomerate of mothering functions as the "subjective object" (1911), an idea that was later adopted by Heinz Kohut in his conceptualization of the "selfobject."[5] Balint (1979) also elaborated on the characteristics of this mothering matrix in his work on the preoedipal character's trauma from the "basic fault." Margaret Mahler (1975) attempted to develop an understanding of the external mother-child relations that characterize normal as well as pathological development when internalized by the child. More recently, Donald Stern (1985) has used empirical research studies of infants to further define the infant's world. Generally, Stern's interpretation of his research findings has enhanced the outlines of the maternal matrix in which a separate and somewhat psychically differentiated infant develops. His view emphasizes how the infant becomes increasingly sophisticated in self-experience and self-awareness through interactive relations with the mother. For this evolution to occur, the mother must be psychically in tune with her infant. The infant's autonomous capacities for attunement to the mother make him exquisitely sensitive to his mother's attunement to him.

## Holding and Attunement

I would describe the essence of the intersubjective matrix of experience in terms of a dialectic of the affect perception of self and other, which object relationists call "contact." This dialectic has varying ranges of mutuality. More independent and interdependent modes of mutuality crystallize over time, reaching a peak mode of organization at rapprochement. Stern has pointed out that an infant's capacity for counterempathic perception of the mother develops prior to the autonomy of Mahler's separation-individuation era (with its subphase periods of practicing and rapprochement). First, there is empathy for the mother as a pleasurable object; subsequently there is a more sophisticated empathy for the mother's process of empathy toward the infant. Both can evolve prior to the cognitive self-differentiation of rapprochement.

From the beginning, the nature of the dialectic responsiveness between mother and infant can vary from sadomasochistic to mutually empathic. If the mother is healthy enough to be open to affect contact with her infant, a resonance can develop between them that does not clearly define either as separate but rather unites each in the mutuality of responsiveness. However, such resonance depends on the mother's ability to be primarily responsive to the infant's cues, which signal his[6] needs and desires.[7] If the mother responds to her own internal cues primarily, subjecting the infant to her needs rather than vice versa, the infant is in danger of developing what Winnicott called a "false self" (1971).

Winnicott spoke of the mother who would substitute her own gesture for the "omnipotent gesture" of the infant. Such a mother disrupts the dialectic between herself and her child. The infant must submit to her because of her need for him; he never has the chance to feel his own true identity through his own self desiring motivation and initiative. What kind of dialectic remains? It is a dialectic not of mutuality but rather one of sadomasochistic dynamics, in which the child who submits totally from the time of development of core self identity becomes a false self or schizoid personality. Narcissistic and borderline personalities are variations on this schizoid personality. All have suffered developmental arrests in self-structure formation that are related to the nature of the internal world.

James Masterson (1981) has spoken of a critical stage in which mothers with narcissistic and borderline pathologies can disrupt such initiating gestures in their children. Using Mahler's schema, he points to the disruption of autonomy during the practicing period, which causes Mahler's "rapprochement crisis" to become a rapprochement abandonment trauma. The child's natural development needs are disrupted by the pathological mother. As the child moves away at practicing, she may either pull him back into an engulfing symbiosis by failing to be available for refueling contact during practicing or cling to the infant in an engulfing manner. During rapprochement, she may have so completely detached from the infant who left her that there's "nobody home" when the infant returns for empathic sharing and reflective mirroring.

Although I find Masterson's phase distinctions enlightening, I also believe that the mother-infant dyad requires maternal attunement to the child's autonomous gestures from earliest infancy. The mother—who herself is engaged in a patholog-ical narcissistic fantasy of symbiotic bliss—may gratify the cravings for holding her child, but she will not have the ongoing empathic attunement for Winnicott's psychological form of holding to take place. This kind of holding is not merely physical; it requires letting go, rhythmic breathing, and internalizing respon-siveness between infant and mother. The mother engaged in her own fantasy of symbiotic bliss may be detached from her infant's cues for responsiveness even during her child's early, symbiotic-like phase of infancy.

Along with the dialectic of resonant responsiveness between mother and infant, there is the dialectic of self-reflection and recognition of the other that is often referred to as a narcissistic function of "mirroring." Margaret Mahler (1975) focuses on this form of dialectic most particularly during the practicing period of development. The practicing period propels the toddler away from the mother, thrusting him toward autonomous play and ecstatic states of exploration.[8] For such reasons, this stage is called "the love affair with the world." According to Mahler, at this point the infant-turned-toddler requires a near-perfect mirroring as he moves away from mother, encased in the intrapsychic fantasy of having mother and all of her powers inside him. He is in the purest state of omnipotence possible at this point, while still being able to move autonomously away from the mother. It is the mother's refueling contact and nurturance when he returns to her that allow him to sustain the fantasy that he is actually self-sufficient, lending a manic quality to his sense of omnipotence. However, as Benjamin (1988) has pointed out, it is not only the refueling contact but also the joy of recognizing the toddler's activities when away that sustain the well-being of the toddler at this time. He needs a validating recognition of his own initiative, even though he is in the outside world, away from the maternal sphere. Without such mirroring reflection or recognition from mother, he is in danger of collapsing into a deflated state of depression that disrupts the aliveness of the interdependent sharing at rapprochement. The mutuality of dialectic at this stage has a particularly narcissistic focus for the toddler. However, such need for reflection by mother, first referred to as mirroring by Winnicott (1971), is—in keeping with the mutual-ity of dialectic between mother and infant as defined by Stern—present in modified forms throughout infancy, including the earlier, more-symbiotic phases of infant experience.

At the period of rapprochement, which follows the practicing period within the overall separation-individuation era, the mother again becomes the prime focus of the toddler's attention. Having somewhat satiated his developmental urge toward autonomy during the practicing period and finding that he is not omnipotently independent of mother, he returns to the external mother to share his experiences in the world. Some deflation of omnipotence is necessary and normal, and minor states of helplessness during the practicing phase allow the toddler to turn back toward the external mother for help and then for sharing during rapprochement. However, too much failure on the mother's part to be emotionally attuned and available for contact will result in the perpetuation of the fantasy of omnipotence (in which mother is unconsciously fantasized as being within the self) as a defense against a traumatic sense of emptiness. Narcissistic defense will then be employed, in which the illusion of being above the empty self is perpetuated by isolation within the cocoon (Modell 1975; 1976) of fantasied self-sufficiency. If the mother does not mirror the child sufficiently to support this omnipotent fantasy from the start, an empty feeling will contribute to an overall sense of depression. Self-deflation will be too extreme, and schizoid withdrawal can result.

If the mother sustains sufficient contact during these phases, the toddler will be able to internalize a whole object mother in relation to a whole self. Part of the mother's job in sustaining contact involves her survival of the child's aggressive demands (Winnicott's "object survival," 1971), allowing her to share in an experience in the world that is now felt as uniquely the child's. The mother's failures in attunement can help the child separate from her if these failures are not traumatic. Enough contact must be maintained so that the child can tolerate the sadness of loss that ensues when he feels the need for a mother who is not always there. His feelings of sadness allow him to mourn the gap between himself and mother so that he can both experience that he is separate from and dependent on her but also continue visualizing her and retaining her image. The mourning during rapprochement can be related to the emotional dynamics of Melanie Klein's "depressive position," which will be elaborated in the next chapter.

## Object Survival

D. W. Winnicott (1971) spoke of "object survival," by which he meant the capacity of the mother to survive the infant's most intensely drive-directed instincts, particularly the aggressive aspects of these instincts. For Winnicott, survival meant the mother's sustaining of a physical and emotional presence in relation to the infant. Further, the mother's survival as an object (specifically as a whole object) implies that she must refrain from retaliating through impingement, abandonment, or detachment.

I expand the notion of object survival to include varying aspects of the dialectic responsiveness of the mother within the intersubjective matrix. The mother or mothering caretaker (who can also be the father) must translate the child's needs and fears implicit behind his cries and rage reactions. The mother must continue to be available for responsive emotional contact at any juncture when rage is resolved into a state of vulnerability and self-observing reflection. Sometimes this involves active modes of engagement on the part of the mother; sometimes this involves a more receptive attunement. Maternal object survival also involves setting limits.

Winnicott spoke of the "environment mother" and the "object mother." The environment mother provides the functions of holding, reflecting, and nurturing, etc, whereas the object mother is the target of instinctual desires and instinctual aggression. The object mother survives within the context of the environment mother's intersubjective matrix. When the object mother survives, she does so by continuing to perform the environment mother's functions of sustained attunement and sustained contact. However, the object mother is distinctly outside the reign of the infant's omnipotent gesture. As she survives the aggressive demands of need and desire, she becomes an outside other who has needs of her own that the child must begin to acknowledge and tolerate. The child learns to be responsive to the outside other and to give up omnipotent initiative after first having had it. The father, as an outside other, becomes an extension of this mother of object survival. He excites by being outside the mother-infant matrix and by offering surprising new modes of interaction from the perspective of a more separate other.

## Mourning

Mourning and object survival are interactive and interdependent processes that take place within the intersubjective matrix. I propose that mourning can follow only sufficient internalization of whole object contact and dialogue. A psychic dialectic is needed to process the grief affects related to mourning. As aggression is modified by the survival of the transitional object, the affect of loss, induced through separation and its frustrations, is felt with a conjunctive awareness of the good in the object. Actually, as Fairbairn (1952) has articulated, it is the entire dialogue of self and other with the parental object that is taken inside the psyche. The object must be experienced as "good enough" (Winnicott 1965) for this internalization of dialogue to occur, contributing to basic self-structure, as opposed to the object being split off as an alienated incorporation or "bad object."[9] Once the dialogue is internalized, an internal psychic dialectic of psychic structure can enhance the capacity to mourn. Object survival and mourning become interactive and complementary aspects of internalization processed through interpersonal contact.

## Dialectic of Psychic Structure

The intersubjective dialectic between child and other, with the mother and father as primary "others," becomes the basis for the core psychic structure. The nature of the psychic structure will determine whether objects will continue to be internalized or whether they will be split off as bad objects. If the latter is the case, they impinge on the subject in a way that is experienced as alien. When they become split off, pathological identifications as well as part object connections form. These pathological identifications, which remain unmodified because of the lack of true affect contact with external others, serve to cause traumatic engulfment and abandonment to be repeated in all interpersonal relations.

Theorists with various views have ways of describing the intrapsychic dialectic that stems from interpersonal and intersubjective experience. For Freud, observations of oedipal-level family interactions may have contributed to him proposing a theory of triadic psychic structure (id, ego, and superego). For Margaret Mahler, a proposed symbiotic phase of development becomes a prominent feature of a theory that views internal psychic structure as forming only as separation proceeds, and differentiated image representations of self and object are formed [which then require degrees of integrating consolidation]. Melanie Klein's theory also proposes a developmental sequence, in which degrees of differentiation proceed along with integration. In contrast to Mahler, for Klein, self-differentiation—rather than preceding and prompting integration—becomes dependent on an affective process of integration that stems from mourning and reparative interpersonal interactions. Instead of the triadic dialogue of Freud or the internalized dyadic dialogue of Mahler, Klein's theory proposes a dialogue within the internal world between an internal object and the person who contains the object. The person containing the object figuratively "speaks" with the internal object on an unconscious level.

Despite the differences outlined in all three developmental theories, there is a common denominator, that is, an internal dialogue of proposed psychic-structure personae that rearticulate a child-parent interaction. For Freud, the superego parent speaks with the id child through the ego. For Mahler, the parental "object representation" speaks with the child "self-representation." For Klein, the parental "internal object" speaks to the child in the adult through unconscious "phantasy." Such dialogue, with its mutual relatedness between self and other, comes about only as early persecutory fears lessen within the framework of the "depressive position" and its mourning process. For Mahler, it comes about during the rapprochement stage of separation-individuation. For Freud, psychic, structural dialogue becomes possible with the establishment of a secure superego at latency. In any case, for all three theorists, externalized reenactments—"acting out"—are the consequence of the absence of such internal dialogue. This acting out prohibits internal integration. Without integration proceeding, compulsive externalization or acting out is perpetuated; it can take place within the work of the creative process as well as within relations with the external world. For the artist who lacks an adequate psychic-structure dialectic and its dialogue of mutuality, self-integration is arrested and externalized reenactments will take place both in the artist's work and in his or her life. The majority of the women writers to be discussed in this study exhibit such parallel modes of reenactment or acting out. They are women who exemplify arrest in psychic-structure development that is related to inadequate intersubjective matrices within child-parent relations.

## The Father's Role

So far my focus has been on the mother as the other in the intersubjective matrix. Where does the father come in?

Quentin Bell's biography of Virginia Woolf describes her strong attachment to her father and writes of the time they spent exclusively together: "This was the time when Virginia could walk out with her father to the Loggan rock of Trem Crom and the fairyland of great ferns which stood high above a child's head, or to Halestown Bog where the osmunds grew" (1972, 34).

In this passage, we can sense the fantasy-enhanced bonding that takes place between a father and a daughter. For the artistically developing daughter, this bond has a significant effect on her creative work.

If we retrace to early development, it seems likely that the initial capacity for creative expression, as well as its pathological form of compulsion, comes not from this father-child bond but rather from the mother-infant bond. Yet following the era of mother-child dual unity, the infant begins to separate from the mother, gradually letting go of the external symbiosis with her by sensing the loss and installing within the self a representation of the early idyllic feeling of oneness. The yearning to rekindle this merger is never lost; "falling in love" is the experience that we carry throughout life as a reenactment of this early symbiosis.

For the girl baby, the motivation to fall in love can affect her relationship with her father from an extremely early age. We know that even during the early stages of breast-feeding, a girl will look over at daddy if he is nearby and will develop a special nonverbal communication tie with him (Spieler 1984). Since it begins so early, the father-daughter bond galvanizes certain functions that the father performs in the development of his daughter. These functions include the father's mirroring, reflecting, and confirming of his daughter's self-image, as well as the father's role in serving as an identification figure for his daughter. At each stage of a young girl's development, her relationship with her father will affect her sense of herself, in terms of feeling pretty and intelligent and, as a synthesis of both of these, in terms of a confidence that she can use and express the creative potential that she has gestated during the era of psychic bonding with the mother.

## Father in Mother and Mother in Father

The father may or may not play a major role in the preoedipal years of his child's development. Like the mother, the father may become one constellation within the overall object as it is internalized. However, most theorists have seen the psychic significance of the father as that of being an outside other who is more differentiated from the child's self than is the mother. Mahler (1975) in particular speaks of the father as an enticing outside object who motivates the toddler to separate from the mother during the critical separation-individuation era. More traditionally, classical analysts have always referred to the father as the differentiated object of erotic longings during the girl's oedipal stage and as the rival for a boy during that stage.

## New Formulations

I propose that the father may at first be experienced as part of the mother, just as the mother is still so much part of the self during what Mahler calls the symbiotic phase of development. This should be seen as a matter of degree and not as absolute. Stern's research (1985; 1989) has alerted us to how an infant can make sensory distinctions between its mother's milk and that of another mother. Therefore, we need to recognize that there is sensory differentiation even before differentiated internal object images are formed. Nevertheless, I propose that prior to the separation-individuation periods of differentiation, practicing, and rapprochement, the father is not clearly differentiated from the mother. Further, it is not until rapprochement that an internal object image of the father is clearly formed and sustained so that object constancy in relation to him as an ongoing other can be maintained. The best evidence for such earlier lack of differentiation between father and mother is seen among the psychologically arrested, for whom the father is a father-mother, with the dynamic of an early mother figure somewhat fused with the father's personality. Borderline characters, indeed all who can be defined as preoedipal (schizoid, narcissistic, or borderline) because of developmental arrest, evidence such father-mother formations in their transference projective identifications.

For the normal child, rapprochement brings a differentiated father, but a father who is still characterized by the godlike idealization typical of symbiotic yearnings toward an omnipotent other. By the oedipal phase, however, the father not only should be differentiated but should be experienced in human rather than in godlike terms, so that erotic desires toward him as an object are not experienced as terrifying and engulfing.

Phases of transition can be seen through the transference phenomena of the clinical situation. Ogden speaks of the "hardness within softness" experienced as maternal transference transforms into father transference. He deduces from this that the father is first experienced as being within the mother, prior to being experienced as a separate other. In Kleinian theory as utilized by Hanna Segal ([1964] 1975), the developmental sequence is always one in which a father-mother internal fantasy forms before a separate father object fantasy forms.

In a situation of developmental arrest, when mothering has been inadequate during the preoedipal phases, I propose that the father remains undifferentiated from the mother. Further, I propose not only that the father can appear as a quality within the mother, as observed by Ogden, but that the mother can appear as a profound dynamic within the personified image of the father. Thus, in symbolic images of many arrested women writers, the father's personality appears fused with the dynamic aspects of a part object mother. One way of referring to this phenomenon, as Masterson (1981) does, is to speak of the father really being a preoedipal mother, since it is the psychic function of the father to which reference is made. Another way to speak of this phenomenon is to label—as Kernberg (1975) does—the transferential object as a "father-mother" figure that recapitulates the internal fantasy drama with an internal father-mother.

When a father obsession and its more generalized phallocentric addiction develop in such preoedipal or arrested females, the craving for a primary "holding" mother can be seen to compel the obsession and addiction. In this case, the father at rapprochement does not become a more-differentiated other who promotes separation, but rather serves as an alternative mother from whom the empathic attunement or holding that was so unavailable or disrupted with the actual mother is now sought. Then, with the emergence of erotic yearnings for the father at the oedipal stage, an already profound craving for the father is intensified and sexualized as he evokes desires for primitive tactile contact that are laced with erotic passion.

The female child's erotic desires for her father cause her to focus the frustrated cravings for her mother on men, particularly on male father figures. All of the women in this book exemplify father obsessions on this nature. Recent feminist concerns have focused on the importance of the mother in development. Sometimes the role of the father is deemphasized. The focus I have pursued in my study of the powerful influence of the father must be seen in relation to its reflection of unconscious yearnings that appear in women. These cannot be dismissed on account of any ideology. Indeed, some women have received sufficient whole object internalization with the mother to mourn and separate from the father through their creative work. However, the majority of the women in my study have suffered severe deficiencies in the intersubjective holding and/ or separation context of the mother-infant relationship; therefore they remain addicted to internal fathers who reflect malignant aspects of the early mother and father relations.

The father becomes the chief figure symbolized in the works of these father-obsessed women. Yet the dynamics of the early mother can be seen within the fantasy transactions between self and father that appear in their creative writings. Since the mother dynamic is contained within the personality features of the father object, the mother as a personality is not studied with the same emphasis that is placed on the father. My study also focuses on the father as an external and internal character, because of the father's critical role in reflecting his daughter's creative talents just as he mirrors her feminine strivings. This will be discussed further in chapter 4.

## The Creative Process as Mother

Whereas the internal father emerges in the form of images and characters within the creative work of women writers, the internal mother may show her presence largely through the form of the creative process itself; her presence is less predominant in the content. For the preoedipally arrested woman writer, the creative process may also offer the allure of providing the developmental mothering that is both needed and lacking. I do not agree with self psychologists such as Kligerman (1980) who see the creative process as actually fulfilling a self-object role, despite the fact that no affect contact and no empathic understanding from an external other are experienced. Kligerman views the creative process as fulfilling the mother's mirroring functions, for example. I do not agree, although I acknowledge the wish for the creative process to substitute for mothering functions. This wish is sorely disappointed time after time for those who have not adequately internalized a good enough mother to begin with.

I believe that the creative process is an experience of interacting with one's internal world. Such interaction can allow the creative work to provide containing and mirroring functions when these functions have already been adequately internalized in infancy so that they can be recreated within the context of the creating process. However, the yearnings for a holding mother and for an adequate mother of separation must be disappointed when no better object than that incorporated during the preoedipal years is provided. What can be projected into both the content and the process of the creative work can come only from what is already within and early internalization processes shape the developmental and reparative functions of the creative process.

## The Father As Demon and Demon Lover

You stand at the blackboard, daddy.
In the picture I have of you,

A cleft in your chin instead of your foot
But no less a devil for that, no not
Any less the black man who
Bit my pretty red heart in two,
        Plath, "Daddy," *Ariel*, 50, lines 52–56

Not God but a swastika
So black no sky could squeak through
                    lines 47–51

I was ten when they buried you.
At twenty I tried to die
And get back back back to you.
I thought even the bones would do . . .
—Sylvia Plath, ("Daddy") (p. 51, lines 58–61)

   When early preoedipal trauma has occurred, a young girl has a pathological relationship with the oedipal father; her mode of internalizing this oedipal father will also be pathological. The yearnings for the early preoedipal mother are transferred to the father as intense and insatiable cravings that also become combined with oedipal-level erotic longings. These longings enhance and exacerbate the intensity of the craving for the object. The young girl will both identify with her father and internalize him. Because of her early problems, she will not have a differentiated sense of self and other, with the result that she is unable psychically to assimilate the father into the self as a whole and differentiated object. Without this assimilation, the father takes on the character of the preoedipal object's archaic, grandiose form.[11] Consequently, interactions with the father are intrapsychically experienced as sadomasochistic in nature, since grandiose objects impinge rather than engage in dialogue. Any narcissistic pathology in the real father's personality significantly contributes to these sadomasochistic dynamics. This is all the more complex and enthralling since the urge toward reenactment of earlier traumatically aggressive interactions also plays a major role in the intrapsychic phenomena that become articulated in creative work. From the preoedipal period, incorporated relations of mother and infant press for reenactment, particularly if a closed system that does not allow modification of external object relations has been created. Without adequate preoedipal interactions with the mother, the father cannot be psychically digested. Father becomes merged with the undigested omnipotent mother and enacts the preoedipal drama as a masculinized tyrant perpetuating its terrors on a defenseless infant self. From Emily Dickinson's perspective:

        He fumbles at your Soul
        As Players at the keys

> Before they drop full Music on—
> He stuns you by degrees—
> Prepares your brittle Nature
> For the Ethereal Blow
> By fainter Hammers—further head—
> Then nearer—then so slow
> Your Breath has time to straighten—
> Your Brain—to bubble Cool—
> Deals—One—imperial—Thunderbolt—
> That scalps your naked Soul—
>
> (no. # 315)

In Sylvia Plath's words:

> Every woman adores a Fascist.
> The boot in the face, the brute
> Brute heart of a brute like you.
> (*Ariel*) "Daddy", 50.

The sadomasochistic torture involves also a partial fusion with the infant self, and this part of the self lends the internal father-mother its dynamic power, as Ogden comments (1986). A dynamically persecutory or abandoning internal object is created. Such a dynamic internal object presses for reenactment, which can take place within creative work as well as within dreams (see Segal 1985) or through "acting out" within life.

The reenactment of these early psychodynamics becomes manifested as demon lover themes in the works of female literary creators. The preoedipal and oedipal father, who can also be seen as a paternally colored early mother, dominates transactions that are compelled to be repeated from within a split-off, sealed-off, internal world.

As long as the engagement with the primary father-mother object remains sealed off from interpersonal contact, no affective awareness of the early traumatic relations can be felt. Therefore, the processes of abandonment depression mourning and of normal developmental mourning are both arrested. The work of women writers who have experienced inadequate preoedipal mothering repeatedly displays paranoid rage, numbness, manic defense, and splitting and disrupting movement toward mournful affect. A hostile internal environment, in which a split-off engagement with a bad object predominates, disallows any space for being open to healing contact with new, good external objects. Without such contact, the abandonment depression mourning (or Klein's depressive position mournings), so necessary to heal and repair the breach within the self—as well as between the self and the external world of interpersonal relations—is never felt and processed. In the absence of such an intense form of mourning, addiction to continuing reenactment, with its compulsive mode of object-seeking activity (which can be creative-process activity), occurs. Just as the father (and father substitutes) may become the source of addiction when he becomes the target of the yearnings for connection that were so frustrated in the early interaction with the mother, so too the creative work can become the source of addiction when it comes to represent the early father-mother internal part object. This work allows the drama with the father, that is inscribed within the internal world to be played out in an external medium; however, transformation of the daughter-father theme is limited, as is self-individuation.

Often, the split-off rage toward the father is most prominent in the creative work. Behind that rage, however, is yearning for the father, which becomes a passionate and compulsive driving force toward continuing engagement with the work. The demon lover literary theme captures the paradoxical dual aspect of love and hate behind the object yearning and its split-off rage. Sylvia Plath's example provides entree into the more detailed studies of Emily Brontë, Emily Dickinson, and Edith Sitwell. By contrast, the resolution of the demon lover theme attained within the creative work of Anaïs Nin leads into the more elaborate study of such resolution within the work and life of Charlotte Brontë. These last two women produced lives and creative work that evidence a higher level of psychological development than is seen in the lives and work of the first group of women. Nin and Charlotte Brontë are capable of mourning to a significant degree within the creative process, promoting separation and self-integration in relation to a more differentiated oedipal-stage father.

Father addiction seems to have been overlooked by self psychology theorists, particularly by Heinz Kohut (1977). Kohut advocates the compensatory aspects of a child's identification with the second parent, who is generally, as in all of Kohut's cases, the father. To see these relations with the father as compensatory when early relations with the mother have traumatically disrupted development of an integrated self is only part of the story. These father identifications, which I call secondary-parent identifications, are potentially addictive, since they become split-off incorporations that demand reenactment once the primary self has been sealed off owing to preoedipal trauma. The addictive ties of preoedipally arrested women to their fathers can be explained on this basis. Two themes coalesce around the origins and consequences of these addictive ties. The first theme is that of the developmental considerations that can limit the reparative potential of the creative process, while the second is that of the demonic role of the internal father within the psyche of the preoedipally arrested creative woman. I propose that incorporating a split-off father object impairs self-reparation even as it promotes the addictive syndrome of creative compulsion.

The lives and works of the preoedipally traumatized women examined here, in contrast to women such as Nin and Charlotte Brontë, suggest the following scenario. As these psychically arrested women invest their creative work with object-related energies and compulsively repeat primitive trauma, they are creatively expressing their aborted attempts to internalize a mothering object and to mourn developmentally. Their struggles to find and to digest an object, carried out through hungry searching for an idealized mother-father figure, remain unfulfilled throughout their lives. Dramatic disappointments color their creative work. Caught up in desperate cycles of searching and yearning, combined with attempts to exorcise the demonic incorporations that are chiefly derived from inadequate early parenting, these women ultimately show psychological degeneration, although they succeed in creating distinguished, indeed often profoundly brilliant, art. Even so, their attempts at self-reparation fail, and their development remains arrested. We will see many shades and nuances of various women writers's reparative struggles, following certain theoretical and developmental discussions that can enrich our observations.

# 3

# Mourning and Creative-Process Reparation

## Mourning As a Developmental Process

Years of clinical practice have taught me that mourning is the essential affective process that promotes self-integration as well as ongoing healthy internalization. If my observations are correct, mourning can be conceptualized as a primary developmental process. According to my view, internalization through mourning begins in the preoedipal stages of infancy and continues throughout the life cycle, changing in quality from childhood to adulthood.

Melanie Klein's psychoanalytic theory is a theory of affective phenomenology that displays the self in process through developmental mourning. Kleinian theory also describes the cognitive process that accompanies affective development within the mourning process, progressively consolidating the self. Such development is seen through the schematic mode of movement from the paranoid-schizoid to the depressive position. This schema describes how the internal representational world manifests self-development along a progressive-retrogressive continuum. Shifts forward into the depressive position are followed by regressions to paranoid-schizoid modes of more primitive functioning, as resistance follows self-integration prior to new levels of self-integration in the depressive position. Yet in the case of developmental arrest, fixation in primitive modes of paranoid-schizoid psychic functioning does not yield to the psychic integration that would normally be characteristic of an organically evolving self. Instead, the affects associated with the depressive position—mainly dysphoric affects—cannot be tolerated by those arrested in the preoedipal phases of development. Tolerating such dysphoric affects means tolerating the painful realization of loss that comes with awareness of the consequences of one's own actions and choices. Such developmentally arrested individuals can be seen as psychically situated in Klein's paranoid-schizoid position. In this position, ongoing archaic rage, manic catharsis, and its accompanying mode of externalization reinforce modes of splitting that deny the passage of time, deny the effects of one's behavior toward others, and deny the loss of the fantasy of paradise and perfection that comes with the knowledge of psychic reality and its ongoing state of ambivalence in love.

## The Paranoid-Schizoid Position

In the phenomenological stasis of the paranoid-schizoid position, one's self is split, as one's object is split, into omnipotent idealized and demonic parts. The omnipotent idealized other reflects the preoedipal fantasy of the primary parental object, which is perceived as godlike.[1] The other side of the split idealized object is the omnipotent demonic object. This demonic part object is experienced in early childhood; in infancy it is sensed in a visceral form that demands defensive retreat. Although for Melanie Klein the demonic object originates from the innate aggression of the death instinct, the demonic object can be also seen as a personified conglomerate of frustrations from ruptures in infant-mother bonding and dialogue (see Ogden 1986). These can likewise certainly be viewed as being enhanced and elaborated by innate aggression.[2]

Along with this split perception of the primary object, the adult who remains developmentally arrested in the paranoid-schizoid position suffers cycles of projecting the demonic part object outward in an attempt to rid herself or himself of distress provoked by terror over the bad object's power to annihilate, destroy, or injure the self, while also seeking fantasy union with the idealized part object for self-protection.[3] In this psychic position, the subject is unable to experience the parent as a whole, with both good and bad or nurturing and aggressive aspects. The invulnerable god ideal is imagined as unlimited in its power to nurture and heal the subject in its craving for the object and for the object's food or "breast."[4]

In psychoanalytic psychotherapy, the psychoanalyst's interpretation of the patient's belief that the therapist omnipotently knows everything can immediately relieve an impasse in treatment when a patient who has reached some capacity for depressive-position ambivalence slips back into the paranoid-schizoid position. The questioning of this unconscious belief—although possibly denied by the patient—can diffuse an oppositional stance to the psychoanalyst, since the fantasy of the analyst as omnipotently powerful is made conscious through such questioning. Once the view of the analyst's omnipotence is seen as questionable, the analyst can be viewed as more vulnerable; the patient can then surrender to his or her own vulnerability.

However, if someone is predominantly arrested in the paranoid-schizoid position, no such interpretation can diffuse the view of the object as omnipotent, because the person does not operate on the level of symbolism at which interpretations have meaningful links to cognitive and affective experience. Responses are visceral and reactive. The person either lives perpetually in a state of fear of the bad (demonic) object, which he or she seeks to expel or exorcise through projection, or is engaged in a blissful fantasy of merger with the ideal object. The effort to rid the self of the demonic object is futile, since it is also a part of the self. In addition, to the extent that the paranoid-schizoid individual cannot interpret his or her own experience, the development of a subjective sense of self is thwarted.[5] Without an adequate sense of one's own interpretive subjectivity, differentiation from the object or other cannot proceed.

The projection process most operative in the paranoid-schizoid position is that of projective identification. The bad part object, (or simply "bad object") is not only projected outward but is also identified with in a primitive, enacted way rather than in a psychic or conscious way.[6] This identification is shown through controlled another so that the object is made to feel what one is avoiding feeling oneself. The subject does not just imagine that the other feels his disowned feelings but actually induces such feelings in the other. Since the effort to expel the bad object and the aversive affects linked to it is futile, cycles of frustrated attempts follow. Yet the intense pressure of persecutory anxiety that comes with these projective cycles can be relieved by periods of blissful union with an idealized other. These are the periods in which fantasy merger is experienced.

In Klein's view, the infant at this beginning stage of preoedipal development is split into alternate states of primitive consciousness in relation to the two part object forms. Therefore, the infant will be undisturbed by awareness of any persecutory bad parent, as long as he feels engaged with the idealized parent. This allows for a state of bliss, so that feeding can occur without terror disrupting nurturance. Still, insatiable need (called "greed" by Klein) and its accompanying affective reaction of "envy" can disrupt the bliss with the idealized breast, turning engagement with it into a persecutory situation again. This can come about since the infant, or the paranoid-schizoid person, does not perceive the vulnerability or limits of the object and may wish for unlimited supplies from it, thus being led to inevitable disappointment. However, Klein does not deal with the role of real trauma in promoting either a sense of insatiable need or narcissistic expressions of envy, which involve devaluing and, more profoundly, spoiling the object and one's experience with the object.

## The Role of the Real Mother

What role does the real parent—generally the mother at this infant stage—play in the paranoid-schizoid situation? Also, what role does this maternal parent play in the infant's psychological changes as he moves from the paranoid-schizoid position to the more advanced depressive position? Klein's theory originally failed to conceptualize the real mother's role in early infant development. The infant was thought to be so engulfed in a world of psychic fantasy that he was not believed to perceive the real mother until depressive-position mourning could proceed. Klein's "mother" was merely allowed a background role as a benign figure modifying the terror of the paranoid-schizoid position through her goodness. However, through what has been learned from modern infant research (e.g., Mahler et al. 1975, Stern 1985) as well as from the contributions of D. W. Winnicott (1965) and Ronald Fairbairn (1952), we can see how early on—perhaps even prenatally—the real mother plays a critical role in psychological development. Therefore, in discussing the cognitive and affective process of the depressive position, I will emphasize the role of the mother's adequacy in relation to determining whether the depressive position can be attained in any stable form and to what extent it may be either aborted or worked through to stages of developmental resolution.

## The Depressive Position

In Kleinian theory, as the infant matures to six or seven months, the split perception of the world related to the paranoid-schizoid position yields to incremental stages of self-integration that constitute the depressive position. It is within the depressive position that whole object perception is attained.[7] The primary mothering parent or breast is now seen neither as a godlike ideal form nor as a demonic bad-object form. The mother becomes perceived as a whole person who has both bad and good qualities. The infant now experiences that the mother is vulnerable, and a sense of concern for her begins to develop. Winnicott (1965), following Klein in his focus on the development of concern, emphasizes the role of the mother in being with her baby as making her a "good enough" mother. A good enough mother can promote both the development of concern and a sustained mother internalization that can facilitate the "capacity to be alone" (1965, 29–36).

At this stage, the infant—or the adult in the depressive position—begins to feel a sense of sorrowful grief, which can alternate with rage derived from the former era of persecutory terror. This sorrowful grief, which manifests itself as feelings of guilt, pain, and the loving sadness of loss, involves a new subjective sense of self, as a conscious sensing of regret and remorse toward the parental object emerges through the mourning process. The mother is now seen as vulnerable to the infant's own aggression. Because she is not split into a hated object and a good object, the infant cannot escape the experience that now his good mother is also the mother at whom he directs his hate, that he is hurting the mother he loves.[8] The infant becomes preoccupied with his own hate; he tries to moderate it and control it through loving affection toward the mother. If love is greater than hate, guilt related to perceived or fantasized injuries against the mother can yield to the mournful sorrow of loss. This is the mourning process that becomes the essence of lifelong self-integration. Such integration repairs and restores the object within the internal world and therefore provides the building blocks of the sense of self.

The subject now feels sadness in the sense of regret that things cannot be undone (see Ogden 1986). One's decisions count now, as do one's mistakes. The harm others can never be totally repaired, although awareness of remorse and loss allows reparative strivings to lead to potential interpersonal understanding. Winnicott, responding to Klein's theory—as well as compensating for what her theory lacked in relation to the real mother—emphasizes the capacity of the mother to "survive" the infant's aggressive instinctual needs in determining whether a child's love becomes stronger than his hate. Whereas for Klein the ratio of love to hate is an innate factor, in Winnicott's theory it is always highly dependent on the role of the external mother. The mother's capacity to sustain contact with her child, to survive aggressive attacks from her child with continuing maternal care, and to be "used" to implement her child's needs and to respond affectively to his "omnipotent gestures" are all critical, in Winnicott's thinking, to determining whether the child's true self survives. The mother's survival is also critical in defining whether archaic aggression is modified into constructive modes of relatedness, including the capacity for concern. Such maternal survival makes the depressive-position mourning and integration process possible.

In my own view, maternal or overall parental survival can be described in terms of a number of factors. Such survival includes containing aggression, translating the child's needs and fears implicit behind the aggression into an understandable form, and ultimately continuing to be available for responsive emotional contact. Sometimes this involves active modes of engagement on the part of the parent; sometimes this involves a more receptive attunement. All of this is critical for neutralizing aggression. Such survival is also critical for modifying splitting and the demons that result from it, so that the good aspects of the parental object can be felt and sustained through internalization.

In Klein's theory, the infant who is in the depressive position because he can experience more love than hate is now able to build an internal world in which the maternal object can be kept alive as a whole object figure. The whole object other also becomes integrated into the basic sense of self through internal identification and attachment, so that a whole sense of self forms. Through sustaining the object inside—whether this is viewed as fantasy or representation—object constancy is made possible, and this reinforces the new whole sense of self. This whole self, similar to that of the new whole object, contains good and bad aspects. As mourning proceeds, a loving tie with the whole object parent is internalized, and a loving and loved sense of the self develops. Healthy narcissism then develops, which, in parallel with healthy object relations, involves tolerance for the ambivalence of love and hate derived from love being more predominant than hate. This more secure self develops images of the self and other ("phantasies" in Klein's term) that are characterized by predominantly good qualities, enabling bad qualities to be consciously acknowledged and tolerated as they become proportionately less threatening. The more loving and better the tie between self and other is, the more successfully the critical affective mourning process can continue. Thus, a developmental process continues, and increasing increments of integration of self and object occur within the internal world of the psyche, forming the psychic structure of image introjects. As loving connections are promoted and internalized, and as loving capacity is expanded, integration of the good and bad aspects of the self representation and of the object representation is increased, and then increments in the process of integration relate to new loving contacts.

This is the way in which I have formulated the transformation of fantasy into structure in Kleinian theory. Mourning involves tolerating and processing the depressive affects of grief, guilt, and loss, as well as tolerating consciousness of depressive fantasies. It is the psychic impact of one's own destructive impulses toward the object that largely constitutes depressive fantasies. To tolerate consciousness of such fantasies involves a sense of anguished loss to the self, i.e., a loss in omnipotence—for the infant is now aware of his intense caring and of the need for a separate object mother that goes along with that caring. One of my female adult patients illustrates this sense of loss and grief related to caring for the mother.

> Ms. P. screamed out "I did it, I did it! It's true! I did it!" at the point at which I interpreted her unconscious belief that she "used her mother up and killed her." She cried and grieved for the first time then, as she confessed her buried hate for her mother that had been shielded by defensive idealization. She felt then that she had not loved her mother enough, that her mother had loved her so, and she had a secret hate that continued to fester inside of her. She could only confess this to me after the height of her expression of hatred towards me. Her hatred of me was followed by her report of a dream, which brought hints of her guilt towards me and its graphic images of sucking the breasts and making erotic love to the lost and longed for mother.

## A Sense of Agency

As mourning facilitates an awareness of one's own "crimes," which are now tolerable even though aggressive, a sense of agency within the self develops, and an urgent wish to make reparation to the injured parental object can be assuaged by an ability to interact with the object in loving ways. What might be enacted in the form of an apology by the adult can be expressed toward the mother, by the infant, through nonverbal and later verbal expressions of gratitude, caring, and generous gestures of praise and love. The child becomes capable of counter-nurturance, and of countersensitivity resonating with the mother's own nurturant attunement.

Here Klein acknowledges the role of the real mother, although she speaks in the broad sense of the primary other as "object." The mother's actions become critical in terms of whether reparation is accepted or rejected (see Klein [1957] 1975). Rejection of reparation causes regressive reactions in the infant, as the love object's rejection of reparation would in the adult. Rather than promote depressive-position integration, rejected offers of reparation cause backlash reactions in which there is a return to depression, with aspects of splitting and paranoia.

## Mourning and Internalization

Mourning and introjective internalization go hand in hand with the dynamics of the depressive position. This phenomenology of the formation of the structure of the psyche and self through affective process can be traced back to Freud's paper "Mourning and Melancholia" (1914), in which he speaks of the introjection of a lost object ("the shadow of the object" falls "across the ego"). Klein extends Freud's thoughts on mourning. Unlike the latter's focus on the pathological aspects of failed mourning, which he spoke of in terms of the melancholic who holds on to his bad internal object (as elaborated by Fairbairn), Klein's interest is in successful mourning. She connects successful mourning with self- and psychic-structure development, since self-integration is defined in terms of the integration of a world of mixed internal objects (both good and bad objects). Klein begins to view mourning as a natural developmental process, in which progressive self-integration becomes the definition of health. As self-integration proceeds and strengthens the sense of self, the developing subject can gradually relinquish the idealized archaic part object and experience a whole object mother or "other." Although Klein does not specifically deal with separation trauma and is apt to subsume separation conflicts under the more instinctual aspects of "weaning," the depressive-position process of self-integration that she describes can come about only if the self has not been sealed off because of separation trauma or because of trauma related to archaic modes of aggression.

When the infant grows into a toddler, his dependence on the parents, and particularly on the parental and caretaking figures who provide mothering, enters the child's conscious sense of self. The affective state of tolerating such awareness of dependence on another is a critical part of Klein's depressive-position experience. From such knowledge, envy and its related narcissistic aspect of shame inevitably result.[9] Again, it is Winnicott rather than Klein who deals with the real mother's impact here. Winnicott writes of the mother's ability to allow the infant to be part of her as the route to modifying envy (1965).[10] The ultimate mode of ongoing modification, which leads to symbolic sublimations, is that of the depressive-position affective mourning process; this continues throughout life, as both a reparative and a psychic-structure-building developmental process. Object internalization, with its complementary aspects of self-integration and -differentiation, is intrinsic to this affective process, thus defining the latter as a developmental process.

## Manic Defense

In the more primitive paranoid-schizoid position, splitting and projection, or projective identification, are the chief defensive reactions to the threat at the preseparation stage of self-annihilation or injury.[11] By contrast, in the depressive position, the chief threat becomes the pain and anguish of the depressive mourning affects and the awareness of the object loss. Related to such pain are the guilt and shame akin to the depressive fantasies that are psychically embedded in painful thoughts and in an array of affects that are largely unconscious. Such shame, guilt, and anguish, as well as the painful sense of grief-filled loss, cannot always be tolerated. Again, Klein fails to mention the impact of the actual mother's behavior here in helping the child build tolerance for such affects. Yet she is acutely aware of how critical such affect tolerance is for self-development (i.e., integration and differentiation) to proceed. Klein was also aware of how often defense arrested the depressive mourning and self-integration process because of the incapacity or unwillingness of the subject to experience this form of pain. She calls the main form of defense in relation to this new depressive-position threat the "manic defense."

Manic defense is a way of warding off vulnerability to affect experience through assuming a position of superiority in relation to one's internal object(s) and the related external object(s)—specifically in relation to the mothering parent in the primal case of the infant. In the manic stance of the adult, one is apt to assume contempt, control, and triumph over the threatening other.[12] The other is devalued and diminished in stature in one's own mind. In this way, by "spoiling" the object, one is able to deny how important the other is and how deeply one feels one's own need for the other. Shame and need intensify the manic state.

The child's need for the mother is total. Yet this can be denied by a reversal of roles in the child's mind, so that the mother is seen as the one who is small, inadequate, and thus dependent on him. This state of denial walls the subject off from the emotional reality of the situation and from the depressive affects that would come with acknowledging the reality of the dependency. The same is true for the adult. Psychically, the subject stands above his or her own needy and vulnerable self in standing above the needed object in his or her own mind, while enacting this defensive stance within external interpersonal relations.

Following from this are certain implications not directly mentioned by Klein in her theory. Most important is that anyone who uses the manic defense stands above any injured part of his or her own self, avoiding affective contact with the object, so that conscious experiencing of past trauma can be avoided. Given external contact with an empathic object, such a defensive stance becomes like bandaging a wound without opening it so that it can heal. Kohut's idea of a selfobject providing contact initiated from the external empathic other does not deal with this critical issue. Kohut does not consider whether the internal self, together with its related object, has been sealed off owing to early trauma or whether it has been opened up owing to consciously reliving the trauma and healing its wound through mourning. In his discussion of the narcissistic personality disorder, James Masterson (1981) seems to be aware of the clinical dynamics of this issue and stresses the necessity for the patient to initiate contact, which opens up the traumatic internal situation that has been perpetuated in relation to the bad-object incorporation from the time of the original trauma, with continual reenactment resulting.

Returning to Klein's view of the position of manic defense, we can see that identification with a second parent or with other figures in the person's life can also be used defensively to wall off contact with the primary vulnerable (needy and/or injured) self, such as a masculine identification with the father in the case of a little girl. This can contribute to the manic position of grandiose superiority.

The manic defense involves a form of control over the object, so that the subject actively attempts to put the object in the position that he or she wishes it to be in. An internal object can be psychically controlled in this way. However, the enactment in the internal world is also complemented by attempted enactment in relation to the real object in the external world. In order for both internal and external manic reactions to take place, the splitting and projective-identification mechanisms of the paranoid-schizoid position are once more deployed. The self-image is split into both a grandiose, omnipotent form and a devalued and impotent form. Then, the devalued part is projected onto the external object so that contempt toward that object can be used to ward off attachment need; this attitude of contempt provides a fantasy power that creates the illusion of triumph and domination. Since the self is relatively more separate from the object at this point, projection rather than projective identification may occur, but attempted control of the other is also evident in the manic stance.

Such manic defense arrests mourning. As long as manic warding off of affect persists, the experience of loss and grief necessary for mourning is arrested. Thus, self-integration and complementary self-differentiation cannot developmentally proceed.

## Manic versus True Reparation

Manic defense extends to Melanie Klein's ideas concerning manic versus true reparation. Klein conceptualizes manic defense as an arrest in reparative mourning by speaking about manic reparation.

According to Klein (1935; 1937; 1940) and her follower Hanna Segal ([1964] 1975; 1985), "true reparation" involves the genuine affective experience of depressive "phantasies." When reparation to the external and internal object is truly made, one can own one's aggressive attacks on the primary internal object and thus can experience a sense of guilt and loss that comes with depressive fantasies of how the other is injured. Sadness is the depressive affect that most clearly articulates this process of internal reparation, since it congeals and interacts with reparative acts toward current external objects. The pain of guilt may be more or less present in this sadness; regret, remorse, and gratitude for the goodness of the object are all experienced along with it. Insofar as love for the object is more predominant than a sense of guilt, sadness will be felt and tolerated. As the sadness is felt, the controls against it relax, and there is a sense of letting go that brings a lessening of paranoia and an increasing openness to contact with others. Thus, the mourning experience brings reparative self-healing and personality growth.

In manic reparation, on the other hand, the mourning experience is not felt. One attempts to restore lost or dead objects without acknowledging guilt or feeling loss. An element of magic is involved. One looks for the quick fix; drugs or alcohol are often used to create the illusion of restored internal objects, without the painful depressive effects of the mourning process being experienced. In manic reparation, there is no letting go of defensive control, in which one tries to control one's internal and external objects. Control is prominent in the contemptuous attitude of the manic state in which one triumphs in one's own narcissistic fantasy over the internal parental objects and over the transferential representatives as they currently exist in external reality. One of my own analysand's clearly illustrated this state of manic defense and its attempt at manic repair.

> As though speaking from some superior height, she rapidly fired a whole list of my problems at me. Agitated by her resented and currently unacknowledged need for me, she attempted to fix me with non-stop criticism. Her attempt to fix me in this manic-paced manner was also her attempt to fix herself quickly,

immediately, because she wanted to be achieving goals in her life that she was not ready to achieve. She couldn't stand being within herself at that moment, for she was warding off the depressive pain of facing all that was still unresolved for her, and facing the emotional reality of who she was at that moment. She could not maintain the illusion that she was her ideal self, yet she made a frantic effort to "fix me" so that I could fix her right away and take away her pain. When in this manic state, my patient seemed cold, closed off, distant, and frantic. She saw me as a "kid" part of her, and yet simultaneously feared that I had omnipotent control over her, and omniscient knowledge as she tried to omnipotently control me. In this manic stance, where rapid assault was a means of manic reparation, this woman gave me no room to respond, and it felt like there was not even any room to breathe. She allowed no "analytic space" between us, so at that moment we could not engage in meaningful dialogue.

The work with this woman also illustrates the movement that can be made from manic defense into true mournful reparation when unconscious projective identifications are interpreted.

In a session following the one mentioned, I said to my analysand that she seemed to think that I knew everything that was going on with us at the moment and she seemed to think that I knew everything that was supposed to follow in the future. When I articulated this, she seemed to just become really conscious, and she agreed that she did believe I had such knowledge. She calmed down, and I could see that she was greatly relieved. I believed that her unconscious fantasy of my omnipotence was tapped, and was being made less threatening as it was addressed in some objective conceptual space between us. Following my comment and her response, she was able to engage in a discussion with me concerning how she thought my problematic responses to her in the recent past could be related to her behavior, as well as to discuss how her reactions to me might stem from my behavior. At that point, I could feel like there were truly two of us in the room, as emotional contact was regained. My analysand began to acknowledge the need she felt for me, which she had been fending off. Feeling this personal need for me made her sad, and with her sadness came a mournful awareness that she could not fix herself quickly, and that she still wanted my help. At this point of mourning, my analysand could let me be with her without fearing my ineptitude or my dominance. In this way, she could begin to more fully internalize me as a good object, who had a loving bond with her. The internalization of this loving connection allowed her fears, fantasies and aggression to become tolerable, and a critical self-integration process was renewed.

My understanding of this mourning process has its conceptual routes in the theory of Melanie Klein. Given Melanie Klein's view of the mourning process as essential to true self-reparation, one can see that this theorist's concept of mourning goes beyond that of Freud ("Mourning and Melancholia" [1917]) to a belief that it is a basic developmental growth process. According to Klein, it is through the experience of true affective mourning that the basic developmental requirements of internalization and self-integration take place. Therefore, it is not surprising that some other psychoanalytic theorists have come to apply the conceptual construct of the mourning experience to a process of evolution that can take place through the creative process, effecting true self-reparation, i.e., reparation of the self through reparation of the internal object.

## A Kleinian Illustration

Hanna Segel ([1964] 1975) illustrates these comparative dynamics of reparation with a play therapy case example. She describes a little girl who expresses rageful aggression toward a play paint set—a paint set that Segal, as the play therapist, interprets to represent symbolically to the girl, her mother and her mother's breasts. After the girl has upset the paints in the paint box ("destroyed the mother's breasts"), she rebels against the loss of the paints by denying it and insisting that the play therapist instantly fix the paints so that they appear perfect again. As she makes this demand on the therapist, she is indignant, impatient, and pushy, illustrating the contempt, control, and assumed superiority of the manic-defense attitude. As the therapist attempts to fix the paint set in response to her junior tyrant's directive, the little girl jumps impatiently from foot to foot, singing her magic chant, "Easy, weasy, let's get busy" (98) over and over as she shouts for the therapist to hurry. She attempts to control the therapist's actions to get what she wants immediately. In Kleinian terms, she treated the therapist like a part object, like an extension of herself or a servant, not like a human being or equal.) This cannot succeed in getting her what she wants, and she leaves the play session angry.

However, the following day there is quite a change in the girl's attitude. She comes into her play therapy session in a subdued and quiet mood. She looks at the paint set with mournful regret and reveals sadness in her eyes and voice. She says, "Isn't it a pity it's so spoilt?" and then suggests to her play therapist, "Let's try to mend it together" (99). She is then able to cooperate with the therapist in a joint effort so that the paints in the paint box can be partially repaired. This time she shows patience and accepts the fact that she has suffered a loss that can never be totally repaired. The paint box will never be as it was. In accepting this, the little girl establishes a closeness with her therapist through the tolerance of mournful—and thus sad and loving—feeling. She can now feel concern for the therapist, and she and the therapist can share and be together. Thus, true reparation has been accomplished, and this openness to her feelings allows her to internalize the experience with the symbolic mother and with the transference father, i.e., the therapist, so that she might learn from her experience and have a more integrated and differentiated sense of self. Her capacity for interpersonal connection has been enhanced.

## Mourning and Reparation through the Creative Process

Melanie Klein viewed creativity as being motivated by the urge to repair the internal parental object, which had been damaged by one's own aggression. Indirectly, this was an attempt to repair the self, since self-reparation depended on having a whole and healthy internal object within one's internal world. In her paper "A Psychoanalytic Approach to Aesthetics," Hanna Segal (1952) elaborates Klein's view of reparative strivings that are expressed through creative work. She speaks about facing depressive fantasies within the process of creativity and begins to conceptualize creativity as a developmental mourning process in which early parental objects—felt to be lost because of anxieties about the damage having been done by one's own aggression—are, in Segal's term, "recreated" (199). The anxieties about object loss are faced with the creative work; in this way the objects can be repaired:

> In creating a tragedy I suggest the success of the artist depends on his being able fully to acknowledge and express his depressive phantasies and anxieties. In expressing them he does work similar to the work of mourning in that he internally recreates a harmonious world, which is projected into his work of art. (196–207)

Commenting again on mourning as a process of psychic structuralization that can be evolved through creative work, she writes, "It is only when the loss has been acknowledged, and the mourning experienced, that re-creation can take place" (199). Specifically in relation to the writer Marcel Proust, she says "Writing a book is for him like the work of a mourning in that gradually the external objects are given up. They are re-instated in the ego, and recreated in the book" (199).

In these quotes, we can see clearly the view of creativity that Segal derived from the Kleinian model of psychological development. She sees creativity as the recreation of the original parental objects that have been lost—not only through one's own aggression, but also through necessary developmental separation. The focus on separation can be seen in relation to Klein's writing (1936) on "weaning" from the breast. Inasmuch as creativity is a recreation from the experience of these losses, it is an act of mourning. Thus, it is the work of mourning—as described in Melanie Klein's "Mourning and Its Relation to Manic-Depressive States" (1940)—to which Segal relates recreation.

In relation to Segal's theoretical comments, we can see that the extent to which a state of blocked mourning can be turned into a mourning process (in which internal objects are assimilated into the self-structure) can largely depend on the degree of mourning that can be achieved through the affective experience of the creative process. It will be seen, as we continue, how the pathological mourning state as briefly outlined in chapter 7 presents a particular problem in this regard.

In Segal's and in Klein's views, mourning is the essential development process of self-integrative internalization, and it continues throughout the life cycle. Psychic structure is created through the mourning process, i.e., through the assimilation of external objects and split-off parts of the self into the psyche so that they can become a fixed part of the intrapsychic structure as internal objects. Internalization thus depends on the affective experience of the depressive affects of guilt and loss; the experience of love allows the guilt and loss to be tolerated. One can look at the bad parts of oneself, which bring guilt and the loss of injury, only when a secure bond of love is felt. Guilt and loss become tolerable as love of a good object is sustained, validating the sense of a good self. Naming the bad parts of one's self and sharing concern about changing one's bad features into more kindness and gratitude toward others are all part of mourning. Thus, mourning and conscious symbolic conceptualization are interactive, as they both developmentally evolve. Insofar as mourning is the prominent mode of developmental internalization, the creative process becomes of utmost importance in the degree to which it allows the work of mourning to be done.

## Mourning through the Creative Process: George Pollock

A view more recent than Hanna Segal's that like Segal's correlates with my own on the interaction of the mourning process and creativity is that of George Pollock, the Director of the Chicago School of Psychoanalysis. In his paper "The Mourning-Liberation Process and Creativity: The Case of Kathe Kollwitz," he writes that

> the artist wishes to express what she feels, sees, and can put on her canvas. This is part of the mourning process. With the expressions comes liberation—internally . . . What remains of psychoanalytic interest is the way in which she was able to make the lifelong mourning process that accompanied these losses serve her artistic creativity. There is no evidence that Kollwitz was able, during any interval of her life, to resolve fully her mourning-liberation process. But there is abundant evidence that she was able to mourn through her creative

products. To this extent, she exemplifies a thesis I have propounded elsewhere, namely, that in certain individuals "great creativity may not be the outcome of the successfully completed mourning process but may be indicative of attempts at completing the mourning work. These creative attempts may be conceptualized as restitution, reparation, discharge or sublimation. Though they may not always be successful in terms of mourning work solutions, the intrinsic aesthetic or scientific merit of the work still may be great despite the failure of mourning completion." (351)

Pollock (1987, 346) elsewhere speaks of mourning in terms of an "adaptational process" that goes on through a lifetime, in contrast to "grief," which is the affective part of that process. Earlier, in 1975, he spoke of all "changes, losses, or transitions" as requiring a mourning process to evolve the normal adaptational process of development. In speaking of changes and transitions as well as losses, he brings self-change—other than that related to object loss—under the umbrella of mourning process and resolution. He also describes the psychic structure that he sees as carrying on this process in terms of an "ego" that perceives and reacts to the "self" (1975, 424). In other words, changes, losses, or transitions in the self—as it appears to the ego in representational form ("component representations," 424)—are affectively processed through the ego, so that new intrapsychic structuralization, or what Pollock calls "reintegration" (1987, 351), can take place.

## Margaret Mahler

Unlike Wolfenstein (1968), who believes that children cannot mourn until adolescence, Margaret Mahler (1975) surmised from her empirical studies on mothers and infants that toddler-stage infants manifest depressive affects akin to mourning. Particularly during rapprochement, (18 to 36 months), infants display a "low-keyedness" and become hypersensitive to separations from others in their world.

My own informal observation of two-year-old infants resonates with Mahler's observations. Loss seems to become a daily experience to be talked about. The toddler's comments often resemble the following expressions: "P. is gone!" or "Where did C. go?" Irritable affect responses are frequently heard along with such comments, ranging from tantrums to perturbed and wistful looks, and sometimes to tears. The ego needs to be quite strong to tolerate the affect of mournful sadness, which Klein refers to as "depressive." Without good mother-infant bonding, such sad affect cannot be tolerated. Thus, we might observe many cases in which mourning is impossible in children and enactment with paranoid rage and repetition takes its place. However, Mahler has helped us become more aware that the mournful sadness that she describes as "low-keyedness" can occur in healthy infants who receive empathic maternal attunement.

## Hans Loewald

In "The Waning of the Oedipus Complex" (1979), Hans Loewald brings the concept of mourning into the realm of the oedipal era. Our guilt over oedipal wishes stirs an enormous need for parental response and survival. This need for parents to endure their children's aggression at the oedipal stage resonates back to Winnicot's (1971) ideas on the need for the mother to "survive" her infant's aggressive attacks during infancy. The mourning process that Loewald speaks of as the "waning" of oedipal conflict can occur only to the extent that parental survival is perceived and assimilated into our awareness. Again, the ability to mourn depends on parental response—now particularly in terms of the same-sex parent's ability to tolerate, and even to accept, murderous wishes directed toward him or her. As we succeed in our accomplishments, Loewald suggests that we enact murder by symbolically murdering the parent with whom we are in competition and by symbolically winning the forbidden object of desire. Throughout life we experience this. The oedipus complex is not resolved; it wanes. Parental survival allows us to let go of our parents and to tolerate the damage that we ourselves have done to them as we surpass and leave them. Yet as Klein and Segal postulate, this letting go is accomplished with regret and a sense of loss. We win and surpass our parents only by paying the price of remorse and grief. The grief is for those whom we can continue to love and be loved by only if we feel with them and for them, rather than wall them off in the defensive state of manic triumph.

In "The Waning of the Oedipus Complex" as well as in an earlier paper, "Internalization, Separation, Mourning, and the Superego" (1962), Loewald suggests that mourning is a developmental process by focusing on the gradations of incomplete resolution that follow from the initial oedipal-stage conflict. Loewald, like Melanie Klein and Kleinians such as Hanna Segal, experiences life as a continuing process of working through guilt and loss. He sees mourning as a continuing process of self-integration. This view of life experience resonates very closely with my own. It is also a view that highlights the need for a primary vehicle by which self-conflict and mournful degrees of resolution can be experienced and expressed. Many have looked toward the creative process to find such a vehicle.

## Edith Jacobson and Althea Horner

In her book and monograph, *The Self and the Object World* (1954; 1964), Jacobson extends the concept of mourning to the adolescent era. She writes of "the significant role of mourning in the struggle of the adolescent, who must disengage himself from his parents and embark on a search for new objects" (1964, 160). She also writes that "adolescence is life between a saddening farewell to childhood—i.e., to the self and the objects of the past—and a gradual, anxious-hopeful passing over many barriers through the gates which permit entrance to the as yet unknown country of adulthood. Beginning with his infantile love objects, the adolescent not only must free himself from his attachments to persons who were all-important during childhood; he must also renounce his former pleasures and pursuits more rapidly than at any former developmental stage" (161).

Although ongoing mourning can be part of development, there are of course critical eras for such normal mourning self-transition that are most distinct during childhood. Mahler has touched on the mourning of the separation-individuation phase, which can be seen to overlap with Klein's depressive position. Loewald has focused on the necessary mourning related to the oedipal era, a mourning that continues throughout life with varying transformations and permutations. This also overlaps with Klein's depressive position. Again, in adolescence the aspects both of separation-individuation and of the oedipal phase are revived with a new instinctual intensity. Jacobson's recognition of this phenomena, as a "drive-structure" or "structural model" theorist is complemented by the work of Althea Horner, an object relations theorist.

In a book entitled *The Wish for Power and the Fear of Having It* (1988), Horner writes of the need for the benevolent survival of the parents in the face of adolescent aggression and claiming of autonomous power. Like Winnicott's stress on the mother's survival of infant aggression, Horner emphasizes the role of the real parents in allowing individuating growth to take place. Ties to parents—and to their power and overall identity—need not only to be renounced, but need to be internalized and preserved within the developing adolescent self with its accompanying ego ideal or "self-ideal". Jacobson's mode of renunciation can take place only if a tolerable level of mournful sadness is induced by the love for benevolent parents that leads to mournful internalization. Jacobson speaks of mourning, and Horner speaks of the psychological threat of overwhelming depression (88) in the face of traumatic parent loss owing to the malevolent use of parental power. The fine line between pathological depression, or pathological mourning, and healthy developmental mourning through the tolerance of sadness in relinquishing parental ties is, I agree with Horner, highly dependent on the parental use of power and on the parents' survival of their adolescent children's power as it is aggressively directed against them. This adolescent use of power against the parents is one transitional avenue that such power must follow before it can be used more effectively for constructive, independent strivings. However, I disagree with Horner that a benevolent attitude of the parents in relation to their own power and to that of their adolescent child can fully immunize the child against depression and anxiety (1988, 88). There is a normal depressive sadness in adolescence, perhaps like the low-keyedness of separation-individuation, with a renewed sturm und drang tone of rapprochement, that can never be alleviated by parental behavior, although parental behavior modifies its form. If this normal sadness is not used experientially to integrate old patterns of relating to parents with new patterns of relating to heterosexual love objects and peers, as well as to differentiate the two forms of relations so that aspects of incestuous family ties are surrendered—if not fully renounced—the necessary developmental transition is not completed. Without such completion, a vehicle for mourning of the parental love objects must be found later in life. For many creative persons who have achieved the adolescent stage of developmental conflict, the creative process may become the vehicle by which residual adolescent mourning can be accomplished.

## A Theory of Creativity Based on Healthy versus Pathological Mourning

My own view is that development, as well as resistance and arrest, can be understood in terms of the mourning process. This includes the developmental prerequisites of the psychic structure for mourning to proceed, as well as the blocks that can inhibit mourning, owing to structural conflicts, when the primary psychic structure has been adequately established.

George Pollock seems to be in accord with my thinking. I believe that we both address a process that can be arrested at various levels of development. Arrested mourning, as viewed through the internal representational world seen in creative work, encompasses all levels of defense and conflict and puts these phenomena under the general umbrella of the mourning process. Arrested mourning would extend along a continuum from pathological mourning, which pertains to the preoedipal person, to mourning aborted by the repression processes and structural conflicts of the creatively blocked neurotic, continuing further to healthy mourning in those capable not only of depressive affects and fantasies but of an organic—as opposed to a magical or contrived—resolution of such depressive phenomena.

I propose that the developmental dynamics of self-experience along Klein's continuum, from the paranoid-schizoid to the depressive positions, can be observed within the creative work of distinguished writers. Biographical trends in the writers can also be seen to reflect the trends in their work.

When I speak of self-experience in such terms, I mean reparative self-striving toward integration, differentiation, and authenticity. Such self-striving can occur on various developmental levels. When we acknowledge that creative work reflects both the creative process and the internal representational world, we can view it to determine whether a developmental mourning process successfully consolidates and finds resolution within the creative work.

## Shades and Innuendoes of Reparation

The primary criteria of true reparation should be based on the degree to which self-integration and self-differentiation have both been achieved, as well as on the level at which they have been achieved. Short of such true reparation, many modes of cathartic, manic, and compensatory reparation can be seen. These might temporarily enhance the cohesion, aliveness, and stability of the self, but I propose that they would not lead to a developmentally sustained growth process as authentic mourning and reparation would.

I will consider the demon lover theme as one symbolic mode in which the reparative motif, as well as its failures, can be observed. When the demon lover theme becomes a demon lover complex, the pathological mourning dynamics of arrested mourning will be apparent and reparative movements will be seen to be disrupted. When the demon lover theme is symbolic of relational and psychic structure conflict, its resolution through mourning within the creative process and its product can be observed.

# 4

# Creative Women and the Internal Father

Very little has been written about distinguished creative women or about creative development in women in general. One exception is a well-known essay by Phyllis Greenacre from 1960, "Women as Artist." Even in this essay, in which an attempt is made to focus on the topic, the female analyst Greenacre dismisses the large majority of female artists with some prejudice. In fact, she writes that for the most part there have been more competent than distinguished women artists.

Having made this assumption, Greenacre then tries to buttress it with Freudian theory. She claims that the anatomical nature of the genitals accounts for men externalizing their genital sensations in artistic form, whereas women keep all their genital arousal locked up inside in the personal and emotional domain, failing to bring these sensations out into the world in impersonal artistic form. Essentially, she claims that on the phallic level women fear exposure of themselves in reference to the "castration complex" (59). She seems to believe that women fail to express themselves and reveal themselves in creative work, because they would experience such exposure as a shameful display of their hidden and internal sex organs.

Greenacre then draws on another explanation as well to proclaim further the artistic timidity of women. She proposes that the need for "infantile diplomacy" in the oedipal daughter, who must depend on the mother with whom she is in rivalry, accounts for a dampening of the "full expansiveness of creative originality" (591). In addition, Greenacre claims that women fear the bisexual elements that they would need to tolerate as "creative individuals" (591).

It is extremely distressing to see one of the rare papers on female creativity reflecting the Freudian bias that female development is psychologically determined by anatomy and drive. If Greenacre indeed wrote this paper in 1960, she should have been familiar with Karen Horney's classic papers on female psychology, which had come out separately as journal articles before they were gathered together and published by Norton in 1967 under the title *Feminine Psychology*. Yet the trend of seeing females as destined to an inadequate, masochistic state of being, which was instituted by Freud and enhanced by early analysts such as Helene Deutsch and Sandor Rado, is evident in Greenacre's analysis of the limited potential in females for creative development. Horney's search for an interpersonal theory of development, which emphasizes a primary drive toward object relations rather than toward narcissistic instinct gratification, seems to have been slighted in Greenacre's focus on women and creativity.

Specifically, Karen Horney contributed the following ideas that should have served to undermine the reigning patriarchal psychoanalytic theory concerning the psychological destiny of females. She was the first to say that all of the early psychoanalytic views of women were invented by men and emerged from a phallocentric view of women as castrated male beings. She was also the first to state that penis envy is not the cause of a girl turning toward her father as a passionately desired love object but rather can be the neurotic outcome of disappointments in love relations with the father at the oedipal stage. Horney thus reverses—and rightly adjusts—the belief in a primary phallus-based causality for personality development in women, stressing effect and consequence from the oedipal era leading to phallic compensation rather than "castration complex" causality. Thus, the loss of the father and the related need to mourn disappointments with the father become the main issue. Wishes for masochistic submission to father or father substitutes and tendencies to overidentify with one's child are no longer seen as inevitable female compensation when the lack of a penis is no longer presumed to be a primary motivating phenomenon.

Horney highlights how the early psychoanalytic theories about female development reflect the societal bias toward reinforcing male dominance and female inferiority. Horney speaks of the joy and bliss of the feminine state in motherhood; she finds male reactions of envy toward women who have the benefits of motherhood within their grasp. To make her case, she employs clinical material from her male patients. Horney further suggests that men need more forms of compensation than women because of their more intense envy and that this may account for motivation toward creative work being seen more often in men than in women. She neglects to account for the crucial role of the father in inspiring creative motivation in a female child (see Kavaler, 1988a). However, she sees oedipal guilt and the related fear of the oedipal mother as often hindering the fruition of the potential for creative work in women, even when motivation is present.

The main contribution of Horney is to see the phallocentric fallacy of viewing female development through the eyes of men, a fallacy which is evident ever since Freud. Horney also counters the view of Helene Deutsch, a psychoanalyst who idealized her father and devalued her mother. She sets the stage for an examination of creative development in women by articulating the potential for natural feminine strength and fruition, which are regarded with suspicion by those who might prefer—or be most familiar with—a neurotically aborted form of female character formation (e.g., as in the "hysteric"). Horney initiates theoretical formulations that counter the view of women as merely passive or reactive with one of women as receptive and gestative. Further, she uses clinical case observation, whereas Freud, Deutsch, and Rado used mere speculation. Critically reviewing her theoretical predecessors, Horney sees the view of the castrated woman as a rationalization for societal disadvantages imposed on women rather than as the result of actual anatomical disadvantages. She points out that anatomical theories of disadvantaged women were being propagated at a time when women were supposed to have "dead" vaginas throughout childhood.

The existence of a view such as Greenacre's which disregards all of the findings of Karen Horney and her followers, seems to suggest the need for many studies, from many viewpoints, to explore creative development in women and to explore the particular psychodynamic psychologies of individual creative women who have won prominent reputations. We need to look at specific women writers and to compare their contrasting character structures and their developmental levels.

An attempt was made by John Gedo to include female creativity in his discussion of distinguished artists from a self psychology point of view. However, a certain minimizing of the importance of the topic is evident here as well. Only one of twelve chapters refers to women artists (entitled "Barefoot and Pregnant"). The other eleven chapters concern male creators in art or philosophy. Gedo's one chapter on women indicates that many obstacles have been placed in the path of women who seek to develop their creative talents. However, even though Gedo attempts to see such obstacles from a framework that considers the attitudes of parents toward their children, he scarcely enlarges the field of study by neglecting to draw on any specific examples of women artists in his book.

As a challenge to this state of affairs, I will use examples of females exclusively. Although there have been psychoanalytic biographies of individual women writers—such as biographies of Virginia Woolf written by Alma Bond and Shirley Panken—they have not comparatively studied distinguished creative women at various levels of development. I believe that we need to account for developmental level as well as psychic structure when comparing a cross range of women. The present study is an attempt to do so.

## The Father's Role in Female Creativity

Although Greenacre (1960) minimizes the extent to which women have distinguished themselves as creative artists while maximizing the nature of the difficulties in female development that contribute to this, she mentions one factor that can tip the scales in favor of creative strivings in women. This factor is the father. A female child's father can help mobilize creative strivings in his daughter, according to Greenacre, particularly if he himself is an artist. Greenacre thus stresses the role of a daughter's identification with her father, particularly during the time of the oedipal romance, when the father is the little girl's prime target for both love and idealization, which promote strong identifications. (Benjamin [1988] attributes such powerful identification to a homosexual attachment to the father prior to the oedipal era.) Other than the one instance in which the father is an artist himself, Greenacre does not refer to any particular attributes of the father that might promote or reinforce creative strivings in his daughter. She does not include any form of mirroring or confirming function as related to the paternal impact on the daughter's creative capacities or strivings.

On the other hand, in his book *Portraits of the Artist* (1983), Gedo deals with the father's role in mirroring, but in a negative way. His references are mainly to the father being an obstacle for the daughter, since the father's envy of his daughter may motivate him to use erotic seduction to deter her from her own creative path. Also, he notes that a daughter is not generally seen as a narcissistic self-extension by her father because of her distinctly different gender attributes; therefore, he believes that she is at a disadvantage compared with a boy, who will be seen as an extension of the father's own strivings for achievement and recognition. Gedo's point is that the father will feel more rivalry toward a daughter than toward a son, since he won't see his own glory reflected in her image. This point would seem to be open to a great deal of contention. Nevertheless, in Gedo's view the female's lot is really a dismal one, insofar as he emphasizes the rivalry not only of the mother but of the father as well.

In contrast to Gedo's negative view of the father and in keeping with Greenacre's emphasis on the father's impact on a female's creative development are the findings of Lora Heims Tessman. Tessman is both a clinician and a researcher who has focused the major part of her research on interviews concerning father-daughter relations from childhood to adulthood. As a psychologist at the Massachusetts Institute of Technology psychiatric service, Tessman has selected a population of highly successful, intellectual, and achievement-oriented women from the Massachusetts Institute of Technology population to investigate the determining factor of father-daughter relations in their development. In a current series of papers entitled "Early Tones, Later Echoes,"[1] as well as in earlier papers, Tessman finds repeatedly that the nature and degree of involvement of the father with his daughter's cognitive, imaginative, and creative efforts are highly consequential in determining the degree of future motivation toward the use and development of these abilities. A particularly important variable within this frame of reference is the degree to which the father allows the daughter to share in his own thought process—his particular form of inspiration and his personal mode of speculation, etc. Tessman emphasizes the permeability of boundaries between father and daughter as they share in one another's cognitive processes, stressing the father's accessibility in particular.

It is through such shared interaction between a father and daughter that the father contributes to the basic ego ideal formation in his daughter. Thus, the father-daughter relationship is structure building in a fundamental way that contributes to the creative development of the female. In a chapter entitled "A Note on the Father's Contribution to the Daughter's Ways of Loving and Working" Tessman (1982) writes, "Because the ego ideal remains more closely connected to desire than to prohibition, a contrast is seen with the forbidding aspects of the superego. Since desire becomes a central component of the little girl's wishes toward the father, the female is particularly prone to involve him in her ego ideal, even when her major identification is with the mother" (p 221). This relating of passionate object-related desires toward the father to the nature of the internal ego ideal as a motivational rather than prohibitive force enhances the developmental connection between creative motivation in women and the father-daughter relationship. This developmental view of the oedipal-stage effects on female creativity highlights the oedipal stage impact, despite any innate or preoedipal origins of creative talent. Yet Tessman also notes that the ego ideal, which is strongly determined by the father-daughter relationship—particularly in its apex during the oedipal period—begins its development at an earlier stage. Despite the preoedipal daughter's need for primary maternal care, the father plays a major role that is not often acknowledged. In Tessman's view (1982), following the internalization of soothing comfort, from the mothering person, there is a natural wish to experience and share excitement with the father.

Appleton (1981) notes the father's impact as the primary parent who engages in play during the preoedipal period. The father is the one who tosses his daughter up in the air or makes a ferris wheel with his legs to spin her or whirl her around. The mother may play a primary role in nurturing, but the father plays in a motoric way that highlights his entrance into his daughter's preoedipal world. The father of play described by Appleton would seem to enter his daughter's world just at the point at which her ego ideal begins to emerge as an internalized entity—prior to the definitive formation of the more inhibitory force of the superego. The ego-ideal is based on desire, and the desires directed at the father are not only erotic oedipal longings, but are earlier longings, called "endeavor excitement" by Tessman (1982, 227), which can be transformed into internalized experiences of vitality in one's work. However, whether endeavor excitement gets transformed into such vitality is highly dependent on whether the father is accepting of the daughter's excitement, as well as whether he is willing to engage with her in her creative efforts.

Appleton's view enhances that of Tessman, for the latter repeats her emphasis on pleasure in object relations as the fabric that forms the ego ideal, as opposed to the narcissistically tinged moral identification with virtue that forms the patchwork of the superego. Images of others, not conceptual edicts, form the ego ideal, and it is the pleasure of object relations that promotes internalization of these ego ideal images.

Quoting other research, Tessman connects the formation of the female ego ideal through involvement with the oedipal father specifically with the capacity for creative work. Tessman cites one study (1982, 222) done in 1954 that stresses the interaction of libidinal excitement and the "benign attitude of the patron" in promoting creative work in females. In doing so, Tessman highlights the critical contribution of the father or father substitute, who is experienced as the chief oedipal object of desire for women, followed by transmutations in father-daughter relations from the oedipal stage and latency periods, and through adolescence and its normal displacements. According to Tessman, an earlier study that she did along with Snyder (see 1989, 222) in 1965 notes the thread of a common theme among creative adolescents and scientists: "the close relationship with an older man who encouraged and sustained the creative one at a crucial period." Tessman quotes Jacobson (1954) to indicate a particular psychoanalytic theorist's view of the intensified meshing of ego ideal formation and the object relations connected with the ego ideal that occurs in females. For females, the quality of the relationship with the father is critical to determining how, as well as whether, there is adequate paternal internalization for healthy ego ideal formation, i.e., the formation of an ego ideal that can sustain pleasure in creative work.

In her 1982 paper on "The Father's Contribution to the Daughter's Ways of Loving and Working," as well as in more recent ones on the effect of the early father-daughter interaction on later patterns of loving and working, Tessman emphasizes the simultaneous and overlapping experience of the little girl along the lines of two forms of excitement: "endeavor excitement" and "erotic excitement" (1989). Although endeavor excitement begins during the second year of life, as striving toward autonomy and individuation come about, it extends into the oedipal period and complements erotic excitement if encouraged rather than stifled. As Tessman articulates, the father can be pivotal for the little girl at this stage in allowing her to tolerate excitement through the partial transformation of that excitement into modes of imaginative and conceptual cognition.

It seems to me that romantic oedipal fantasy can cause creative imagination to flourish, particularly if the father-daughter communion of this period is lush and fecund without being overly stimulating. Further, conceptual cognition as out-lined in the work of Piaget can be propelled by the father's sharing of the process of thought with his daughter as she grows. The father-daughter communion is thus transformational and structure building rather than just erotically enthralling.

Tessman writes of the father that "his contribution revolves around his simulta-neous role as object of her excitement and model in its transformation" (1987). If there is a good enough father, he would serve as both an object for instinct desires and as an interpersonally interactive facilitator for his daughter's psychological growth. He would need to be able both to receive and accept his daughter's erotic oedipal desires and facilitate the transformation of endeavor excitement into pleasurable activities and creative cognition (Kavaler 1988a). This would involve the father having capacities for mirroring, attunement, sharing, permeability of his own thought processes, and availability for identification and admiration. Tessman emphasizes the pleasure in "affect tone" (1982, 2) that needs to accompany tolerance for impulse. The internalization of such pleasure, combined with tolerance, could very much depend on the father's relative freedom to interact with his daughter. Severe character pathology of any kind, particularly narcissistic or schizoid pathology, would interfere with this (see Kavaler 1988a). The father must welcome and not repel or oppose excitement, while also involving himself in the creative endeavors of his daughter and allowing his daughter to participate in his own endeavors. Tessman (1982) alludes to the importance of participation when she points out that the traditional oedipal fantasy of getting or receiving a baby from father is more accurately described as a wish to actively "make a baby with father." As the girl grows into a woman, it can be her creative work—not only the biological creation of a baby—that is most significantly experienced as "making a baby" with father (see also Mendell 1988). Through interviews and clinical cases, Tessman presents many examples of how endeavor excitement is stimulated and sustained by the father's acceptance and encouragement. Such excitement appears also to be contained and cognitively assimilated through such paternal acceptance and encouragement. The combination of erotic and endeavor excitement makes the often-described phenomenon of "creative ecstasy" more comprehensible in developmental terms, without it necessarily being assumed that endeavor excitement is derived exclusively from erotic oedipal excitement (as traditional instinct theory might assume). The simultaneous experience of erotic and endeavor excitement by the oedipal-stage daughter would explain how she could be stimulated to ecstasies both of love and of creativity.[2]

## Discussion of Innate Factors

Since creative expression and achievement seem to be founded on a degree of innate potential as well as on developmental experience, the question arises as to whether the father's motivational role in stimulating female development—and particularly creative development—also has some innate, predisposing input. This input might be a priori imprints, images, or fantasies that could facilitate father-daughter interaction, and that could even motivate the female child toward interaction with her father.

Jungians speak of innate archetypes in which masculine and phallic energies and imprints play an important role. Monick (1987) specifically writes about a spiritual phallic force that he sees as motivating men toward sexuality and women toward creative productivity. He implies that there is a universal reservoir of phallic spiritual energy that emerges from a collective unconscious, endowing us all with certain aggressive and expressive energies. Melanie Klein, in a similar vein—on account of a combined drive and object relations theory orientation—speaks of innate a priori "phantasies" of paternal, phallic, penetrative forms. Although traditional theorists are wary about such speculations and object relations theorists following Klein have failed to adopt her view of an a priori psychology, even discounting practically all consideration of innate psychological input in an effort to rid themselves of the formerly all-too-weighty concept of "drive," I do not believe that the idea of innate psychological predispositions can be totally disregarded. Whether fantasies begin to form prenatally or postnatally, we are much more aware now than in the past that a good deal happens on the level of psychological fantasy prior to oedipal-stage occurrences. Thomas Ogden (1986) attempts to account for Kleinian views of a priori psychic predispositions by noting Noam Chomsky's psycholinguistic theory of innate linguistic grammer, i.e., of innate, psychologically built-in limits that prescribe the boundaries and possibly even the global directional outlines of our cognition. Piaget (1969) and Inhelder and Piaget (1958) have talked about a presumably imprinted roadmap of developmental cognitive growth, with predictable stages of cognitive dynamics that occur through interactive modes of assimilation and accommodation between organism and environment. All of these theories raise the question of the innate contribution to a human development that unfolds with a certain rhythm, dynamic, and direction, given the necessary interpersonal experiences between child and parents and child and environment. Regarding females and their creative development, this question can be specifically applied to the female predisposition for an interaction with her father. I find myself asking why little girls, as well as the little girls that we discover clinically within adult women, seem to expect their fathers to play a certain role in their development, even if they haven't received good enough father care. Is this just a wish and its affectively formed fantasy, or does that wish extend to an expectation which is so universal that some root aspect of it must be innate? Is there a built-in image of an ideal father with which all women must contend?

One day a female colleague told me about a recent dream that related to her burgeoning desires to involve herself in an artistic endeavor. She told me in particular because she knew of my interest in fathers and daughters and how their relations effect female creative motivation. In her dream, her father appeared to her as a figure who encouraged her to move into her creative work. She mentioned that her father had died when she was twelve and that she never remembered him as having played such an encouraging role in her life.

Since this woman was a colleague and not a patient, I do not have access to any information concerning the veracity of what she said about her father not having actually played the role in her life that he played in her dream. I can therefore only speculate by way of putting forth useful questions. Perhaps this woman did receive encouraging facilitation of her cognitive and creative growth during her childhood but doesn't remember it. On the other hand, perhaps this woman's wish for her father to play that role is sustained despite his absence in that regard. However, could it not also be that her dream brought some archetypal image of her father to consciousness, a specific image conjured up by a psychological need that extends beyond the power of human desire, even as it may create human desire?

Even though such questions cannot be answered, they remain with us. There are innate components to creativity that we know interact with the interpersonal relations between children and parents, and which therefore must interact with the internalizations and incorporations of parental functions by children. Whether there is a particularly masculine aspect to these object-related desires that become transformed into creative desires and intentions, can be only a matter of speculation. Jungians, Kleinians, and Freudians have all posed theories that beg us to ask whether there are innate phallic creative energies or innate a priori fantasies (or images) of mirroring father figures. If not, the paternal role in the oedipal-stage era could be all the more determinant of female creativity. As Tessman suggests, the internalization of that role by young girls and of the interaction with the father in that role may be the critical variable in determining whether innate and preoedipally induced creative potential is actualized in later years. However, for a women truly to express her unique feminine form of creativity (see Chicago 1977), she would need to integrate her father into her own sense of self, which depends on a survival of the feminine self in its initial stages of development during the preoedipal era. Not to integrate the father is to suppress feminine creative capacity and potential, even if motivation owing to the incorporation of the father is strong.

## Developmental Arrest and the Failure of Ego Ideal Formation

Whatever innate creative capacities and motivational forces there may be, it seems to be at the critical oedipal stage—when the love affair with father takes place—that both innate and preoedipal creative capacities begin to be transformed into manifestly creative endeavors. This transformation can take place through an active engagement between the father and his daughter, in the case of female development, whereas it might take place between the oedipal mother and her son for male creative development. Such engagement—with its tranformative potential for developing psychic structure—would then continue in alternate forms of father-daughter transaction throughout latency and adolescence (see Kavaler 1988a). Tessman's theory of structure building indicates how this particularly female transformation takes places. She places special emphasis on the erotic and endeavor excitement aspects of the father-daughter attachment. In the theory that she has formulated through her research with women, the father-daughter interaction and its overall affective tone of pleasure and desire become internalized as both a structural and a motivational force,[3] which can have a major impact on a women's creative process as well as on the content of the creative work. A critical time for such internalization is during the oedipal period, but it extends prior to and beyond it. The critical structure formed through this internalization is the female ego ideal.

Yet what happens in the case of preoedipal arrest, when the female child comes to the father with a diffuse and unconsolidated self? What happens when the little girl comes to her father still undifferentiated from her mother, not yet integrated from within at a primary level? In such a case, I propose that two main structural dynamics can be observed.

One structural dynamic is that the father's personality is incorporated as a masculine identification that presses for dominance within the intrapsychic world, instead of being neatly contained within the integrated structure of the ego ideal. Thus, the primary and feminine self either can become submerged within the masculine personality or can coexist in an unstable state that tends toward personality diffusion or self-splitting. James Masterson (1981) has given examples of borderline people who exemplify such self-disorder personality diffusion in the form of alternate self-states that are reexperienced as a mother-self and a father-self. I speak of incorporation rather than internalization in this case, because the masculine identification has both a compensatory and a defensive role in the intrapsychic world. The masculine identification may provide an alternative form of cohesion or vitality when the primary self is fragmented or enfeebled, but it can also strongly suppress the more natural primary feminine strivings in the female. Unlike the integrated ego ideal formation, this compensatory and defensive secondary self exists half in the self and half in the internal object, so that the self and object do not exist in free interaction but rather in a restrictive form of fusion that is unstable.

Despite pathological preoedipal fixations that prevent the triadic oedipal structure from forming, the oedipal energies of erotic and endeavor excitement are felt; they tend to have an archaic intensity, since mourning, separation, and intrapsychic structural differentiations have not modified or neutralized the preoedipal oral cravings. Therefore, the father is not only yearned for by the little girl; in the case of developmental arrest, he is orally craved as well. The oedipal yearnings and preoedipal cravings become diffusely mixed; the oedipal and preoedipal psychic structural formations thus become mixed as well. As the object of both oral and oedipal desires, with cravings for maternal modes of tenderness intermingled with oedipal yearnings for romance and for genital penetration, the father becomes mammoth in his tantalizing power of attraction for the little girl. This is the second structural consequence of the premature psychological use of the father by the arrested little girl. As seen in the essay on Sylvia Plath, "daddy" becomes the colossus and the Gothic god-daddy, extending to divine as well as to demonic proportions. In Kleinian theory, this is merely the cloaking of the father's clothes over the primary mother's idealized and demonic dimensions. However, in studying the internal-world revelations of creative women, it will become clear that the external father's unique personality can play a significant role in coloring the early mother's form.

## Summary of Developmental Issues

In order clearly to conceptualize the developmental issues that effect overall female growth, female creative development in particular, and the pathological vicissitudes of such development, I will now summarize preoedipal and oedipal object relations dynamics by reviewing the following: (i) healthy women, (ii) women suffering from preoedipal arrest, and (iii) oedipal-stage object addiction in women. This summary can help clarify the self-process and/or arrest in the distinguished women writers whose cases will be presented for study.

### Healthy Development

In healthy development at the preoedipal stage, the child internalizes a good enough primary mothering object. This requires adequate mother-infant bonding beyond the symbiotic period (Mahler et al. 1975) and into the critical separation-individuation era, from differentiation through practicing and rapprochement. According to Mahler, it is during the rapprochement phase that the representations of self and object are consolidated as clearly separate, and it is during this phase of the separation-individuation era that such representations become integrated within themselves. A synthesis of Mahler and Klein can be made, since the integrative work of the Kleinian depressive position is seen at work in Mahler's rapprochement phase. Through this depressive-position mourning process, the mother comes to be perceived as a whole object, as someone who is good enough in the sense of having tolerable inadequacies. The mother, and then the father as well, need no longer be archaically idealized within godlike, infant-perceived dimensions. On an affect level, ambivalent feelings for the mother become tolerable as her overall goodness is conceptualized through a representational figure of the mother existing within the internal world. The mother's "holding" or empathic functions are internalized as well. Consolidated self-structure is formed, as the maternal holding environment is internalized, and the mother's object features are assimilated into a whole object image form. Contact between self and other is needed on a continuing basis for this to occur; such contact brings frustrations and disillusionment that move separation forward through an affective mourning process. In this way, the process of Klein's depressive position progresses, with the affects of mourning allowing integration of images of the object and self as ambivalent perceptions are worked through.[4] As the representations of self and other are differentiated and consolidated, the ongoing interpersonal dialogue between self and mother is internalized so that differentiated structures of ego and self are formed; these structures continue their dialogue within the internal world. This internal dialogue signifies that the level of intrapsychic conflict and intrapsychic, interactive integration has been reached. If this internal dialogue is free and dynamic, affective interpersonal encounter in the external world will be encouraged. This healthy development differs from psychic arrest, in which the internal structures become fused in a perpetual state of reenactment because of early trauma. In the case of arrest, the fused internal structures will inhibit affect encounter and dialogue, not only in the external world of interpersonal relations but in the transitional world of an artist's creative work as well.

At the oedipal stage, the female child who has successfully navigated through the self-integrations of the preoedipal period is ready to encounter her father as a differentiated whole object figure who is erotically desired. Endeavor excitement, as well as erotic excitement, is stimulated through a dialogue between self and father for the little girl. Such excitement propels internalization of the father as a differentiated representational form within the internal world. The female's central self (Fairbairn's "central ego") assimilates the father's form as it is experienced in interaction with her self. Given that the preoedipal mother has been adequately internalized during the separation-individuation phases of development, the father can be adequately internalized as well. His actual form can be assimilated into the preconscious areas of the central self, instead of being split off in a sealed-off internal world within a haunting, visceral form.

I believe, along with Tessman, that the desired father is particularly structuralized into the oedipal female's evolving ego ideal. The father's impact on the ego ideal is powerful on account of the oedipal dynamics of the female. Disillusionment with the father at the critical oedipal stage is felt as disillusionment with an idealized romantic figure of human dimensions, as opposed to prior disillusionment that centers on the father who is perceived as a god. In creative women, the image of the object as a muse can be experienced either in preoedipal archaic ideal forms, as an omnipotent god-daddy, or in oedipal-level erotic and human ideal forms. Tolerable, as opposed to traumatic disillusionment allows mourning (see Loewald 1962). For the oedipal female, tolerable disillusionment with her father will allow her to differentiate herself from him and to develop her own unique capacities, although she retains a level of motivation related to her internalized engagement with her father. Inevitable oedipal-stage disappointments in a daughter's wish to be exclusively adored by her father and to outrival her mother and sisters lead to disillusionment. The greater the freedom from earlier preoedipal trauma, the more the actual personality of the father will play a role in this disillusionment process (see Kavaler 1988a).

## Preoedipal Developmental Arrest

Unlike the course of healthy development, when a pathological mourning state persists the constellations of self and object within the internal world never become integrated. No good enough primary internal object is formed, and self and object representations remain split. Because of inadequate maternal attunement, particularly during the critical separation-individuation era, the object is incorporated rather than properly internalized, i.e., rather than assimilated into the nuclear self. Such incorporation perpetuates split-off or part object formations within the internal world of the psyche. Such an incorporated object is not assimilated into the nuclear self, which is also the basic feminine self for a female. This incorporated object can appear to exist half in the self and half in the other in interpersonal relations, so that cycles of projective identification occur (see Kernberg 1975) in which a part of the self is projected onto the object yet is still experienced as a part of the self). Boundaries between the self and the other remain diffuse, although on a cognitive level the distinction between self and other is known. Primitive affect cravings for merger with the object serve to blur that distinction. However, desires to merge with the object are motivational only when the object is seen in an idealized, godlike form. When the object is perceived as a demonic object, escape from it is sought, even as it is also held onto because one's primal identity has become fused with it. Attempts to escape through internal-object exorcism can be seen in the poetry of such psychically arrested female writers as Sylvia Plath. Inevitably, an idealized god turns malicious and malignant, for in the state of desire, when merger is sought there is the threat of self-loss that comes with the desired merger. This "bad" object now is felt to be intruding through strangling or to be devouring through some form of primal erotic swallowing and rape. It can also be felt as suffocating, or as abandoning by means of coldness, remoteness, and indifference. Instead of object representation within the internal world, the archaic object (also called the part object) is felt viscerally as a concrete, affectively engaged and dynamic figure. The primitive object is projectively expelled and identified with simultaneously; this can be seen through interpersonal behavior and through transitional-world artistic expression.[5]

When the developmentally arrested little girl reaches the oedipal stage, she incorporates the father as a split-off bad object and as an idealized counterpart. In this case, the father is still archaically idealized, unlike in normal development, during which the erotic father replaces the idealized god-father. When the female is developmentally arrested, the father is erotically desired while remaining idealized as an omnipotent god. This erotic desire for the father cannot be tolerated, since the psychic structure that is necessary to process yearnings and frustrations into the form of self and ego ideal structures does not exist.[6] The father is not internalized within an integrated ego ideal structure but remains split off, taking the manic and intrusive form of the bad primary object. The incorporated father—who is not adequately internalized or assimilated into the interpersonally related central self—is experienced unconsciously and in a projected form as possessing a demonic nature that is colored by masculine and erotic features. Unconscious fantasies of this half-in-the-self and half-in-the-other demon lover are found in the creative self-expressions of preoedipally arrested women; artists may demonstrate this addiction to their demon lovers through a compulsive mode of engagement with their creative work and its process. The creative woman then revels in and rebels against a sense of being possessed by a masculine demon-god. Since the father has become fused with the primary mothering object, an engulfing object is colored by a new masculine object. The engulfment, with its alternating consequence of abandonment, remains a perpetual psychic theme in the internal world of the woman, becoming a literary theme for a woman writer, inasmuch as her internal world is given external articulation in the transitional-world realm of her creative work. The transitional world of creative work is not necessarily just a mirror for the internal world. In fact, in relatively higher-level women, the creative process transforms that internal world (see case of Charlotte Brontë). However, for the preoedipally arrested artist, the creative process is more constricted, since that process itself is driven by the artist's compulsion to externalize the viscerally dynamic internal-world enactment. A brilliant creative mind may provide infinite variations in form and image, etc., but the basic dynamic theme of the creative work will to a large extent mirror the sealed-off situation of the internal world in the case of preoedipal women.

Fused with the primary object, and often derived from the narcissistic pathology of the actual father, the internal father will persist as a demonic or bad object within the psyche of the developmentally arrested female. The antidote is then often sought in the form of an idealized male rescuer.

## The Oedipal-Level Woman

Women who pass through the preoedipal stages of development without arrest in differentiated psychic-structure formation become engaged in interpersonal relations with a whole object father. This occurs since the preoedipal mothering figure has already been internalized as a good enough whole object. However, much depends on the personality of the father in determining whether the young three- to five-year-old girl will reintegrate and finish self-consolidation at the oedipal stage, and whether she will move on the superego refinement during latency and to nonincestual heterosexual development during adolescence. If the father fails the daughter as an adequate oedipal-stage father, or if he dies, the little girl may not be able to mourn him, to separate from him, and to internalize him as an integrated good enough object. In this case, a state of addiction to the oedipal father develops and persists. This becomes a phallocentric form of addiction that easily becomes generalized to other men onto whom the paternal image is projected. Since she lacks an adequate interaction with the oedipal father, the little girl does not form a mature ego ideal and consequently becomes overly dependent on external male father figures as she lacks the internal relationship with an adequate father figure.

As long as this psychic situation is not resolved, the adult woman will be compelled to seek reassuring confirmation from male figures, a type of mirror addiction that may be expressed in the need to prove that men will fall in love with her or merely to seek male approval and support in an excessive way. Yet such a woman is separate enough to seek mirroring for a differentiated, albeit immature, self, rather than for a grandiose and undifferentiated self. The men she may become obsessed with—which may be confused with falling in love— are erotically desired human figures, not godlike muses or their tyrannical counterparts. The love object's real personality is to a significant extent accurately perceived by such a woman. Also, her own creative development can proceed when a good enough external father figure, with whom she may resume interaction and self-development, is found. Such a woman is capable of creating the man into a good enough figure within her internal world of objects and their representations, despite awareness of his significant inadequacies. She can employ her good enough preoedipal representations as a psychological format or blueprint and does not need to deny these inadequacies, since she can counterbalance them in her mind with his good qualities when she can begin to allow mournful disillusionment with the father to whom she has remained psychologically addicted.

The creative process can be used extensively to work through mourning and to separate from the father who is defensively idealized. It can be used to sort out the real inadequacies of the father and to differentiate the female artist from her father, as well as from the men who carry the father projection. Through the creative process, she can realistically encounter her father's inadequacies, while still selectively choosing his admirable assets for her identifications with him. However, disillusionment with the father must be tolerated so that mourning and its accompanying object internalization and integration can take place.

## The Internal Father in the Preoedipal-Level Woman

For the preoedipally arrested woman, there is a second structural consequence of the self becoming masculinized. The father is incorporated in a split (idealized and malevolent) form, rather than internalized in a whole object or three-dimensional form that would reflect integration. Because of preoedipal arrest, the good and bad aspects of the father—and the erotic and aggressive instinctual aspects of his form—are not integrated. The good father, like the primitive mother of Kleinian theory, remains profoundly ideal and is sought out for defensive and compensatory merger. The bad father, also like the primitive mother of Kleinian theory, remains severely malevolent or villainous. The father also appears as an androgynous mother-father, since the preoedipal and oedipal objects are merged rather than differentiated and integrated. Also, the father-object halves are partly fused with the self-parts. The result is that free interaction in external relations cannot develop, since internal relations are not free. The bond of self and father object becomes constricting. Free motivation is thus bound in compulsion. This extends to creative motivation, since the little girl's creative strivings are so influenced by her infatuation with her father, particularly as the oedipal stage impacts on development.

As the little girl becomes a creative woman, she may thus be propelled into two opposite directions by her fused engagement with the split paternal object. On the one hand, she may be inspired toward intense creative expression by the idealized half of the father. However, this expression will be bound by a compulsion that drives her to manically exhaustive and partially defensive orgies of productivity. On the other hand, she may be pulled toward self-submergence in a primitive masculine identification that can either block or numb her creative expressions or drive her simultaneously to self-destructive and creative acts.[7] As the preoedipal female embraces the malevolent form of the father—which she cannot avoid doing, for he comes in tandem with the idealized father from whom she seeks rescue—she becomes psychically possessed and she can also become masculinized.[8] This is true for the preoedipally arrested woman, because owing to the sealing off of her internal self she cannot succeed at interactions that could result in integrative self-transformation.

## The Muse and the Demon

The creative woman in particular will often experience her split-father engagements as male muse and demon forms. Perhaps that is why when we consider creative literature, we find myths that reflect both the idealized and the malevolent father in the form of the demon lover. The demon lover can appear in one moment of self-expressive experience as a muse god and at the next moment as a devil. The muse is both inspirational and erotic. He can inspire the "creative ecstasy." Yet for the creative woman suffering from preoedipal psychic arrest, the villainous demon takes possession of her, turning the creative ecstasy into a suicidal frenzy or into the cold frigidity of isolation and death. Images of death then abound. Alternatively, an idealized muse father is once more recreated through manic and narcissistic modes of defense. The vicious cycle must continue. Only despair, sickness, death, or suicide can end the cycle, as long as the preoedipal arrest is not modified. I propose that as long as this arrest remains, the necessary curative mourning cannot be accomplished though the work of the creative process alone. When we look at further cases that illustrate this, the terms muse and demon will be used to encapsulate all that is represented by the part object idealized godfather and the part object malevolent or bad father respectively. The myth of the demon lover must be discussed first, for the muse and demon father appear in this myth in both literary and psychodynamic forms.

# 5

# The Demon Lover Theme as Literary Myth and Psychodynamic Complex

## The Myth of the Demon Lover

The myth of the demon lover has appeared both as a significant literary theme and as a prevalent psychodynamic complex. It is exemplified by an epic poem that appeared in Blackwood Magazine in Emily Brontë's day. According to Winnifred Gerin, Emily Brontë's biographer, the poem later appeared in the Oxford *Book of Ballads* as "The Daemon Lover" (Gerin 1971, 48, note). Gerin's version of the opening and ending shows both the yearning and the tragic demise of this poem:

> where hae ye been, my long, long love,
> These seven long years and more?

asks the . . . the Catherine-like deserted woman of her returned love.

> O I'm come to seek my former vows
> That ye promised me before

asserts the bold lover, recking nothing . . . of her new ties as wife and mother; and bewitching her away with promises:

> I hae seven ships upon the sea,
> And the eighth brought me to land;
> With mariners and merchandise,
> And music on every hand.

Only when she has left her home and sailed with him does his true daemonic nature appear in the final gesture that destroys them all:

> And aye as she turn'd her round about,
> Aye taller he seem'd to be;
> Until that the tops o' that gallant ship
> Nae taller were than he.

He strack the top-mast wi' his hand,
The fore-mast wi' his knee;
And he brake that gallant ship in twain,
And sank her in the sea.

(49)

This ballad reflects the demon lover myth's theme of abandonment in its most treacherous form. Coleridge's well-known poem "Kubla Khan" reflects the same theme. Written under the influence of opium, Coleridge's demon lover poem seems to come straight from his unconscious:

In Xanadu did Kubla Khan
uA stately pleasure dome decree
.......................................................
But oh! that deep romantic chasm which slanted
Down the green hill athwart a cedarm cover!
A savage place! as holy and enchanted
As e'er beneath a waning moon was haunted
By a woman wailing for her demon lover!

(Abrams et al. 1962, 198)

## The Demon Lover Psychodynamic Complex

Jungians see this literary theme of seduction and betrayal, as a myth derived from the collective unconscious. In their view, the theme becomes a diagnostic description of a psychodynamic complex. In a book entitled *On The Way to the Wedding* (1986), Linda Schierse Leonard writes about this theme in terms of the Dracula vampire story, in which possession by oral eroticism is emphasized, showing the importance of the preoedipal determinants within the complex. Another woman analyst, Marian Woodman, writes about this demon lover theme in terms of a malignant father-daughter complex in the father-obsessed woman. In her book *Addiction to Perfection: The Still Unravished Bride* (1982), she writes:

If she succumbs to her inner lover, he comes between her and genuine relationship, making a real man appear contemptible and sexuality seem like prostitution. . . . She is vulnerable to the suave manner, the eloquence with words, the perfectionism and ideals with which she endows him, and her own hold on life is so tenuous that she sets herself up for murder either by the man who is carrying the projection or by her own inner lover.
Ironically, at the core of that father-lover complex is the father-god whom

she worships and at the same time hates because on some level, she knows he is luring her away from her own life. Whether she worships him or hates him makes no difference, because in either case she is bound to him with no energy going into finding out who she herself is. So long as she can fantasize her love, she identifies with the positive side of the father-god; once the fantasy is crushed, however, she has no ego to sustain her and she swings to the opposite pole where she experiences annihilation in the arms of the god who has turned against her.

(136)

Woodman continues: "Female writers are particularly prone to the demon lover; Emily Brontë, Emily Dickinson, Virginia Woolf, Sylvia Plath" (136).

Woodman's views corroborate my own findings, and the female writers that she mentions are among the ones whom I have chosen to study. I would like to add to her comments that only when the idealized father figure is taken inside the woman's psyche at the level of primitive omnipotence, where he becomes a god or mammoth muse upon whom early symbiotic longings are focused, does the father of necessity turn into a demon or "daemon." Incorporating him at this level,[1] in an attempt to compensate for the lack of an adequate good maternal object, causes a symbiotic illusion[2] including wishes that must inevitably meet with traumatic failure. If wed to this frustrating and omnipotently idealized figure[3] a woman is addicted to an internal object, which she holds on to in an attempt to seek rescue or repair. When early impairment in self-development has already resulted from the engagement with the primary mothering figure of earliest infancy, a woman remains vulnerable to a psychic incest marriage with an internal father. As the female child becomes bound in a closed-off internal system, autonomous self-development through external interpersonal relations is further inhibited. Already injured by her infant-level encounter with her primary mother, she easily becomes addicted to the father who holds out the promise of rescue through erotic enthrallment. Consequently, she seals herself off from the nourishment with others—who might actually be more adequate compensatory figures than the father (including psychotherapists). This results in a splitting of her self. One part of her self is left to engage in sterile or repetitive external relations, while another part of her self serves as a container for psychic blueprints of early-life dramas and somatic reactivity. On account of her split, her somatic reactivity lacks the connection with others necessary for an emergence into modes of spontaneity and autonomous self-expressiveness.

In 1985, Marian Woodman published another book, *The Pregnant Virgin: A Process of Psychological Transformation*. Here, Woodman further elucidates aspects of the demon lover complex, broadening out understanding of the type of father-daughter relationship that contributes to it and also connecting it with the factors of inadequate mothering that interact with the father-daughter internal-ization. Here, she writes of the complex with particular relevance to the creative woman, whom she defines as "one who is compelled from within to relate to her own creative imagination" (35). According to Woodman, a creative woman who becomes psychically entrapped in the demon lover complex through her emersion in the creative imagination, which is so near to the unconscious, is a woman who is merged and bound with her internal father in a psychic incest marriage. Contributing to the power of this intrapsychic mergence with the father is the lack of an adequate maternal internalization. She speaks of the mother of such a woman as being either absent or in rivalry with her daughter. However, the absence may be psychological, not actual. The early mother-daughter bonding has been insufficient, and the daughter has no adequate feminine force residing in her core (Klein's good maternal object). She is wooed by the seductive spirituality of the father, and a father-daughter psychic fusion results. The incest is spiritual for the creative woman, not actual. Her unconscious is merged with that of her father. She strives to make life a perfect work of art; she lives in art, not in the world.

The following description by Woodman of the creative woman's demon lover complex gives a special emphasis to the preoedipal dynamics not seen in her earlier book.[4] She writes:

> Her sexuality and femininity foundered on the reef of her primal relationship to her mother. The "puella" mother who has never taken up residence in her own body, and therefore fears her own chthonic nature, is not going to experience pregnancy as a quiet meditation with her unborn child, nor birth as a joyful bonding experience. Although she may go through the motions of natural childbirth, the psyche/soma split in her is so deep that physical bonding between her and her baby daughter does not take place. Her child lives with a profound sense of depair, a despair which becomes conscious if in later years she does active imagination with her body and releases waves of grief and terror that resonate with the initial primal rejection.
>
> (1985, 37)

Given this primal mourning experience, which both Woodman and I deem necessary for self-reparative integration, one would wonder whether the active imagination experienced within the use of the creative process could ever contain or hold it. When the bond with the mother has not been securely established, the engagement with the shadow side of the idealized father becomes profoundly dangerous and leaves an explosive emotional force threatening to erupt from within. Body boundaries remain diffuse. Early needs for merger with the mother have been traumatically frustrated so that such a woman grows up with no sense of her own body's dimensions and "demarcations" (37).

Not being able to differentiate herself from her mother on such a basic level, the daughter certainly cannot then differentiate herself from her father with whom she may commune intuitively, intellectually, or spiritually. Of course, such communion may also take place with a father substitute.

The father or father substitute becomes the woman's fantasy savior. As Fairbairn (1952) has pointed out, the split in the self is not only between external and internal object relations; internal relations are split as well, splitting the self a second time. Woodman refers to this split in terms of a psyche-soma split, implying that the psyche of the woman's self becomes addictively and incestuously wed to the "spiritual" or idealized father, while the soma of the woman's self remains merged with the primary mother. Fairbairn also indicates in his papers that he believes self-splitting can take place between attachments to the father and mother as bad part objects, not just between attachments to split parts of the mother.

The father's role as the spiritual drug for the woman's psyche can have dire consequences for the developmentally arrested creative woman. If the father supports such a woman's creativity, he gives her the possibility of psychic survival through symbolic self-expression, even if she cannot sustain the day-to-day contact of relationships within the interpersonal world. Consequently, she cannot help becoming addicted to the creative process and being compelled to create, for she is unable to communicate in any other way. She is split off from her body and from interpersonal relations with other people. This reflects a basic self-split that both I and Woodman have described. Through this self-split and through symbiosis with the father there develops a phallocentric (male-oriented) addiction that lives only through the woman's link to her creative work. The creative work provides the "transitional space"[5] for communion with the incorporated, internal father, with whom she is merged. However, the woman's intrapsychic symbiosis with her father can easily become a malignant symbiosis, as any disappointment with this father as muse-god immediately reactivates the early preoedipal trauma with the mother. Also, her continual need for paternal and male approval makes her wish to become what he would have her be. Yet to be his image is to lose herself. The creative process can be the arena for this conflict between her need to find herself and her addictive craving to please her father. She becomes victim of her craving to keep winning male admiration, an admiration she seeks as a drug substitute for the primary love that has eluded her.

Another aspect of the creative compulsion, based on an addiction to an internal idealized or omnipotent father, relates to the reification of the creative process itself. The woman's art—whether literary or otherwise—becomes the concrete expression of the symbolic spiritual marriage with the idealized father. To create and to keep on creating become the source of an idealized image of the self—as it is experienced through the bond with the idealized father—and reassure the woman artist that the bond with the idealized father still exists. The art can be psychically (and often unconsciously) experienced as a sex substitute; it then becomes compulsive to the degree to which the woman is wed to her internal idealized and demonic father as a lover. The woman artist's sexuality then becomes split off in a closed system so that external male lovers are often sought only when they resonate with the projection of the internal god-demon father. Often, there is no desire for lovers of flesh and blood; the internal father is the exclusive lover whose spiritual form calls for "copulation" through the creative process of the art. In the less-extreme case, when external men are desired, it is only insofar as they resonate with the internal ideal father (or are the opposite of the actual bad father) and serve as "muses," inspiring the woman to create.

The creative woman can cultivate her psychic intimacy with her father—or with the husband, lover, or brother who carries the projection from the originally desired father—through the use of the creative process. Thus, she can come to live artificially within the creative process or transitional-space realm (see Winnicott 1953). Creative women who become entrapped in this realm are those who have no leverage to come and go from it, because they have no containment within their bodies and its physical relations with others owing to an absence of early maternal internalization. There is no good inner core object to which to return. The maternal holding environment is not found within the inner world, because the disruption of maternal bonding was too profound. A good enough maternal introject is lacking, since this exists only in the company of a good enough maternal holding environment. Therefore, the creative woman who is imprisoned within this complex becomes sealed off in an isolated psychic domain, in which the only nourishment is increasing psychic intimacy with the idealized father-muse, thus perpetuating an untimely and addictive symbiosis. Woodman describes these dynamics as follows:

> Psychic intimacy and physical intimacy go together naturally, but, where they have been split apart at a pre-verbal level, the instinct is isolated. . . .
>
> The distortion in the body/psyche relationship is compounded by the symbiotic relationship between father and daughter. There is a primal confusion between the spiritual and instinctual depths because the love she received from her father is the very energy which sustains her life. . . . Locked in her musculature, her feminine feelings are not available to her; thus, if she is threatened with abandonment, she may become virtually catatonic with unexpressed terror, and subject to strange physical symptoms. She is losing herself, physically and spiritually. Abandonment becomes annihilation because her body with its welter of undifferentiated feeling cannot provide the "temonos," the safe place, to protect her ego. Nor can the collective world offer support. Her preoccupation with the world of the imagination makes her view the mundane world with scorn and fear. It is a cruel, illusory world in which unreal

people clutter their lives with superfluous objects, and clutter is unendurable when the inner world is dismembered.

(1985, 38–40)

Woodman is attempting to articulate here something like the sense of "jumping out of one's skin," a sense that a creative woman can feel and transmit when caught in the terror-driven compulsion to keep going, to keep creating, when the thin artery of connection to the world through connection to her father or his male derivative is severed.[6] The break in the ambiguous and tortuous yet salvaging bond can come with any disappointment in the father, no matter how slight it may appear to others.

Any disappointment with the father, or with the male onto whom the father image is projected, can be experienced as traumatic abandonment, because it is felt as a recreation of the earlier preoedipal abandonment by the mother during infancy. It is of no consequence whether the disappointment is because the father does not live up to the daughter's idealized image, which she projects onto him as a substitute for early mothering, or whether the disappointment comes from an actual rejection from him.[7] Either way, the daughter reexperiences the primary level of abandonment; without her compensatory link to the idealized father she becomes suicidally engaged with the dark or demonic side of the tantalizing father.

According to Woodman, "Cut off outwardly from her environment, cut off inwardly from her positive masculine guide, the woman identifies with the dark side of the father archetype—the demon lover. There is no one to mediate between her terrorized ego and the chaos through which it is falling. The abyss is bottomless" (40). Woodman refers both to Sylvia Plath and to Emily Dickinson. Both were preoccupied with images, thoughts, and themes of death—craving to know whether death was a dark abyss like the emotional void within them in their living death, or whether it would bring reunion with the muse-god father and free them from the demon father. Suicide, however, as seen with Sylvia Plath, can be an embracing of the demon, a yielding to his death kiss. Woodman writes:

> Suicide is a final stroke of vengeance against the savage god who has abandoned her. Paradoxically, it is affirming what he has done to her ego: God has taken her out of life, so killing herself is affirming him. Suicide is a Liebestod, a death marriage in which she embraces the dark side of God—a negative mystical union. Psychologically, it is marriage to the demon lover. The relationship of the woman to the demon is sadomasochistic, and her battle with him fascinates because it has within it the elements of violent eroticism.

(1985, 41)

Accidents, fatal illness, even suicide win out against the creative life in women who continue to renounce life and who continue the schizoid sealing off and burying of primal pain. Since their renunciation cannot lead to an active affective mourning through their creative work, eventually their creativity wanes or dies, although temporary compensation has been provided. Woodman quotes Dickinson in terms of this perpetual sealing off, referring to an isolation within the internal world with one's masculinized internal object, which I believe can also be seen in terms of a pathological mourning state. This theme of sealing off is seen to be prominent in the work of Plath, as symbolized in the title of her one novel, *The Bell Jar*. Woodman refers to Plath's suicide as well as to Dickenson's adherence to a renunciation of life.

Considering these two distinguished creative women writers, we must ask whether a woman caught in a cycle of creative compulsion and demon lover addiction can ever be cured and—unlike Plath and Dickinson—move toward life. Woodman refers to the possibility of psychic reparation: "If, on the other hand, loneliness leads to insight and illumination, the ego may establish a creative relationship with the inner world and release its own destiny" (1985, 42). Yet Woodman fails to cite any of the developmental or interpersonal factors that might be necessary for a positive outcome to take place. She speaks of loneliness turning to insight, but what makes such loneliness tolerable enough for insight to take place?

One might surmise that if a woman is already arrested because of a lack of early maternal contact and bonding, which implies failure to internalize a maternal holding environment, the conscious experience of loneliness would bring extremely intense and implosive affects, similar to those described by James Masterson (1976; 1981) when he writes about the abandonment depression of borderline and narcissist patients. To tolerate such affects, which erupt as a particularly severe form of mourning, such a woman would need containment and contact. It is questionable whether the creative process alone can provide this. The creative process allows contact with internal objects, and with split-off parts of the self; it does not provide embodied contact. The creative process can—but does not necessarily—provide the interactive dialogue of self-transformation, but it does not offer the mode of consistent intersubjective attunement that an external other offers. The creative process cannot provide the visceral sense of affect containment that two people who are in a room together can provide, when one experiences the feelings of the other concurrently with the other. Involvement with creative work can activate a good early holding environment during engagement in the creative process but only if such a holding environment has been internalized early in life.

Insofar as the literary or artistic theme of the demon lover can be viewed as both a symptomatic design and a diagnostic sign related to the psychological function of the work of creative women, the enlargement or diminishment of the theme gives us clues as to whether mourning resolution and self-reparation have taken place during the course of any particular woman artist's creation of her work. If the expression of the creative process shows a resolution of the demon lover complex, this may indicate the potential for mourning and for self-integrative development. On the other hand, the development of the demon lover theme without resolution may indicate that the demon lover pscyhodynamic complex, as well as its corresponding pathological mourning state, is not reparable through the use of the creative process. The developmental factors in the life of any particular creative woman can be observed. Through the study of creative work, we can draw comparisons along the lines of developmental arrest versus neurotic defensive regression and neurotic blocking owing to structural conflict.

## The Symptomatic Demon Lover Literary Theme

In women writers, the demon lover literary theme can be a symptom of unmourned internal objects, which persist as persecutory objects in the psyche. Such persistence of bad objects promotes a state of pathological mourning in which excessive aggression counters healthy strivings to love as well as to mourn the early objects of one's first primary ambivalent attachments. The occurrence of the themes of masculine demons and female victims can be diagnostic in assessing to what degree self-reparative strivings succeed or fail in the life of a particular female writer. In terms of Melanie Klein's psychodynamic theory, the demon lover theme is evidence of a fixation in the splitting mechanisms of the paranoid-schizoid position. The internal object remains too "bad" to promote an integration of a whole good (good enough) self.[8] Thus, split-off bad and devalued components of the object remain predominant in internal-world dynamics. The whole good object and the subjective sense of self of the depressive position fail to develop in any sustained manner.

From Ronald Fairbairn's theoretical perspective (1952), the demon lover theme is evidence of a failure to resolve psychopathology that inhibits healthy self-integrative growth. The demon lover theme symbolizes tenacious and addictive attachments to bad-parent incorporations. From Fairbairn's view, the theme illustrates how instinctual relations with internal objects can predominate over external whole object relations. Such unmodified relations with internal bad objects are due to the sealing off of the self within a closed system perpetuated by unmourned trauma. This reenactment is a form of pathological mourning in which ties to early traumatizing objects cannot be relinquished.

I propose that the demon lover theme appears in the work of women artists particularly because the primary maternal attachment of infancy is replaced by a primary libidinal attachment to the father during the oedipal era of attachment to the erotic object. If preoedipal mothering has been significantly inadequate, the more likely the attachment to the oedipal father will reflect an eroticization of longings for maternal nurturance. Consequently, the internal father becomes fused with the internal mother, manifesting as a combined father-mother figure in symbolic expressions of the internal attachment. When mothering has been severely inadequate, as in the cases of female writers such as Emily Dickenson (Kavaler-Adler, 1991a), Edith Sitwell (Kavaler 1992b), Sylvia Plath (Kavaler 1985; 1986), or Anne Sexton (Kavaler 1989a), the symbolized internal father-mother will appear as more godlike than human. However, if preoedipal mothering has been less severely deficient or has been compensated by maternal substitutes, the eroticization of longings for parental care will be combined with normally intense erotic passions, and the father will be seen as a differentiated man. In the case of significant failings on the part of both parents, the bad-object symbolization of the demon lover literary theme will be promoted in a female writer's work, and the internal father will be psychically experienced as a malevolent god. Sufficient mourning and separation from the internal parents are necessary to resolve the situation; a creative woman may ambivalently strive for such resolution in her work.

When the demon lover theme is resolved into themes of three-dimensional whole objects, which involves a general sustaining of healthy psychodynamic connections between internal and external objects, we can see reparative strivings to be at work. This is accompanied by a diminishment of destructive aggression, as seen in symbolized literary form (in terms of characterization, narration, and plot). Such diminishment of aggression may be apparent after themes of destructive aggression are consciously faced by the artist. Good-object experience, which can appear as Klein's "recreation" of the good after depressive fantasies are faced (Klein 1940; Segal, 1957), is seen to survive. However, if mourning of the original bad objects is not experienced and processed—either in the life or through the work of the women artist—the artist is vulnerable to a regression into a state of bad object relations and its pathological fixations. When such vulnerability persists, new and particularly traumatic disappointments will promote regression into pathological relations with bad internal objects, causing a detachment in external interpersonal relations. External relations will be characterized by attempts to compensate for bad internal object relations by attaching to idealized external objects or "muses," but the reenactment of the sadomasochistic drama of the internal world is inevitable.

## The Demon Lover Complex and the Work of Annie Reich

Jungians are not the only psychoanalysts who speak of the demon lover complex, although they are the only ones who label it as such. Annie Reich is a distinguished Freudian analyst who spoke of the dynamics related to the demon lover complex in women by focusing on the male as the extension of the narcissistic self. Her work describes milder versions of the complex, in which suicide and self-deterioration are not in evidence and the symptoms assume a more neurotic nature, although the borderline level of the problem can also be seen by the skilled diagnostic eye.

In her book *Psychoanalytic Contributions* ([1940] 1973), Reich highlights the narcissistic mother-daughter bond as it is re-enacted throughout a woman's life in the form of narcissistic fusions with men. In "Narcissistic Object Choice in Women" ([1953] 1973), Reich describes women who perpetuate a grandiose compensation for their own lack of self-development through repeated experiences of merger with idealized men. Frequently through the sexual act, these women seek to reinforce their identification with the image of their male ideal. Here, the more common sexual ecstasy is evident in lieu of creative ecstasy. In "A Contribution to the Psychoanalysis of Submissiveness in Women" ([1940] 1973) Reich depicts cases of women who seek similar narcissistic fusions with their male ideals through submission to their control, identifying with their male persecutors. The women whom Reich describes in her essays do not seem to have the creative capacities that the women writers explored in the present book have. In fact, they seem to have lacked any normal level of creativity or of self-identity. In seeking a grandiose compensation for this lack through narcissistic relationships with men, they appear to pay a significant price. They pay either through continued disillusionment with their men that must be denied through cycles of continuous merger or through continued masochistic suffering, as a way of defending against such inevitable disillusionment with their male god-demons. Despite the differences between the women studied by Reich and the prolifically creative women in this study, they all share the fate of an imprisoned self that cannot become fully differentiated from a male figure to whom they are psychologically bound. The women described in Reich's paper on narcissistic object choice are more consciously engaged with the idealized god-man father, whom creative women seek as their muse. The "extremely submissive women" whom she describes seem to reflect the enmeshed internal and creative relations that addicted creative women have with the other side of this split, and idealized male, the demon lover, under whom they erotically suffer and against whom they rebel.

## Other Theorists

Other psychoanalytic theorists have touched on theory relevant to the demon lover complex. Fairbairn and Klein are the object relationists who prepare the way for such theory by describing a battle with a possessive and persecutory object within the intrapsychic world. In "Mourning and Malancholia" (1917), Freud also contributed by acknowledging the role of the sadistic internal object in the intrapsychic world, when mourning is unresolved and melancholia results. However, Jungians have been the most articulate in describing a state of conflict that is particularly related to female development, as well as to female father obsession and addiction. Marian Woodman is the only Jungian who has specifically related this complex to creative women, leading to the studies that I pursue here.

## Studies of Distinguished Women Writers

In the essays that follow, we can see the emergence of the demon lover theme in the contexts of the biography that has shaped each woman and of the literature that each woman has shaped through her symbolic expression of her inner world. As with Ronald Fairbairn's (1952) and Harry Guntrip's (1976) patients' dreams, we can see creative work as a display of the inner world's dynamic form. The movement toward reparative self-integration can be contrasted with the arrests in such developmental process as the dynamics of mourning or aborted mourning are observed. If mourning and reparative development are arrested, then reenactment and externalization will be expected to dominate the picture presented through the creative literary expression. However, if mourning proceeds through the use of the creative process, it seems likely that transformation and whole object symbolism will evolve. We can observe whether the work of the creative process then moves its author toward or away from interpersonal life.

# 6

# Portraits of Two Kinds of Creative Women

Anaïs Nin and Sylvia Plath are two writers whose psychological uses of the creative process provide a striking contrast in the study of object relations. Their lives and work allow us to differentiate success from failure in the psychological use of the creative process. I will use both writers as introductory examples to my overall thesis about the developmental factors that influence the degree of self-repair that may be achieved through use of the creative process.

## Anaïs Nin

Anaïs Nin was born in Paris on February 21, 1903. Her father was a concert pianist, and her family traveled widely throughout Europe. When Nin was nine, her father deserted the family. She moved to New York with her mother and two younger brothers in 1914; she began a diary in which she used to write letters to her absent father. Although Nin later studied and worked as a dancer and as a psychoanalyst (following a training in analysis with Otto Rank), she continued to write.

Nin hoped to reach her father through her writing and bring him back. Her diary became invested with wishes for rescue, self-repair, and magical cures through her father's love. Nin endured unrequited love through the psychic realm of her diary, which became the chief resource for all her later literary work. In fact, the diary itself has been considered her major work. Within it, Nin created female characters who served as alter-egos and who expressed her own psychological struggles.

It is significant that Nin's diaries report her mothering to have been so favorable. Her mother's resilient nature shines forth despite the abandonment by her husband. The mother's continuing nurturance and empathic involvement with her daughter's growth suggests a healthy vitality and capacity for attuned relatedness. Telling perhaps is Nin's report of her mother's ability to express joy and enthusiasm for life, despite the poverty and adversity endured after the departure of her husband. These human qualities are seriously lacking in Nin's father, who exhibits narcissistic character pathology.

In her diaries and short stories, Nin struggles with her father, who has become a ghostlike internal object. Although she idealizes her father, he is more than a part object whose godlike features turn pervasively demonic. Nin faces the realistic failings of her father and in doing so develops a differentiated view both of herself and of him. Her capacity to do this suggest that she achieved whole object relations during infancy and separation-individuation. Presumably because of good enough mothering, Nin resolves a separation process in relation to her father, in spite of the intense frustration of her oedipal passions. She recovers from the trauma of her father deserting her and ultimately recovers from the pathological cravings for men who can be used as alternative father figures. Such cravings impeded her capacities for self-integration before their resolution through creative-process mourning.

In *Winter of Artifice*, a novella derived from the original diary writings, Nin sets up an encounter so that she can face her father. In another novel, *A Spy in the House of Love*, Nin shows her struggle with regressive narcissistic fusions with men. Within her creative work, she demonstrates how she has used men as self-extensions, just as her father had used her as an extension of himself. It is through the process of her work that Nin ultimately resolves the loss of her father, allowing her to move past her narcissistic involvement with men and past her narcissistic injuries. These injuries could have been only accentuated with abandonment. Yet when Nin's father actually did abandon her, she was already in the latency stage and had completed the self-development of the preoedipal and oedipal periods.

Although Nin's reaction to the traumatic loss of her father suggests that there could be earlier issues of maternal abandonment during the preoedipal years, other factors make it appear unlikely that the preoedipal difficulties reached traumatic proportions. Nin is able to reflect on herself within her creative work and to find her way to whole object relations through this creativity. This indicates that Nin's mother was able to facilitate a primary cohesive self-structure during the preoedipal period. Nin's psychic conflicts reflect oedipal-stage narcissistic difficulties, as opposed to predominantly preoedipal dilemmas. From Nin's descriptions of her father, we can infer that she suffered severe oedipal humiliation, seductive paternal exploitation, and her father's use of her for his own narcissistic mode of mirroring in which he sought a compulsory reflection of his own grandiosity. Nin's anguish, confusion, and manic and depressive reactions to despair [1] indicate normal deflation of her own grandiose self following the practicing period and during rapprochement. This implies adequate development up until rapprochement, so that her narcissistic features appear as regressive symptoms rather than as products of developmental arrest. Such symptoms can be reactions to the oedipal-stage frustrations of adoring a father who coldly deserted her at the age of nine. Nin's literature is a creative expression of her psychological dynamics.

A major theme throughout Nin's writing is her relationship to her absent father. Each of Nin's female characters reflects this relationship. In her novella, *Winter of Artifice*, Djuana stands as an alter-ego heroine who waits for her father, as Nin had waited for her reunion with him: "She is waiting for him. She was waiting for him for twenty years. He is coming today . . . " (p 67). At thirty, Djuana consummates a fantasy reunion with her father, resembling Nin's own reunion. As with all meetings based on idealized images, her expectations will lead to disappointment and deadness before separation and release. Disappointment brings back the hurt of the past: "At nine years old, Djuana has sensed his impending exit from her life. . . . Suddenly, moved by an acute premonition, she threw herself on him and clung to him passionately. Don't go Father! Don't leave me!" (60).

His departure left an emptiness that filled Djuana with fantasies of a tender, nurturing, and understanding father—qualities that her real father never possessed. Her father's cold, narcissistic contempt was converted into such a fantasy ideal through Nin's intense yearning for her father's return. Djuana-Nin thought of her father when God was spoken of in church, and she wrote religiously in her diary. She imagined that her writing would reach her father, the man whom she now turned into a god. She yearned for her father's admiration and longed passionately for him to see her. Her diary became her symbolic mirror as she looked toward her fantasy father, and ultimately toward the men who were to replace him, for a reflection of herself.

At first, Djuana-Nin maintains the illusion that her identity will emerge through fusion with her father rather than through separation. She fantasizes that she will give up all her power to him and through him will merge into greatness, gaining herself through his power: "She, being woman, had to live in a manmade world, could not impose her own, but here was her father's world, it fitted her. With him she could run through the world in seven-league boots" (72). As Djuana-Nin deals with the emerging realities in this tale, her idealization of her father and her merger with him are shattered. She realizes that her child's view of her father is based on distortion. His abandonment of her aborted the process of coming to know her father as a differentiated personality. She was left with an unmourned fantasy ideal and a sense of being incomplete without her father's mirroring reflection. This realization comes as Djuana-Nin wakes up to the realities of her adult needs. The pathology of her narcissistic wishes and of her father's narcissistic character structure then emerges. Facing him, she begins the mourning process in which she lets go of the ideal father of her fantasy. Through mourning, she faces the truth about who her father really is. In doing this, she begins to face the facts of the person she can be if she can just separate from her father by differentiating herself from his narcissistic traits.

Her father's pathology becomes clear as he demands exclusive possession of her. After demanding that she give up all men in her current life so that they might devote themselves to each other totally (74), Djuana-Nin experiences her father's jealousy of her past loves as well:

> Her father's jealousy began with the reading of her diary. He observed that after two years of obsessional yearning for him she had finally exhausted her suffering and obtained serenity. After serenity she had fallen love with an Irish boy and then a violinist. He was offended that she had not died completely, that she had not spent the rest of her life yearning for him.
>
> (79)

Yet more threatening than his demands on her was the split within his own character:

> Through this mask of coldness which had terrified her as a child she was better able as a woman to detect the malady of his soul. His soul was sick. He was very sick deep down. He was dying inside; his eyes could no longer see the warm, the near, the real. He seemed to have come from very far only to be leaving again immediately. He was always pretending to be there. His body alone was there, but his soul was absent. . . .
>
> (94)

Djuana-Nin begins to face her father's falseness. She faces the split between a cut-off inner self and the outer self he showed the world. Behind his mask of aristocratic pride, she sees the weak and cowardly inner being hidden behind a mask: "It was difficult for her to believe, as others did, that the mask tainted the blood. . . . " (97). Djuana-Nin seeks to get beyond the division of self observed in her father. By self-reflectively confronting herself with her illusions, she can face the reality of her own pain and can avoid being divided within herself. Through awareness and self-reflection, she avoids incorporating her father's self-division.

To stay with her father means not only to lose the boundaries of her own identity but to live with lies that deny her true self as well as her lifelong attempt at self-definition, begun in her diary. To find herself she must face her own injuries and face the real nature of the father who inflicted these injuries, even though up until now she had blinded herself so as to preserve a fantasy father who promised no pain. Djuana-Nin returns to her father's desertion, despite his denial that his acts toward her need have consequences. She faces her rage by facing the vulnerabilities within herself that her father would prefer not to see.

She surrenders the wish for his support—and faces herself alone—through her personal writing: "He did not know that this feeling was so strong in her that anything which resembled abandonment created a violent inner storm . . . : a door closed on her too brusquely, a letter unanswered . . . " (72).

Djuana-Nin also remembers his coldness, his critical slights, his contempt for her dancing, and his accusations that she was a fraud when she claimed to be sick. As her vision of these realities is sharpened, she begins to sense a freeing up of the bond of narcissistic fusion: "Realizing more and more that she did not love him, she felt a strange joy, as if she were witnessing a just punishment for his coldness as a father . . . " (105).

Djuana-Nin leaves her father as he had once left her. Nin makes this emotional separation graphic. Djuana leaves on a trip despite her father's protests that she is abandoning him. Although Nin's stories turn on the symmetry of Karmic justice, in which the punishment fits the crime, leaving her father clearly goes beyond retaliation. Her fictional abandonment does not come from vindictiveness, but rather comes through her own growing insight into herself and her own needs. She proceeds with her mourning, facing the lonely but liberating truth that her father is not the fantasy father who she believed could heal the little girl in her. She mourns not only the fantasy father but the little girl within whose reactions to her father she needs to understand to integrate the past and to move into her own adulthood. As she faces the loss of not having had a father who loved her when she was young, she lets go and surrenders to her pain. Through this surrender, she feels her needs as a woman.

Nin symbolizes the mourning of the little girl within by mentioning her literal loss of a girl baby whom she had miscarried (119). She uses the actual events of her life to portray Djuana's psychology within her literary format. She uses her diary writing, and the story that evolves from it, in *Winter of Artifice*, to work through the separation of her own needs from the narcissistic wishes that her father had imposed on her, as well as from her own childhood fantasy wishes.

Nin can never have the father whom she did not have in reality, but she can face loss and move beyond it to better relationships with others in her life. She does this by moving from worshipful relations with male writers such as Henry Miller and D. H. Lawrence to creating an art of her own, which she begins to share with other artists. Her differentiation and separation from her father, explored and worked through by means of creative work, allow her to create a unique art and identity of her own. This process also allows her to relate more fully within interpersonal relations. Increasingly, she adopts a nurturing attitude toward others, whereas earlier she had scorned such nurturance because she connected it with her mother and her mother's fate.

In *Collage Dreams*, a biographical study of Anaïs Nin and her work (1977), Sharon Spencer discusses Nin's acceptance of the nurturing aspects of herself that she formerly denied. Differentiating herself from her father's narcissistic attitude toward others, she was able to integrate more of her mother's nurturance into her own personality. She did this while still not surrendering the healthy narcissism represented by her father because of his dedication to artistic creativity.

Nin integrates herself by mourning her father. Separating from him through mourning, she moves beyond her fear of identifying with her mother. She begins selectively to identify with those aspects of her mother with which she had already unconsciously identified. She no longer has to defend against a whole part of herself; she no longer has to disown her nurturance and hide it from awareness. As she strengthens herself through mourning, she is able to be a nurturer in her own way, no longer fearing dominance by her mother's personality. She adopts a nurturing role with artists, because she had chosen to be an artist as her father had. Through mourning, Nin can selectively own identifications with both her father and her mother that suit her true inner nature.

Nin's writing reveals another journey that parallels the one just described in *Winter of Artifice*. Within her work she struggles with her own narcissism and with the self-fragmentation that this seemingly defensive narcissism brings. In doing so, she struggles to go beyond the defensive character traits that are so connected with her identifications and relations with her narcissistic father. The mirror becomes the symbol for her narcissistic neurosis, it is used throughout her novels, stories, and diary writing to describe the forces that inhibit her.

In *The Mirror and the Garden*, she speaks through Djuana and observes:

> Djuana let her eyes melt into the garden. The garden had an air of nudity, of efflorescence, of abundance, of plenitude.
>
> The salon was gilded, the people were costumed for false roles, the lights and the faces were attenuated, the gestures were starched. . . .
>
> The eyes of the people had needed the mirrors. . . . All the truth of the garden, the moisture, and the worms, the insects and the roots, the running sap and the rotting bark, had to be reflected in the mirrors.
>
> (12–13)

Only as Djuana-Nin frees herself from these mirrors of the narcissistic world can she truly define herself. In an earlier prose poem, *House of Incest* (1958), Nin expresses the chaos within that she feels as narcissistic fusion and boundary loss oppose potentially individuated identity. Through the explorations within her work, she discovers that such regressions into undifferentiated states are the consequence of living through image reflections in the way her father always did. Nin repeatedly uses the theme of the mirror to symbolize her imprisonment: "I am ill with the obstinacy of images, reflections in cracked mirrors . . . " (29). "When I sit before my mirror I laugh at myself . . . I cannot tell how all these separate pieces can be ME. . . . I do not exist. I am not a body" (47–48).

We can speculate that Nin disowns her body because of oedipal trauma in relation to her father. Nin is forced to live through image reflections of herself, and she looks to men to mirror her. Any loss of a mirroring male brings a sense of not existing as a whole. However, when she seeks out a masculine other, she is caught in a trap of interlocking projections. In *House of Incest*, she experiences this in relation to her brother. Both undifferentiated form and content pervade *House of Incest*, and the struggles are carried into her other work, although she moves from the undifferentiated images in a prose poem to the somewhat more differentiated form of characters within a novel. In *House of Incest*, the female narrator has only an intrapsychic relation to the other characters. All references to others are reactions to introjective entities within the solipsistic world of the narrator's mind. There is no sense of self, and since the self is defined in relation to others, there are not others. Nin is showing the sense of psychic chaos that comes with a sealing off of the inner self. For her, this sealing off seems regressive and defensive, instead of being as fundamental as it would be in the case of developmental arrest, for Nin is able to move beyond it through active and self-observant struggles in her other works.

In her other novels, the extremely narcissistic form of her writing changes. The narrator adopts a semi-object orientation, a relation to a person who responds to part object others. There is still an intrapsychic focus, in which others are part objects rather than whole objects. Yet the solipsistic air of *House of Incest* is transcended. In novels such as *Ladders to Fire* (1959), *Children of the Albatross* (1947), *Four Chambered Heart* (1966), *Solar Barque* (1958), and *Seduction of the Minotaur* (1961), the female heroines react and respond to others who exist outside the self. Still, those others are presented through the experiences of the heroine and reflect her subjective view. There is no sense of other people as having an existence apart from the heroine. In *A Spy in the House of Love*, (1954; 1974) the part object others are erotically inflamed male reflectors who mirror various aspects of the self. The whole issue of yearning for and raging against them is reflected in content as well as in form. Sabina, the heroine of *A Spy in the House of Love*, expresses her narcissistic dilemma: "Sabina wants to be what Allan wants her to be.

At times Allan is not certain of what he wishes. Then the stormy, tumultuous Sabina waits in incredible stillness, alert and watchful for signs of his wishes and fantasies" (17).

Allan mirrored only the little girl in her. To seek the comfort of his steady and protective presence, she relinquished all of her erotic and passionate features. In order to reclaim these other parts, Sabina had to seek out other lovers to mirror and reflect them. Nin, in the form of her alter-ego Sabina, again becomes trapped in her mirror image as it is reflected by part object male others: "But when she wished to end a role, to become herself again, the other felt immensely betrayed, and not only fought the alteration but became angered at her. Once a role was established in a relationship it was almost impossible to alter (89). Toward the end of *A Spy in the House of Love*, some prospect of separation from these male mirrors is hinted. Sabina meets the Lie Detector, the only man in her life who does not insist that she conform to an image. Although terrified of being truly seen, Sabina begins to reveal herself to this man, who, we are told, helps her to face her inability to love. In this manner, Nin sets the stage for self-integration and for relations with whole object others. The development of the capacity to love implies the acceptance of a whole other rather than the mere use of the other as a mirroring reflector for one's own mirror image.

Although *A Spy in the House of Love* was published late because of the difficulty in finding a publisher during the 1950s for such an erotic tale, it was actually written during Nin's middle period, when her narcissistic struggles were at their peak. The resolution of these struggles comes in her later work, *Collages*.

The stories in *Collages* (1964) show further progress in the struggle toward differentiation of self and other. Nin goes beyond the part object reflections of her middle period to show a spectrum of separate and whole characters. The whole style of narration changes. The sense of fine perception of one female heroine is lost as well as transcended, and the flavor of internal sensing is changed. There is an opening of the world of objectivity and interpersonal relations and a considerable diminishment of the intensity of the internal drama of narcissistic struggle.

In *Collages*, Nin devotes a section to the tale of Varda and his daughter. Nin's writing no longer emanates from the internal locus of the female psyche. Varda and his daughter are in conflict and also in relation to each other. They have equal weight as whole objects. Varda loves his daughter and wishes her to see and experience the vital world displayed in his painting. His daughter resists and mocks his efforts to appeal to her through his stories and anecdotes. However, by a twist of the narrative, his daughter is allowed to discover his world. Through the experience of taking the drug LSD, her senses open up, and she begins to reflect in her own manner of dressing the brightness and color of her father's world of painting. There is a new understanding reached and communicated between them. In essence, there is dialogue rather than merger. Exclusively intrapsychic struggles are absent from this work, because such struggles have been resolved in separation and in the accompanying mutuality of interpersonal relations.

Thus, the journey from *House of Incest* to *Collages* represents a symbolic exploration that helped Anaïs Nin to transcend her rage at her father and to mourn through her yearning for him. Having sensed the loss she was able to go beyond it.

## Summary of Nin

Nin worked through her wounds and self-injuries by a combination of poetic and analytic exploration, as demonstrated in her writing. She recreated her father and confronted the fallacies of her idealization as well as the suppressed anger that kept her enslaved in wishes for his mirroring admiration.There was no way for Nin to escape injury. After her father's departure, she scrutinized herself for flaws, trying to discover a reason for her father's desertion, which was felt as betrayal. Yet the humiliation was modified by some knowledge of the narcissistic bind that she was in and by evidence that her father was unworthy of the kind of worship that she clung to from childhood.

Nin used her creative work to express her struggle and navigated her way through it. Her creativity grew out of this psychic struggle; her creative work was her format for self-investigation. Nin shows capacities for self-reflection. She is the interpreter of her own experience (see Ogden 1986), differentiating internal-object fantasies from the reality traits of a parental object. She contains and symbolizes the related affect experience. Given these preoedipal developmental capacities, Nin was able to resolve the narcissistic conflict between exposing her true self and living through projected idealized images (see Kavaler 1985; 1992a). When she lives through the projected idealized images of men, she enacts romantic, erotic, or childlike roles that capture only an element of her true nature and freeze that element in time, as behind a mask.[2] With separation from her father— and from the men who serve as father-figure displacements—Nin comes to accept all parts of herself and to integrate herself from within.

As Nin gains increasing insight into her own needs, she separates and differentiates from her father, as well as from her father's mode of narcissistic defense. By seeing her true father, she is able to give up living in a hall of mirrors. She lets go of her internal-object fantasies, the relics of her past and enters a mourning process that is based on both awareness and acceptance of the disappointments inherent in these idealized internal-object fantasies. Mourning disappointments bring about perceptions of whole objects that are internalized as structuralized mental representations within the nuclear self. Nin's creative works give evidence of the developmental achievement of such structuralization, as in *Collages*, in which characterizations of the whole object self and male other are developed. As Nin surrenders the narcissistic fusion with a defensively idealized father part object, which is accomplished through the affective process of mourning, she reclaims split-off incorporations of the more realistically inadequate father. She recalls vivid memories of childhood neglect by her bad rather than good enough father. This allows Nin to gain affective awareness of childhood traumas so that they can be resolved.

## Contrasts with Nin: The Case of Sylvia Plath

The progress that Anaïs Nin made in her creative work opened up new interpersonal experiences in her life. This was a progressive developmental process which led to complementary whole object relations and to self-integration. It cannot be assumed that because Nin was successful in this self-integrative task, other artists will enjoy such success. Sylvia Plath stands in sharp contrast.

Plath is a poet whose work displays an aborted and ultimately pathological mourning process. I have described the vicious cycle of reenactment in Plath's work in several journal articles (Kavaler 1985; 1986). Plath exhibits severe narcissistic pathology in both her life and her work. Developmentally, her narcissistic pathology seems to fall at a borderline level. Within her creative work, we can see how Plath became possessed by the archaic part object for which she yearned, instead of mourning such an internal object presence so that self-transformation through self-integration could become possible.

Plath was born on October 27, 1932, the first child of Otto and Aurelia Shober Plath. Her father was a German professor who had been born in the Polish Corridor. His doctorate was in entomology (he was an expert on bees). Professor Plath's book *Bees and Their Ways* gave him a notable reputation in his field.

Plath's mother, Aurelia, was twenty-one years younger than her husband. She and Professor Plath met at Boston University, when she was pursuing a master's degree and he was her teacher. The age difference and the roles of student and teacher suggest a strong need on Otto Plath's part for an idealized position.

At age two and a half, Plath was traumatized by the birth of her younger brother. In her own words, as recorded by Butscher, (1976), she declared: "A Baby! I hated babies. I who for two and a half years had been the centre of a tender universe felt the axis wrench and polar chill immobilize my bones. I would be a bystander, a museum mammoth. Babies!" (7). This reaction to her brother's entry into the world suggest a preoedipal narcissistic disturbance. With an established vulnerability, this early blow may have had some impact on Plath's developing self-split and on the narcissistic preoccupation that is so vividly presented in her poetry. Yet it was the double-edged wound of her father's life and death that most prominently stamped her work and altered her "axis." Otto Plath's roles as both his daughter's narcissistic mirror and her idealized god-tyrant are documented in fact and fiction by the poet. Plath embellishes the fact with her own psychic myths and creates a demon lover father who serves as her tyrannical muse. Throughout her poetry, Plath shows a craving for an archaic god-demon father, resulting in bulimic incorporations and expulsions expressed through her poetry. The following is taken from "Lady Lazarus," one of her well-known *Ariel* poems:

So, so, Herr Doktor.
So, Herr Enemy.

I am your opus
    I am your valuable,
The pure gold baby

(8)

Herr God, Herr Lucifer,
    Beware
    Beware

Out of the ash
    I rise with my red hair
And I eat men like air

(9)

Here Plath attempts to retaliate against her father by eating men and being reborn. Later she turns to attempts at exorcism. However, she has no alternative finally but resignation and petrification when struggling with her internal father demon and his mammoth elaborations in fantasy. The more optimistic note of manic triumph at the end of this poem, in which the poet sees herself as conquering her father through incorporation within a state of "red hair" rage, is to degenerate into self-annihilation as the archaic god-demon's grandiosity keeps him beyond her grasp. She becomes imprisoned within her own system of part object father idealizations, which are incorporated early-object forms that seem to combine a preoedipal primary mother object with a masculine paternal form. Plath, like Nin, lost her father during latency, following his death; however, unlike Nin, she was unable to mourn and differentiate from him through her creative work.

Plath's part object is not just a regressively defensive constellation; it is an early rather preoedipally arrested object form. Her poetry reflects the archaic level of her father idealization. Appropriate to this preoedipal-fantasy dimension, Plath labels a poem about her father "Colossus." She imagines her father as a Roman ruin:

O father, all by yourself
You are pithy and historical as the
Roman Forum . . .
. . . . . . . . . . . . . . . . . . . . . . . . . . . . . . . . . . . . . . . . . . . .
Nights, I squat in the cornucopia
Of your left ear, out of the wind . . .

(*The Colossus*, 21)

In her later *Ariel* poem "Daddy," her father is

> Marble-heavy, a bag full of God,
> Ghastly statue with one grey toe
> Big as a Frisco seal.
>
> (49)

To ward off the power of her stifling erotic idealization, Plath negates her father as a god and turns him into the devil—a Nazi devil. By turning her adoration into hatred, she hopes to free herself:

> Not God but a swastika
>     So black no sky could squeak through.
> Every woman adores a Fascist,
>     The boot in the face, the brute
> Brute heart of a brute like you.
>
> (50)

The poet holds herself tight in her own protective and stifling idealization, as her inner self remains sealed off behind its reflecting-image play and addiction. The needy self of the child, behind the mask mirrored by the idealized other, threatens to drain away her life from behind its schizoid barrier:

> Open-mouthed, the baby god
>     Immense, bald, though baby-headed
> Cried out for the mother's dug
>     The dry volcanoes crouched and spit
> Sand abraded the milkless lip.
>     Cried then for the father's blood. . . .
>
> (*The Colossus*, 39)

Turning from mother to father, she is again in the power of an idealized other who mirrors her but who cannot respond to her hungry cravings for affective contact. As exorcism follows incorporation, Plath tries to kill the connection to her father or else to kill her father himself. Caught up in her own need, Plath clings to her father as she attempts to destroy him:

> So daddy, I'm finally through.
>     The black telephone's off at the root
> The voices just can't worm through
>     If I've killed on man, I've killed two—
>
> (*Ariel*, 5)

While she clings to her father, the poet's sadistic revenge can never be complete. She clings to the man-god who has been incorporated as an early extension of her own self, and his destruction becomes her own. The villagers stamp on daddy. There's a "fat black stake in his heart" (*Ariel* ["Daddy"], 51). Still he is not finished. He rumbles with power despite the poet's attempt at a tantrum rage assassination. The bitch goddess continues wailing against a wall of blocked grief. Plath uses many images of fragmentation as her inner self fragments. Often they are mixed with the bloody red wound: "A dozen red lead sinkers round my neck" (*Ariel* ["Tulips"], 11). There is no revenge without self-annihilation.

Plath's differentiated self is lost; she uses the word "somebody" to refer to her now alienated experience (*Ariel*, 28–29). In a continuing progression, her poems all move from similes and comparisons to the annihilation of identity and to merger. The sadistic male daddy is victimized by the queen bee feminine self, who in turn is threatened with death by young virgins; her salvation leads to the death of the author.[3] All are ultimately equalized by extinction.

As one split-off part of Plath kills off another, with victim and victimizer merging through mutual annihilation, the voice of her internal parent is heard in the background: "The woman is perfected. Her dead" (*Ariel*, 84). The victim is the part of her that lives falsely through the mirrored image of the other. In "Death and Co." Plath writes "Bastard, Masturbating a litter, . . . " (*Ariel*, 28). She rages against the male tyrant who can see her only through his own image, in a masturbatory way.

As her rage erupted, Plath's poetry came fast, in a manic intensity. Plath writes in "Kindness" (*Ariel*, 82),[4] "The blood jet is poetry, there is no stopping it." She arose at 5:00 A.M. to express her rage in poetry. But behind the rage was the terror, where nobody ever reached her. Her move from hiding in false images, turned to a manic intensity, and ultimately became a withdrawal into death.

As the poet withdraws into her suicidal state, she writes "Edge," a poem in which she recoils into herself, undoing the birth of her own children. Her poem "Last Words" (*Crossing the Water*, 40) involves a repudiation of her narcissistic mirroring relation with her father, leaving her alone to die with "words" (*Ariel*, 84) that become "dry and riderless."

The final performance is played out all too perfectly. In *The Savage God*, A. Alvarez proposes that Sylvia Plath's last suicide attempt, at thirty, was not intended to succeed. Ironically, it was set up with signs of ambivalence not seen in her earlier attempts. Plath left a note with the telephone number of her doctor next to the oven in which she exterminated herself.

Plath's poetry was perhaps more final than her last thoughts. Her creative-process attempts to purge herself of her demonic death-father by catharsis were never successful. The rage to retaliate was increasingly weakened, until the failure to mourn brought fixation on the wound, and ultimately its draining into the aridity of death.

## The Role of Plath's Mother

Both Sylvia Plath and Anaïs Nin had narcissistic fathers, rather than fathers who would qualify as good enough. We get a glimpse of the father-daughter relations in Butscher's biography (1976) when he describes Plath's father showing off his three-year-old daughter's precocious ability to memorize and recite poly-syllabic Latin names. Plath always wrote about her relationship to her father in terms of a scene of performance. Biographers other than Butscher, such as Wagner-Martin (1987), have attested to the stage of performance that dominated the poet's early relations to this professorial father, who died when she was eight. The narcissistic dynamics could become Plath's narcissistic defense, as was true in the case of Anaïs Nin. A critical distinction between Plath and Nin, however, resides in the difference between their mothers and in the distinction between their mothers' capacities for maternal relatedness.

It seems from Plath's own descriptions that her mother was as narcissistic as her father.[5] Like Otto Plath, Aurelia Shober Plath seems to have continually encouraged her daughter to strive for perfect mirroring through academic and social performance. In fact, Mrs. Plath apparently played a large part in her daughter's false-self persona. Plath writes of her mother's sugary falseness in her poems (see "Kindness" in *Ariel*). In letters to her mother, she herself is false, grandiosely being on top of everything. When Sylvia writes in her poem "Edge," "The Woman is perfected. Her dead" we wonder what part her mother played in her suicidal addiction to perfection. In an essay from 1981 entitled "Fusion with the Victim: A Study of Sylvia Plath," Shelley Orgel gathers the data concerning the effect Plath's mother's had and highlights her lack of emotional responsiveness as described by Plath herself in her autobiographical novel *The Bell Jar*. Orgel describes a mother deadened within herself, who has perhaps never mourned, as Sylvia Plath herself proclaims in her creative work. All of the evidence indicates that Aurelia Plath was cut off from her own inner self and lacked spontaneous emotional response. How much this affected the daughter during her preoedipal dependence on her mother can only be guessed. How emotionally constricted Aurelia may have been after her husband's death can likewise only be surmised. Most significantly, however, Plath's poetry suggests an inadequate early mother, since the poet never seems to transcend primitive part object relations.

## Plath and Other Psychically Arrested Creative Women

As the poet rages at her father-god, her hatred makes him demonic. Sylvia Plath's creative work fits into the split archaic ideal and archaic demon described by Melanie Klein in her clinical observations of part object relations. These part object relations signify the prominent self-split of the borderline personality structure. The poet invests both her creative work and her own father within that work with godlike powers. Then, the poet attempts to swallow her god whole. This incorporative mode leads only to exorcistic expulsion of the magic object,[6] expulsion of an archaic part object that cannot be integrated into the poet's own sense of self. This expulsion is accompanied by cathartic expressions of rage that allow the poet to rise above her own injuries and needs and above the position of dependence on an object that could potentially lead to self-structuralizing internalization. These dynamics reflect Klein's descriptions of the self-disruptive paranoid-schizoid position, as well as the manic dynamics that she describes as eluding reparative object engagement, since dependent vulnerability is eschewed. The paranoid-schizoid position is a psychic dynamic expressed through vicious cycles of splitting and exorcistic catharsis.[7] Manic cycles of contempt also annihilate both the self-contact and the interpersonal contact needed for mourning and self-integration. As Plath continues to rage rather than mourn, frustrating cycles of such preoedipal-trauma reenactment propel the intense agony that vitalizes her creative work. The cycles become degenerative, and self-fragmentation ultimately leads to schizoid retreat and to the act of suicide,[8] in which the merger with the demonic father-god is completed. Erotic yearnings commingle with cravings to merge with and destroy the mammoth other who becomes a recalcitrant extension of herself. Plath's oral erotic craving for the demon lover father becomes a yearning for merger through death and is eroticized by oedipal and incestuous longings.

This sequence can be seen in Anne Sexton's work (Kavaler 1989a) and in the works of several other female writers whom I will study as I proceed from theory to individual cases. The poets Emily Dickinson, Emily Brontë, and Edith Sitwell display a similar degenerative sequence, which becomes an antiprocess, since the potential developmental mourning process is undermined. Such an antiprocess sequence can be called pathological mourning, because in object relations terms, the attempt to mourn the external parental object and its fantasized dimensions as an early internal object turns to incorporative psychic swallowing and expelling.

The idealized object is not a good object. It is a compensatory fantasy replacement for a mother who was not "good enough", i.e., who did not provide affectively responsive object contact, while allowing autonomy. Without the internalization of a good enough mother,[9] loss does not turn to reparative developmental mourning. Rather, a vicious cycle of primitive idealization and villainizing of the object occurs. The compulsion behind this self-destructive cycle involves terrors of self-annihilation. Repetitive themes of abandonment, engulfment, rage, and bereavement characterize the creative work of those who exhibit this form of pathological mourning as they reenact preoedipal-stage developmental arrest. Psychic-structure limitations contribute to this aborted and pathological mode of mourning, as will be discussed later in my description of the kind of early mothering necessary for mourning to proceed.

Why do many artists spend their lives locked up in their work, while others use the creative process in their work to move toward interpersonal relations? Anaïs Nin progressed toward healthy interpersonal relations through her creative work, as did the nineteenth-century novelist Charlotte Brontë. The latter, like Nin, was able to mourn and differentiate through the creative process. In contrast to such women are women who are unable to mourn within their creative work and who are also unable to progress toward self-integration and mutual interpersonal relations. Generally, my studies show that pathological mourning leads to an addiction to creativity itself, a syndrome I address as "the compulsion to create." Women writers who cannot mourn write of being locked up in cells that often symbolize their fathers' bodies or houses. In the opening of "Daddy," Plath writes:

> You do not do, you do not do
> Any more, black shoe
> In which I have lived like a foot
> For Thirty years, poor and white,
> Barely daring to breathe or Achoo.
>
> (*Ariel*, 49).

Emily Dickinson and Emily Brontë both withdrew into seclusion within their father's homes. Dickinson wrote of being shut up "in prose . . . Because they liked me "still" (*The Complex Poems* No. 613, 302). In one way or another, women who cannot mourn and individuate through their creative work withdraw from the world through seclusion or suicide. Sometimes, as with Edith Sitwell, that withdrawal does not come until late in life. However, deteriorating relations with others, along with an addiction to creativity that increasingly promotes isolation, often lead to suicidal despair and/or to death from disease.[10] Writers such as Plath, Dickinson, and Sitwell become the victims of their most valuable assets, their creative talents. Without the capacity to mourn through the creative process, artistically gifted people can remain endlessly trapped, unable to experience how creativity can move them toward a richer interpersonal life.

Although exceptions exist, these people may not turn to psychotherapy to resolve the early traumas that have sealed off their internal and intrapsychic worlds from interpersonal relations, and thus from developmental mourning and self-growth. These are the people who may harbor a defensive narcissistic fantasy of self-sufficiency (Modell 1975; 1976). They believe that they can heal themselves from within through the creative process; they may unconsciously wish to find themselves through their work. They may even unconsciously wish to use their work in the service of mourning the early preoedipal objects to which they are tied. However, they are generally compelled to reenact preoedipal dramas and traumas, since they are unable affectively to experience trauma so that mourning can lead to healing the wounds of the past. When the inner self has been sealed off from interpersonal contact at the earliest developmental stages of life, prior to self-formation through differentiation and integration, a schizoid barrier promotes seclusive and/or suicidal behavior. Mourning and self-formation cannot then proceed unless the early trauma can be experienced through the containing presence of an "other" in psychotherapy.[11] This is true when a failure in healthy modes of internalization leads to unassimilated or split-off incorporated part objects entering the internal world. Such part objects lack any capacity for intrapsychic dialogue and therefore oppose the developmental progress that requires mourning for self-integrating structure building during engagement with the creative process.

# 7

# Charlotte Brontë: Biography and *Jane Eyre*

During her lifetime, Charlotte Brontë published one collection of poetry and four novels. Her earliest novel, *The Professor,* written in 1846, was published posthumously in 1857. Her second novel, *Jane Eyre* (1847), established her fame. An overnight sensation, it set London literary circles buzzing with curiosity as to the real identity of the author who hid behind the male pseudonym Currer Bell. Nearly 150 years later, *Jane Eyre* remains Charlotte Brontë's most celebrated work. Her third novel, *Shirley* (1849), a tribute to her sister Emily, was based on memoirs and fictional elaboration that contained social and political satire. The novel deviated from the personal style of female psychology that marked *Jane Eyre*. In her last and most artistically mature novel, *Villette* (1853), Brontë returned with even greater acuity to the psychological realm. Here, Brontë narrated in fictional form her unrequited love for the French professor with whom she had studied for two years (1842–43) in Brussels. It is a theme with which she had attempted to deal in *The Professor* but which needed the passage of time and the crystallizing of feeling to come alive. *Villette* was written after the death of all of Charlotte's siblings, after a lifetime of caring for her demanding and now aged father, and after years of disappointments occasioned by attempting to establish herself independently in a patriarchal and socially prejudiced society. Sobered and reflective after losses, Brontë used the writing of *Villette* to mourn for and to separate from her father. After its completion, she was able at the age of thirty-eight to consent to marriage for the first time. In marrying Arthur Nicholls, her father's curate, she relinquished forever her fantasies of being united with the hero of her adolescence, the man who had defeated Napoleon at Waterloo. In 1855—less than a year after her marriage—Charlotte Brontë died, apparently from a combination of tubercular diseases related to pregnancy.

Brontë's recent biographer, Margot Peters (1986),[1] writes of her subject:

> [A]s a subjective novelist whose chief business is to convince the reader of one individual's capacity for love, hate, suffering, pride, self-discipline, and triumph, she is hardly equaled, if indeed she is equaled, by any other English writer. Had she lived to write one or two more novels like *Jane Eyre* and *Villette*,

she must have occupied a separate but equal niche across from Thackeray and George Eliot, for it is because of her slender output, not the quality of her work, that she suffers in comparison with the prolific Victorians.

(413)

Peters also remarks that Charlotte Brontë "filled her novels with the tensions of her own ambivalent desires" (414). In the following discussion I attempt to chart precisely what these desires were and to show how, through heroic effort, Brontë moved toward resolving them personally and artistically.

When Charlotte Brontë was five, she arrived at Haworth Village, where her father set up house at a parsonage as town curate. Haworth was in a rugged area of Yorkshire, 10 miles from Lancashire, surrounded by marshes and moors. Because of poor town sewerage, health conditions were abysmal.

Within the year, Patrick Brontë's wife died of cancer, in great emotional distress and unable to keep her religious faith, as she was torn abruptly away from her "poor children" (Peters, 1986, 4). At her death, the widower was in a state of shock. He was unprepared to raise five girls and one boy by himself and thus settled for the help of his dead wife's sister, Aunt Branwell, who came to live with the bereaved family. Fridgety, fussy, and cold, Aunt Branwell was also an intellectual sparring partner for her brother-in-law; she set an example of female intellect if not warmth.

The order and reserve of this household was occasionally broken by paternal rampages. Charlotte Brontë's original and classic biographer, her novelist friend Elizabeth Gaskell [1857]; 1983), describes a vivid scene in which Patrick Brontë raided the children's closets, seizing the gay-colored boots and garments they had retained in the midst of poverty, expelling from their house all apparel that he judged frivolous. One wonders whether the male characters in the novels of both Emily and Charlotte, who demonstrate intrusive and threatening attitudes as they enter a room (Heathcliff in *Wuthering Heights* and Professor M. Paul Emanuel in *Villette*), found the blueprint for their behavior in such "holy" raids.

Outside the household lay the vast world of nature. From quite a young age, the five sisters ventured out on the English moors—hand in hand. For Charlotte, the outer world of nature offered strong contrasts to the inner world of her imagination. Reading and writing addictively from childhood, she put her thoughts into words, composing tales, stories, plays, and poems. Enchanted with her brother Branwell's toy soldiers, she named one of them after the macho military hero of the day and of her romantic dream, the Duke of Wellington. Tory politics and royal battles of passion and bravery filled Angria, the fictional

African Kingdom that she and her brother Branwell created,[2] while Emily and Anne wrote their poems and tales of another imaginary place, Gondal.

As his children grew, Patrick Brontë realized that they needed to be educated outside the home. Poverty limited their options. The new Clergy Daughters' School at Cowan Bridge that had been established for the daughters of poor clergymen turned out to be a tragically cruel experiment for the Brontë girls. Charlotte's most famous novel, *Jane Eyre,* immortalizes Cowan Bridge.

Malnutrition, rigid regimentation, lack of warmth, inadequate clothing, and poor sanitary conditions constituted the school environment. The administration rationalized such hostile deprivation by declaring this to be the proper approach to saving Christian souls. Charlotte's scathing attack in *Jane Eyre* describes how the school's demigod, Mr. Brocklehurst—whom she labeled "the Black Pillar"— considers a child's early death her quickest avenue to heaven. To starve the body and to blister it with the chafing of brittle shoe leather in an icy winter's walk to church are deemed the kind of Christian suffering necessary to chasten the soul. Yet no such martyrdom is prescribed for the "Black Pillar's" children. Bedecked in velvet, silk, and furs, they appear before the skimpily dressed and nearly famished school girls in *Jane Eyre.*

Charlotte survived such rigid and irrational discipline and, ultimately, the typhoid epidemic that swept the school. Her grief and rage were understandably great even years later when she looked back on the horrors that had taken Maria and Elizabeth from her forever. The character of Helen Burns in *Jane Eyre* is her eulogy to Maria. As the girl who turns the other cheek, Helen functions as an admired and idealized spirit but also as a sharp contrast to Charlotte's own creed, which appears more like that embodied by the Israeli cry "Never again!" Through her character Jane Eyre, she displays the vehemence of despair turned to rage and retaliatory pride. Although Charlotte suppressed outward expressions of her rage in her interpersonal life, inwardly this rage seethed along with the anguish of her restrained passions. Thus, she wrote to her best friend, Ellen Nussey (Peters 1986, 159), that she was a "hearty hater." She did permit her suppressed rage to appear overtly in the sharp satiric thrusts of her fiction. In public, she kept herself in check, I suspect, because of a supersensitivity to social exposure and extreme fears that social humiliation would be the consequence of any narcissistic exhibitionism. One exception was the occasion at which she trumpeted a few furious blasts at her former literary idol, William Makepiece Thackeray, embarrassed and disappointed by his self preoccupations, following the achievement of his own fame. Her rage rarely elicited the feared hostile response: when expressed in her novels, instead, it assumed a highly integrated form.

When the seven-year-old Charlotte left her term of torment at Cowan Bridge in May 1825, she still needed and wanted an education. Her insecure position in the social-economic world in fact made it imperative. The daughter of a poor clergyman, with several younger siblings dependent on her, she required future employment. Although the available options were narrow, they were at least specific. To gain a position as governess or teacher, a female of her background had to possess a certain level of scholarship. Therefore, after five years of being tutored at home by her aunt, the anguished Charlotte left her family and all of the games of imagination associated with them to enter another school twenty miles away from Haworth. Roe Head was not, like Cowan Bridge had been, an educational experiment. A small but established school for refining young women, it was run by the four Miss Woolers; of these the eldest, Margaret, would become the future employer and friend of her former student. At her new school, Charlotte grew to adulthood, graduating from the position of student to that of teacher; she also met her two lifelong friends, Ellen Nussey and the vibrant feminist Mary Taylor.

Although preoccupied with scholarly tasks at Miss Wooler's school, Charlotte did not allow her imagination to rest. At nighttime she arose histrionically to taunt and terrify her ten fellow boarders with ghost stories. Her tales were so vivid that she scared herself; soon her storytelling was banned.

As a teacher at Roe Head, Charlotte was even more stifled than as a student. Her hours were long and tedious. There were always pupils to instruct or sewing or some other tasks awaiting her. Just as when she later became governess in aristocratic homes, Charlotte had to perform many odd jobs that completely filled her time, effectively preventing her from enjoying any personal life. Her internal life was strangled too. During this period she suffered continual somatic and psychic agonies. Occasionally, in a five-minute burst of freedom, she would peer out a window and dream of the seashore she had seen once or more generally fantasize about finding permanent freedom.

During those years, there was no writing, only dreaming. Peters describes Charlotte, finally alone in the late hours of the night, after she had finished heaps of sewing and lessons. Then, her mind could explode with dramas suppressed during the day. Yet these stories remained internal because she was too exhausted even to lift a pen. In 1841, when Charlotte briefly returned to her father's home after approximately seven years of serving as a teacher at Roe Head, and as a governess at various establishments, she decided that the only way to avoid being buried alive was to found her own school, with the aid of Emily and Anne. For this task, she sought her aunt's financial assistance. Painstakingly practical and responsible, Charlotte appealed to Aunt Branwell and won her confidence. To run her own school, she herself needed more schooling in music and foreign languages. Ambition roused her to action.

In the meantime, Charlotte was conscious of her literary aspirations. Having composed her own juvenilia, she never totally abandoned the desire to write. This was especially true as her suppressed imagination swelled up and tantalized her. In December 1834, she wrote a letter to the current literary god, the poet Lord Robert Southey, begging him to read and evaluate some of her poetry. His response was predictable at a time when the *word* itself was considered to be solely a masculine endowment, given from God to the male sex only. In his reply, Southey made it plain that women's place was not in the literary world. Southey allowed that in her quiet moments—the time between domestic tasks— a woman might jot down a few poetic rhymes. He even acknowledged Charlotte's talent for them. However, to transform such creativity into art, he stressed, would surely constitute a betrayal of her sex. He left her with his best wishes.

Charlotte initially reacted submissively and compliantly. She thanked Southey, "however sorrowfully and reluctantly it may be followed,"[3] and promised to obey his instructions. Her conscious attitude was deferential, just as it had been when her father admonished her to perform her "appropriate" female obligations, such as darning her brother's socks and sewing his collars and cuffs. Deep inside, however, she could not be silenced. As the years brought increasing disappointment and pain, her talent was to erupt in a more vivid form.

Before this happened, the future author received and rejected a proposal of marriage in early 1839 from Ellen Nussey's brother Henry. Charlotte's visions of a future bridegroom did not include stifling her flippant wit, in an effort to be a demure wife to a sedately bourgeois clergyman. She wanted someone more like her childhood hero, the Duke of Wellington.

To prepare for a school of her own, Charlotte persuaded her family to allow Emily and herself to go to school in Brussels. They hoped to learn French and some German as well. Emily reluctantly agreed to join her older sister. Patrick Brontë personally accompanied his daughters to Brussels in a show of support for Charlotte's plan.

At the Pensionnat Héger, Charlotte met the charismatic professor (her true-life Byronic hero) who would become both the magnet of her life and the chief cause of her long-term wound of unrequited love, which later became the source for her creativity. Constantine Héger and his wife were the directors of the school. This paternal, and passionately intellectual man appealed to the deep craving inside Charlotte for male recognition and affirmation that had been so frustrated in her relationship with her generally indifferent father. Monsieur Héger was to become the male center of *Villette* in the character of Monsieur Paul Emanuel, or M. Paul.

Charlotte's experience in Brussels fanned the flames of her hidden passionate nature. On hearing that their Aunt Branwell had died in October 1842, the two sisters hastened home from Brussels. On their arrival, they found their brother Branwell without work and descending rapidly into drunken and drugged dissipation. Their father repeatedly excused Branwell's blatant and eggregious faults and bewailed the fate of his "brilliant and unhappy son." So preoccupied was the father with the grandiose self-flagellations and the haunting fears that kept his son awake all night that he never considered his daughters' frustrated but potent talents. The irony was all the greater after Charlotte became London's most celebrated author upon the publication of *Jane Eyre*. When she finally showed her father a copy of the book everyone was talking about, his only words were: "It's more than likely." He even expressed some degree of astonishment that Charlotte had managed to write a book. Brontë never realized the actual extent of his Charlotte's success. Nevertheless, he didn't hesitate later to take advantage of her fame.

Before her literary success, however, Charlotte longed to return to her professor in Brussels. Although Emily declined to accompany her after the interruption of their aunt's death, Charlotte remained determined. Invited cordially by both the Hégers to teach at the school while continuing her own studies, she overcame all obstacles, and returned in January 1843. By April, Charlotte's relationship with Madame Héger had deteriorated, for the older woman had guessed her secret and strove quietly and successfully to prevent, without her husband's knowledge, any direct intercourse between Charlotte and himself. Thus Charlotte began to lose all the cherished attention that she had come to receive from her adored professor. Without acknowledging to herself the love she felt for him, she suffered the insult of his withdrawal; yet she was paralyzed to do anything to change the situation until she roused herself enough to depart from Brussels permanently in January 1844. Héger responded to a few of her letters, then following that corresponded in a formal manner. Following an impassioned letter she wrote to him in January 1845, he failed to ever reply again. Charlotte sunk into despair. In November 1845, she wrote her last letter to him.

The rest of Charlotte Brontë's life reads like a history of tragic loss and fairy tale success. Having finally acknowledged her defeat by the emotional starvation calculated by Madame Héger, she returned to a funereal atmosphere at home. Her father was going blind, her brother continued on his self-destructive course, and unknown to anyone, Emily and Anne were on the verge of fatal illnesses. Branwell finally died in September 1848, wasted from his insatiable bouts of opium and drunkenness. Less than three months later, Emily Brontë died from consumption; five months later, Anne succumbed to the same illness. Before these tragedies, Charlotte was in limbo, anxiously awaiting some word from her professor. Her plans to start a school with her sisters could not be completed, since Patrick Brontë's failing sight made him dependent on them to stay at home. Branwell's dissipated habits rendered a school at home equally impossible. Reduced to a state of vegetation from her unfulfilled plans and hopes, Charlotte immediately rallied to action after she chanced upon Emily's poetry. Braving and overcoming Emily's scorn for this intrusion, Charlotte pursued her new project: the publication of a book of poems by herself, Anne, and Emily. Because of the prejudice against female authors, the three sisters chose male noms de plume: thus were born Curer, Ellis and Acton Bell. Although Emily's poetry received an excellent review, the actual book sales numbered two (the volume had been published at their own expense).

Charlotte turned to novel writing in hopes of more favorable public reception. Her first novel was rejected by six publishers and never published in her lifetime. It was her second novel, *Jane Eyre,* that won her rave reviews and brisk sales in London and beyond. The fairy tale side of her life began. Yet the fairy tale was already irrevocably marred by the pain she felt on behalf of Emily, whose novel *Wuthering Heights* received unsympathetic, even cruelly castigating reviews (Anne's novel had been published simultaneously by the same firm). Despite expanding social horizons that took Charlotte out of her seclusion in her father's home and village, her life was simultaneously becoming brutally depleted. In less than six months she lost her three surviving siblings. Thus, at the age of thirty-three, Charlotte was bereaved in the bleak and funereal remains of the Brontë household, alone with a seventy-two-year-old father, who simultaneously clung to and shunned her. The silence at Haworth Parsonage became haunting and ominous. Isolated entirely and irrevocably from the sibling companionship that—with the exception of Branwell—had nourished and sustained her, Charlotte was nearly overcome by the feeling of morbidity in the house, feeling that resonated with her internal state of despair and further stressed her already fragile state of physical health. Other than a brief visit to her friend Ellen Nussey between October 24th and 31st of that year, Charlotte was isolated with her detached and depressed father at the parsonage. Luckily, at this low ebb, her young publisher George Smith invited her to his mother's house in London, where she arrived at the end of November.[4]

Although her identity as the author of *Jane Eyre* and *Shirley* was beginning to be known, she failed to light up the salons in the London social scene. Morbidly shy, she left many of those whom she met amazed that hers was the pen that produced brilliantly witty dialogue.

After her exposure to the public arena, Charlotte was relieved to return home; yet such feelings did not last long. The loss of her sibling companionship, of which she was reminded everywhere in the parsonage, left her in agony; even writing was torturous. During her sisters' decline, she had sought solace in writing the historical-political *Shirley,* which evolved into a partial eulogy of Emily. However, the effort involved in personal and social drama was a strain for her, and she questioned that novel's artistic value. Charlotte's literary talent lay in the personal psychology realm. For her next novel she thus returned for inspiration to her life, that is, to the unrequited love that until her siblings' deaths was the source of her greatest sorrow. *Villette* was to be the work that was most chastened by suffering and the most articulate in its faith in emotional survival.

A year after *Villette* was published, Charlotte Brontë now thirty-eight, married her father's curate, the Reverend Arthur Nicholls, despite her earlier rejection of him. She married mainly to put an end to her loneliness. Although he lacked the dimensions of her charismatic and romantic heroes, her husband gradually became the object of her sincere respect and even admiration. Considering him her intellectual inferior, she nevertheless appreciated his decency and determined love for her.

To marry Nicholls, Charlotte had to overcome her father's intrusions and vetoes, for Patrick Brontë condemned her suitor as unworldly. Where did she discover the strength for this last lonely battle? Perhaps finally we can attribute it to the reparative aspects of the creative process and Charlotte's success at reporting her inner states to the outside world through it. She was able, I believe, to use this process to mourn her many losses. Through it she survived and triumphed. Still, the somatic and psychic battles took their toll. Married less than a year, Charlotte Brontë died at the age of thirty-nine, leaving behind her two grieving men, her husband and father.

## "The Silent Tyrant in Her Life"

When the novelist Elizabeth Gaskell published the original biography of Charlotte Brontë after her friend's death, she was restricted on certain issues. The biography had been commissioned by Patrick Brontë shortly after his daughter's demise. Gaskell presents Charlotte's devotion to him as one assumed voluntarily through a sense of endearment. However, one receives a quite different impression from reading Margot Peters, a more recent biographer. Peters emphasizes Charlotte's enslavement to her father's control. Not always overt, this control was reinforced by her father's hypochondriacal capriciousness and petulance and by the daughter's unconscious guilt bond. The trap of paternal possession was never more manifest than when Charlotte was considering a proposal of marriage from Arthur Nicholls. Brontë's "rage against Nicholls was deep and relentless" (Peters 1986, 362). The older man's fury was clearly narcissistic, revealing his wish to use Charlotte as a narcissistic extension of himself:

> When a father has martyred a daughter and enjoyed her sacrifices so long, he does not willingly give her up to another master. . . . That penniless opportunist who dared to better himself by plotting an alliance with his famous daughter! . . . In his youth Mr. Brontë had been an ambitious man: he had struggled up from Irish poverty to distinguish himself at Cambridge; he had imagined himself a man of letters until failure and consciousness of mediocrity had warped him into misanthropy and alienation. For the last five years he had lived his own

thwarted ambition through Charlotte's fame, goading her to contacts with the rich and famous, fretting when her writing did not progress. Was Currer Bell's glory to be wasted on a mere curate? The match would be a degradation; his daughter would be throwing herself away. . . . So the old white-haired man raged, spitting out the unlucky curate's name with contempt.

(361)

In Charlotte's letters to Ellen Nussey, Peters has found clues to the daughter's reaction to the father's overt cruelty during this period. Charlotte saw the "selfish and materialistic motives" (363) behind her father's opposition to her marriage. She tried to be a peacemaker between the two men, to squelch her resentments as she had in the past; but now they rose up to full consciousness. Her father's narcissism and desires to control could not be overlooked at this critical time. Peters surmises what was in Charlotte's mind:

Much as she cherished her father as the last of the family that had been all in all to her, much as she disciplined herself to obey his wishes, she was forced to admit his injustices. Her poor frail mother, six children in almost as many years, his aloofness to them all, the Clergy Daughters' School, her dead sisters—none of it his fault, exactly, yet inextricably linked with him neverthe-less. His unfairness to her: his obliviousness to her needs because she was plain and a girl; his unimaginative exhortations to "womanly duties"; the hours of writing time she had sacrificed to please him; his external restraints on her freedom. The time, when she was nineteen and would have been thankful for an allowance of a penny a week, and she asked him for a tiny sum, and he said, "What does a woman want with money?" How Aunt's money, not his, had paid for Brussels, and the school prospectuses, and the paper and ink for their writing, and the publishing of the poems and of *Wuthering Heights* and *Agnes Grey*. His greed for her fame, his fret when her writing would not come, his snobbery, his misanthropy, his selfishness, his silence. Her endless sacrifices. . . .

(380)

Peters thus identifies a general pattern of indifference and paternal narcissism haunting Brontë throughout her life. Charlotte may have only admitted it to herself late in life, but in her novels, its effect is quite evident. Her male characters always possess two main traits: an insistence on the subtle tyranny of masculine dominance and a self-centeredness that detracts from their capacity to appreciate and affirm the substantial intrinsic nature of a female character.

The observant Gaskell was aware of the paternal abandonment to which Char-lotte was subjected but felt that she had to censor this observation from her biography. In one of her letters, Gaskell comments:

We dined—she and I together—Mr. Brontë having his dinner sent to him in his sitting-room according to his invariable custom, (fancy it! and only they two left). . . .

Each day I was there—was the same in outward arrangement—breakfast at 9, in Mr. Brontë's room—which we left immediately after. What he does with himself through the day I cannot imagine! . . . He was very polite and agreeable to me, paying rather elaborate old-fashioned compliments, but I was sadly afraid of him in my most inmost soul; for I caught a glare of his stern eyes over his spectacles at Miss Brontë once or twice which made me know my man; and he talked at her sometimes; he is very fearless. . . . Moreover to account for my fear—rather an admiring fear after all—of Mr. Brontë, please to take into account that though I like the beautiful glittering of bright flashing steel I don't fancy firearms at all, at all—and Miss Brontë never remembers her father dressing himself in the morning without putting a loaded pistol in his pocket, just as regularly as he puts on his watch. . . .

(Peters 1986, 382)

After quoting this letter, Peters adds, "Comparatively free herself, Mrs. Gaskell was shocked at Charlotte's subjection to her father. On long walks over the brown hills, during intimate confidences by the fireside, she urged Charlotte to escape" (382).

It is interesting to speculate why Gaskell decided not to reveal any of this in her biography. Perhaps in keeping with her fear of Patrick Brontë, as noted in her letter, she steered clear of any intimations that Charlotte suffered from his reign over her. On the contrary, Gaskell's biography esteems Charlotte for the devoted sacrifices she made for her father. Perhaps Gaskell hid her own acute observations, sacrificing veracity for the comfort of her patron. If so, it may be said that in a sense she repeated Charlotte's own mistake.

Charlotte's close friend Mary Taylor was another critic of Brontë's hold on Charlotte. As Gaskell had done, she urged Charlotte to escape. Taylor herself had fled from England to New Zealand to escape the general male domination typical of English culture. A staunch feminist, she wrote many letters to Charlotte, pressing her friend to free herself from what Taylor viewed as a self-enforced martyrdom. Charlotte, in other words, indulged her father's use of her.

Charlotte had never openly rebelled against her father. She channeled much of the lust to do so into her creative work, in which her heroines attempted what she did not dare. Yet her father's cruel and contemptuous rejection of Arthur Nicholls, combined with his obvious indifference toward her own prolonged loneliness, kindled a fire in Charlotte's soul which until then had rarely burned outside her fiction. She decided to confront her father face-to-face and to ask him to show some favor to Nicholls rather than to act behind his back. Risking Brontë's wrath and the possibility of even greater withdrawal from her company, she unflinchingly spoke her mind and broke the cord binding her to him. Later, I will show how her creative work apparently paved the way for this confrontation.

Peters quotes Charlotte saying, "Sheer pain made me gather courage to break it" (383) and describes the scene between daughter and father:

> She entered his sitting room in great fear and stood before her old father, whose face had grown hard and cold with enraged pride. She spoke very quietly.
>
> "Father, I am not a young girl, not a young woman even—I never was pretty. I now am ugly. At your death I shall have 300 pounds besides the little I have earned myself—do you think there are many men who would serve seven years for me?"
>
> In scorn and impatience he cried out, would she marry a curate?
>
> "Yes, I must marry a curate if I marry at all; not merely a curate but your curate; not merely your curate but he must live in the house with you, for I cannot leave you."
>
> The old man pulled himself to his feet, trembling with rage, his silver hair bristling.
>
> "Never," he shouted. "I will never have another man in this house!"
>
> He did not speak to her for a week.
>
> (383)

Brontë finally consented to his daughter's marriage, but only when he was forced to feel the strength of her will. His obligatory consent did not prevent him from inflicting one last wound on Charlotte, on her wedding day. During the period prior to it, when Charlotte was overwhelmed with the arrangements, Brontë had already contributed to her stress by experiencing a mysterious and "sudden attack of deafness" (Peters 1986, 393). Now, on the day itself, his final and most acute abandonment came. According to Peters (394), Mr. Brontë declined to attend Charlotte's hard won wedding. He claimed he was unwell.

So Charlotte walked down the aisle with her old schoolmistress, Margaret Wooler. Brontë's hypochondriacal excuses were transparent but unopposed. This ultimate slight was symptomatic of the whole paternal pattern. Although Charlotte's father demanded that she fit herself into a woman's role, he refused to yield to her wish to marry. Her creative work, on the other hand, was recognized by her father not for itself but for the vicarious fame it brought him. Charlotte's (and indeed Emily's and Anne's) attempts at writing and publishing were all launched without inspiration or support from their father, although during childhood he had permitted an environment in which their imaginative capacities could grow. Only after *Jane Eyre* received great acclaim and popularity did Charlotte show it to him. Peters contrasts Patrick Brontës mild display upon reading Charlotte's book *Jane Eyre* with the overinvolved worship characteristic of Brontë's response to his son.

Her father's combination of exploitation, possessiveness, and abandoning indifference made a deep imprint on Charlotte Brontë's internal world. In her novels, unrequited love was a constant theme.

## Charlotte Brontë's Novels

In response to her intense yearning for her father's love and recognition, Charlotte Brontë channeled her ache and tension into her creative work. In doing so, however, she went beyond merely reproducing Patrick Brontë's narcissism, indifference, and alienation from her. That is, she reproduced her internal father object, but she also created characters that explored dimensions beyond it. In these creations, Charlotte the writer found resolutions for the woman's unfulfilled yearnings. Through her work, Charlotte was able to mourn the loss of her father and separate from him.

Although more famous than *Villette, Jane Eyre* lacks the psychological veracity of her final novel. *Jane Eyre* is romantic, action-oriented, and fast-paced; its plot turns on external accident instead of unfolding through the interior design of authentic character development. Because *Jane Eyre* therefore offers a more limited view of Charlotte's psychological growth, my comments on it will be considerably briefer than those on *Villette*.

*Jane Eyre* concerns a young governess who grows up in a harsh school environment that resembles the infamous Cowan Bridge. Impoverished, orphaned, and rejected from her family of rich relations, the young, constantly victimized heroine Jane Eyre struggles to maintain a sense of integrity. Her victimization begins with a rejecting aunt but is ultimately symbolized by the demonic male patriarch who is treasurer and manager of the school for young orphaned girls. Jane Eyre—calls this tyrannical and malicious male authority, Mr. Brocklehurst, "the Black Pillar." More granite rock than human, he symbolizes the arbitrary and sadistic control exerted in a patriarchal culture. Brocklehurst, expressed as a cruel and indifferent demigod by Charlotte's Jane Eyre, employs twisted religious philosophy to justify niggardly practices that promote starvation and abuse, even causing the deaths of many of the school's young female student boarders. These events mirror the author's actual experience at Cowan Bridge, where her sisters Maria and Elizabeth had died.

The Black Pillar praises those who die young in his hands for their Christian purity. In effect encouraging their deaths, Brocklehurst deprives his charges of adequate food and clothing. The appearance of an ornament on a girl's clothing or a decorative lock of hair on one of their heads allows him to launch into self-righteous, condemnatory lectures to the offenders. Meanwhile, his own daughters parade before the shivering students in velvet, silks, and furs. His hypocrisy is highlighted by Charlotte Brontë's satire. The reader can only speculate about what hidden anger toward the author's own father was invested in her male villain.

Brocklehurst's character is unrelieved by any good qualities. He seems to emerge from the author's imagination as an archetypal demon father, that is, from an unconscious realm in which preoedipal part objects reside. Yet as the narrative progresses, this black patriarch fades into the background, and is replaced by a more ambiguous male figure. From an intrapsychic perspective, this process parallels a basic development progression. In this developmental process, archaic figures originally inhabiting the individual's world are superseded by more-integrating levels of internal figures who tend toward whole object construction. This process naturally occurs when normal repression provides a cushioning barrier against the primitive nightmare phantoms of the person's infant past.

After her experiences at school, the heroine becomes a governess and meets the man with whom she is to find a degree of mutual and requited love. Mr. Rochester, the owner of Thornfield Hall, where Jane is employed as governess to his illegitimate female child, is her superior in a hierarchical and calibrated society. The author apparently believes that as an artistocrat and as Jane's employer—Jane calls him "Master"—this male must be humbled. Thus, when Jane first meets him, as well as at the end of the novel, he is placed in a position of dependence on her. In both instances, external accidents of fate leave him injured and somewhat castrated. These events and their consequences counteract the domination that Rochester can and does exert over Jane because of his superior economic and social status. However, Rochester's dependence is based solely on external catastrophes which preclude the kind of inward male transformation that occurs in *Villette* through interaction with the opposite sex. When Jane encounters Rochester for the first time, he has just been thrown from his horse and is temporarily lame. At the novel's end, Jane is free to marry him only after he has been permanently maimed and blinded in a fire. The reader wonders why Brontë didn't see Jane as capable of standing up to a sustained encounter with a whole man. According to the feminist critics Gilbert and Gubar (1979), Jane is able to "handle" Rochester, as she demonstrates by fending off his control with deft repartee and by insisting that she will continue to work and have an independent income if they should marry. Jane does this and more. She also resists her own cravings to spend every moment with Rochester after he lets down his barriers and proposes marriage. Moreover, she resists his attempt to seduce her into being a narcissistic extension of himself by refusing to accept his ornamental presents of clothes and jewels. Jane even stands up for differentiated beliefs of her own. For example, she immediately decides not to stay with Rochester on learning that he has a mad wife in the attic and is not free to effect a legal and religiously sanctioned marriage. Nevertheless, despite Jane's great strength of character, Brontë does not allow her heroine to surrender to her love for Rochester until he is crippled in a fire. Although Jane holds out for a love based on a man's respect for her intrinsic virtues it is not these virtues—including her moral and spiritual strength—that develop her tale and determine her fate. Brontë makes Jane's fate depend on a third party, who descends like a deux ex machina from "heaven" (or in an ironic thrust, "hell"), i.e., from the attic. God thus gives Rochester the freedom to marry by killing off his mad wife in the fire that also destroys Thornfield Hall. God or fortune (Gilbert and Gubar, 1985, 733, speaks of "fortunes" of the characters), also arranges that Jane inherit wealth from a forgotten uncle's estate, thus enabling her to gain a rough economic and social equality with Rochester. It is finally a miracle—the sound of Rochester's voice calling to her—that sends Jane back to him. God and fortune are pulling the strings of Jane's destiny.

This deux ex machina resolution prevents Jane in the end from being complete as a whole object, or a whole woman, for she is not the predominant agent of her own fate. Jane does not direct her life course through a fully developed subjective sense of self, nor does she resolve her conflicts through self-reflection. In this, I believe, she mirrors the author's own incomplete psychological development when she wrote *Jane Eyre,* although the novel shows a heroine who has made some strides toward differentiation and toward a sense of authentic female and individual identity. When working on *Jane Eyre,* Brontë had not begun to grieve her losses; not until the creative process of *Villette* did she begin to do so. She had not yet stood up to her father and confronted him about her future husband in what was to be a pivotal act of separation. At the time of writing *Jane Eyre,* Brontë wished desperately to flee the misery of her life and to be rescued by a masculine god. She craved to speak her mind freely and authentically. The character of Jane Eyre begins to do exactly that, but the author's deeper issues of personal identity do not come into focus until *Villette*.

The character of Rochester also reveals the incompleteness of Charlotte Brontë's own psychological developmental journey. As the created father figure of her literary fiction reflects the evolution of the author, in whose psychological realm the internal father resides, so too does the paternal lover's formulation reflect the inhibition in the female heroine's growth. Rochester, like Jane, is incomplete as a whole object. Unlike M. Paul in *Villette,* he does not stand by himself as a three-dimensional figure. Because he is seen solely through Jane's eyes, Rochester is alive only in her reflective vision. The reader observes Rochester through Jane's report, as he taunts and tests her by flirting with another woman or as he woos Jane herself with promises and compliments. Even though Rochester engages in dialogues, these seem studied and formal, never spontaneously responsive to Jane. The reader has difficulty imagining him existing without her.

Rochester bears the complex stamp of Charlotte Brontë's yearnings for a father, for a man of her own, and for the combination of paternal affection and recognition that she craved from her real father. Unlike the male characters in *Villette*, Rochester is purely fictive. It is hard to conceive of any real man acting as he does. His acceptance of Charlotte's alter-ego Jane—especially in light of the social barriers between them—is implausibly quick. Rochester's magnanimity in transcending all external barriers to marry Jane seems to be a product of Charlotte Brontë's original fantasy wish fulfillments rather than of an internal working through of conflicts over wishes and losses. Rochester is therefore flattened into a one-dimensional form. He fails to emerge out of the author's (and heroine's) internal developmental process or from an interpersonal interaction among characters.

As a creation then, he is symptomatic of Charlotte's limited use of the creative process when she wrote *Jane Eyre*. She was not yet mourning through her work as she was to do later. Her wishes were achieved via the magic of fictional wish fulfillment rather than by reparatively working through the depressive position. Thus, the author's alter-ego heroine does not feel emotional injuries and does not experience internal conflict. Instead, she impulsively acts and reacts. She flees from Rochester when he is not free to wed her, risking death so she will not have to stay with him long enough to feel the pain of her object longings manifested in yearning for him. The panic of Jane Eyre's manic flight is evidenced by the acute danger of her penniless state after she absentmindedly leaves the parcel containing all of her assets on a coach while making her escape. She has time neither for thought nor for internal dialogue.

The ending of *Jane Eyre* is also tainted by magic. It is too perfect, too idyllic. Jane is now free of her need to use intellectual sparring and distancing to protect herself from Rochester's domination. Again, this change is the result of external events rather than internal developments. The reader feels that Jane has been freed because of two changes in the balance of power between her and Rochester. First, her inherited fortune has shifted the economic balance of power, and second, Rochester's new physical impairments have shifted the physical balance of power between them. The reader is hard-pressed to believe that this new married state is auspicious and that the two will live happily ever after. Rochester is now blind and his arm is crippled. His arrogance has supposedly been modified, as has his will to dominate. Only now, in his state of dependence, can he be a perfect male companion for Jane. This is the stuff of which fairy tales are made.

We are left with questions about *Jane Eyre*, because Brontë has had God orchestrate all of the dynamics for a mutually respectful love between a man and a woman in this novel. She has not trusted in her own alter-ego's character. At the end of *Jane Eyre*, her father's ghost still haunts the author's inner world. The paternal ghost leaves behind the following question. Can Charlotte ever overcome Patrick Brontë's patronization, control, manipulative dependence, and grand indifference to her needs for affirmation? Six years later, the publication of *Villette* provided the answer.

# 8

# Villette

When George Eliot read *Jane Eyre,* she was—along with the rest of the book-reading public—impressed. On finishing *Villette,* Brontë's fourth (but third published) novel, Eliot waxed even more enthusiastic. "It was," she wrote a friend, "preternatural" (Gilbert and Gubar, 1979, p. 408). According to Gilbert and Gunbar, Eliot "majestically testified to her fascination with *Villette*" (408). Completed five years after *Jane Eyre, Villette* truly is more wonderful than *Jane Eyre,* with a sustained power and profundity lacking in the earlier novel. Although not as consistently intense or fast-paced, *Villette* possesses a reflectiveness that makes it a more internally powerful work than *Jane Eyre,* the excitement of which derives largely from its boldly dramatic plot. In contrast, *Villette* seems to emerge out of the vivid, visceral consciousness of its author, stretching tautly from her nerve endings to our own. The writing conveys an almost somatic sense of repression. Periodic eruptions of suppressed affect punctuate the novel's neurotically hesitant movement. The emotional progression and regression of the heroine Lucy Snowe are charted with developmental verisimilitude. Her intrapsychic struggle is exceptionally vivid. Throughout, Lucy's satire of other characters, such as the doll-like Paulina (Polly), is muted by her own conscious despair. Lucy's psychic growth is morbidly slow and frequently disrupted; her female vulnerability is exquisitely exposed. Still, at the novel's end, the mourning and working-through processes have been effective. The author's alter ego, Lucy Snowe, suffers self-risk, and maintains her faith, ultimately leading to personal triumph. *Villette* depicts the unfolding of a separation-individuation process. After the labor pains of differentiation, a female identity is born.

Much of *Villette's* triumph comes from Brontë's decision to employ a mixture of third-person and first-person narration. In *Jane Eyre,* all characters and events are experienced through the subjective first-person awareness of Jane. In contrast, Brontë alternates in *Villette* between the first-person narrative of Lucy and third-person objective narration. This use of third-person narration allows the other characters to acquire three dimensionality when they are not interacting with Lucy. Operating within this wider arena, Lucy is like Jane, Brontë's alter-ego, offering the reader much insight into the author's own life struggle.

## Lucy Snowe

Like Jane Eyre, Lucy Snowe is an orphan—perhaps even more so, since she has no uncle who can leave money to her or any cousins. Born of alienation, she lives a shadow's life, never revealing her passionate nature until it emerges through the consecration of a man's love—a love based on genuine mirroring affirmation. However, this love is severely modified and limited. In *Villette,* Brontë did not condescend to popular taste to produce a conventional happy ending. The disappointments of paternal and related modes of masculine love severely diminish Lucy's gratification, for she yearns for male recognition. The male characters are drawn from life, and Lucy Snowe suffers life's real rejections. Nevertheless, she triumphs.

Lucy's alienation is reinforced by her life circumstances. First, she is a caretaking companion for Miss Marchmont, a dying old lady. Then, she is a teacher in a French school in which the English are mocked and scorned. The school is located in the town of Villette, where Lucy's experiences are reminiscent of Brontë's own period in Brussels at the pensionnat Héger. There, the foreigner Lucy is continually subjected to exclusion and emotional exile. She must fight to forge an identity in this environment; the extreme difficulties that such a task presents highlight her intrapsychic and interpersonal struggle. From her childhood as a shadow person—that is, living in benign resignation as an observer in another child's home—Lucy's sense of being an outsider has been established. Her room in that home is compared to a submarine cabin. It is a womb into which she descends to hide from inspection. Yet the room's security is false, because it is a hideaway in the home of another. The child Lucy has no identity and no home of her own.

How faithfully Lucy's alienated condition reflects Charlotte Brontë's own circumstances can be only guessed. Clearly its emotional veracity stems from the author's own self-perceptions. The inability and/or unwillingness of her father— in whose home she lived most of her life—to see and value Charlotte must have made her feel at times like a reluctantly dependent boarder. His condescending devaluation of her because she was female and the related restrictions that he imposed on her freedom[1] must have caused her to see herself as a servant and as a shadow of a human being—someone who existed to clean, cook, and sew her brother's clothing. Furthermore, the elder Brontë's incommunicativeness (as reported in Mrs. Gaskell's letters) must have helped convince Charlotte that she was an unseen shadow.

In *Villette,* Lucy Snowe moves from the English home of her godmother, Mrs. Bretton, to that of the arthritic and elderly Miss Marchmont, who employs her as a lady's companion. Her passive interactions with Miss Marchmont emphasize Lucy's role as shadow. The older woman's old sad tale involves thirty years of suffering the loss of the only man who ever loved her. Her life is, like Lucy's, a premature entombment. Signs of Miss Marchmont's death-in-life existence are her rigidifying arteries and memory. In Lucy Snowe's odyssey, Miss Marchmont symbolizes the cost to the female self of alienation from the fertile juices of life.

Her employer's death precipitates a life crisis for Lucy, forcing her, despite all her fears, beyond the role of shadow. Stumbling, starting, and pushing herself forward, she finds new employment at Madame Beck's school in Villette.

## Monsieur Paul Emanuel

Monsieur Paul Emanuel enters the scene as a pugnacious professor whom the school's mistress, Madame Beck, consults in her attempts to evaluate Lucy. Already, he displays a certain flamboyant aspect in her world, with an even slightly magical overtone. He is said to possess the transcendental seerlike dimensions of a psychic.

M. Paul's initial entrance into Lucy's life is brief; it is followed by a long delay before their next meeting. In the interim, Lucy takes a significant step away from the obscurity of her position as nurse-governess to become an English teacher. It is significant that Lucy makes such an advance before entering into any deeper entanglement with the brilliant and demanding professor. This move prepares her for his challenging intrusions into her secluded world.

Once a teacher, Lucy is not only favorably receptive to Professor M. Paul's intrusions, but she actually initiates some steps of her own into his world. Constantly meeting up with this "little dark man," Lucy takes in his character, frequently reassessing it. As the novel progresses, the reader is shown varying snapshots of him that are modified and elaborated, until an initially demonic visage yields to a tender and benevolent one. But since M. Paul is shown from many different angles, it becomes clear that all of these snapshots are true: he is a complex, multidimensional man. Sometimes he appears as a mixture of contradictions, because he is a man who changes the tenor of his attitudes with the impact of genuine interpersonal contact, even though such contact may seem combative at first. He can be influenced by Lucy to the extent that his growing surrender to intimacy with her markedly softens his character.

Lucy's first encounters with M. Paul paint him as a Napoleonic despot. He intrudes on her privacy, dictating morals and principles of self-sacrifice to her. On hearing that she became physically sick and mentally weakened (to the point of delusions and unconsciousness) by her isolation at the school during a vacation where she was mandated to care for a retarded child, he reprimands her for not having nobly risen to a saintly role of self-sacrifice and caretaking. On a visit to a museum, he exhorts Lucy to live the secluded life of a lady, and urges her to follow the example of a nun. His patronizing attitude is emphasized in this scene, in which he freely gazes on a nude painting of Cleopatra, while directing Lucy to guard her female eyes from such a sight. In this early encounter, he sets up rules to restrict Lucy and then surveys her in his self-appointed role of censor and guardian.

During this encounter, Lucy observes M. Paul:

> [H]e merely requested my silence and also, in the same breath, denounced my mingled rashness and ignorance. A more despotic little man than M. Paul never filled a professor's chair. . . . M. Paul showed a phase of character which had its terrors. His passions were strong, his aversions and attachments alike vivid; the force he exerted in holding both in check, by no means mitigated an observer's sense of their vehemence. With such tendencies, it may well be supposed he often excited in ordinary minds fear and dislike; yet it was an error to fear him: nothing drove him so nearly frantic as the tremor of an apprehensive and distrustful spirit; nothing soothed him like confidence tempered with gentleness. To evince these sentiments, however, required a thorough comprehension of his nature; and his nature was of an order rarely comprehended.
>
> (278–79)

Lucy sees M. Paul's narcissism, and then suffers his projection of it onto her. Later, she observes M. Paul at a concert, as he places himself in the center of the orchestra to gain attention. She comments to the reader: "Insufferable to him were all notorieties and celebrities: where he could not outshine, he fled" (289). His accusations against her are projections of this trait:

> [H]e accused me of being reckless, worldly, and epicurean; ambitious of greatness and feverishly athirst for the pomps and vanities of life. It seems I had no "devouement," no "recueillement" in my character; no spirit of grace, faith, sacrifice, or self-abasement. Feeling the inutility of answering these charges, I mutely continued the correction of a pile of English exercises.
>
> (387)

M. Paul is satisfied only when he can arouse Lucy into passionate indignation. He employs forced entries, spying, and insults toward her in class, ridiculing her in front of the students to provoke an emotional reaction from her. In the process, Lucy continues to observe him closely: his "unspeakable looks leveled through a pair of dart-dealing spectacles" (409); "his teeth clenched," his visage turning from "a mask to a face" (407). He "hisses" at Lucy (193) and mocks her in front of another man, calling her a flirt and a "coquette" (193). His forced intrusions are also meticulously described: "The closed door of the first class—my sanctuary—

offered no obstacle; it burst open, and a paletot, and a bonnet grec filled the void; also two eyes first vaguely struck upon, and then hungrily dived into me" (201).

The professor, as Peters asserts, reveals his male chauvinism by relenting in his provocations only after he has aroused Lucy to rage or countercursing, or has made her commit a fauxpas.[2] It is also true that he cries with sadness only after having humiliated Lucy, forcing her to experience her pain. At this point he displays a patronizing pity, as when she breaks down from the strain of reading a difficult French passage. These harassments obviously evidence his need to dominate and his male chauvinism.

On the other hand, M. Paul is also the man who brings Lucy's fiery soul out of hiding. His provocative poses and exhortations challenge her to struggle against her neurotically rigid self-limits. His joy in provoking her from placidity to rage and reactive retaliatory passion mobilizes a level of reactivity that she previously had sealed off and buried.[3] The professor wishes to prove his masculine prowess by being the one to affect her; in so doing, he also challenges her to surpass an inhibited and strangled sense of self. In one of their first encounters, he insists that she aid him by playing a part in a school play. Lucy reluctantly yields to his vehemence. On stage she begins to lose herself in the masculine role assigned and to glimpse the potential passion within herself. Terrified of her own expansiveness, she withdraws to her chambers following the performance; but she has now had a taste of her ability and pleasure in acting and exhibiting herself before the world. Earl Knies comments: "He makes Lucy study subjects which do not interest her by scoffing and sneering at her, and in her desire to crush the mocking spirit of M. Paul she develops her own capacities and personality as they had never been developed before" (194). Lucy gradually loses her early impulse to recoil from M. Paul and starts to act naturally and to feel comfortable in his presence. As Knies observes, " 'quite happy—strangely happy—in making him secure, content, tranquil' (II 201) and experiences moments that she did not believe life could afford. The fiery 'salamander' (II, 130) thaws Lucy's icy reserve" (194).

We experience Lucy's previously ambivalent regard for M. Paul as distinctly changing. The first, demonic view of him as a simple Napoleonic despot, is modified. Lucy comes to a new understanding of the professor, and of his provocations, as she psychologically apprehends him:

> And he took forth and held out to me a clean silk handkerchief. Now a person who did not know would naturally have bungled at this offer—declined accepting the same—etcetera. But I too plainly felt this would never do: the slightest hesitation would have been fatal to the incipient treaty of peace. I rose and met the handkerchief half-way, received it with decorum, wiped therewith my eyes, and, resuming my seat, and retaining the flag of truce in my hand

and on my lap, took especial care during the remainder of the lesson to touch neither needle nor thimble, scissors nor muslim. Many a jealous glance did M. Paul cast at these implements; he hated them mortally, considering sewing a source of distraction from the attention due to himself. A very eloquent lesson he gave, and very kind and friendly was he to the close. Ere he had done, the clouds were dispersed and the sun shining out—tears were exchanged for smiles.

(320–21)

Lucy continues to carefully observe his faults, such as envy and jealousy; but note that she views these demonic qualities with some sense of the conditional:

No; he was naturally a little man, of unreasonable moods. When over-wrought, which he often was, he became acutely irritable; and, besides, his veins were dark with a livid belladonna tincture, the essence of jealousy. I do not mean merely the tender jealousy of the heart, but that sterner, narrower sentiment, whose seat is in the head.

(436)

Lucy observes the traits of the male chauvinist in the professor:

I used to think, as I sat looking at M. Paul, while he was knitting his brow or protruding his lip over some exercise of mine, which had not as many faults as he wished (for he liked me to commit faults: a knot of blunders was sweet to him (as a cluster of nuts), that he had points of resemblance to Napoleon Bonaparte. I think so still.

In a shameless disregard of magnanimity, he resembles the great Emperor. M. Paul would have quarrelled with twenty learned women, would have unblushingly carried on a system of petty bickering and recrimination with a whole capital of coteries, never troubling himself about loss or lack of dignity. He would have exiled fifty Madame de Staels, if they had annoyed, offended, out-rivalled, or opposed him.

(436)

Then Lucy describes the opposition his chauvinism excited in another female teacher: "Whether he expected submission and attention, I know not; he met an acrid opposition, accompanied by a round reprimand for his certainly unjustifiable interference" (437).

The professor causes Lucy to commit errors in her work so that he might sustain the appearance of superiority. He cannot tolerate aggression from a female when it is not hysterical.[4]

Yet Charlotte Brontë attributes certain redemptive qualities to this demonic father figure. The professor grows in complexity. First, he tolerates Lucy's rage and even welcomes her outbreak after inciting it; moreover, it is not always hysterical rage that he invites. Having insulted Lucy in class by hurling vindictive comments against the English, he is pleased and even relieved when she retaliates (429). For the first time, Lucy overtly displays her fiery nature in a direct attack. She curses the French, decrying their stupidity.

M. Paul still needs to be in a superior position, which requires that Lucy commit errors in her work for him to correct. However, the professor also inspires Lucy to move beyond stasis. Lucy notes the professor's inspiration for her to own her talents:

> Yet, when M. Paul sneered at me, I wanted to possess them more fully; his injustice stirred in me ambitious wishes—it imparted a strong stimulus—it gave wings to aspiration.
>
> In the beginning, before I had penetrated motives, that uncomprehended sneer of his made my heart ache, but by-and-by it only warmed the blood in my veins, and sent added action to my pulses. Whatever my powers—feminine or the contrary—God had given them, and I felt resolute to be ashamed of no faculty of His bestowal.
>
> (440)

At first she does not see M. Paul's flattering appraisal of her beneath the taunting tone of his insults. Yet he is finally the one person who comes truly to recognize her essence. Lucy may glance and balk when he calls her a coquette and flirt in front of Graham, but secretly she is flattered. Opposing Graham's and her own perception of herself as an unobtrusive shadow, M. Paul sees Lucy's hidden passion and fire. He first notes these qualities when she acts in the school play. Later, when he apparently insults her, it is implied that he perceives her much more vividly than anyone else, even though he uses aversive labels such as "coquette" and "social climber" in his assessment. Ultimately, M. Paul reveals his real vision of Lucy. He tells her that he senses her secret passion, her savage and fiery soul. At this, despite herself, she melts and warms up to him. It is M. Paul's growing love for her that enables him to penetrate her inner soul. His sensitive antennae probe beyond the limits she herself has dared to pass. Although during much of the novel he is portrayed as a despotic intruder who attacks the resistances of his students to open their hidden inner selves, with Lucy the genuineness of his love ultimately makes him appear more a ravisher than a rapist. The professor's love emerges along with his growing awareness of Lucy's love for him. Their interactive play encourages each to change and to become more deeply and overtly themselves. Lucy unfreezes,[5] while he sheds much of his dark, demonic aspect and begins to exhibit a mature tenderness, joy, and generosity that formerly existed in a potential and hidden state. On another level,

M. Paul's surname—as Knies points out—is "one of the Biblical names for the promised deliverer of the suffering Hebrews" (192). In keeping with his name, M. Paul delivers Lucy, the tortured soul of *Villette*. That is, the love of this father figure delivers Lucy from her nunlike seclusion into the open arms of the world,[6] for M. Paul's recognition of her is directly responsible for her taking steps toward life and toward self-individuation.[7] Lucy creates an identity as the professor discovers her hidden wrath and yearnings. He spies the passions that Lucy had repressed, or that she suppresses anew as they seek to emerge.[8]

As M. Paul's tenderness appears, Lucy experiences a gentleness in his nature that she had never before discerned. This revelation shakes her because of her newly found vulnerability:

> I hid my face with my book, for it was covered with tears. I asked him why he talked so; and he said he would talk so no more, and cheered me again with the kindest encouragement. Still, the gentleness with which he treated me during the rest of the day, went somehow to my heart. It was too tender. It was mournful. I would rather he had been abrupt, whimsical, and irate as was his wont.
>
> (475)

With her new vulnerability comes a new vision of him. She sees new qualities in him, for example, on spying him praying: "I had never seen him pray before, or make a pious sign; he did it so simply, with such child-like faith, I could not help smiling pleasurable as I watched; his eyes met my smile; he just stretched out his kind hand, saying, 'Donnez moi la main! I see we worship the same God in the same spirit, though by different rites' " (474).

However, to win his admiration fully, Lucy has to differentiate herself from him. This must be effected through employing the discord that had always existed between them, because the task is so difficult. It is made particularly hard by M. Paul's assumption, as he begins to care for her, that they are essentially alike. His narcissism dictates this belief. Thus he says, "Do you observe that your forehead is shaped like mine? . . . Do you hear that you have some of my tones of voice? Do you know that you have many of my looks? I perceive all this, and believe that you were born under my star" (457).

Lucy's feelings of differentiation and separation first emerge during a religious dispute between M. Paul and herself. As part of his caring for her, he tries to convert her to his religion, to make her a part of him. Yet when she defends her own religion and its intrinsic connection to her inner self, he shows his respect for her by affirming the bond between them.

> "I did not like it,' " I told him, "I did not respect such ceremonies; I wished to see no more."

And having relieved my conscience by this declaration, I was able to go on, and, speaking more currently than my wont, to show him that I had a mind to keep to my reformed creed; that the more I say of Popery the closer I clung to Protestantism; . . .

When I had so spoken, so declared my faith, and so widely severed myself from him I addressed—then, at last, came a tone accordant, an echo responsive, one sweet chord of harmony in two conflicting spirits.

"Whatever say priests or controversialists," murmured M. Emanuel, "God is good, and loves all the sincere. Believe, then, what you can; believe it as you can; one prayer, at least, we have in common; I also cry—'O Dieu, sois appaisé envers moi qui suis pécheur!' "

(516–17)

Following this scene, M. Paul proves to be a protector and a benefactor. His behavior is, of course, dissimilar from the miserably disapproving denouement in the author's real life, in which, instigated by his wife, Monsieur Héger ultimately rejected her totally. By expressing paternal affection, the fictive M. Paul, allows Charlotte Brontë to transcend the disappointments experienced in her unrequited love for Héger. Nevertheless, the degree of affirmation that Héger managed to give her—far exceeding that of her father—allowed Charlotte to recreate him in M. Paul. Brontë was able to use the partial love she did receive to transcend her actual paternal relationship.

In *Villette*, Charlotte Brontë makes M. Paul the chief agent of Lucy's newly individuated identity. As Lucy differentiates from him, he gives birth to her. The professor defends his right to say good-bye to Lucy against the intrusive force of Madame Beck, a defiance that the actual professor, Héger, never dared in the face of his formidable wife. Brontë, then, creates the kind of man whom she can respect, whose paternalism yields to her growth, and who aids her escape from a competitive and cold mother figure (perhaps reminiscent of her own Aunt Branwell and Madame Héger). Before Lucy leaves the school in Villette, M. Paul bestows a gift that sets Lucy free from Madame Beck's control.[9] He secretly arranges a private home to be rented for Lucy, which is to be divided into private and school quarters. His generosity then enables Lucy to live independently on her own terms. The author's realistic wishes (she once hoped to set up such a school with her sisters) are met through her created heroine; however, in contrast to *Jane Eyre*—in which the happy ending is more like a magical wish fulfillment—here the characters' emotional developments support the quieter outcome. Charlotte Brontë receives a realistic form of aid from a man through her alter-ego, Lucy Snowe, a support for her own development that she never received from her own father. Further, Charlotte-Lucy gains recognition of her true nature. M. Paul must leave Lucy for a voyage to Guadaloupe, part of a three-year project proposed by Madame Beck and her coconspirators to banish the teacher from the vicinity of his favorite pupil. Before leaving her, M. Paul promises that she will be "his lady" on his return. Although the promised happy romantic ending is unfulfilled—returning to England, M. Paul dies during a storm at sea—Lucy is consecrated by his love and affirmation of her true self. He has acknowledged her inner power and independent growth. For the three years before his death, Lucy continues to develop and prosper in his absence, sustained by the loving affirmation of his letters.

The ending of *Villette* implies that the experience of being loved for one's true self is what genuinely counts and that the continued existence of the external object relationship is secondary. Thus the novel closes on a note of implied respect for psychic internalization.

Unlike Charlotte, Lucy receives an affirmation that is neither withdrawn nor denied. In her real life, Brontë waited in torment for over six months for Héger to reply to her letter of January 6, 1845, perhaps the penultimate one she wrote to him. The prototype for M. Paul was quickly intimidated as soon as Charlotte revealed her true feelings, her anguish, and yearnings for affection. His withdrawal was instant and total. Like granite, the idealized father figure of Héger— her own Duke of Wellington—was obdurately silent just as Patrick Brontë had become during his prolonged pathological mourning after Branwell's death. Charlotte wrote the poem "He Saw My Heart's Woe" to express the frustrated anguish that Heger's implacability caused:

> He was mute as is the grave, he stood stirless as a tower;
> At last I looked up, and saw I prayed to stone;
> I asked help of that which to help had no power,
>     I sought love where love was utterly unknown.
>
> Idolater I kneeled to an idol cut in rock!
>     I might have slashed my flesh and drawn my heart's best blood:
> The Granite God had felt no tenderness, no shock;
>     My Baal had not seen nor heard nor understood.
>
> (quoted in Peters 1986, 171)[10]

In *Villette*, Charlotte Brontë transcended her acute disappointment with Héger. She never devalued him, but instead built him up into a good object. She made her lost love into an oedipal father who romantically affirmed her. The ending of *Villette* allows this internalization to stand on its own and leaves Lucy free to lead a separate life apart from M. Paul. If the lovers had been reunited, could they have been wed and lived happily together? Certain of M. Paul's traits make this outcome doubtful. As a benevolent father, M. Paul successfully helps Charlotte, through Lucy, to repair her paternal disappointments—with her own father and with Héger. Yet as a lover and husband M. Paul would probably fall short of the mark. For he is far more afraid of Lucy's sexuality than of her aggression. In one exchange, he tells her that she is becoming loose and dangerous, as indicated by the flowers she now wears in her bonnet. Lucy responds that they are only little flowers. The professor exhorts her to keep them little. The scene, though quaintly within character for someone with his provocative nature, also reveals his fear of her female sexual development, even as he helps her to grow. Brontë's real professor may have been similarly threatened by her development; in her fictive recreation, he is threatened by her sexual growth.

In the finished novel, Charlotte created an ingenious resolution to her real-life predicament. She derives from her half-fictional, half-real professor[11] a reparative love that moves her beyond paternal disappointment, as well as beyond the painful paralysis of her unrequited love for the actual Professor Héger. Brontë the writer keeps her fictive professor from entering into a marriage that had every possibility of evoking intense guilt and oedipal conflict. Through this reparative resolution in her work, Brontë herself moved beyond her father by marrying a man who was far less narcissistic and despotic. Thus, Lucy awakens from her emotional hibernation and takes on an active life, like her creator.

## The Character of Graham (Dr. John) Bretton

That Lucy loves another man in *Villette* was a matter of some concern to at least one of Charlotte Brontë's contemporaries. How could a woman love two men at the same time? The man who posed this question to the author, Charlotte's publisher George Smith, was the model for the character of Graham (Dr. John) Bretton, a fact of which Smith was well aware.

To Smith, Charlotte defended the truth of her depiction of a woman able to love two men, just as she defended the veracity of the novel's slow and spasmodic pace. She wanted *Villette* to breathe life, not to be constructed artificially to gratify the reader's fancy. Smith's inability to see her point and his subsequent niggardly payment of five hundred pounds to her for *Villette* after the successes of *Jane Eyre* and *Shirley* (indeed, it could be said that *Jane Eyre* put his publishing house on the literary map) reflect his blindness, a blindness depicted in Graham Bretton. In drawing this character, Charlotte did not neglect to show his charm and warmth and bask in his generosity, since she was ever ready to restore and even honor the image of a man who had grievously disappointed her. Yet such acknowledgments never dissuaded her from a poignant portrait of the real man's faults.

The character of Graham Bretton highlights what Tony Tanner refers to as the "subtly pervasive tyranny of the male in this world" (1985, 17). Through a nearsighted misreading of facts, Bretton unwittingly seeks to force women into a role—ever so gently. His subtlety stands in contrast with the outlandish, despotic outbursts of M. Paul. Like George Smith, who cannot imagine a woman loving two men at once, Graham cannot see the true dimensions of Lucy's character. He takes her defensive disguise as the real thing and describes her as being "inoffensive as a shadow" (*Villette*, 403). At one point, he seeks to force Lucy into a role as his desexualized confident, asking her to assist him in courting another woman, reinforcing his wish for her to be a neutralized "shadow." Lucy's response is distinctly articulate in her anger:

> In this matter I was not disposed to gratify Dr. John: not at all. With now welcome force, I realized his entire misapprehension of my character and nature. He wanted always to give me a role not mine. Nature and I opposed him. He did not at all guess what I felt: he did not read my eyes, or face, or gestures; though, I doubt not, all spoke. Leaning towards me coaxingly, he said, softly, 'Do content me, Lucy.'
>
> (404)

As Lucy is about to put Bretton in his place, M. Paul comes by and hisses "coucerette, coquette" in her ear. The timing is exquisite, because although M. Paul acts like a pestering insect (unlike the smooth, seductive Graham), he is truly responding to Lucy's feminine passion. Graham laughs at the professor's comments, thereby making clear his own naïvité.

From the beginning of the novel, Graham is portrayed as the very image of assuming masculine dominance. Unlike the professor, he needs not display any tyranny, because he goodnaturedly assumes that this dominance is his birthright, for which he has no need to fight. Graham's first scene with Paulina, the "Daddy's girl" who comes to stay at his home during their childhood, illustrates the dominant role he unconsciously assumes. Tanner describes the incident: "[H]e suddenly picks Paulina up with one hand and holds her up in the air, an action full of 'disrespect' presaging the dominant power of the male" (33).

Much later in the novel, Lucy still sees Graham as a symbol of male dominance. She says, "In two minutes he would have had my secret; my identity would have been grasped between his never tyrannous, but always powerful hands" (*Villette*, 554). Earlier, Lucy desperately searches for a letter from him that she thinks has been lost. It emerges that he has snatched the letter away for his own amusement, in a kind of subtle taunting:

> Curious, characteristic manoevre! His quick eye had seen the letter on the floor where I sought it; his hand, as quick, had snatched it up. He had hidden it in his waistcoat pocket. If my trouble had wrought with a whit less stress and reality, I doubt whether he would ever have acknowledged or restored it. Tears

of temperature one degree cooler than those I shed would only have amused
Dr. John.

(327)

Lucy had seen Paulina, as the child Polly, subject to such dominance by
Graham. Lucy regards Graham's dominant behavior with a dispassionate contempt, reflecting a more passionate envy. On the one hand, she is mesmerized
by the despotic airs of the Napoleonic professor Emanuel (as the young Charlotte
was by the Duke of Wellington). On the other hand, when Lucy is the actual
object of the presumptuous male's game, she rebels—if not always overtly.
Humiliated by the examination of two male professors whom M. Paul has without
warning inflicted on her, she comments: "I myself appeared to be shaken or
emptied out of my chair as a solitary and withered nutmeg might be emptied out
of a spice-box by an excited cook" (492). Yet her rebellion surfaces in the essay
that she is asked to write on "injustice." In it she flares into fiery articulations,
creating a narrative space for herself—and therefore an identity—as she pours
out her venomous wrath against the arrogant male professors.

Lucy's rebellion most succinctly expresses her anger at Graham after he asks
her to betray herself and to become his handmaiden in his courtship of the adult
Paulina. Although she never verbally confronts him on account of the professor's
intrusion at that moment, she nonetheless says to herself, "Nature and I opposed
him." She shows her resistance to Graham by then refusing to accommodate him.
Her behavior strongly contrasts with Paulina's, who in relation to Graham and
to her father is the caricature of the woman who never separates from men and
their will to dominate.

## Paulina and Her Father

A young heiress, Paulina is provided for in every paternal way by her father,
Monsieur de Bassompierre. She is described as a pixy or a faun, dispensing her
charm before men as a translucent lamp exudes a magical light. She is both
protected and imprisoned by the circle of male dominance around her. But Paulina
never feels imprisoned, since she is so compliantly a part of these men, merging
with them in perfect attunement. Because of her dependency, she is occasionally
bereft when the men she adores must leave her behind to enter their own world
of masculine affairs or of scientific pursuits.

Paulina never challenges her father. She generally gets whatever she wants by
seductive persuasion; when she cannot, she collapses. This behavioral mode is
never clearer than in the scene in which she confronts her father's opposition to
her marriage with Graham. Lucy, observing the scene, narrates:

She stood looking at him a minute. She wanted to show firmness, superiority to taunts; knowing her father's character, guessing his few foibles, she had expected the sort of scene which was now transpiring; it did not take her by surprise, and she desired to let it pass with dignity, reliant upon reaction. Her dignity stood her in no stead. Suddenly her soul melted in her eyes; she fell on his neck:—" 'I won't leave you, papa; I'll never leave you. I won't leave you, papa; I'll never leave you. I won't pain you; I'll never pain you!' " was her cry.

(528)

When Paulina experiences an inner thrust toward separation from her father, she is threatened. Attempts to vocalize her need to separate result in her collapsing; she can win only by being the frail and pitied female victim, essentially by default. This scene is meant to contrast with the one in which Lucy separates emotionally from M. Paul by defending her own religious views. It also contrasts with Charlotte's confrontation with her father over her freedom to marry Arthur Nicholls.

## Arrested Mourning

Tanner writes:

> Throughout *Villette,* there is a tension between a need to mourn, so as to renew a capacity for love, and an inhibiting suppressive and repressive force, which emanates from the author's psyche. As the inability and suppressive psychic forces oppose a natural need to connect with others through the process of mourning one's losses and disappointments, the protagonist, Lucy Snowe, buries objects such as Graham's letters, that symbolize her love. With such "premature entombments" (Tanner, 16), Lucy Snowe arrests the self integrating process of mourning. Lucy's symbolic self burials are echoed by the legend of a nun who was buried alive and the professor's burial of his life through sacrifice for other people.

To bury one's love is to bury one's self. When Lucy buries Graham's letters, rather than mourning her love for him, she has the impulse to bury herself. "[B]ut all this was nothing; I too felt those autumn suns and saw those harvest moons, and I almost wished to be covered in with earth and turf, deep out of their influence; for I could not live in their light, nor make them comrades, nor yield them affection" (*Villette,* 230). Remember that during Lucy's employment as a companion to the aging Miss Marchmont, we see the younger woman encased in a life-in-death experience. She lives as a shadow to a woman who is herself a shadow, since Miss Marchmont has endured thirty years without any desire to go forward with her life—thirty years of arthritic rigidification within a body that has, with equal rigidity, held on to an unmourned internal object. Additionally, from childhood until her encounter with M. Paul, Lucy lives in an "oppressively domesticated world,"[12] in which she is forced in upon herself, for there are no opportunities or connections for her in the outside world. She lives interred within the cemetery of minute domestic concerns, where the passionate life is sealed off.[13]

Then, as Lucy changes and gains some emotional distance, she sees all of Villette as an Egyptian mirage in a vision she has while drugged on an opiate slipped into her drink by Madame Beck. Lucy's acquaintances in the town now appear in a carnival setting. Despite their levity, her vision is of the ancient land, where all life was a preparation for entering the tomb:

> In a land of enchantment, a garden most gorgeous, a plain sprinkled with coloured meteors, a forest with sparks of purple and ruby and golden fire gemming the foliage; a region, not of trees and shadow, but of strangest architectural wealth—of altar and of temple; of pyramid, obelisk, and sphynx; incredible to say, the wonders and the symbols of Egypt teemed through the park of Villette.
>
> (550)

Each apparition of the waking dead seems to carry the same symbolism in relation to Lucy's intrapsychic state. To bury life as she has been forced to do, to become like the legendary nun who was buried alive, to bury a love when it is unrequited as she is forced to bury her love for Graham through creating an earthen tomb for his prematurely arrested missives—all of these are symbolic reference to the psychically arrested mourning state in which Lucy (and Charlotte) is encased. This state is characterized by looking backward when there is nothing to look forward to, imagining oneself buried underground because one is numb from lack of human contact. Such a mental state cannot be overcome until the person is touched from the outside; only then can mourning begin. Only then can depressive despair be tolerated consciously, enabling an active sense of loss to be worked through so that one can take steps toward rather than away from life.

## Mourning

Unlike Emily Dickinson and Emily Brontë who we will study in the next chapters, Charlotte Brontë moved toward life. She did not select entombment when she had a choice. She did not choose an internal object over external ones in her own life. Therefore, she did not end up married to her demon lover. She was touched from the outside. Despite her final rejection by Héger, she felt recognized and affirmed by him. He saw and acknowledged her depth, brilliance, and passion. Through writing Lucy Snowe's story, the only surviving female Brontë relived and enlarged this paternal-object-related gratification. Through the creative process, she allowed the awareness of the touch that brought her to life. The creative process opened up her sense of loss, changing it from frozen despair to the fluid affects of felt grief. This opened up her potential psyche space, latent since early development. (see Ogden, 1986). Charlotte Brontë thus made choices toward activity and life, and away from passivity and internal emptiness.

Although *Villette* reveals Charlotte in her state of arrested mourning, it also describes her evolution from it. *Villette* is an exegesis of the mourning process as it unfolds in fits and starts. In the novel, tension between passivity and activity is played out, as is that between withdrawal and aggression and suppression and sexuality. During the resolution of these tensions, endured suffering evolves into the fluid venting of sorrow. In contrast to her sister Emily, Charlotte endures but never cherishes her suffering. Life is chosen at the cost of emotional risk.

To describe *Villette,* Tanner uses a quote from Samuel Beckett: "The periods of transition that separate consecutive adaptations . . . represent the perilous zones in the life of the individual, dangerous, precarious, painful, mysterious and fertile, when for a moment the boredom of living is replaced by the suffering of being . . ." (7).

In *Villette,* Lucy Snowe's vulnerability in response to suffering is most exquisitely exposed during her solitary stay at the school during the long summer months:

> I lay in a strange fever of the nerves and blood. Sleep went quite away . . .
>    I err. She came once, but in anger. Impatient of my importunity she brought with her an avenging dream . . . sufficing to wring my whole frame with unknown anguish; to confer a nameless experience that had the hue, the mien, the terror, the very tone of a visitation from eternity. Between twelve and one that night a cup was forced to my lips, black, strong, strange, drawn from no well, but filled up seething from a bottomless and boundless sea. Suffering, brewed in temporal or calculable measure, and mixed for mortal lips, tastes not as this suffering tasted. Having drank and woke, I thought all was over: the end come and past by. Trembling fearfully—as consciousness returned—ready to cry out on some fellow-creature to help me, only that I knew no fellow-creature was near enough to catch the wild summons—Goton in her far distant attack could not hear—I rose on my knees in bed. Some fearful hours went over me; indescribably was I torn, racked and oppressed in mind. Methought the well-loved dead, who had loved me well in life, met me elsewhere, alienated; galled was my inmost spirit with an unutterable sense of despair

about the future. Motive there was none why I should try to recover or wish to live; and yet quite unendurable was the pitiless and haughty voice in which Death challenged me to engage his unknown terrors. When I tried to pray I could only utter these words;—

"From my youth up Thy terrors have I suffered with a troubled mind."

(*Villette*, 231–32)

Tormented by being left utterly alone, Lucy does not refuse companionship when it finally comes in the form of M. Paul; later she is able to let him truly see her and deeply touch her. She never seals herself off. This communion is made possible by her capacity to suffer actively, that is, to experience that within and then to let go. The occasions during which she vents tears of sorrow inform us of this capacity. One such scene is when she risks the unknown following the death of her first employer, Miss Marchmont. Terrified of moving forward, out of the seclusion enforced by her position as companion, she nonetheless embarks on a voyage that symbolizes her transition. Before she arrives in Villette, she spends the night in London:

All at once my position rose on me like a ghost. Anomalous; desolate, almost blank of hope, it stood. What was I doing here alone in great London? What should I do on the morrow? What prospects had I in life? What friends had I on earth? Whence did I come? Whither should I go? What should I do?

I wet the pillow, my arms, and my hair, with rushing tears. A dark interval of most bitter thought followed this burst; but I did not regret the step taken, nor wish to retract it. A strong, vague persuasion, that it was better to go forward than backward, and that I could go forward—that a way, however narrow and difficult, would in time open, predominated over other feelings; its influence hushed them so far, that at last I became sufficiently tranquil to be able to say my prayers and seek my couch.

(107)

Lucy is relieved from her isolated suffering, which has brought her to the point of unconsciousness, by the rediscovery of her former godmother and the latter's son, Graham. Both take her into their homes and their lives. On leaving them to return to Madame Beck's school, Lucy's tears escape her internal censor.

When Graham's letter seems lost, Lucy again openly sobs in pain. Only in response to such overt grief does Graham return the letter he has playfully snatched (326–27). Lucy lets him soothe her, although his kindness is intermingled with masculine taunts about his ability to seize the letter again: "A warm hand, taking my cold fingers, led me down to a room where there was fire. Dr. John and I sat before the stove . . . he was as good to me as the well is to the parched wayfarer— as the sun to the shivering jail-bird. I remember him heroic. Heroic at this moment will I hold him to be" (327). She receives his warmth despite his hostility of a moment before. When Graham's letters stop coming, Lucy's bereavement is intense. She seeks to curtail it by burying the letters she possesses. In one sense she faces her loss squarely, a necessary part of the working through of the depressive position. Yet, in another sense, she is hurrying the process, because the anguish of feeling her suffering is at this juncture too great. Therefore, an incipient piece of mourning is arrested. Lucy is left with "sad, lonely satisfaction" (380) on burying the letters, the few written to her before Graham's interest has been transferred to Paulina. "But I was not only going to hide a treasure—I meant also to bury a grief. That grief over which I had lately been weeping, as I wrapped it in its winding-sheet, must be interred" (380). Because Lucy has rushed the act of mourning, aggression supersedes loss. She turns that aggression against herself and buries the letters from Graham that she had so treasured:

> Well, I cleared away the ivy, and found the hole; it was large enough to receive the jar, and I thrust it deep in. In a tool-shed at the bottom of the garden, lay the relics of building-materials, left by masons lately employed to repair a part of the premises. I fetched thence a slate and some mortar, put the slate on the hollow, secured it with cement, covered the whole with black mould, and, finally replaced the ivy. This done, I rested, leaning against the tree; lingering, like any other mourner, beside a newly sodded grave.
>
> (380–81)

Despite this premature burial of feeling and its object, Lucy-Charlotte has felt the keen cut of her loss enough for conscious grief to yield to love. Despite her self-suppression and her indirectly aggressive assault on the man contained within her internal burial ground, her suffering is experienced. Love emerges within the context of mournful suffering:

> Alas something came rushing into my eyes, dimming utterly their vision, blotting from sight the schoolroom, the garden, the bright winter sun, as I remembered that never more would letters, such as he had read, come to me. I had seen the last of them. That goodly river on whose banks had sojourned, of whose waves a few reviving drops had trickled to my lips, was bending to another course: it was leaving my little hut and field forlorn and sand-dry, pouring its wealth of waters far away. The change was right; just, natural; not a word could be said: but I loved my Rhine, my Nile; I had almost worshipped my Ganges, and grieved that the grand tide should roll estranged, should vanish like a false mirage . Though stoical, I was not quite a stoic; drops streamed fast on my hands, on my disk: I wept one sultry shower, heavy and brief.
>
> (377–78)

Through conscious despair (her endured suffering), Lucy creates meaning in her life—even in the absence of bonding and support from her environment. As Lucy Snowe creates meaning in her fictional life, Charlotte Brontë constructed a narrative space for herself in a literary world ruled by men. She refused to conform to the male idea of what women's writing should be, and she refused to be an imitation male, although she felt compelled (given Southey's earlier reaction) to use the pragmatic tool of a male pseudonym when she published. For this reason, reviews of Charlotte's books were controversial. Although those of *Jane Eyre* and *Villette* were mostly favorable, Brontë was sometimes accused of being an "unnatural" woman for her "male" writing, while simultaneously being criticized for her domestic detail, considered to be "proof" of a female who had violated her proper role by becoming an author. The greatest criticism of *Villette* came from a woman who was of her own Tory political persuasion. Peters reports a women's review of *Villette:*

> "We want a woman at our hearth," sneered Anne Mozley, "and her imperson-
> ations are without the feminine element, infringers of modest restraints, despis-
> ers of bashful fears, self-reliant, contemptuous of prescriptive decorum; their
> own unaided reason, their individual opinion of right and wrong, discreet or
> imprudent, sole guides of conduct and rules of manners,—the whole hedge
> of immemorial scruple and habit broken down and trampled upon. We will
> sympathize with Lucy Snowe as being fatherless and penniless . . . but we
> cannot offer ever the affections of our fancy (the right and due of every
> legitimate heroine) to her unscrupulous and self-dependent intellect. . . ."
>
> (Peters 1986, 371)

Recording this review, Peters comments: "Ironically, Charlotte's bitterest ene-mies were women. Male critics were often severe with Currer Bell, but only a woman, unsheathing her claws to defend traditional femininity, slashed with such fury" (371). Like Lucy Snowe, Charlotte Brontë faced her own Madame Becks.

Lucy Snowe reflects the tenacity of Brontë's own struggle. Continually grief-stricken, frequently deserted, and sometimes cruelly abandoned,[14] Lucy neverthe-less mourns enough to move on. She constantly takes steps toward separation from an inner male tyrant, and she becomes individualized through creating the understanding permitted only by felt grief. In the process, she stays open to the men in her life no matter how greatly they disappoint her. When M. Paul first has an insight into her passionate nature, she allows his affirmation to spur her on in the direction she had begun when she risked coming to Villette. Later, his affirmation encourages her to try her capacity as a teacher. She leaves her shadowlike existence behind. Thus, after M. de Bassompierre asks her to be a paid companion for his daughter Paulina, Lucy refuses, remarking to the reader,

"I am no bright lady's shadow." This assertion, Knies suggests, is "quite in contrast to the Lucy who had submerged her personality in Miss Marchmont's to 'escape the great agonies' " (192). Lucy's view of herself begins to change, as does her willingness to risk the great agonies rather than to be buried in tedious domestic routine. When M. Paul insists that she perform in public, Lucy initially resists but then yields mostly to please him and to keep the peace. Once on stage, her hidden ardor emerges and M. Paul is able to glimpse her vibrancy. Afterward, she quickly pulls back. Fearing any expansiveness unleashed in herself, she is terrified that she will otherwise lose her integrity. She must inwardly consolidate. Nevertheless, Lucy has been aroused, and each time she emerges anew, she finds it harder to suppress her real self.

Lucy needs to be a teacher to confer on her self an identity in a world of external form.[15] She has no social or financial status or any family bonding to define herself. Lucy's family has vanished in a shipwreck—a metaphor for Brontë's own family situation—All are dead, except for her father and herself. She seizes the opportunity M. Paul offers her to have her own home and school, because she is ready to move out further on her own. Although Lucy sometimes envies Paulina's security, she also has contempt for her lack of autonomy and self-definition.

In contrast to the compliant Paulina, Lucy has embarked on a psychic voyage, reflected in the physical voyage she must take to arrive in Villette. When the novel begins, she is presented in her cocoon, a cavelike room called a "submarine home," where she lives in isolation despite the presence of her godmother and her son. During *Villette,* she leaves this inner psychic cocoon and then withdraws again with each step of growth, demonstrating the emotional reality of all psychic growth. Each oscillation of progression and retrogression becomes an overall rebirthing and working-through process. As Charlotte Brontë recreates herself in the novel, her alter-ego heroine Lucy exhibits the growth process and its stages of the working through of grief experiences that ultimately create meaning.

Although there seems to be some collusion to keep Lucy suppressed and shadowlike[16]—particularly in reference to Graham, Madame Beck, Miss Marchmont, and Pierre Silas—she constructs a narrative space for herself. She does this against the male chauvinism of M. Paul, as well as in defiance of the three opponents just mentioned, just as Charlotte Brontë writes her book about Lucy from a position of defiance of the literary world, in which language itself was seen as masculine. Lucy articulates herself in speech, and her author Charlotte Brontë in written words, yet both claim the power of words, to assert their views, and to fight against the male chauvinism that demands that a woman silence herself, and retire to being a caretaker of others.

The progress of Lucy and Paul's relationship does not run so smoothly from association to adhesion to amalgamation, but it is still, even at its most abrasive and argumentative, a matter of her establishing a place in his language with her own tongue. Thus when he tries to convert Lucy to Catholicism she admits she cannot meet his arguments, "but I could talk in my own way. . . . She must be able to talk in her own way, no matter how falteringly, otherwise she will simply be submerged in the surrounding alien language. She can only be herself to the extent that she can speak herself. And speaking in her own way within the book is related to narrating the book itself in her own way. . . .

(42)

Charlotte Brontë's struggle for her own language (voice) is mirrored in Lucy's struggle. Just as Charlotte defies the Victorian male's image of what a woman should be by continuing to write, despite Lord Southey's (and Wordsworth's) advice, Lucy fights against playing an assigned role. Thus Lucy's sharp response to Graham's classifying image of her ("Nature and I oppose him!"), Tanner suggests, relates to Brontë's work in *Villette* and her own need to individuate through the "renaming" that is central to Lucy's development. This renaming of Lucy's is a critical part of her author's mourning process (see Segal on mourning and naming [1964] 1975)

It is in part an act of retrospective exegesis but more than that it is the creation of a narrative context of private semantic amplitude and significance to set against the social context of constricted and insufficient meaning which she had to endure. . . . Just as Charlotte Brontë hands over to Lucy Snowe the right to rename her actual environment (Villette, Labassecour, Boue Marine, etc.) so her whole book is an act of renomination. As she composes her book she is composing herself, and what that book shows us is not just Charlotte Brontë in a refracted light but the imagined figure of Lucy Snowe refusing to have her experience named for her. . . . Lucy Snowe, depicting herself in various stages of ignorance, illness, and incompletion finally defines herself in her "heretic narrative." The meaning of the life only finds itself in the completing of the book . . . thus her arrival "at some definitive state of being."

(50–51)

Tanner is acknowledging narrative truth that creates historical truth, rather than vice versa. With Lucy's mourning and individuation process comes the working through of object loss, self-loss, and rebirth. Similar to all working through processes—characterized in Kleinian theory as the depressive position and in Mahler's theory as separation-individuation—Lucy's process is only partially successful. Still, it allows her to open up to M. Paul's love and affirmation and to strive toward her own autonomy. In creating this process for Lucy, Brontë permitted a parallel development for herself. In other words, as she wrote *Villette*, Brontë carved out an identity for herself that went beyond the scintillating opinions in *Jane Eyre*, to an ongoing, reflective self-analysis. It was in fact through some combination of the self-affirmation she received through her self-created father figure and her own ability to face her losses and suffering without denial that Brontë opened to life and to self-agency. Lucy opens toward life and goes on to prove her capabilities and to prosper. Marriage does not seem to be her fate; the ambiguous ending of the novel lets us know that despite the reader's wish to deny another loss, M. Paul's death prevents any further relationship between him and Lucy. Still, it is the experience of the relationship itself that is critical. Lucy develops a capacity to love as she is loved, and the mutuality within love is internalized. Charlotte Brontë seems to have developed an intuitive sense of such internalization processes through tolerating the painful affects of mourning as she wrote.

What other specific effects did this mourning and rebirth process, experienced through the character of Lucy Snowe, have on her creator? Apparently, Brontë was able to use the affective vividness of the mourning within the creative process of this novel to move toward life, just as Lucy did. Charlotte opened to the possibility of marriage. She broke the constricting bond with her father; in his external and internal forms. I speculate that her power to do what her sister Emily could never do was related to a higher level of psychic development. Her writing demonstrates that she achieved a level of neurotic conflict (for example, conflict over aggression) and was not split at a primary-self level as the more schizoid Emily was.[17] Such higher-level development could obviously be derived from the longer period in which she experienced her mother prior to her death. As Emily's older sister, Charlotte had her mother throughout the stages of basic self-consolidation during the separation-individuation phases of development, losing her only later at the oedipal stage. As will be seen, Emily Brontë was not so fortunate. Freeing herself of her father's hold on her, Charlotte moved toward Arthur Nicholls following the creation of *Villette,* finally coming to accept his offer of companionship through marriage.

## Reparation of the Object in the Working-Through Process

In examining Charlotte Brontë's working-through process, we need to consider another element in *Villette:* how it shows reparative strivings operating within the working-through process of the depressive position. These reparative strivings can be seen by the way in which the two chief male characters, Graham Bretton and M. Paul, are initially constituted and then reconstructed by the author.

Despite her awareness of Graham's failings, Lucy never responds to them by devaluing him even when his behavior pains and injures her. Instead, her highly ambivalent view of Graham is reworked always in flattering terms. As indicated, she sees him as heroic when he shows tender consideration for her during the incident of the lost letter. Her anger at his manipulation is dispelled by his tenderness. Even mocking threats fail to provoke her: "If you don't tell me," he taunts, "you shall have no more letters. . . . I will again take away that single epistle: being mine, I think I have a right to reclaim it. . . . You may hide it, but I can possess it any moment I choose. You don't know my skill in sleight of hand" (*Villette,* 328).

Lucy doesn't deny Graham's taunting, she remarks of it, "I felt raillery in his words: it made me grave and quiet; but I folded up the letter and covered it from sight" (328). Despite Lucy's awareness that he can be provocative, the reader senses that she keeps intact her heroic image of him, perhaps holding the two impressions simultaneously. Thus, Lucy inserts a reparative comment to compensate for each of her criticisms of Graham. This is reparation rather than reaction formation, because she retains an awareness of Graham's character flaws.

> [T]o feel, and to seize quickly another's feelings, are separate properties; a few constructions possess both, some neither. Dr. John had the one gift in exquisite perfection; and because I have admitted that he was not endowed with the other in equal degree, the reader will considerately refrain from passing to an extreme, and pronouncing him un-sympathizing, unfeeling: on the contrary, he was a kind, generous man. Make your need known, his hand was open. Put your grief into words, he turned no deaf ear. Expect refinements of perception, miracles of intuition, and realize disappointment.
>
> (264)

Additionally, when Graham, with impeccable timing, rushes in to propose to Paulina and to appeal to her father for consent, Lucy notes that he is both lucky and simple. She makes a similar observation on seeing him impervious to the affective impact of the demonic actress, whom she calls Vashti (341). Lucy's last comments on Graham, after his desertion of her and his engagement to Paulina, follow the same pattern:

> Graham's thoughts of me were not entirely those of a frozen indifference, after all. I believe in that goodly mansion, his heart, he kept one little place under the skylights where Lucy might have entertainment, if she chose to call. It was not so handsome as the chambers where he lodged his male friends; it was not like the hall where he accommodated his philanthropy, or the library where he treasured his science, still less did it resemble the pavilion where his marriage feast was splendidly spread; yet, gradually, by long and equal kindness, he proved to me that he kept one little closet, over the door of which was written "Lucy's Room."
>
> (555)

Lucy engages in the same construction and reconstruction of M. Paul's character, restoring and repairing it constantly. Brontë was writing of her love for her real professor in the aftermath of his cruel and complete abandonment. Her first literary response to this disaster came in such poems as "He Saw My Heart's Woe," and the novel *The Professor*. Written shortly after M. Héger's letters to her ceased, the latter novel lacks the analytic distance attained in *Villette,* which greatly refined her view of M. Héger. During its writing, she apparently mourned his loss, so that she was no longer stuck in the frozen state of bitter devaluation. The image of the professor changes as M. Paul Emanuel grows from someone demonic to a compassionate and loving friend whose only remaining flaw, in regard to Lucy, is his paternalism. His fears of her sexuality explain why he still needs to view Lucy as a child. Their last meeting is tender, with Lucy feeling immense gratitude for his love. Having faced her defiance of M. Paul, her distrust of him,[18] her occasional wrath toward him, and her differentiation from him, Lucy becomes free to experience the full range of her appreciation for his loving qualities. Her openness to him at their last meeting illustrates that psychic reparation of the formerly hostile internal male object has occurred. Lucy can now remember M. Paul as a true and golden friend. During this meeting, Lucy narrates her reactions: "Warm, jealous, and haughty, I know not till now that my nature had such a mood; he gathered me near his heart. I was full of faults; he took them and me all home. For the moment of utmost mutiny, he reserved the one deep spell of peace" (591).

Despite her real reasons for bitterness, Lucy repairs the images of Graham and M. Paul, without needing to deny either man's faults. Simultaneously her view of God as a male is repaired. At the peak of her sufferings, Lucy explains her view of God:

> With what dread force the conviction would grasp me that Fate was my permanent foe, never to be conciliated. I did not, in my heart, arraign the mercy or justice of God for this; I concluded it to be part of his great plan that some must deeply suffer while they live, and I thrilled in the certainty that of this number, I was one.
>
> (229)

Although such a view may be seen as a rationalization and a reaction formation disguising repressed rage, a positive image of a paternal male is retained, and the devaluation characteristic of a more primitive mode of splitting does not appear. Moreover, when the subject of the male-object restoration is M. Paul, there does not seem to be a defensive projection. Lucy's restoration of her paternal male objects does not diminish her own sense of self but enhances it. The end of *Villette* shows that M. Paul is held in such esteem by Lucy that she calls him her king (587). He is a benevolent king, a muse of her own self-creation, not a king of demonic masculine domination nor a king defined by external appointment. Her heart, in interaction with M. Paul's own, has bequeathed him the title of "king."

## Charlotte Brontë's Level of Psychic Development

Unlike most of the other authors of my study, Charlotte Brontë developed to an oedipal level. This enabled her to use the creative process for mourning, separation, and individuation. *Villette* provides evidence for the level of psychic development that she attained.

Charlotte Brontë's fictional characters, expressive of her internal world, are available for contact rather than remote. The main characters in *Villette* can integrate dialogue with each other and also within themselves. Through her alter-ego heroine Lucy Snowe, Brontë demonstrates that she can be both immediate and reflective without becoming abstracted from herself. Her primary internal object, this suggests, has been assimilated into her psychic structure, and ongoing integration[19] continues to be developed through her creative process, particularly in *Villette,* in which grief and loss are felt and tolerated.

Thus, Charlotte Brontë can experience in the immediate moment and yet generalize her experience through reflective thought that leads to conceptualizations and generalizable hypotheses and conclusions. She appears to have reached Piaget's (1969) stage of formal operations. Her character symbolism is not stereotypic but interactively alive. Her part object male characters develop into whole objects as she moves from *Jane Eyre* to *Villette,* as they also do within *Villette* itself. In *Villette* the reader sees how a rigid and dominating man grows into a personality that can tolerate a complex ambiguity and an ambivalence of emotional experience. Also, self-integration is enhanced by transformative interaction between whole object female subjects and whole object male others. Differentiation of self and other proceeds along with self and other integration, according to the normal developmental growth process within the creative process. The latter process itself becomes a means to confront disillusionment and to work through mourning and its related integration.

Further, Charlotte Brontë progresses beyond a transitional-stage use of the creative process to an oedipal-stage resolution. This allows her to move toward a sustained interpersonal connection with a real man, as a follow-up to the process of engagement with her creative work. Such movement in her interpersonal life testifies to the achievement of reparation, revealed as incremental stages of differentiation and integration of self and object, leaving their imprints within the internal world.

In contrast to preoedipally arrested authors whose self parts oppose each other through splitting and fragmentation, Charlotte Brontë exhibits intrapsychic conflict. Lucy Snowe carries on an inner dialogue between two female voices: reason and imagination (307–9). The voice of reason represents an internal masculinized female, who is perhaps an internalization of the author's aunt Branwell or of her father.[20] The other voice, Lucy tells us, represents the internal resources of imagination. This latter voice appears as a deeply intuitive and feminine resource within the female author who portrays it. Imagination is the freeing expression of the inner self, or the libidinal ego. Reason is the controlling antilibidinal ego persona, here appearing as a voice that threatens to suppress or seal off the libidinal ego. Yet reason is overthrown. Conscious rebellion occurs. Repression—and its mode of sealing off affect and creative desire—is defeated. Good enough early mothering can be hypothesized in relation to the emergence of the feminine inner voice and its feminine intuitive capacity. Charlotte Brontë is able to contact this feminine resource within herself.[21] This ability demonstrates that Brontë's primary self has not been sealed off from interpersonal contact. The affective contact of her infant femininity and its tie to a feminine maternal figure are overtly available. The kind of internally reflective and psychically conflictual dialogue that Charlotte demonstrates through her fictional characters will be seen to be absent in the work of the other women to be studied in this volume, those with preoedipal level arrests in development.

Imagination is the softer voice in Charlotte Brontë, confirming the evolution of a matured object internalization, which can only be born through the experience of integration of self and object. This voice of imagination represents the feminine self insofar as it is an inner expressive self. Imagination also represents the true, spontaneous self, as described by Winnicott (1965) and Masterson (1981). According to Fairbairn (1952), imagination is the libidinal ego in conflict with the antilibidinal ego. The imaginative voice represents a creative self possessing free motivation, which itself is produced by the ebb and flow of unconscious feeling and thought. This self is in touch with the primary process, that is, with the inner urge toward connection through self-expression. The creative self is not driven by the compulsion symptomatic of a primitive superego or "anti-libidinal ego" (Fairbairn 1952). It is not derived from either a split-off self and object combination or an "orbital object." The creative part of the self emerges organically from within; in feeling it, the person feels his or her needs, fears, and other vulnerabilities that lead to experiencing depressive pain and its integrative insights.

Charlotte Brontë grows within her writing as she moves from *Jane Eyre* to *Villette*. In *Villette* she begins to create characters who express choice instead of reacting to deterministic outer forces. God and nature prevail in the earlier novel, but psychological awareness brings self-determination and choice to the latter.

God's fateful gestures no longer determine the heroine's psychological fate. The female psyche has survived despite his interventions, not because of them. We see this at the end of *Villette,* when the professor's death by shipwreck is suggested but is also ambiguous. Lucy had internalized her beloved and integrated their dialectical relationship into her own psyche. The purpose of this physical survival is not necessary. He has psychologically survived through Lucy's psychic internalization of him. Reactive tendencies in the heroine grow into choice through interpersonal transformation. Lucy's interaction with the professor promotes emotional awareness that transforms depressive pain into active mourning. Love encourages a more fully realized sense of self. Yet this amplitude would be impossible if the professor did not come into being out of a capacity for whole object relations on the part of his author. Unlike Rochester in *Jane Eyre,* M. Paul is a separate and relatively autonomous character. The developmental journey that Brontë creates in *Villette* is not contrived. It unfolds from within the characters' organic developmental processes. Brontë's self-growth, as it occurs through her creative process, consists not only of external separation and autonomous action but of the mournful growth of the inner expressive and needy self, which creates its unique identity.[22] Open needing and self-expression flourish in tandem. In *Villette,* an oedipal crisis crowns the evolution of the self, as Madame Beck intrudes on the heroine's relationship with her reparative father. Although Lucy still represses her erotic desire for this father figure, it reveals itself in her shocked and indignant reaction to Madame Beck.[23] Such involvement in an oedipal triangle requires a highly structuralized level of intrapsychic conflict, reflective of object constancy, sexual differentiation, an advanced level of defenses, and sustained whole object perception. The preoedipal desire for reparative self-healing by the father figure predominates with its mode of tenderness, but the reparative transaction elicits oedipal fantasies of marriage and courtship. The oedipal crisis consolidates the power implicit in Lucy's exposed vulnerability, revealing a resilient self with capacities to heal its wounds through emotional contact and sustained connection. Narrative and historical truth move in parallel, because the reader is witnessing an integrated self creating and developing itself anew.

This journey of a woman's self-evolution parallels the development from part object to whole object experience and its internalization within the internal or intrapsychic world. Once the external contact heals and nourishes the inner needy self, an assimilation of external objects can occur. The psychic journey of *Villette* shows a developmental readiness for such assimilation, as opposed to a compulsive cycle precipitating extrusion and exorcism of incorporated objects that are felt to be persecutors.

The characters in *Villette* encounter one another; such meetings can occur only between whole objects. As Lucy Snowe, the author confronts her whole father figure and integrates him into her own psychic structure, repairing the lack of a good enough father internalized (creating the "ego-ideal") that stems from her oedipal-age interactions with her real father. In the vicissitudes of life, Charlotte Brontë allowed herself to be touched by another, her male French professor. She created M. Héger, similarly to the way in which Winnicott (1953) describes transitional-stage infants creating their absent mothers. Through her alter-ego representational form, Brontë creates a man who transforms her more fully than her experience in actual life has done. Brontë resonates with her life experience through the "recollections in tranquility" of her creative work. Using the vehicle of her own narrative, she allows the interpersonal encounter in her lived, historical life truly to penetrate her psyche, transforming her sense of self. This narrative encounter recreates the historical interpersonal encounter as her creative-work transformation enables her to move on to a successful heterosexual relationship and to marriage.

In developmental terms, Charlotte Brontë was able to evolve through an ongoing creative process that was organically progressive until the end. We will see how this contrasts with the narrative evolution of her sister's output. Emily Brontë distinctly failed at such organic resolution in her novel *Wuthering Heights*. Unlike her sister, Charlotte Brontë does not attempt transcendence of trauma through archaic idealization and merger; rather, in opening to mournful effect, she is able to allow transformation through interaction. Thus, her reparation is true, not manic.

In *Villette,* we also see the transformation of the masculine human element and its integration with the feminine. The demon or bad part object male—the Black Pillar—disappears into the background, making way for the hero, Professor Paul Emanuel. Initially, he is extremely demonic in his contempt and arrogance, which indicate an unintegrated character and the probability of a repressed paternal idealization remaining unintegrated in the author's psyche. Yet as the novel proceeds, integration occurs. In seeking to encounter Lucy Snowe, the professor opens to tenderness. The author's tendency toward psychic splitting is reduced, while her capacity for integration and thus for internalization is enhanced. Her evolving whole object male comes to appreciate the feminine power evinced in assertion, intellect, and ultimately in open vulnerability and needing, although in his fear of her sexuality, he also seeks to diminish her and to keep himself above her. More importantly, however, Lucy Snowe survives and transcends the negative aspect of the professor's character. She gratefully accepts this father figure, proving how loving gratitude is reparative and integrative (see Klein 1957).

The created world of *Villette* reveals Charlotte Brontë's capacity to tolerate depressive despair. Manifesting the diagnostic signs of oedipal conflict and its inhibition, this writer ultimately displays the same kind of assertion that restores self-esteem that we have seen in Anaïs Nin, who also works at the developmental level of the depressive position. To achieve this, Brontë had to endure the depths of grief characteristic of the self-integrative depressive position. Within the depressive position, Charlotte Brontë's evolving self-structure and femininity each have an organic power. By tolerating depressive affect and fantasies, she changes despair into mourning and self-integration. Through her work, the author internalizes the split-off aggressive part of her self that she apparently failed sufficiently to own and integrate during her oedipal-stage development. We can hypothesize that such oedipal-stage failure was perhaps due to a lack of adequate engagement with her real father,[24] whose narcissism did not yield to transformation as her created father's narcissism did. Here, in the creative work and its inner psychic process, narrative truth reaches beyond historical truth as Charlotte Brontë creates her own good enough father, in spite of Patrick Brontë's pathology. Unlike the erotically enthralling professor father whom she created, Charlotte Brontë's father was a "silent" tyrant. He either fused with another in a narcissistic merger (as with Emily) or remained alienated, unrelated and unempathic to the separate needs of his daughters. Such lack of awareness of his daughters' separate identities is related to Brontë's wishes for his son to mirror his own grandiose or self-idealized image. He never accepted the reality of Branwell's failings (Peters 1986), nor could he recognize his eldest daughter's profound psychic strengths and creative talents. He only glimpsed, as previously suggested, a reflected image of the success he so desired for himself, seeing Charlotte as a psychological extension of his own idealized self.

In contrast to arrest within the creative process, itself characteristic of psychically split and arrested preoedipal women, Charlotte Brontë's developmental self-process reflects an evolving creative process. Therefore, her creative work was able to result in a self-integrative resolution at both preoedipal and oedipal levels, as both internal and external object relations became integrated. Having completed the mourning process with *Villette,* Charlotte was finally ready to marry a man suitable for her.

In *Villette,* we can see the working through of the demon lover theme, which, for Charlotte Brontë, resides on the level of whole object relations. The level of this integration process contrasts with that of the part object or "archaic object" demon lover theme, visible in the work of preoedipally arrested writers such as Emily Dickinson, Edith Sitwell, Emily Brontë, and Sylvia Plath. Whole object reparation of father figures allowed Charlotte Brontë to leave behind her oedipal infatuation with male father figures, such as the Duke of Wellington and Héger, and evolve toward the more mature love necessary for marriage. The novel reveals her inner growth as she moves toward marriage to an "ordinary" man.

As Charlotte Brontë's whole object father figure becomes integrated into her own sense of self and as her male and female characters encounter one another and live through grief to attain communion, the reader can relate to her symbolic characterizations through her capacity for reflective insight, as evidenced by Lucy Snowe. Lucy is not only a heroine; she is also a narrator who observes, contemplates, evaluates, draws conclusions, and generally struggles with psychic conflict.

Further, object attachment is sustained within the transitional world of *Villette* despite the loss of the desired father figure. Since Charlotte Brontë's major male character dies in *Villette,* the author seems to be making a statement about her own capacities for internalization. A possible interpretation is that the literal survival of the object is unnecessary for a woman's primary self-development. Instead, the capacity to internalize a female-male object attachment at the depressive-position level of whole object attachments determines such development. The resulting internalization—based on the primary experience of love, not on idealization or mirroring from a part object—makes ongoing self-integration, developmental mourning, and self-individuation possible. This mutuality is the key ingredient needed to permit mourning, object internalization, and self-individuation, even though such mutuality is facilitated by these processes as well.

Charlotte Brontë's "use" of her father, in Winnicott's sense of the use of the transitional object ([1969] 1974), seems related to her ability to oppose him and consequently to risk losing him. She maintains his survival within her internal world through a continuing capacity for internalization that had already been developmentally established at an earlier level. This integrative mode of internalization is distinguished from incorporation of an object so that it remains a split off part-object.

In *Villette,* Paulina represents the author's unconscious fears that she could lose her ability to internalize her father and therefore not become free or separate from him. By creating Paulina, Brontë faces this fear and its related depressive fantasies concerning her father. In encountering the intimidated part of herself, the author of *Villette* uses the creative process for psychic encounter rather than for reenactment or cathartic exorcism.

With the words "Nature and I opposed him!" Lucy Snowe separates herself from Graham just as Charlotte separates herself from her father in her actual interpersonal relations.

I hypothesize that Charlotte Brontë experienced successful differentiation from her mother during the preoedipal phases of development. This is confirmed by the psychic development of the creative process, with its capacity for repression as well as for insight. Brontë demonstrates a dynamic intrapsychic life, which would have required her early mother to be adequately "used" for differentiation and self-integration. Because of such primary internalization on Brontë's part, her oedipal-stage father could also be used for differentiating and integrating the self functions, while simultaneously serving as the subject of erotic desire—if her actual father was indeed too narcissistic to be adequate for such psychological use. In the person of the real professor whom she encountered in Brussels, she was able to find a substitute father figure who was more capable of empathy and of being affected and transformed by her engagement.[25] Despite later disappointment, she did not devalue M. Paul through a split view of the object, as the preoedipally arrested women writers I discuss repeatedly did. Instead, her earlier internalization of the good enough object, derived from the preoedipal stage with her mother, enabled her to retain the positive experience with her substitute father and to recreate and elaborate it through her creative work. Having internalized a separate embodied mother, she could be touched by the good aspects of a father figure—even if he was a substitute for her original father. Consequently, Brontë's image of her father appears to have survived disappointment.

It appears that for Charlotte Brontë, the creative process is distinctly tied to the father in its motivational roots, that is, in terms of instinctual object desire for the father derived from its oedipal-stage origins.[26] Brontë psychologically used a father figure more adequate than her actual father. She also used the creative process for varying developmental aspects of self-formation. Identification, integration, differentiation, and an overall internalization process of psychic object assimilation can all proceed through an intense engagement with the creative process. Additionally, Brontë merged with the creative process as she fused with her female heroine Lucy Snowe. Yet between merger with the process and separation from it, the author had to use her creative work to mourn for the grief of individuation. Only then could she escape the internal demonic father of her phallocentric addiction. Moreover, to transcend this phallocentric demon lover complex through mourning involves a capacity to tolerate disillusionment in relation to the father object. This allows reparation of the object, as accomplished by Charlotte Brontë in relation to her father through her use of the professor.

We can conclude that for this reparation to be possible, Brontë must have been able to internalize the functions of the preoedipal maternal holding environment, as described by D. W. Winnicott (containing, mirroring, soothing, nurturing, and so forth). The maternal holding environment is internalized particularly during the symbiotic era. Yet to be able both to separate from and to merge with her father, Brontë must have also been able to internalize the transitional-stage[27] or rapprochement-stage[28] mothering functions. In other words, she must have internalized an embodied respondent or a "mother of separation." The paranoid-schizoid women writers, with whom Brontë is contrasted, may to some extent have internalized the "symbiotic holding mother." They apparently failed to internalize an adequate mother of separation. This would be a mother who could provide refueling throughout the practicing stage and sharing interaction during rapprochement and who could relate to their own separate subjectivities.[29] The biographers of these women believe that the mothers in question were not psychically developed enough in themselves to relate in the manner appropriate to the "other's" needs during these stages.[30]

Since Charlotte Brontë apparently enjoyed adequate transitional-stage mothering, she could internalize a differentiated father figure at the oedipal stage and could then generally construct differentiated characters within her creative work. She could create vivid interpersonal contact and dialogue between her characters, which involved authentic affect. Such veracity in describing the affect life in itself is an indication that Brontë was not split off from her internal self. Her inner life, although suppressed or repressed by neurotic strictures, was ultimately available to her in a very personal way through her introspective mode of writing.

Another contrast with preoedipally women arrested writers is that Charlotte Brontë's alter-ego female characters are not perpetually persecuted by a demonic male, although they encounter good and bad males. This balance demonstrates a higher level of splitting, a neurotic level that surpasses the more archaic level of profound idealization-devaluation or villainization. Even Charlotte Brontë's negative male characters possess the traits of assimilated objects. For the most part, her male characters are not intrusive, split-off persecutors. They do not have to be perpetually ingested and then vomited up through cathartic extrusion or exorcism.

We can view Charlotte Brontë's internal world through her creative output. That world reveals a softening of persecutory assault within the narrative progression of each novel, as well as from one novel to the next. Because of a sense of agency and a capacity to tolerate depressive affect, Brontë does not remain fixated in a state of persecution that promotes compulsion. Her alter-ego heroines do not need to cling addictively to an archaically idealized object for protection or for compensatory and defensive functions. Also, to the extent that Brontë does show a phallocentric addiction to Héger, who so preoccupied her life and work, it is manifested at an oedipal level, where the father is differentiated, and is not craved as an extension of the author's self. Brontë's adoration of heroic male figures, such as the Duke of Wellington, is normal adolescent idealization, not the archaic idealization apparent with paranoid-schizoid fixated women writers or those with preoedipal arrests. Her idealization has the character of adolescent infatuation, perhaps made acute by her father's detachment from her (as Peters 1986 comments). In such a case, addictive phallocentric yearnings are particularly malleable.

## Summarizing Conclusion on Charlotte Brontë

Charlotte Brontë employs the creative process as something transitional to the extent that she can both "marry" and separate from a paternal figure within her novel and move on from both her father and from the creative mode of encounter to an interpersonal marriage in the "external" world. This progression does not imply that her creativity is regressive or that she would not wish to create again. It means only that she has used it as a vehicle toward more mature interpersonal relations. In fact, during the year of marriage that Brontë sustained prior to her untimely death, she contemplated writing another novel (as reported by Peters 1986). She clearly wanted to create; perhaps these abilities were even freed of the compulsion that dominated when she had no intimate relationship in her life. Following her journey of developmental growth in *Villette* and her marriage, she may have felt an even greater motivation to write. The compulsive need to create, formerly based on an unresolved and phallocentric addiction to the father, had been resolved through her creative work. Charlotte Brontë's compulsion—to the extent that it was a compulsion—was on the level of neurotic dynamics, not of a reenacted pathological mourning state apparent in the work of preoedipally arrested women. Brontë therefore showed a capacity to use the creative process to mourn and to separate from a father fixation with its derivative symptoms of love addiction. Although she needed the empathic touch of a real man (Héger), she transformed herself though an encounter with the male character that she herself created, without any external supportive relationship to provide a holding environment or external transitional-stage maternal functions.

Brontë's ability to integrate her father figure provides more evidence of her openness to the developmental process within her internal world. Her integrative capacities reflect a primary self-structure that is open to object relations contact. This self-structure is not sealed off behind a schizoid barrier. Brontë's work reveals a primary differentiation and integration of self that allow her to integrate herself and her male other—in the forms of Lucy and Professor Emanuel—in an interdependent relation to one another, reflecting depressive-position whole object relations. Self and object internalizations have obviously shaped internal objects into assimilated introject forms that serve as imprints for ongoing levels of developmental integration.

Charlotte Brontë's ongoing growth in observing-ego reflection goes hand in hand with the development of subjectivity and agency and the capacity for mutuality and interaction. Her creative evolution can be seen in terms of integrative internalization and in the enduring suffering of mournful awareness of self and of other. Engagement with the creative process allowed unconscious split-off parts of the internal world to become conscious members of the subjective self and its object world.

# 9

# Emily Brontë I: The Messenger of Hope and the Demon in the Nightwind

Emily Brontë was born in 1818 and died in 1848. Despite her short life, she produced a large collection of poems under the title of the "Gondal" dramas, which she and her younger sister, Anne, constructed together. She wrote various other poems, including "The Prisoner," which was written close to her death. *Wuthering Heights* was her sole novel and was written with the intention of publication. A posthumous collection of her poems was published in 1850 by her sister Charlotte. Although Emily resisted publishing her poems during her lifetime, she resigned herself to the publication of a book in 1846 that contained a combination of her poems along with those of her sisters Anne and Charlotte. Emily also wrote seven essays, called "French Devoirs," during her stay with Charlotte in 1843 at the Brussels school where the two sisters went to learn composition and language in the hopes of opening their own school for children. Following this, the poet returned home because of her aunt's death and chose to remain there, ultimately withdrawing into seclusion.

Reluctantly, Emily Brontë had taken a job in her earlier adulthood owing to financial necessity. As a governess-teacher, she stayed at Law Hill for only six months, beginning in 1837 and extending into 1838 (Gerin, 80–84). *Wuthering Heights* is a crystallization of the landscape and mythic atmosphere that she imbibed there. It was at Law Hill that she was first emotionally transported by her muse, which she experienced as an external masculine power. Brontë's biographer Gerin writes that it was "as of a real presence breaking in upon her bondage and challenging her to surrender to its liberating power" (1971, 86). From that point, Brontë's source of creative and literary inspiration was to come from outside.

To picture Emily Brontë is to picture a being turned inward—away from the world—and toward the internal imaginings and sufferings that brought her close to nature and to the sibling symbiosis of her childhood. Yet she can be seen clinging to her internal objects of suffering: "Torments and madness, tears and sin!" (no. 149; poetry, quotations are from *The Complete Poems of Emily Jane*

*Brontë* [1941]). Fixed in this rigid pose, mourning never comes, although the writer is frozen in the pose of a mourner, and her poetry has frequent funereal episodes. Instead of the movement of depressive-position mourning, there is confusion of gender identity, of self- and object-directed wishes, and of erotic and aggressive desires. Characteristic of the paranoid-schizoid-position split, masculine internal objects cannot be integrated and the idealized muse always exists in counterpoint to the malignant form of the demon lover.

When her mother first became ill, Emily was probably only around one and a half. Thus, she may have lost her mother during the critical separation-individuation phases, suffering an abandonment trauma that was never healed and developing a symbiotic cocoon fantasy that kept Emily imprisoned behind a self-protective wall, continually yearning for a return to a happier era of symbiosis.

The biographer Gerin repeatedly informs us of Emily's yearnings for merger with her male muse, which was experienced as a "visionary spirit" and as a "messenger of hope." In her nineteenth year, when she was in residence as a governess at Law Hill, the poet had her first mystic experiences while communing with nature as she had always loved to do. In the following years, her visionary spirit visited her more often and inspired her creativity. As a young girl she had written poetic dramas in her Gondal notebooks based on the epic themes and Byronic tales of her day; however, when her male muse took possession of her, her level of poetic awareness intensified, and her poetry took on a much more personal coloring. At the height of her spiritual communions with her muse, she became intensely prolific (1846). She wrote a credo that declared the life within her to be an invulnerable poetic force with which she was impregnated through her soul-merger with the "eternal heart" of the universe (Gerin 1971, 246). The life within was sharply divided from the one without, and she sought to shield the former from exposure. Coming from her internal world, her poetry was sacred; she felt traumatically violated when her sister Charlotte convinced her to allow publication of it. However, the novel at the time of her greatest creative productivity, *Wuthering Heights,* was a dramatic tale meant for publication. It was less directly revealing of her intrapsychic marriage with her male muse than the poetic recall of the visits of her "God of Visions." Nevertheless, it was in her novel that the split-off demonic part of her male muse was most developed.

At the climax of her faith in her masculine spirit, the poet saw death as the fulfillment of all her desires. Death was imagined as the ultimate road to marriage with her masculine idol. However, shortly thereafter her idol deserted her and her creativity dried up. By 1848, her vision of death as the ultimate form of transcendence had turned toward paranoia and doubt. The traditional views of heaven did not console her. Without the creative inspiration of her male muse, she looked toward death as the only way out of the imprisonment she now felt in her body and in her whole earthly existence. Her last years (ending in 1848) were ones of disillusionment and creative blocks. Formerly she had what she hoped would lift her out of an isolated body barricaded against emotional contact with other humans through a mystical fusion with her masculine muse-god. That hope became a source of disillusionment as her body decayed and emotional isolation took its toll.

Within Emily Brontë's poetry, we can see how any poetic and spiritual sense of transcendence could not be sustained. The literary critic Margaret Homans (1980) remarks that the poet settled for possession when she could not attain transcendence. Emily Brontë's male muse possessed her, which suggests an early failing in psychic individuation. Instead of the projection of a differentiated male part of her that she could merge with in transcendence, she was stuck in a more primitive projective identification cycle, that which she projected out remained an undifferentiated part of her. The sense of possession rather than transcendence seems to come from this. The poet, therefore, could never own her male muse's power as male poets were apt to own the power of their female muses. Possession was followed by desertion. Perhaps these were the cyclical reverberations of early mother loss so typical of borderline trauma. Was Emily's experience with her muse a reliving of the preoedipal-era abandonment in an unconscious reenactment? Although her biographer simply states that "her god of visions ceased to come" (Gerin 1971, 246), Emily had an expectation of her fate. Gerin leaves us with an emphatic conclusion that leads into my literary analysis of Brontë's psyche: "The tragedy of Emily Brontë, as her last years show, did not lie in an early death or literary failure; but in the loss of her 'God of Visions,' in the departure of her 'radiant angel' when she most needed him" (166). Perhaps Emily Brontë's fearful anticipation of a fateful desertion by her male muse-god was based on the unconscious blueprint from the critical separation-individuation developmental era. The aggressive aspect of her involvement with her muse reflects the demonic form that her muse ultimately took. Brontë thus reveals herself as one of many women writers enmeshed in a demon lover literary theme, a theme which reflects its psychodynamic origins.

## The Male Muse and the Demon Lover

At first the voice of imagination is a kind voice, not yet defined as a masculine one. In "To Imagination" (composed on September 3, 1844), Brontë writes:

> When weary with the long day's care
> And earthly change from pain to pain,
> And lost and ready to despair,
> Thy kind voice calls me back again—

O my true friend, I am not lone
While thou canst speak with such a tone!

So hopeless is the world without,
The world within I doubly prize;
Thy world where guile and hate and doubt
And cold suspicion never rise;
Where thou and I and Liberty
Have Undisputed sovereignty.

(no. 174)

Although the voice is seen as a relief from the ugly real world of truth and fact, which crushes the flowers of "fancy," it is also distrusted as its phantom aspect is contemplated. The poet's perception reveals a false split between the external and internal worlds. She is lured by a figure derived from her internal world as she writes: "I trust not to your phantom bliss." Hints of the demonic aspect of the voice are then first cited. Yet quickly the poet returns to her only hope of salvation from her life-in-death real world, by claiming it to be a benign power once more:

Yet still in evening's quiet hour
With never-failing thankfulness
I welcome thee, benignant power,
Sure solace of human cares
And brighter hope when hope despairs.

(no. 174)

Following the distrust in the phantom spirit of imagination shown in poem no. 174, Emily Brontë writes in another vein (October 14, 1844):

No, radiant angel, speak and say
Why I did cast the world away;
Why I have persevered to shun
The common paths that others run;
And on a strange road journeyed on
Heedless alike of wealth and power.

(no. 176)

The poet experiences guilt and perhaps fear as she sees herself betraying the way of the world—the world of interpersonal relations—for the worship of her private masculine kind:

So with a ready heart swore
To seek their altar stone no more,
And gave my spirit to adore
Thee, ever present, phantom thing—
My slave, my comrade, and my King!

The royal king now changes form once more, becoming the muse-god:

And am I wrong to worship where
Faith cannot doubt nor Hope despair
Since my own soul can grant my prayer?
Speak, God of Visions, plead for me
And tell why I have chosen thee!

In her essay on Brontë, Margaret Homans writes: "There is no apparent reason for inflating this figure into a king, since at the same time she so overtly makes it a part of herself and easily governable. Her insistence on intimacy must be concealing some unexplained alienation, of which the terror 'king' is the trace" (1980, 114).

We are put in mind of Emily Dickinson's inner king, to be discussed, who rises up as a benevolent internal object in her dreams and empowers the poet with a creative strength, only to become a demonic god who taunts, defeats, and leaves her. Emily Brontë's king remains even more alien. He does not endow her with creative power. When addressed as "thee" or "thou," her muse grows more externalized until it is the restless "God of Visions" with which she wrestles for control of the poetic imaginative power, wrestling also for the word that defines her as having a poetic voice. The loss of her voice becomes a theme, since she cannot internalize the power of this muse now called the "God of Visions."

According to Homans

Many of her poems dwell on the masculine figures of alien power, elevating them from the status of agency to that of the major subject. This arrest itself suggests that she is not confident of having obtained the visitant's support, and the content of these poems is a continuous effort to wrest the visitant's power away from them and make it her own. It is not inherent in the concept of the masculine muse that he should take and keep more power than does the traditionally feminine muse, but in Brontë's poems he does. . . . The poet defends herself from the danger of becoming a feminine object by aligning her poetic self with the stage in feminine development in which the mother is rejected in favor of a turn toward masculine objects, but that turn cannot become an identity.

(105–7)

The turn to father results in the attempt to use the male as a masculine self-extension. This seems to be a masculine substitute for a poorly consolidated female identity. The author is left with a part object incorporation (a split off or "orbital" object) rather than an integrated internalization, and the incorporation takes demonic hold. We are presented with the literary myth of masculine possession. In reference to this myth, Homans notes the Gothic and Byronic male figures who inhabit Emily Brontë's world in her Gondal poetry. The female victims and the tantalizing male demons seem possessed by passions that they do not control (109). Homans addresses a deficit in the poet's own sense of agency, which she reveals in the expression of her inner world through her creative work. The poet's primary feminine self lacks agency and thus seeks a masculine compensation.

As Emily Brontë turns from poems about her fictive land of Gondal to ones about her own mind, she retains the myth of possession. There is no dialogue of mutuality or flight into transcendence. The masculine muse can only possess (see Homans). When the poet tries to own the male muse's power, it vanishes. Homans writes:

> In assuming the powers of the figure she once pleadingly invoked and worshipped, she finds that its powers vanish. Its powers resided in its defiance and in her desire. . . . As before, she does not conceive of a poetic power that would be both her own and powerful.
>
> (111–12)

The poet seeks to heal a split between the external world, which she experiences as "sad reality," "truth," and things "hopeless" (113), and the internal world, which she condemns as "escapist" (113), through imaginative power in the creative moment. However, she fails, for she has only the imaginative power of the creative moment as it is again externalized and associated with sources of power in the "real worlds"—implicitly real worlds that house males and masculine forms. According to Homans, "she increases the pools of her imagination by associating it with 'real worlds,' but the cost of that gain in power is the voice returning to a source outside the self" (113). The poet cannot sustain inner experience. The consequence is that a developmental internalization and integration process is continually disrupted by the externalization of the inner power in an intrusive form. Later, in *Wuthering Heights,* the poet uses the character of Heathcliff to personify this externalized force.

The voice of the muse returns to an alien, masculine source. The external world is perceived as alien and masculine, while the internal world is seen as a resource of imagination devoid of reality. This false split of inner and outer worlds follows the line of a primary schizoid self-split. Both imagination and reality elude internalization by this splitting dichotomy.

As the poet moves from a voice of imagination to an external "God of Visions," the myth of possession takes hold. In other words, she wins the power of the perfect or idealized object—"I'm perfect because I'm part of you"—only by submitting to him. She submits to an externalized and masculinized vision of the idealized self, submitting to a king, and seeking to have the king as a slave. She is possessing only by being possessed. She settles for submission and ultimately for a renewed imprisonment because she cannot truly surrender (her self is too undifferentiated and insecure).

Why does Emily Brontë submit to a male force that she perceives and creates as all-powerful? Homans points out the sociological and feminist perspective in terms of the ownership of language by the Victorian male, which forces female poets to submit to male power as a means of attaining the power of language. My own view, however, considers how the psychological dynamics of female submission can be seen in terms of Emily Brontë's developmental object relations.

Brontë's poetry expresses a premature turn toward her father. Presumably, this premature turn came about because of her mother's death during the separation—individuation phase of her development. It is clear that she turned toward him prior to an adequate separation from her mother, with the result that self-differentiation and integration were severely compromised. This female poet's submission to male power can then be seen as preoedipal mother worship combined with longings to be both nurtured and erotically stimulated by the fantasied paternal rescuer. In the case of preoedipal psychic arrest, this male rescuer is also needed to complete the sense of self. The premature turn toward the father provides a masculine compensation, which is imprisoning when the basic feminine self has not been formed. The muse is the preoedipal mother-father who still appears as godlike on account of the early level of fantasy involved. Merger with the muse is sought not only because the poet believes that the muse owns language and its creative power of inspiration but also because a compensatory masculine identity is sought, and erotic desires toward the father intensify the cravings behind the psychic need for identity. Yet when a compensatory masculine identity is sought, it must be a false and grandiose identity that lacks grounding in a primary integrated self. This leads to the bravado of the masculine figures in Emily Brontë's work and to their lack of affective sensitivity or empathy. When the woman does not become a man, the woman becomes a submissive victim to the false grandiose self, personified in the images of male antiheroes, male villains, and male victimizers.

It is within these object relations dynamics that we can see how Emily Brontë distrusts her own power over language (Homans, 115). Language is seen as an alien power from a masculine realm, as "the Word" was considered the property of a masculine God in religious texts. Since Brontë possesses the "God of Visions," he is devalued from "mine idol" to "sweet thing" (115). The power of language is also lost, since the male muse's power over language is based on his alien masculine "otherness," reflecting the general nineteenth-century prejudice that competent authors are necessarily masculine. Homans writes: "Mastering and containing the power undoes it, and yet to see it again as external threatens the poet's existence as a poet." (115)

Emily Brontë loses the power of language as well as the imaginative voice. The poet seems to be saying that there is no mutuality of poet and muse in her vision, just as there was no reciprocity in the male-female relationships in the world which she inhabited. The choices are submission or dominance. If the woman chooses dominance, she loses the power of self-expression that is considered a masculine gift to her. Yet if she chooses submission, she must secretly withhold herself (both in terms of sex and language) to prevent surrender, since surrender implies self-loss when the surrender is to a patriarchal, masculine god. Also, one cannot surrender without a differentiated and integrated self.

Another poem (from outside the Gondal collection) that highlights the conflictual wishes and fears in relation to the male muse—(166)—The poem "Julian M. and A. G. Rochelle" opens with the line "Silent is the House—all are laid asleep" (no. 190). Dated October 9, 1845, it was written at a later period than the poems discussed above. This poem again shows masculine possession as the only alternative to total imprisonment in the male dungeon of the "real" external world. The antihero in this poem is "Julian," who is full of self-aggrandizement and self-flattery. His character resembles that of Emily's brother Brandwell, another male to whom she turned when her mother died.

Emily depicts the passive position of the female as proclaimed throughout. At first the heroine, Rochelle, waits chained in Julian's dungeon, which is both safe from the cold blizzard outside the jail door and separated from the dreamed-of liberty lying beyond. Ironically, the security of the female is at its height. Rochelle is walled and chained inside a prison, which is owned by a male who is supposedly her former childhood friend. Julian seems to have carelessly deposited her there many years ago, for some unknown reason that he has apparently forgotten. Meanwhile, Rochelle rots in prison and suffers the agonizing tyranny of her iron chains. Her only escape from physical and mental torment comes after dark, when her imagination transcends her psychophysical state, and she is both haunted and tantalized by a vision of the "messenger of hope." Rochelle is haunted because the "messenger of hope" threatens to bring death. Yet she yearns for death, praying that some transcendent world lies beyond it. She looks toward this masculine force for liberty, passionately proclaiming that "visions rise and change which kill me with desire" (line 72). Nature is used to invoke the Gothic forms that usher in the masculine spirit, which she hopes will be both a transcendent muse and a messenger that can bring the promise of a liberating death:

> He comes with western winds, with evening's wandering airs,
> With that clear dusk of heaven that brings the thickest stars;
> Winds take a pensive tone, and stars a tender fire.
> And visions rise and change which kill me with desire.

The moment of visionary revelation seems analogous to the moment of possession by the phantom imagination or God of Visions described in Brontë's other poems:

> Then dawns the Invisible, the Unseen its truth reveals;
> My outward sense is gone, my inward essence feels—
> Its wings are almost free, its home, its harbour found;
> Measuring the gulf, it stoops and dares the final bound!

The poet informs us here of the loss of physical boundaries that accompanies the creative moment, when subject and object become one: "my inward essence feels." We hear echoed the transcendental view of Emerson, who in his essay "Nature" describes bypassing the ego and becoming a "transparent eyeball" (Bradley et al. 1900, 1005) or of Wordsworth who speaks of how "Our souls have sight of that immortal sea, which brought us hither" (Abrams et al. 1962, ●●●). Brontë, however, exhibits an element of doubt that expands to despair. As Homans comments, the transcendental moment of creative power is easily overcast with a threat of death. This is true since creative power for Brontë comes from a projection of the masculine object, and this male object is reduced to a grandiose self for the female who lacks an essential feminine and preoedipal identity. Masculine possession, combined with dissolution of the female self, threatens as the female poet-heroine merges with the masculine god. A few stanzas later, Brontë declares that the messenger of hope's liberty comes at the price of a quick and agonizing death. In this dynamic constellation, the female voice, or the female self, must die. Thus, as we move into the next part of the poem, the tantalizing "God of Visions" becomes the arrogant male Julian, whose self-bravado silences all female expression. The voice of Rochelle is silenced; the female subject becomes a mute victim, paying the price of male rescue as compensation for an arrested self.

In the first part of the poem, there is an amorphous figure called the "Wanderer." As Homans points out (120), the wanderer is a visionary being, who—like the messenger of hope—promises to bring creative inspiration to the poet. However, he may bring the threat of death as well as the visionary power of creative imagination, for this power comes from without, and the merger that is required to attain it can annihilate the female poetic self, particularly when all female expression depends on the lack of differentiation of the external masculine form. Homans notes that the "Wanderer comes through a waste of winter snow" (120), which could symbolize regions of death similar to the regions from which the messenger of hope is experienced as coming from. These regions of death are an ominous sign of the ultimate extinction of a female form through the annihilation of female voice.

The visionary spirits of this poem are analogous to the male muses in Emily Brontë's other poems, in which she struggles with the tantalizing power as well as the agonizing fear of her own imagination (see Homans, 122). As with most preoedipal characters, Brontë suffers from terror of her own unconscious, which is projected and projectively identified with. Since the poet's creative power always comes from without and ultimately from a masculine form, the inchoate spirit of the Wanderer is transformed into the male form of Julian. Her power of speech comes at the mercy of this ambiguous but ultimately masculine wanderer. The masculine figure's external control over her language makes it an alien control that is subject to withdrawal. This is what makes the wanderer as well as the messenger of hope simultaneously so tantalizing and threatening.[1] The extinction of the poetic voice is death to the female poet; merger with the male muse continually threatens her with this fate. Yet the merger is still craved, for inspiration from without beckons and the poet has not been able to sustain a sense of imagination, which would require a fluid dialectic between the external and internal worlds (see Ogden 1986). The creative moment thus has the same Janus-faced nature as the moment of sexual orgasm (see Stolorow and Lachmann 1980, 42). To the degree that self-differentiation and integration are not securely defined, to the degree that a dialectic cannot be maintained between self and other, the yielding to the other threatens self-extinction. Rather than surrender, we find the terror of submission to self nihilation. Brontë's difficulty as a female poet who always feels the victim of the externalized muse's subjugating power reflects her own preoedipal-character problem in interacting with the narcissism of her father, in particular of her incorporated father. Brontë may very well also be influenced by her sociological position as a Victorian female in a world dominated by men. Within the internal world of the preoedipally arrested female, however, the domineering male becomes the omnipotent, grandiose self-structure that obstructs feeling and feminine imagination while simultaneously promising empowerment. Within Emily Brontë's literature, we see a female artist's identification with a narcissistic father following the traumatizing loss of her mother. The defensive grandiose self, used to protect against the conscious experiencing of this trauma, must consequently appear to us in masculine dimensions.

As the poem continues, the interpersonal dynamics between Rochelle and Lord

Julian depict the external form of the internal conflict of the poet herself, as her preoedipal self reacts to her incorporation of the male part object. The theme of masculine possession unfolds, even as Rochelle is released from the male's literal prison. Although Julian liberates Rochelle from his concrete dungeon, he annihilates her identity by defining all that happens to her (see Homans, 119–20). Rochelle's eloquent speech is never heard again following her description of her nightly awakenings, when the "messenger of hope" comes to her with visions of imaginary rewards for torments that can bring quick death. Early in the poem, Rochelle's initial scorn for Julian had turned to poetic eloquence, as she imagines rescue coming from her approaching God of Visions. Her wish for rescue appears as a wish to transcend herself, but when thoughts of transcendence turn to thoughts of death, the female subject ceases her eloquence—and in fact ceases all speech. This is noted distinctly in the text of the poem:

> "And robed in fires of Hell, or bright with heavenly shine,
> If it but herald Death, the vision is divine."

> She ceased to speak, and, unanswering, watched her there,
>
> poem 190

The next fifteen stanzas of the poem are all Julian's. When he sees that Rochelle is near death, he immediately thinks of liberating her. Yet before releasing her he hesitates, fearing that his instant love for her will not be returned. If he releases Rochelle, she will no longer be his subject. She may even reject him. Homans has noted that such self-serving reflection is "appalling in a dramatic hero" (117); this may relate to why Emily Brontë's romantic heroes have been labeled antiheroes. Antiheroes could easily have been derived from elements of the father's and brother's narcissistic character structures.

Julian dismisses his own thoughts as "selfish love" and releases Rochelle. Rochelle is then seen to stay with Julian because she is a "wounded dove" (Homans, 119) and not because she reciprocates his desire or feels love for him. However, as Julian then narrates his own tale, he flamboyantly assumes that Rochelle must love him. Apparently propelled by his own solipsistic vision, Julian neglects state affairs and soldiering in war to care for his chosen woman. We never hear from Rochelle herself again. Life with Julian is mute, as she sinks into a passively reactive form to meet his image of her. She is now seen completely through the male's image of her, as revealed through his speech. Rochelle is now immured in a prison even more profoundly than before, as she is compelled passively to exist in terms of the male rescuer's image of her.[2] Homans writes:

> Feminine figures rely on masculine figures for their speech, and the poet herself defers first to the Wanderer and then to Julian as his chosen speaker. The poet

has no rebuttal for Julian's deceptively cheerful interpretation of the final state of events. The poem never returns to her, as if she had set in motion a self-sufficient machine.

(122)

The "self-sufficient machine" to which Homans refers might be analogous to the compulsive reenactment of Emily Brontë's closed schizoid system, in which early relations with her internal father-mother are continually reenacted following the early loss of her actual mother.

In the end, Julian claims that his devotion won Rochelle's love, but surely there is room for doubt, since his summary declaration comes at the end of a list of self-praising proclamations. The narcissistic aspect of Brontë's muse and of her internal-male father-brother may be seen here. Rochelle never gives voice to her own love. Julian ends the poem;

> It needed braver nerve to face the world's disdain
> And by the patient strength that could that world defy,
> By suffering, with calm mind, contempt and calumny;
> By never-doubting love, unswerving constancy,
> Rochelle, I earned at last an equal love from thee!

## The Night Wind

Emily was most free to pursue her writing at night. Frank (1990) describes the exhilaration that would overtake the poet as the evening hours came. She became inebriated with the vast night world where she could be alone with nature. Nature itself then became part and parcel of her spiritual quest, a quest of escape from the outer world of interpersonal relations, a world oppressive to those split in such a way that outside contacts takes them away from their inner selves. As darkness and nature enclosed her in an imagined haven, that which unconsciously might be experienced as a cocoon of safety (Modell, 1976), she felt the titillating arousal of her male muse through the "night-wind".

In this poem, male muses and captors are seen in an altered but analogous form when nature becomes an alluring and deceptive spirit. In a poem about the night wind (no. 140 (A7) [1840]), a demon lover theme emerges in fuller form and foreshadows the development of Heathcliff:

> But still it whispered lowly,
> "How dark the woods will be!

The thick leaves in my murmur
Are rustling like a dream,
And all their myriad voices
Instinct with spirit seem."

(140)

Homans (124–25) writes of the night wind's fatally seductive charm. The night wind seduces the maiden and poet into regions of erotic darkness that promise death, not transcendence. As with Plath, Dickinson, and Sexton (see Kavaler 1986, 1988, 1989), the demon lover becomes death itself. The preoedipally arrested female cannot contain the instinctual desires for the muse. She is too disconnected from her body. Her desires become split off parts of the other, intruding upon her, and ultimately extinguishing her. The suicides (whether active or passive) of these women can be seen as the part of them that is projectively-identified with the demon lover taking the life of the other part (the female child self.)

The night wind, or demon lover, claims an inexorable power that belies his apparent gentleness:

The wanderer would not leave me;
Its kiss grew warmer still—
"O come," it sighed so sweetly,
"I'll win thee 'gainst thy will.

(#140)

The speaker resists all of these efforts because she understands what they mean. Unconsciously, the poet knows that the night wind's seductions, just like those of the male muse and of the male mortal Julian, must end in possession, not in transcendence and self-enhancement. The female's inability to internalize the male power is a direct consequence of her own lack of self-agency, a primary aspect of developmental arrest.[3] The result is either death-in-life or actual death. The poem's ending is like that of another poem, "Aye, There It Is," (#148, *Complete Poems*) with an "explicit image of death" (Homans, 125):

"And when thy heart is laid at rest
Beneath the church-yard stone
I shall have time enough to mourn
And thou to be alone."

#140

Instead of ecstatic merger, the poet experiences possession or death. The yearned-for symbiotic other half does not exist. The narcissistically omnipotent male spirit on whom she focuses these yearnings is experienced, repeatedly, as a seducer and betrayer. As an arrested female turning toward a narcissistic father or brother, Emily Brontë can never imagine herself receiving a facilitative attunement from another, but rather becomes subject to a coercive domination. Her phantom's promises of an ecstatic loss of self result only in a voidlike, life-in-death loss of self. Internally, the demonic male can be seen as the rigid schizoid barrier itself, with its grandiose overtones of manic control.

# 10

# Emily Brontë II: *Wuthering Heights* and the Demon Lover

The basic psychodynamics of the demon lover theme, as they are manifested in Emily Brontë's poetry, also appear in her only novel, *Wuthering Heights*. Since this theme can be seen both as a symbol of the author's psychopathology, and as a metaphor for her developmental strivings, it is worth considering how this theme carries through from the poetry to the novel. In addition, the novel reflects the reparative strivings and limitations of the creative process as it is used by someone of Brontë's constitution.

The story line of *Wuthering Heights* reflects a particularly violent demon lover theme. It is a theme in which Heathcliff appears as an archetypal muse-demon, or demon lover. Emily Brontë's own split off aggression can be seen to manifest itself in the character of Heathcliff. Her vulnerable child self, which can be seen as an arrested ego, manifests as the female victim, Catherine.

If Heathcliff and Catherine are seen as two parts of the author, Emily Brontë, it can also be seen that the preoedipal years of the author's history are quite probably reenacted in her novel. I propose that Emily Brontë experienced an early good mother during her infancy, which is recaptured in the symbiosis of Heathcliff and Catherine when they were children. (The author's childhood symbiosis with her brother Branwell can also be represented here). The disruption of this proposed maternal symbiosis, without any adequate separation-individuation era transition, due to the mother's death, can also be witnessed in the proposed reenactment in Emily Brontë's novel. We can see the toddler child part of the author raging against its severance from the mother part of the author, each part of her psyche frantically craving reunion, as Heathcliff frantically craves reunion with a psychically possessed Catherine. Although Heathcliff can be seen as the demonic form associated with an abandoning mother, he is also the child victim. When, towards the end of the novel, Catherine threatens to leave him through death, he cries, "You loved me—then what right have you to leave me?" (*Wuthering Heights*, 197). Catherine too, is both child victim and anguished mother who rages against her fate, wishing to escape into death to extinguish her pain, and yet tantalized by the connection with her childhood self extension or adopted brother, who is experienced in moments of longing, and of forced separation, as her other half. Catherine feels the arousal of all her body felt passions in relation to that connection as we can see in the following scene. The narrator, Nelly Dean, who is modeled upon the Brontës' nanny and servant, Tabby, sees the effects of physical arousal in its degenerative stages of agitation. She quotes Catherine as follows:

> "I shall not be at peace," moaned Catherine, recalled to a sense of physical weakness by the violent, unequal throbbing of her heart, which beat visibly, and audibly, under this excess of agitation.
>
> (196)

At the crescendo of the novel, when the push-pull dynamics of a traumatic and tortuous separation culminate in a scene between Catherine and Heathcliff, Heathcliff's voice ultimately extinguishes that of Catherine, just as Julian's formerly extinguished Rochelle's in "Rochelle and Julian," the poem beginning with "Silent is the House. . ." After the agitation described by Nelly Dean, Catherine faints. As Catherine's voice is extinguished in this manner, as she lays unconscious after fainting, Heathcliff's voice rises to its most eloquent and articulate pitch:

> You teach me now how cruel you've been—cruel and false. Why did you despise me? Why did you betray your own heart, Cathy? I have not one word of comfort—you deserve this—You have killed yourself. Yes, you may kiss me, and cry; and wring out my kisses and tears. They'll blight you—they'll damn you. You loved me—then what right have you to leave me?"
>
> (204)

Following this, Catherine remains in a comatose state as she gives premature birth to Linton's child, and then dies.

Prior to this, Catherine has proclaimed Heathcliff to be another half, a self extension of herself:

> "Nelly, I am Heathcliff—he's always, always in my mind—not as a pleasure, any more than I am always a pleasure to myself—but as my own being."
>
> (22)

Yet, Heathcliff seems more like a masculinized container for Catherine's (Emily's) split off oral aggression and oral lust and passion than for her soul. He is described as "foaming at the mouth" and "gnashing his teeth" (197) in his lust for her, which appears to highlight the oral incorporative level of his author's own frustrated cravings. Catherine's soul is attached to Heathcliff because he contains the elements of life in a human body that she herself cannot contain in her body, although these elements erupt from him rather than flow forth, thus implying his own lack of psychic and body integration. When Catherine leaves Heathcliff during adolescence to be courted by the aristocratic patriarch, Edgar Linton, she disrupts a symbiotic merger between herself and Heathcliff that poisons Heathcliff, leaving him without a heart. He must return to Catherine to seek his heart again! Without his heart he has become a demon, a former muse turned sadist, through calculated motions of seduction and abandonment. It is the demon within him that not only bankrupts and destroys Catherine's brother, but which also seduces, impregnates and then shuns Isabella (his wife of one night of marriage). He also clings so vehemently to Catherine that he physically and emotionally dominates her to the point where her voice, and ultimately, her life are extinguished. Yet, he is driven to the state of being a demon through his intolerable state of emptiness. We know of his emptiness as he is quoted as seeing the world as a void. Without Catherine, who was his heart for him in childhood, the world is a void and his soul is empty and turns black. In losing Catherine as the extension of himself who contains a heart, he loses all the heart's tender capacities for love and human connection.

When the symbiosis is aborted between Catherine and Heathcliff, Catherine becomes the lost heart of Heathcliff and Heathcliff becomes the lost body of Catherine. Initially, Catherine had asked her father for a whip when he went to town, on the fateful day when he found the orphan Heathcliff. Catherine's brother Hindley had asked his father for a violin. It is the interpretation of several authors, including Gilbert and Gubar (1979), and Katherine Frank (1990), that Heathcliff embodies the elements of aggression symbolized in a whip as well as the elements of passion symbolized in a violin. As such, he can seem to embody instinctual elements that can easily arouse and tantalize the child of a Victorian society, where instinct is repressed and disowned, as well as arousing the child of developmental arrest, whose instincts have gone underground due to separation-individuation trauma. Having been both forms of this child, Emily Brontë as author, can easily have created the character of Catherine out of her own state of being, a state where heart and instinct are severed, and where, therefore, the child never grows through adolescence into the integrated state of a true and authentic adult. Instead, she becomes a false self of role adaptation, when called upon to perform the part of an adult person, wife, and Victorian lady.

From adolescence on, encased in the compulsive role playing of the false self, Catherine Earnshaw could not help being a victim. She could not help wishing for death as an escape, an escape both from a false marriage to Linton—the passionless patriarch—and from a regressive symbiotic merger with her childhood other half, the manically arousing Heathcliff. In a scene of frenzy, where the physical presence of Heathcliff arouses her beyond any tolerable level of psychic containment, Catherine cries out in desperation that she will die and go to a place where she will be above and beyond Heathcliff. In this fantasied other place, she declares that she will be "in it." In my interpretation of this phrase, she means that she will be contained in a way that she cannot be in a human body. Her dilemma of being split between instinct and heart, between passion and socialized intellect (represented by Linton, the husband she leaves Heathcliff for), prevents her from being "in it" while in human form. To be at home in her body would mean to go through a self integration process that her author's aborted separation-individuation period has prevented her from successfully navigating, so that her alter-ego character, Catherine, demonstrates the result of this failure. Although Emily Brontë, as author, could most probably not have consciously remembered this original period of separation trauma during the time of her mother's illness and death, she could remember some repeated form of it during adolescence, reacting to it with anorexia (see Frank, 1990), suicidal fantasy, and seclusive withdrawal just as her created alter-ego character, Catherine, did. In her novel, Emily Brontë recreates this adolescent trauma, giving it voice and image. It is Emily Brontë's creative genius that allowed her to become both Heathcliff and Catherine, so that she might face her two false selves: the compliant post-adolescent Catherine and the oppositional Heathcliff. It is her creative genius that allowed her to become both Heathcliff and Catherine, so that she could describe the two split aspects of a potentially integrated, related, and thus true, self. I see one part self as the oral aggressive passion of a body self aborted from further growth, growth that would move towards romantic yearnings and lustful passions after separation. This body is disowned at adolescence as Catherine submits to be molded into the adult female mode of Victorian dress. The other half self is the heart that could feel the yearnings for connection—through fantasies of out of body mystic harmony, and through fantasies of an inner essence not dependent on external relations. With such fantasies, expressed vividly in poetry and now in her novel, Emily Brontë, in the character of Catherine, wards off the sensory contact that threatens to bring the unbearable pain of unmourned trauma. When Catherine cries that Heathcliff is her world, and Heathcliff cries that he cannot live without Catherine, they are both right. The manic frenzy created by their cravings to have each other, and yet to escape from one another, is the frenzy of two part selves who can never unite since they are not separate beings that are integrated within themselves. Therefore, they cannot marry within the interpersonal world. They both end up looking to death for some kind of unknown answer, and the demon lover scenario again turns to the tragedy of merger with the muse who is the inspiring other half of one's being, which ends in death. The separation trauma cycle is complete.

As a novelist, Emily Brontë tried to save her novel from the Greek tragedy demise of an internal world blueprint being inevitably reenacted. She tried to provide a "deux ex machina." She did so by creating the children of Catherine Earnshaw and Edgar Linton, of Heathcliff and Isabella Linton, and of Catherine's brother Hindley and his wife. She narrates a tale of their survival. However, the "deux ex machina" solution is an artificial one, and the lack of organic character development as resolution is obvious in this novel. The second generation characters manifest as part-objects, not as whole objects. They are flat, one dimensional, often being known only through the voice of an observer, Nelly Dean, the family nurse and narrator. At first represented as ruffians, who are narcissistically self absorbed, belligerent and alien to interpersonal contact, they are then presented to us by the narrator as transforming and reaching a mature state of tender caring and relatedness. In this way, the author attempts to rebuild the world, rather than leave it in desecration. The author's plot tells us that Catherine's daughter ultimately yields to receiving the written and verbal approaches of Heathcliff's son. We, as readers, are then led to believe that this ends happily in marriage, and the world goes on, with no more traces of destruction and loss, even after the nightmare of the demon lover tale of manic arousal and death.

I, as a reader, am left unbelieving. The ending seems contrived and thus false. There is nothing in the characters of these female and male second generation characters that makes them any more capable of sustained human connection than that of their parents. They are one dimensional in lacking a capacity to feel ambivalence or psychic conflict, to anticipate the reactions of another, to empathize or understand another, to be aware that they are interpreting the world and creating their own subjective meanings. Without awareness that they are constructing meanings they cannot undergo the organic change of re-constructing meanings, and therefore of recognizing that the same other person can become different from who he or she was before. To believe, therefore, that they have come to an acceptance of each other is hardly possible.

Hanna Segal (1952) has said that the artist, unlike others, can face the depressive fantasies, i.e. the unconscious images of their own destructive aggression, and can survive them by recreating a new and less destructive world through their art. I believe that Emily Brontë was attempting to do this. Yet, unlike her sister Charlotte, who wrote *Villette,* I believe that she failed. I believe that she failed to recreate an authentic world that survived, and that her contrived ending stands as a false ending. Her authenticity is not in finding a more true self in her writing, but rather in her literary creation of a psychic trauma from she could not escape. Her search for an early good mother is seen in her quest for a muse. Her early true self, presumably established in the symbiotic era with her mother, can be seen in her depiction of a childhood symbiosis between Heathcliff and Catherine that is represented as a fortuitous evolution of nature. Heathcliff's name is linked with that of the beloved "Heather" that Emily Brontë found in her natural surroundings. He is linked in his origins with nature, and is mysteriously found and mysteriously transformed into a rich man who can seek sadistic revenge.

Heathcliff is both nature and magic, but fails in authenticity where Klein's mode of "manic magic reparation" (see segal, 1975) substitutes for the true reparation of change, true reparation requiring the mourning of loss and the letting go of childhood attachments that are traumatic and/or regressive. The part of Heathcliff that is nature, and not magic, seems to echo an early real communion between his author, Emily Brontë, and her mother of infancy. However the part of him that is magic, seems to be a false resolution to an abrupt separation that is abortive of the self. Heathcliff must inevitably turn demonic and seek reunion with his female heart only in death, for life only repeats the trauma of aborted interpersonal connection. Therefore, I see Emily Brontë's novel, just like her poetry, as aborted rather than resolved. In this sense her work mirrors her life.

## Heathcliff as Demon Lover

Although Heathcliff is an inspiring masculine spirit to Catherine in childhood, he fails to survive as a muse when he loses Catherine. As an adult he is described in terms that highlight his demonic character as it manifests through instinctual dynamics that are cut off from any loving object connections. Heathcliff is described in terms of anal sadistic epithets and anal sadistic scenes. He is also characterized by adjectives related to the oral biting stage. He "grinds his teeth" (195), according to Nelly, the nurse and narrator in the tale, and foams at the mouth "like a mad dog" (197). He is surrounded by dogs with long sharp teeth. In one of his manic articulations he cries: "I have no pity! I have no pity! The more the worms writhe, the more I yearn to crush out their entrails! It is a moral teething, and I grind with greater energy in proportion to the increase in pain!" (189).

Heathcliff is also as handsome as the Prince of Darkness is said to be. He is irresistible. His combination of blatant cruelty, and an addiction to power and vindictiveness, can easily erupt into careless and seemingly motiveless sadism (e.g., when he hangs Isabella's dog). Like the archetypal demon lover, he seeks possession above all else and goes mad with rage when his childhood love eludes his grasp. Yet Catherine does submit to him through death. Although she never fully yields her emotional being to him in life and speaks of transcending him in death, Heathcliff is never content till he holds the dying Catherine in his arms. Still alive, Catherine threatens Heathcliff with the narcissistic wound of betrayal, since she has left him to marry a more socially acceptable and elevated man. Yet what Heathcliff originally lacks in fortune and social pedigree is eventually compensated by his tantalizing passion and by his manic-erotic power.

Again in the archetypal vein, Heathcliff tantalizes the heroine. He draws her away from the world and her husband to his own shadowy cave, where death awaits. In interpersonal terms, he is the macho Victorian male who absorbs the female into himself rather than yields to a reciprocal relationship with her. Intrapsychically, he is the omnipotent, grandiose internal object that imprisons the libidinal self or feeling ego. For instance, as the infatuated Isabella is aroused to a frenzy, Heathcliff sets off his imprisoning snare as one would hunt a dog. As the woman gives her heart and soul, Heathcliff merely seeks possession and proceeds to mold her soul to his own designs. Once he has power over her, he demands exclusive rights; he then rather quickly cuts the cords that link his female victim to others in the external world. As he possesses her, he binds her from within, remaining within her as a psychic tapeworm.

Heathcliff also seeks omnipotent control over Catherine. The scene between Heathcliff and Catherine at the point of her approaching death illustrates the manic and demonic intensity that highlights Brontë's entire novel. Passions erupt as evidence of explosive forces from within that are rebelling against the constricting walls of an intrapsychic schizoid barrier. Heathcliff and Catherine can be seen as two parts of the self erupting in this fashion. The metaphorical manifestation of this is the imprisonment theme in all of Emily Brontë's poetry. The counterpart to the imprisoned self is the eruption of instinctual cravings in manic frenzy. According to David Daiche (1965), Heathcliff is always acting on others, generally creating a sense of frenzy: "We get no direct presentation of Heathcliff: he is seen almost always as a force acting upon others, and it is to his effect on others that we wish to come to the heart of the mystery" (18).

Daiche also highlights the sadistic image we are given of Heathcliff by the author:

> This is not the only time that Heathcliff is presented in the act of forcing an entry or an egress. . . . He is handsome and savage, surrounded by fierce dogs and in some sort of intimate association with a girl, or the spirit of a girl, whose appearance arouses a sadistic impulse in Lockwood and a mixture of rage and longing in Heathcliff himself. His aged servant speaks the language of religion, but is obviously a sadist. A further point about him appears to be significant: the cold inhospitality of his demeanor is a variance with the blazing warmth which Lockwood finds at the domestic centre of the house.
>
> (21)

## Heathcliff As Mirror and Man

Is Heathcliff a part of Catherine, a mirror of Catherine in masculine form, or a differentiated male object? Daiche suggests the first. Catherine's cry to Nelly demonstrates the narcissistic nature of her highly ambivalent bond with Heathcliff: "Nelly, I am Heathcliff—he's always, always in my mind—not as a pleasure, any more than I am always a pleasure to myself—but as my own being" (22). When Catherine is irate at Heathcliff's response to her—as during the torrential scene of her approaching death—she negates his actual existence to negate his response and claims her own form of him as an internal part object, apart from his external reality: "Oh, you see, Nelly! he would not relent a moment to keep me out of the grave! *That* is how I'm loved! Well, nevermind! That is not my Heathcliff. I shall love mine yet, and take him with me—he's in my soul" (196).

Although this statement is strong evidence for Catherine's own narcissism, it begs the question as to the entire nature of her attachment to Heathcliff. Is it purely on narcissistic grounds? Is this momentary cry merely a narcissistic defense against the helpless and injured feeling she might experience if she acknowledges her real attachment to Heathcliff as an object separate from herself? Given her other statement about him being herself, the overall narcissistic dynamic cannot be dismissed simply as a moment of defense. What makes the problem so complex, reaching beyond Daiche's declaration that Catherine's love for Heathcliff is merely a form of self-love, are other innuendoes of heterosexual visions. Heathcliff's masculine form is essential. He is not merely a mirror for Catherine or a twin in Kohut's terms of a mirror transference.[1]

In fact, Margaret Homans (1980) is quite emphatic in her view that Catherine's love for Heathcliff is a heterosexual yearning that goes beyond the intrapsychic need for a mother and distinctly enters the oedipal realm. This heterosexuality can be related to Homans's remark that Emily Brontë's poetry represents the point described by Freud "as the feminine turn from mother to father":

> The reunion that Cathy and Heathcliff seek is not primordial, but a reunion with each other as consciously known and loved individuals, however the reader may qualify that love.
>
> Instead of an investment of belief in transcendence after death, images of continuance in the novel are all invested in heterosexual love, regardless of how the reader judges the specifics of Cathy and Heathcliff's relationship.
>
> (149–61)

Both the heterosexual oedipal level and the narcissistically imprisoning part object bond are seen in the relationship between Catherine and Heathcliff. On account of the complex interplay between these two levels, seen generally in those of developmental arrest (borderline, narcissistic, and schizoid patients), there is a manic intensity that reflects the extremes of compulsion and ambivalence. If Heathcliff is a mirror or a twin for Catherine, he can be seen as a split-off masculine part of her own self, as is the "God of Visions" or the male muse. In addition, Heathcliff can be seen as a separate male other for whom Catherine yearns. His erotic power to tantalize is never described in explicit sexual terms; in fact he seems to prefer the power of possession to any sexual union. Yet despite his preference for narcissistic control over sexual power, he can serve to draw out sexual desires from Catherine. Daiche quotes one critic who declares that Heathcliff serves to motivate all of the external sexual forces that are in the novel, bringing new life to fruition (25). Thus, the two levels of narcissistic part object alliance and oedipal attachment can coexist. This coexistence is created by a heavy emphasis on eroticization of an early narcissistic psychic structure and its narcissistic part object. There is continual allusion to this eroticization, since Heathcliff is described as irresistible to all of the characters, particularly to Catherine and Isabella. Daiche observes:

> It is perhaps curious that Emily Brontë shows no sense of the otherness of the other person in a passionate relationship between the sexes. Ultimate passion is for her rather a kind of recognition of one's self, one's true and absolute self in the object of passion. ("Nelly, I am Heathcliff!" "I cannot live without my life! I cannot live without my soul!") This notion makes contact with the suggestions of incest in the novel.
>
> (28)

Putting aside traditional views of purely distinct developmental levels and using a more-complex object relations perspective, in which both parental objects and levels merge, we can integrate Daiche's and Homans's views with the emphasis of the present book. We can see the oedipal eroticization of the narcissistic-level psychic structure as it manifests itself in an internal male object in women, going back to the father.

## Degrees and Limitations of Reparation As Seen in the Novel

To judge the nature of an author's internal world and of her psychodynamic developmental position by studying her creative work can be a difficult task. There is certainly room for a grand margin of error. However, an author's work is a reflection of that author's internal world just as dreams are. With this in mind, I will examine the form and content of Emily Brontë's novel, attempting to evaluate to what degree her use of the creative process can be seen as reparative. The demon lover theme that we see in all of her work expresses a psychopathology that begins at a preoedipal level and is then reinforced at an oedipal level. If symbiotic yearnings from an earlier era are still urgent because of developmental arrest, they are generally directed toward the father, particularly when a young girl reaches the oedipal stage. Such a view is in harmony with the demon lover complex, as it was earlier outlined in relation to Marian Woodman's theory.

I have been repeatedly attempting to show how the literary theme of the demon lover expresses a particularly psychodynamic theme and to demonstrate its pathology as evidenced in the works and lives of various women writers. Thus, my focus has been on the father-daughter relationship, which deeply influences the creative strivings of a woman. My focus has also been on the incorporated childhood father as he exists in the internal world, often appearing as a fused mother-father internal object on account of the layered nature of this object relations dynamic. In the process of demonstrating this female syndrome within the creative work itself, I have also been considering the extent to which use of the creative process is reparative along the lines of self-differentiation and self-integration, as seen within the context of Melanie Klein's two major psychodynamic self-states, i.e., the paranoid-schizoid position and the depressive position.

From the psychodynamics of *Wuthering Heights*, I conclude that Emily Brontë remained fixated primarily in the paranoid-schizoid position and that the success of her reparative strivings—as seen in her use of the creative process—was therefore very limited. The evidence I see for the primary intrapsychic status of the paranoid-schizoid position is as follows. First, there is an ongoing cathartic, externalizing, and exorcising emphasis to the novel's dynamic intensity. The two main characters in particular are engaged in an ongoing process of projective identification with each other, in which they force volatile aggressive impulses upon each other. Further, no loving tie beyond disappointment is ever sustained. Retaliation and revenge are set off by disappointment, which is always experienced as betrayal, particularly by Heathcliff, who is the most primitive and narcissistic character. Relentless and vindictive attempts at revenge are set in motion within the overall plot, which circulates around Heathcliff. Murderous and suicidal rage alternate, which is characteristic of the borderline psychodynamics of Heathcliff's character. The object of hate is also always a part of the self, given the dynamics of part objects that are experienced as self-parts through projective identification. Also characteristic of the paranoid-schizoid position, guilt and loss can never be tolerated. Both Catherine and Heathcliff attempt to expel or exorcise such internal experiences as though they are persecutory internal objects. The attempt at such exorcism through externalization always leads to increasing fears of persecution, especially since what is attacked is also a part of the self, and the attacking rage and accusations are felt to injure one's own person.

Split part objects rather than whole objects are apparent. For instance, Edgar Linton is all tenderness without passion and Heathcliff is all passion without tenderness. Heathcliff is also a profoundly diffuse character, lacking both differentiation and integration, like the diffuse male characters in Emily Brontë's poetry. Heathcliff is male-female, father-mother, and brother-self in relation to

Catherine. Catherine too is both male and female. She has demonized masculine features that are aroused by Heathcliff's passionate archaic aggression. Catherine and Heathcliff can be seen as two part object halfs of the author herself. They are part objects in the sense of being diffuse conglomerates of masculine and feminine attributes and of libidinal and aggressive forces that are not well-differentiated from one another.

There are in addition the flat characters, who are predominantly reactive in nature. They do not have the motivational subjective selves of whole object persons. They cannot reflect on or interpret their own actions. All of the descendents of the primary characters who inherit the world within the novel could qualify part objects in this respect. The ending seems extremely contrived because of the dynamics of the part object characters that appear. In fact, the ending seems more like the magic solution of manic reparation (see Segal, 1975) than any true reparation that could come about through the working through of an affective process within the lives of the primary characters. Catherine II and Hareton are brought together in a behavioral compliance through Nelly's attempt at peacemaking, not through any inner or intrinsic sense of chosen value in relation to the other. They are used as props to restore order in the world when the borderline-level retaliatory response has destroyed all of the primary characters. There is no subjective self-motivation toward reparation of self and other or any tolerance for facing guilt within a grief process. There is only a traditional Victorian servant's (Nelly's) attempt to replace all things as quickly as possible. This precludes the experience of loss following massive destruction of human relationships. It is only the outer form of society—its outer shell—that is reestablished. On the level of the self, it is the false self that is reestablished, not a true or subjective self. Feminist critics Gilbert and Gubar (1979) speak of the false patriarchy that wins out and is called "civilization" only by the last spokeswoman, Nelly. She narrates the conclusion from her own false-self position as the part object daughter of the patriarchy and is a woman who lacks the vitality of a truly integrated self; her femininity is therefore stereotypic rather than organic in form. We never see her tenderness, although it is reported to exist by herself at the end.

Is there a capacity for ambivalence shown by the characters in this novel? Not if ambivalence is traditionally defined as a capacity to love and hate the same object over time. Both Heathcliff and Catherine serve as tantalizing and rejecting objects for one another.[2] Neither can tolerate mixed reactions toward the other. Each switches back and forth in his or her affective responses—one moment painfully longing for the other, the next trying to destroy the same object. There is hardly a pause between these opposite reactions and no psychic space (Winnicott's "potential space," see Ogden 1986) for the integration of these alternating states of feeling. They are operating out of an enactment of the paranoid-schizoid position merger with the unconscious, in which opposite states of mind co-exist and alternate but are never experienced as contrasts that create a sense of psychic conflict.

At one point Catherine comments, "That is not my Heathcliff. I shall love mine yet, and take him with me—he's in my soul" (196). When Heathcliff does not behave as she wishes, she denies his reality as an external object; with the swiftness of manic magic, she conjures up her own version of Heathcliff. There is no experience of psychic conflict in Catherine's reaction.

This unrelenting affective intensity by itself is a sign of the perpetuated paranoid-schizoid state of mind that can come from a developmental arrest in the author. Brontë's incapacity to experience ambivalence is another sign, and this incapacity compounds the intensity of the novel. Unrefined rage and hysterical mania predominate over any tenderness and harmony that might emerge from mutuality. The novel's era of peace, to which Nelly alludes when she speaks of Catherine's marriage to Linton while Heathcliff is away, is only momentarily sensed as actually existing in the present by the narrator. There is also allusion to Linton's tenderness, but it is never experienced firsthand. What is experienced firsthand is the autistic form of pseudodialogue between Catherine and Heathcliff, which has the constant intensity of manic eroticism and murderous rage. Also, the void of the borderline trauma is prominent in Heathcliff's speech. He declares that his idealized and demonic[3] object's death drops him into an abyss. His references to an outer void strongly suggest that he has no sense of an inside. Without an inside, Heathcliff can only enact despair; he cannot feel it and subjectively define it.

The more refined depressive-position affects of guilt, concern, grief, sadness, and loving loss are never felt or expressed directly by any of the novel's characters. Without such affects, there can be no subjective sense of self or any secure sense of self-agency. There can be no mournful working through of love and hate, the prime elements of relational conflicts. Therefore, no capacity to tolerate ambivalence and thus to sustain interpersonal connections within and without can be achieved. The characters in Emily Brontë's tale appear diffuse in form while they also exhibit confusion. This confusion is not felt, however, but is defended against with narcissistic rage. Most prominently narcissistic in nature, Heathcliff wards off internal confusion and an externalized void by creating the persecutory plot of a paranoid. The plot's characteristic betrayal, as expected, leads to annihilating revenge that is relentless, as it is for most narcissistic characters who enact their rage at a borderline (or developmental arrest) level, presumably due to developmental arrest (see Masterson, 1976).

Even if the author of *Wuthering Heights* was withdrawn and controlled during much of her actual daily life, in her creative work she gives vent to borderline acting-out tendencies against which schizoid withdrawal and narcissistic insulation (Modell's 1975 [1976] cocoon state) defend. These acting-out tendencies can be seen within her novel to spell out revenge and retaliation on a repeated basis. They mark the relentless tread of the schizoid-narcissistic character who cannot cry or mourn and who lacks true internal whole object dialogue, presumably on account of developmental arrest.

Both Catherine and Heathcliff display the manic defenses against depressive-position affect as described by Melanie Klein and Hanna Segal. These manic defenses are shown through interpersonal attitudes that interfere with true relating, which are expressed through airs of contempt, control, and triumph (see Segal, 1975).

Catherine taunts Heathcliff with her scornful claim that she will supersede him through death, triumphantly declaring that she will go beyond "you all." She will go beyond the horizon of death, where she can finally be "really with it and in it" (197). This manic wish to rise above an emotional reality that feels too painful and yet to feel "in it" is a psychic defense against feeling out of it, or out of one's body, as Catherine obviously feels. Catherine splits off from her body, particularly as she is aroused to a lustful frenzy for the magnetic idealized male that she can never have.

Heathcliff too defends with an air of manic triumph. He displays a general air of cynical contempt, scornful accusation, and belligerent disdain. His attempts to control all those around him also illustrate the level of a delusional narcissistic omnipotence that denies all separation. Everybody is essentially treated as an extension of his own body; thus Heathcliff feels that he is entitled to control people as one would control an arm or leg. His belief that Catherine has betrayed him is felt not as a subjectively defined interpretation but as a reification that cannot be contradicted. It is an interpretation based on his assumption that Catherine would marry him when they grew up, although no such marriage had been discussed or promised. These manic operations are based on the paranoid-schizoid processes of splitting and projective identification, which can be seen as signs of developmental arrest as well as of defense. Like Piaget's (1969) egocentric youngster, who demonstrates this aspect of the paranoid-schizoid position, neither Catherine nor Heathcliff can see the other's view and their own at the same time (see Bach 1985). Thus, cognitive aspects of psychic arrest perpetuate the ongoing torment of continual accusation. For those suffering from such arrest, all self-serving behavior on another's part is seen as betrayal and selfishness— never as need or necessity, but only as effrontery.

The arrest displayed by Emily Brontë's characters echoes that of their author. *Wuthering Heights* reminds us of Brontë's poetry, in which the poet is unable to internalize the powers of the male muse.

At the end of *Wuthering Heights,* we see the degree to which Brontë lacks the development of a subjective sense of self, a lack which reflects her failure to achieve the depressive position. This impasse in the novel seems necessarily to reflect the author's own internal process. If the only forces active in the novel are the superego and id, where is the mediating ego, the ego which contains the overall subjective and self-reflective self? Certainly, the magnetic id seen in Heathcliff and the superego compliance seen in the characters of Catherine's daughter and Hareton, are never integrated in any way that would form a subjective self. Such integration could come about only through the mutuality of relationship, the interpersonal mutuality that could prompt and sustain a mourning process. No such process is seen in this novel. Thus, the ending appears contrived because of the author's mechanistic and magical attempt at repair.

Two further aspects of the paranoid-schizoid position are apparent. The first is an incapacity to adequately perceive and test reality as seen in Emily Brontë's character of Catherine. Catherine wishes to die to be born and to kill Heathcliff without truly having him disappear. She opens the window to breathe in the natural scent of the moors at the expense of a fatal chill. Nelly, in contrast, represents reality in that she closes the window. The second aspect of the developmental-arrest position is the trenchant intrusion of the omnipotent object, implying a disrupted preoedipal-level holding environment (see Ogden, 1986).[4] This intrusion is seen when Heathcliff imposes his presence as a sudden and malevolent apparition.

### Speculations on the Internal and External Father-Daughter Relationship

Winifred Gerin's biography describes the relationship between Emily and her father, showing the special bond between them. This bond crystallized during a period in which the two lived alone together at Harworth, while Emily's other siblings were away at the respective homes in which they were employed. Gerin writes:

> Between Emily and her father a new closeness grew up in the year of their isolation together. His deteriorating eye-sight made him dependent on her about the home for more than reading. It affected not only his clerical avocations, his reading and writing, but the daily discharge of his pistols over the heads of the gravestones in the churchyard.
>
> (147)

For the ritual of firing off a loaded pistol every morning—a tradition carried over from the Luddite emergency of 1811 (continued through 1812)—the reverend turned to his daughter Emily to help him. He also considered this ritual an act of defense in the rough moorland terrain. Emily, who had imagined the land of

Gondal in her girlhood and who had invented "the fighting gentry," seems to have responded warmly to her father's idea for her to learn to shoot. Gerin quotes a passage from John Greenwood's diary, in which a local neighbor witnessed this father-daughter event:

> Mr. Brontë formerly took very great pleasure in shooting—not in the way generally understood by the term, but shooting at the mark, merely for recreation. He had such unbounded confidence in his daughter Emily, knowing, as he did, her unparalleled intrepidity and firmness, that he resolved to learn her to shoot too. They used to practice with pistols. Let her be ever so busy in her domestic duties, whether in the kitchen backing bread at which she had such a dainty hand, or at her ironing, or at her studies, raped [sic] in a world of her own creating—it mattered not; if he called upon her to take a lesson, she would put all down; his tender and affectionate "Now my dear girl, let me see how well you can shoot to-day" was irresistible to her filial nature, and her most winning and musical voice would be hard to ring through the house in response, "Yes, papa" and away she would run with such a hearty good will taking the board at him, and tripping like a fairy down the [sic] to the bottom of the garden, putting it in its proper position, then returning to her dear revered parent, take the pistol, which he had previously primed and loaded for her. "Now my girl," he would say, "take time, be steady." "Yes papa," she would say taking the weapon with as firm a hand, and as steady an eye as any veteran of the camp, and fire. Then she would run to fetch the board for him to see how she had succeeded. And she did get so proficient, that she was rarely far from the mark. His "how cleverly you have done, my dear girl," was all she cared for. She knew she had gratified him, and she would return to him the pistol, saying "load again papa," and away she would go to the kitchen, roll another shelful of teacakes, then wiping her hands, she would return again to the garden, and call out "I'm ready again, papa," and so they would go on until he thought she had had enough practice for that day. "Oh!" he would exclaim, "she is a brave and noble girl. She is my right-hand, nay the very apple of my eye!"
>
> (147–48)

This quote beautifully encapsulates the relationship between Brontë and his daughter. It suggests how close and special the two were to each other. Was this the same cold, narcissistic, patriarchal tyrant who—according to her biographer Margot Peters—ruled Charlotte with his sadistic withdrawals and guilt-provoking whining? Of course Emily might have enjoyed a relationship with her father quite different from that of her older sister. Also, this scene was observed while several of Brontë's children were still alive; even if his grief from his wife's death and from the death of his two older daughters may have been insufficiently mourned, he had not yet encountered the deaths of his son, of Anne, and of Emily. Perhaps his withdrawal from others was not as extreme at this time as later, and he was thus more available for his daughter Emily than he would later be for Charlotte.

There might be an alternative or perhaps an additional explanation for this discrepancy. Emily's need to be special to him may have been enacted in a way that he could respond to with the kind of father's affirmation that Charlotte had always craved and never received. Emily seemed ready to please him at all times. She cleaned his house, cooked his bread, and did his ironing, apparently not minding it the way Charlotte always had.[5] She was ready at a moment's notice to shoot his pistol for him. Emily had no desire to leave home and leave him behind. Also, more than any of the others, she cared for the idolized son, Branwell. For herself, Emily asked only to go off on the moors so that she might meet her muse and be inspired to write. Emily's father could even share this love for the moors. After all, he had exposed Emily to his own love of nature in the first place, as well as to the poetry that he had written in response to it.

Furthermore, there were some special things that father and daughter shared. When Emily played the piano, it was her father who communed with her. She could read literature to her father in which both shared an interest, and she must never have forgotten that he first introduced her to the literary world through *Blackwell's* magazine, and through related books that the whole family shared when she was a child (see Gerin). No doubt she was grateful that he had shared in the world of Gondal that grew out of her own imagination and that he was willing to let her worship God on the rough natural moors instead of going to church—despite his being a clergyman. Finally, her father shared in her love of animals. From his point of view, perhaps Emily was the one who shared in his personal preferences, and to the extent that she did, or to the extent to which she may also have identified with him, his narcissistic needs may have been met sufficiently for him to favor her as a special daughter—perhaps even as an extension of himself.

How does this relationship between Emily Brontë and her external father relate to the inner-world relationship between herself and her father? This is where biographical fact and anecdote end and speculation begins. Such speculation is essential to understand how both the idealized muse and the demon lover figures seen in her creative work developed from this internal world. It also helps us to see how using the creative process can be channeled into a compulsion by the developmental need of the self to repair itself.

As already stated, Emily Brontë's mother became fatally ill during her infancy. We can judge the dynamics of her trauma during those earliest years only by seeing how it manifested itself in her relationship with her father, and consequently in her use of the creative process to express her inner world. From the dynamics of the demon lover theme, as well as of the theme of the demon lover's other half, the male muse, it seems that two levels of development became merged. This scenario reflects that of the internal worlds of several other women writers of this study. A primary maternal symbiosis seems to have been disrupted, leaving arrested symbiotic yearnings that were later transferred to the father. This in turn created a fixated need for an idealized part object, which was intermingled with erotic longings for the oedipal-stage father. Like Emily Dickinson, Emily Brontë may have needed to identify with her father and consequently with the masculine aspects of his character. Her willingness to shoot pistols, her Gondal fantasies of waging war, and her need to portray the male demon lover Heathcliff as an extension of herself, as well as her cravings to be inspired by a male muse or by a masculine night wind, may have all been derived from her wish to join her father (and possibly also her brother) to herself as a symbiotic other half. Related to this would be the narcissistic mode of carrying out such a symbiotic yearning through an image identification. However, Emily was unable to carry out this masculine identification as a successful compensatory reparation in her creative work, let alone in her life. Her symbiosis with her male muse, and perhaps originally with her ill mother, was apparently too aggressive in nature. Within her literary work, her attempts to merge continually meet with possession, psychic imprisonment, and psychic splitting, rather than with a mutuality that can success-fully result in self-integration and internationalization. This seems like the reen-acted psychic blueprint of her infancy. Perhaps the aggression seen in this malevo-lent symbiosis is also a result of the attempt to merge with a narcissistic father who not only may have treated her as special but who, in his unwillingness to be deidealized, may have conveyed an aggressive resistance to her wish to merge with him—particularly when he was not in control of the manner in which the merger took place. Such narcissistic resistance to a daughter's disillusionment could also have the effect of an aborted developmental idealization, resulting in devaluation and in a splitting of object experience into the form of part object relations.

We will see that in contrast to Emily Brontë, Emily Dickinson had more success in forming a compensatory masculine identity through creativity. We can speculate that the actual death of Emily Brontë's mother was more traumatic than the consistently schizoid detachment of Dickinson's mother. In Brontë's internal world, as expressed through her creative work, there are torturous battles to break free from the male muse's power that follow precipitously upon contact with that muse. Dickinson could dream of her "dream king" and have him inside her all day while she created her own masculine and aggressive forms in poetry. Brontë was unable to internalize her muse's power. Her masculine forms wiped out her females, as in the male hero's extinction of Rochelle's voice in "Silent Is the House," or in Heathcliff's triumphant survival that leads to Catherine Earnshaw's death.

In Emily Brontë, we see the dynamics of a lower-level borderline, or of a schizoid character with narcissistic features. The poet seems to have formed a narcissistic defense through mirroring from her father following from a separation-individuation arrest with her primary mother. She refers to her heroine's marriage in *Wuthering Heights* as entrapment, reminiscent of lower-level borderline's fears of engulfment that can be reenacted at any critical stage of separation, and especially during adolescence. Gilbert and Gubar (1979) attribute Brontë's sense of entrapment to a general female reaction to Victorian patriarchal male culture, which according to them begins its treachery most insidiously when a pubescent young girl is abruptly molded into a Victorian "lady." This view does not account for the level of psychopathology expressed in the character of Catherine Earnshaw, which from a psychoanalytic perspective of development regresses to a state of preoedipal developmental arrest that is related to Klein's paranoid-schizoid position. After all, Brontë was seemingly compelled by the part object situation of her internal world to create Heathcliff as a masculinized half of Catherine. Heathcliff could not be properly internalized by Catherine, nor could he be joined to her as a separate and differentiated figure. This pattern reflects how the author could not psychically negotiate relations with men or with her male muse. I suggest that the adolescent separation trauma that Gilbert and Gubar observe in the character of Catherine is a screen memory for the earlier trauma of an aborted maternal symbiosis. This may be a repressed or split-off trauma of the author that is inherited by her creation, Catherine.

Like Emily Dickinson, who is yet to be discussed, Emily Brontë seems to have developed the syndrome of being the father's "spiritual bride." Never leaving her father's home, she was susceptible to the psychic-incest merger, which could have fueled her creativity and made her envision a spiritual male muse. This psychic incest merger carried over the earlier level of symbiotic cravings to the psychic oedipal level of marriage with a man. However, such a psychic-incest situation also results in the compulsion to use the creative process to expel the malignant part object counterpart to the male muse, i.e., to expel the demon lover as he exists, split off and unintegrated, in the internal world. Thus, the creative process not only becomes the route to the idealized mother-father and the format for the fantasy of self-repair through the search for that internal figure via the creative work, but also takes on the malevolent manic intensity of a compulsion to exorcize the demon lover counterpart. Because of the preoedipal level of arrest, movements toward depressive-position mourning and working through are unsuccessful within the work of the creative process. Thus, there does not appear to be any integration and differentiation of self and other. Splitting remains prominent, along with projective identification, as seen in Catherine Earnshaw and Heathcliff.

## Conclusion

When she was dying from consumption, Emily Brontë would not consent to see a doctor, to stay in bed, or to try prescribed remedies. In her poetry, she cries "No Coward Soul Is Mine" (no. 191 ●●●) and faces death with the grandiose presumption of narcissistic self-sufficiency (see Modell 1976). Since her creative peak, she had witnessed her brother Branwell's degenerative demise and death. She had heard his tales of woe, and encountered his bitter denouement. Through seeing her brother's weakness her own contempt for humanity was reinforced. In *Wuthering Heights,* Brontë evidences both her contempt and her despair. Her brother's swearing is repeated in the cynical disgust of Heathcliff and in the drunken dissipation of Catherine's brother Hindley. Both these fraternal characters express the blackness of Brontë's own disillusionment, as well as the degree to which she was imprisoned with both her father and her brother in a paranoid-schizoid-level projective identification. They express her own split-off rage. Such rage continually turns inward when there is no creative outlet.

Without the reparative integration of a depressive-position mourning process in her creative work and without a renewed creative catharsis, despair and its unmodified rage seem to have combined with physical sickness to defeat Emily Brontë. The loss of her idealized male part object—her male muse—left her bereft. The failed symbiosis with her muse may have reopened the old wound of the lost maternal symbiosis, one lost too traumatically when no transitional object, reminiscent of the holding environment mother, was there to receive her and to allow for a whole object maternal internalization.

Although her poetry and prose exhibit manic defense and manic reparation, it is the splitting processes upon which the manic defense is based that really defeat any movement toward developmental mourning. Aggression remains a split-off rage in a masculine and eroticized form, and this prevents a sense of agency from developing. As Homans so clearly analyzes in terms of Brontë's poetry, the poet cannot internalize power; this relates to how she cannot internalize any good-object interactions through external relations. The bad object, infested with raw primitive aggression, remains malignantly inside. One can therefore speculate that the result of poetic exorcism may lead to the malignant form emerging as fatal somatic illness.

Speculation concerning the dynamics of the poet's illness aside, the literary work of Emily Brontë speaks for itself. It displays pathological mourning, rather than developmental mourning. This appears as disappointment in the reparative power of an idealized male muse, which continually leads to despair, expressed in persistent thoughts of death. The idealized male spirit becomes the demon lover, who becomes death itself. Since the splitting and projective processes of the developmental arrest undermine any mournful working through of guilt, rage, and loss, Emily Brontë remains in a prison of paranoid-schizoid dynamics. She fends off any interpersonal relations that might allow her an affective avenue to escape her prison. In her poetry, she continually cries for "liberty" but looks to a split-off male part object for rescue as she projects his idealized form. When her male muse does come, she may experience the recreation of an early symbiotic state in which she felt nourished in a mother-infant cocoon of "dual unity." This brings the birth of creative inspiration. However, such a state of creative inspiration cannot be sustained without interpersonal contact. Emily Brontë never yielded to such contact. Perhaps affectively sealed off since her preoedipal years, she viewed interpersonal contact—which differed from the narcissistic mirroring of her father—as an invasion into her rich inner world. She probably feared total loss of self as reflected in the extinction of her female heroines. Therefore, it is not surprising that the poet reinforced her schizoid barrier against contact with external objects and held to her paranoid conviction of outsiders as invaders—a conviction that could only intensify when she faced disillusionment with her spiritual male muse.

Emily Brontë's paranoia convinced her that doctors could bear only poisons. Furthermore, both her poetry and her novel display a long-term yearning for death that was not just a search for some comfort after a lonely existence in this world but that is also symptomatic of her belief that death would bring an ultimate reunion with her male muse. However one interprets this belief, it resonates with the beliefs of many other suicidal female poets. Sylvia Plath, for example, saw death as a reunion with her dead father.[6] She is reported to have seen a "wonderful dream, a marvelous vision" just prior to her suicide (Wagner-Martin 1987, 245). In her final hours, Emily Brontë's vision of death as a magical reunion with her idealized male muse seems to have failed her. It was a vision stitched with doubts, as revealed in her poetry. Unlike Heathcliff, Brontë did not go to her death with an ultimate conviction that it would bring her salvation through love. In these last hours, she asked for a doctor, but it was too late.

Emily Brontë forever remains, for those attempting to view her, inside a narcissistic cocoon where she can cherish the woe (#149, p. 166) of her masochistic sufferings. Within this cocoon, she views even her pain as an inner "tenant" (#149, p. 167) or, in Melanie Klein's language, as a sacred internal object. In fact, she speaks possessively of her "torments and madness, tears and sin." (#149, p. 167) Although she decries her imprisonment, she worships the suffering derived from her chains. She tries to assure herself that it will bring her a heaven beyond the grave. Yet this assurance is never convincing. Although her cry is for "liberty," she depends on the male "messenger of hope" for her deliverance; yet she cannot be liberated by an externalized projection of her self, even if it is merged with an idealized part object derived from her father. The poet may seek to internalize power, but she is not dealing with an external object. Presumably, she is dealing with a split-off part object projection derived from her own internal world. Thus, the creative power remains outside her in the form of a male muse. The minute he is incorporated, his power is lost. He cannot be adequately internalized, nor can he be used to modify an internal demonic form. Brontë does not appear capable of processing the affects necessary for transformation and integration, because she has erected a wall against the contact needed for mourning resolution to take place. Her way of protecting herself is her way of imprisoning herself and perpetuating arrest. In sum, this female poet is a good example of Winnicott's infant who dreads being "found" and yet who despairs if not found (Winnicott 1965).

Emily Brontë died in 1848 from a bad cold that escalated into tuberculosis. Perhaps, as Joyce McDougall writes in *A Plea for a Measure of Abnormality* (1980, 346), the victim of tuberculosis opens herself (her lungs) to tubercular bacilli rather than to grief. McDougall describes patients who, like Brontë, had suffered losses so early that they could not be mentally symbolized and therefore could not open themselves to an essential mourning process. Her description of these patients reinforces the speculations of Brontë's biographer Gerin (1971), who suggests that the poet chose to die when she no longer "hoped for" the appearance of her muse. Instead of retaining the perception of a muse, and unable to grieve its loss, just as she could not grieve the loss of a mother who had no mentally recorded form, the poet was left with an inner ghost that appears to have manifested itself in somatic form. Gerin's descriptions make it clear that Emily Brontë experienced a ghostlike presence that tortured her from within (248). This ghost can easily be seen as the split-off archaic internal object that enacts a role complementary to that of the idealized muse, i.e., that of the demon lover. Emily Brontë leaves the world with these words:

> And I am rough and rude, yet not more rough to see
> Than is the hidden ghost which has its home in me!
>
> (Gerin, 248)

Perhaps the demon-lover ghost is the mother of separation who precipitated trauma when she abandoned her daughter through her literal death. I have proposed that in the face of such early trauma, Emily Brontë could not sustain the illusion of her muse. She could not sustain the psychic recreation of an early holding environment mother of a safer and more symbiotic time. Because of her primitive psychic split, resulting in her inability to integrate both external and internal worlds, this creative woman failed to integrate a self that could promote relatedness. Instead, she was left with narcissistic psychic fusion and self-annihilation. Given her acute preoedipal trauma, no mourning process could unfold through the creative process.

Emily Brontë offers impressions of disrupted states of self. Her creative work offers evidence not of object mourning and self-integration through mourning but rather of the reenactment of self-trauma as frantic striving for contact with the inner self is sought. This striving appears frantic and disruptive because the inner self is suppressed and sealed off from contact with external objects. In this sealed-off state, there is not enough affective contact for sustained internalization of external others, and therefore mourning and integration of those others into a primary self cannot successfully occur. The following phenomenology can be observed.

Brontë switches from moments that are felt with the body (such as "My outer sense is gone, my inner essence feels,") to externally abstracted moments of remote verbal symbolization, as when she speaks from the view of an external male other or of "external worlds" in her poem (Julian M. and A. G. Rochelle, "Silent Is the House") (#190). This switching from the body locus to an external locus, which is expressed in abstract language, seems characteristic of the border-line mode of functioning that Emily Brontë displays. She shows the personality diffusion and psychic splitting that Kernberg speaks of in diagnosing the border-line character (Kernberg, 1975), and also the manifestations of developmental arrest highlighted by Stolorow and Lachmann (1980). The self is split between an inner voice and an external, detached viewer, who can also become grandiose and hostilely intrusive. As the self is split, the self and other lack differentiation and the more abstract voice, or the more intrusive persona appears as both self and other.

Borderline extremes of opposition are also seen in Emily Brontë's work. For example, her poetry displays diffuse mixtures of female-male, sex-aggression, and god-demon symbolizations. This diffuseness shows a lack of differentiated self-structure. Given such diffuseness, dialogue between a differentiated self and other cannot be achieved. In the absence of such dialogue, there is no contact with the internal self to stimulate a mourning and healing process.

All this can be related to the nature of Emily Brontë's relationship with her father. Perhaps the poet remained perpetually dependent on a narcissistic fusion with him. She took on the role of her father's special daughter, and a state of mutual mirroring of the idealized self was enacted. This in turn seems attributable to an earlier arrest in self-development, possibly stemming from a separation-individuation era when her mother died.

Brontë must have encountered her father's narcissistic need to have her mirror him following an earlier period when her inner self became sealed off. It follows that if the poet attained her father's idealizing mirroring by being his special daughter and by reflecting his idealized image, she would reactively give up her strivings for autonomy and for a potential individuated identity. With a sealed-off primary self, her relation with her father would be based on fusion, not on differentiated relations that could allow autonomy as well as individuated authenticity. The consequences of such false-self development would then become severe, and they might require a compulsive antidote of self-expression through creative activity on a continuing, incessant, and sustained basis. Yet without the ability to mourn and differentiate from an adequately internalized internal object, there would be no ultimate resolution.

Perhaps it was only because of an early death from consumptive disease that Emily Brontë's reactions to her sense of imprisonment never turned to suicide.[7] However, her consumptive disease itself (as the word suggests) might be seen as a malignant object exerting its suicidal force from within. In her lengthy essay on Brontë, Homans (1980) indicates the suicidal trends that did exist. She describes an essay written when Brontë was a student at the school in Brussels with her sister. In this essay, the poetic character dies from maternal neglect, because she cannot dare to offend her absent mother with an open expression of need for care and contact. Such a suicidal trend, in which one cannot express one's needs to the mother one is totally dependent on, can also be seen in *Wuthering Heights,* in which Catherine is driven to starve herself to deny the need she has for Heathcliff, resulting in death. Catherine's anorexic symptom, which reflects Emily Brontë's own (see Frank, 1990), mirrors her psychic state. Just as she refuses to eat and digest food, so too is she unable and/or unwilling to take an object inside of herself for psychic digestion. She cannot digest her male love object. Therefore, this parallels the case of Sylvia Plath, who could not digest her god-daddy, a god-daddy whom she alternately swallowed and spit out (see Kavaler 1985, 1986), exhibiting psychic bulimia, as Emily Brontë exhibited psychic anorexia.

It is not surprising then that Emily Brontë's fictional characters do not survive, as seen in the deaths of her primary characters in *Wuthering Heights*. Their deaths symbolize the author's failed attempt to create and articulate a subjective sense of self. She is unable to bridge the gap of interpersonal communication. As Catherine and Heathcliff scream out their rageful and egocentric views at each other, they merely echo themselves. They do not speak through symbols, their use of words is reactive, not symbolic, they are not separate from that which symbolizes their objects, and they do not create meanings. Neither character reaches the other; there is no bridge of receptive empathy. Faced with the ashes of this failure, Brontë attempts to rebuild her inner and transitional world by depicting an alternate heroine and hero, both of whom are portrayed as surviving. Yet such survival seems contrived. The new characters themselves seem manufactured rather than created. Unlike Catherine and Heathcliff, they show some ability to reconcile their differences. Yet what the narrator reports as tenderness seems to come not from inner evolution, but rather from a form of compliance to the narrator's dictates and to the novel's contrived plot. No interpersonal understanding or reception of an "other's" subjective view is reached. Consequently, there is no organic resolution, as might hypothetically be derived through the mournful letting go of old-self and object reenactments, so that reception of the new can be taken in and empathically perceived. Death itself becomes hope when it is associated with the fantasy state of psychic merger, as is the case for the suicidal Heathcliff. Only a regressive resolution of merger can be sought when differentiation and self-integration fail. Both Heathcliff and Catherine turn toward death as their author does in yearning for a muse that might come from the realm of death or in surrendering to her consumptive disease without a fight. The yearned-for muse becomes the demon lover image of death at the psychic level of borderline preoedipal arrest, with its paranoid-schizoid-position mode of thinking.

# 11

# Emily Dickinson: Muse and Demon

## Early Background

Emily Dickinson was born (1830) and died (1886) in her father's house in Amherst, Massachusetts, the first female and the second surviving infant of the Dickinson family.

From the beginning, the future poet seems to have experienced what it is like to be engaged with an absent presence or a present absence.[1] In the gaps and blocks between her and her detached, preoccupied mother, Emily Dickinson may have felt the empty spaces that became images of voids, lacunae and ellipses in her cryptic form of poetic self-expression.[2]

Several biographers have told of Emily Norcross Dickinson's depression throughout her daughter Emily's infancy and on into her childhood. John Cody, who wrote a psychoanalytic biography of the poet, speaks of the many losses that the poet's mother had suffered in her own family just prior to her daughter's birth. Cynthia Griffin Wolff, Emily Dickinson's most recent biographer, makes clear as well that the mother's depressive and hypochondriacal reactions were part of an overall schizoidal-depressive character problem. Not only was she shocked into numbness by a sequence of deaths and disappointments, but she was by character a withdrawn, inhibited, and unexpressive personality. Although functioning adequately at times as a housewife, she was hopeless, dependent, and passively resistant from the beginning of her marriage (see Wolff 1986). In Wolff's view, Mrs. Dickinson's willingness to marry at all was a submission to an inevitable fate that she seemed no longer able to forestall through her inertia. Edward Dickinson's conviction that she would fit neatly into the role of his wife— a role carefully calculated into his blueprint of life—won the day. According to Wolff, it was precisely this blueprint rather than any interpersonal developments that prompted wedding plans. This was not an auspicious beginning for a family, and for a female child it had its particular hazards in that the chief figure for identification left a "gap" or "void" as her trademark. It is no wonder that in growing up to creative self-expression, Emily became preoccupied with defining an "absent presence," which she described as an "eclipse" (Wolff 1986). This was not the "present absence" of a tranquil "environment mother" (see Ogden,

1986), who can be adequately internalized, it is the "present absence" of a physically present, but emotionally absent parent. Also, the image of an absent father, mingled with the early maternal image to create an internal object most truly characterized through the term "eclipse" (Sewall 1974, 62). The father's more overtly dominant personality could easily color the experience and image of the primary maternal object within the internal world.

Emily Dickinson wrote, "One need not be a chamber to be haunted" (Wolff 1986, 463). As the poet struggled to see into a mysterious "eclipse," she revealed the haunted chasm that she felt inside. Her poetry spun a web of intrigue within the chasm as her internal father colored the empty inner scene. Her maternal void became colored and eroticized by a patriarchal and yet highly emotionally dependent father.

Edward Dickinson was a man burdened with both shame and stunted ambition. According to Wolff, he was the son of a highly idealistic Puritan, Samuel Fowler Dickinson, who had made impassioned and inspired economic investments for the founding of Amherst College, hoping to establish a religiously inspired community. To do so, he had extended himself to the point of bankruptcy and disgrace. In response, his oldest son, Edward, became obsessed with caution and crazed with a desire for respect and legitimacy. Every move that Edward made was calculated as part of a strategy to reestablish beyond question the sanctity of the Dickinson name. As a hard-working attorney, he managed to win renewed reverence for his family. He also earned back the lost family property with its stately homestead, and he served perpetually as the competent treasurer of Amherst College. However, as Wolff points out, his fear of passion never ceased to undercut the sway of his ambitions, which took on a political form. As a stalwart Whig Party member, his opinions were plodding and his thinking was mediocre; he was a lost wanderer among the taller political giants he followed and revered. Yet he sought fame and political adventure in the Massachusetts senate, far way from home, and he therefore became for his daughter Emily an absent presence, a phantom who would serve as an intrapsychic film negative which could be imprinted with all the idealistic forms that his daughter needed to seek in a male extension of herself. With this background in mind, I will examine Emily Dickinson and her father in terms of their evolving father-daughter bond and its psychic imprint. From biographical facts, we can speculate in the service of finding meaningful questions and theories, even when definitive answers may not be forthcoming.

## Emily Dickinson and Her Father

As a girl, Emily Dickinson engaged in no overt play or flirtation with her father, since his stern and remote manner forbade it. Yet her father's dominance left an indelible mark on her poetic mind, since she struggled with an authority figure who kept hidden a profound affection and an even more profound and deeply hidden need. This was all the more arousing in that the oedipal triangle had a devalued and self-effacing link, that of Emily Norcross Dickinson. Through her vision of her mother, Emily might have surmised quite early that marriage could effectively submerge a woman's character. Emily never did marry, nor did she emulate her mother's example of womanhood. The mother's apparent lack of intellect and general detachment and lethargy, must have aroused anxiety in her daughter about any need to identify with her. Emily's poetry displays tremendous ambivalence about being a woman. Her satire about the craving of women to win the esteemed role of "wife" reveals the fear of loss of self behind her view of the socially acceptable persona:

> I'm "wife"—I've finished that—
> That other state—
> I'm Czar—I'm "Woman"
>  now—
> It's safer so—
>
> How odd the Girl's life looks
> Behind this soft Eclipse—[3]
>  (199) [c. 1860]

Again the word "eclipse" brings us back to self-loss and to the void, now seen as part of an inevitable submission by women to men. The "abyss" of which Dickinson writes in her nature and death poetry sharply resonates with the metaphors of male and paternal eclipse that become analogous to a masculine god's eclipse. To prevent a husband's eclipse, the poet could only refuse to marry. Even after the mutual desires that arose in a late-life love affair, Emily Dickinson would recoil from marriage.

To avoid being like her mother or the stereotypical wife, Emily could turn toward identification with her father. This afforded Edward Dickinson's personality a prominent role in her psyche, a role which all but eclipsed that of her mother. Edward was a more active and visible figure, presenting an example of a person of intellect.[4] He was far less distasteful to her than her mother, and far more interesting. Sewall's classic biography quotes many of her comments about him, such as her view of him as deficient in the "low enjoying power" (p. 55). Here, the poet notes her father's inability to play, which created a lack of the paternal form of contact that is generally most prominent during a daughter's early childhood (see Appleton 1981, 8).[5] She spoke of her father's voice coming from a sort of "foreigner" who seemed very far away each morning. With awe and reverence, she added that his heart was "pure and terrible." Emily was aware of her father's detachment from her. She noted, "Father is busy with his briefs," and she spoke of his increasing estrangement from contact with his family.

The less conscious side of the poet's reactions emerge in her poetry; various biographers have noted these as well. The psychoanalyst John Cody writes: "Her deep interior linkage to Edward Dickinson, through blocking her completion as a woman, stimulated her to use her mind" (1971, 103). Helen McNeil notes that Emily Dickinson seemed to assume the role of her father's "spiritual bride"! "Edward seems to have selected Emily to stay with him, rather the way Emerson chose his clever daughter, Evelyn Tucker" (1981, 92). Cody reinforces this view with his comments about Edward Dickinson's indirect and guilt-provoking messages to his daughter concerning his need for his children to stay perpetually near him and his home. Wolff (1986) refers to the unconscious effect of the father's often contradictory behavior, since he held on to his children while simultaneously maintaining extreme distance from them in both an emotional and a literal sense. She writes that Emily was left with the kind of rage toward him that had to be buried, since it was consciously unacceptable. She links it to the poet's continual battle with an indifferent and sadistic god, which Emily Dickinson perpetuates throughout a major period of her poetry. Emily Dickinson's male and paternal god became the "metallic god" who "drills his welcome in" and the faceless god who sadistically turns his back on the poet and drops her into an abyss. Thus

> Edward Dickinson in his elder daughter's renderings of him is principally the mirror in which her own feelings have been reflected. And yet, since such images of a father are essentially childlike, unamended into some more accurate, comprehensive, adult evaluation, the persistence of this way of perceiving him suggests that the relationship was relatively static. Her anger at his absence and his unavailability never intrudes into her letters (for unlike mother, she does not voice even qualified unhappiness). Instead, rage is entirely separated from "my father, Edward Dickinson"; it finds expression only in the poetry, directed toward a "Father" in Heaven whose face we never see and whose voice we never hear.
>
> (Wolff 1986, 63).

In this statement, Wolff notices the static position in which Emily Dickinson was frozen in relation to her demonic god.

This static position is an obvious sign of the internal fixation of pathological mourning and its object relations drama. We need to understand how Emily's reaction to her father was imposed on a preoedipal trauma related to her early mother, a trauma which I propose left Emily with a split god and demon object in her psyche. Her father's personality came to color this split-object imprint, which remained unmodified from the preoedipal era because of early arrest. Whether her split object was innate and archetypal (as Klein or Jung might maintain) or merely due to developmental arrest, it was perpetuated by the maternal-abandonment trauma that appeared incessantly in her poetry, both in its subjects and in its forms. Her poetry became a poetry of recorded disruptions, abortions, and breaks that could resonantly echo repeated breaks in early maternal bonding, some of which may have occurred in the critical rapprochement era, disrupting a potential capacity to mourn and individuate. As any reader of Emily Dickinson knows, her poems repeatedly terminate on a note of disruption and psychic void. Despair is seen in the abortive cut-off that culminates the sequence in each poem. The sense of the endless "zero," the poignant abandonment into a void, and the image of being "dropped" into a black abyss disrupt every vision of harmony, unity, and intercommunal connection. To imagine this motif through the eyes of developmental theory conjures up visions of aborted symbiosis, rapprochement trauma, and self-annihilating terrors of separation closing in like death. Always the one note of self-oblivion comes even as it is feared and foreboding. Such poetry reenacts the trauma as it symbolizes it. It also replaces the object of abandonment with the image of the father where the preverbal sensation of the mother may once have been. More importantly, however, the poetry also testifies to the aborted urge toward developmental mourning that is arresting the poet, keeping her immured within a transitional world and preventing her from moving forward into an adult interpersonal life. Dickinson's mode of receiving Nature reveals the trace of a break in developmental mother-infant bonding, possibly for the rapprochement period (no. 1400). Although birds are dear and dependent creatures in Dickinson's poetry, it is a bird that avoids and eludes relatedness with the poet and flees, reproducing the harshness of separation:

> He glanced with rapid eyes
> That hurried all around—
> They looked like frightened Beads,
> I thought—
> He stirred his Velvet Head
>
> Like one in danger, Cautious,
> I offered him a Crumb
> And he unrolled his feathers
> And rowed him softer home—
> (#328)

Here, the poet's gesture of kindness is repulsed, and rapprochement with nature fails. In another poem, about a snake, the withdrawal is on the human side:

Several of Nature's People
I know, and they know me—
I feel for them a transport
Of cordiality—

But never met this Fellow
Attended, or alone
Without a tighter breathing
And Zero at the Bone—

                (#986)

When the poet creates an ideology for this failing in nature that she so acutely perceives in her psychologically vulnerable state, it is a sadistic God who becomes the agent of the aborted connection between living creatures. This view came to reflect an overall rejection of religious faith during a period that marked the heyday of group and individual "rivivals" meetings meant to arouse a new spirit of commitment to Christianity in Puritanism. The poet continually asks whether God is planning to plunge her into an abyss, even as he proposes new myths of heaven and paradise. With her doubting mind eating away at her, she declares, "narcotics cannot still the tooth that nibbles at the soul" (Ferlazzo 1976, 35). In the chasm of her gap-ridden faith, the poet pictures the abyss in a well to envision the possible fraud of a promised eternity. Maybe eternity is only a big black hole, a bottomless abyss that swallows up our tenuous souls after death:

What mystery pervades a well!
That water lives so far
As neighbor from another world
Residing in a jar

Whose limit none has ever seen,
But just his lid of glass—
Like looking every time you please
In an abyss's face!

The grass does not appear afraid,
I often wonder he
Can stand so close and look so bold
At what is awe to me

                (1400)

The poet implies that because she is human, she is unlike the confident blade of grass that is not afraid since it is part of nature. She is separate, apart, and alienated. Her internal abyss, imprinted within her from infancy, seems in this poem to be externalized. Although her mother may initially have deserted her, the poet's reenactment of the trauma is related to her father, who in his distance and detachment has created within her the view of an indifferent and casually cruel God. Nature is at the mercy of this God as she herself is. In another poem, God's cruel indifference murders just as blindly as it creates an abyss or void to terrify the frail creatures of mortal dependence:

> Apparently with no surprise
> To any happy Flower
> The Frost beheads it at its play—
> In accidental power—
> The blonde Assassin passes on—
> The Sun proceeds unmoved
> To measure off another Day
> For an approving God.
>
> (1624)

The poet sees God as cruel; she takes on a mission to oppose, defy, and even educate him through her poetry. All that she never said to her father is said in her poetry toward her paternally imprinted God. She never gives up her love for her God or for the father from whom her view of God is derived. Yet she sees God as a betrayer, a promise-maker who defrauds on his promises:

> How ruthless are the gentle—
> How cruel are the kind—
> God broke his contract to this Lamb
> To qualify the Wind—
>
> (1439)

Each time she attempts to trust and revere him, mistrust wins out and the rage she never openly expressed to her father bursts forth. The ongoing battle that she displays toward her God can take on the quality of a little girl's tantrum. Although she could never kick her remote external father in the ankles, she can kick her God in such a manner through her poetry:

> Of Course—I prayed—
> And did God Care?
> He cared as much as on the Air
> A Bird—had stamped her foot—
> And cried "Give me"—
> My Reason—Life—
> I had not had—but for Yourself—
> 'Twere better Charity

To leave me in the Atom's Tomb—
Merry and Naught, and gay, and numb—
Than this smart Misery.

(376)

## Father Obsession

Emily Dickinson's life was that of a recluse. By her thirties, she had fully withdrawn from the world. An interesting aspect of this lifelong seclusion is that it not only served as an escape from the outer world, but also allowed Emily permanent residence in her father's home. Her withdrawal from the world was a withdrawal into the world of her father.

Sewall (1974) informs us that Emily mended her father's slippers and played music for him. After one year at Mount Holyoke College, she remained in her father's home, writing guilt-provoking letters to her brother, Austin, who had departed to teach in Boston. In her letters Emily spoke of the heavenly home that awaited her brother's return. Cody in particular (1971) indicates how Emily was her father's agent in seeking Austin's return. It becomes clear that Emily's need for her father was not one-sided. He may have seemed remote, but Edward Dickinson made his desires known to his daughter, who was all too willing to read his subliminal and perhaps even unconscious messages. Significantly, Edward would not eat any bread unless it was baked by Emily. Mrs. Dickinson's sole vocation as cook was thus usurped by her father-obsessed daughter, and Emily cultivated a recipe learned from her mother into a special form of "black bread" that she baked exclusively for her father.

Emily's ritualistic obligations to her father seem to have extended beyond a bond to that of a collusion, creating symptoms of an unconscious bind. Perhaps the poet's jealous desire for the kind of demonstrative adulation that her father lavished on her brother (Cody 1971; Wolff 1986) gave her cause to collude with her father, from whom she longed for similar gifts, gifts of intense recognition.[6] A preoedipal condition of psychic vulnerability in response to a detached and inadequately responsive mother would dramatically exacerbate such desire. Her lack of preoedipal identity differentiation would cause her to cling to her father at the expense of becoming herself secluded from the outside world. In her own words, she reports herself to be a victim possessed, without acknowledging the tenacious possessiveness she herself contributes to the father-daughter bond.

They shut me up in prose—
As when a little Girl

> They put me in the closet—
> Because they liked me still—
>
> (613)

At home, her father could become the muse, the god, and the demon that emerged in her poetry. Yet even in her daily life she revealed her addiction to her father and to his concerns. Beginning in high school, she would refuse invitations to go out by saying, "Father is in the habit of me" (Sewall 1974). According to Sewall, Emily believed that her father would miss her and would want something in her absence. Emily may have been projecting her own yearnings for her father. Yet Sewall, like Cody, Wolff, and McNeil, is impressed by the father's nonverbal mode of influencing the development of his daughter's addiction to him.

> As his family slipped away from him whether geographically, intellectually, or emotionally, Edward showed his disappointment, or grief, not in words whose effect might have been restorative, but in what seems to have been a general moroseness and anxiety, the pensiveness that Vinnie noted. Emily refused invitations because father was "in the habit of me"; she felt he would miss her, would want something in her absence. Once she reminded Austin that "this is a lonely house, when we are not all here." Eventually, of course, they all stayed in Amherst—Emily and Lavinia in the Homestead; Austin with his wife, next door—partly perhaps, out of loyalty to this lonely, hard-working, melancholic and dedicated man.
>
> (63–64)

Despite the rumblings of rage in Emily's poetry, where she kept her secret self immured from her father's world, within her external life at home she made it her priority that her father not be displeased. To sustain her father's pleasure, she outwardly complied with all his rules and routines. Although she had been the last holdout against religious conversion in her year at Mount Holyoke, she nevertheless followed her father's religious rituals. Each morning she would attend family prayer meetings and "think her own thoughts," while "he addressed 'an Eclipse' " (Sewall 1974, 62).

In fact, Emily attempted to fit into her father's mold as perfectly as possible. She maintained an outwardly compliant false self devoted incessantly to her father's pleasure. Her secret inner self lived only in her poetry, where her father addiction emerged in its hostile and negative form. Her father's increasing detachment with age is reported by the poet herself: "My father seems to me often the oldest and oddest sort of a foreigner. Sometimes I say something and he stares in a curious sort of bewilderment though I speak a thought quite as old as his daughter. . . ." (quoted in Sewall 1974, 66). Like Emily, her father had a public self, one he devoted to political duty as much as he could. Yet he had no transitional world of creative expression for his inner self, and so his potential inner self seems to have died long before he did. His obsessional character seems to have deteriorated into an increasingly schizoidal state of detachment, a pattern that his daughter's own character was to repeat with age. After his death, the daughter that had been so dutiful to him was left to endure years of silent anguish. However, his death was also to bring a new awakening in Emily Dickinson's internal relations with him.

## Father's Death

On June 16, 1874, Emily Dickinson's father died in a hotel in Boston, where he was attending the state senate. Just the day before he had been at home with Emily. They had a brief meeting that Emily herself eclipsed. She writes of her last moments with her father, in which she seeks to exclude her mother: "The last afternoon that my father lived, though with no premonition—preferred to be with him, and invented an absence for mother, Vinnie being asleep" (quoted in Sewall, 69). Emily would usually have withdrawn to her room after a family meal, but on this particular day, in keeping with her unconscious intuitive response to her father, Emily decided to visit with him alone. She then became embarrassed by her father's pleasure in her company, and perhaps afraid of sexual feelings at the point when her father remarked with uncharacteristically intimate feeling that he "would like it to not end" (69). In response, Emily suggested that her father leave her to walk with her brother. Then he was gone.

Edward Dickinson's death hit Emily very hard, as can be seen in Sewall's recall of her own words:

> Emily was shocked to find how shocked she was: "I cannot recall myself [she wrote to her Norcross cousins]. I thought I was strongly built, but this stronger has undermined me. . . . Though it is many nights, my mind never comes home."
>
> (69)

Her home had been always with her father; now he was gone. Her mind could not come home to his absence. Reality became confused, since the boundaries of her world had always been set by her father's measure. She had become increasingly reclusive, but after her father's death she refused to go outside the house at all. Sewall writes that "three years after his death she avoided a family reunion because," in Emily's words, as she was "accustomed to all [the relatives] through Father, they remind me too deeply of him for Peace" (69).

Although she had frequently worn white, after her father's death she wore white exclusively. Perhaps she was more determined than ever to appear virginal, as though transgressions of virginity severed her forever from the special honor of being her father's pure little girl. Her sense of herself as bad must have been deep, given that she had to protest her innocence so dramatically. If her father's heart was "pure and terrible," as she remarked after his death, she may have surmised that she must remain absolutely pure in order to meet him again after her own death. She was wed to him as his spiritual bride. Intellectually and creatively compelled to commune with him and his image, she had to freeze her sexuality more than before.

Emily grew to love her father even more obsessively after his death, and much more overtly. She now said that she had known the world only through his eyes. How could she live now that he was gone? For two years she dreamed obsessively about him. She wrote: "I dream about father every night, always a different dream, and forget what I am doing daytimes, wondering where he is" (Cody 1971, 91). After he died, Emily shed the ironic detachment and caricaturing attitude that she had formerly adopted toward her father, as when she described the jauntiness of his stiff pride: "Father steps like Cromwell when he had the kindlings" (Sewall 1974, 634). Although her satire had no doubt been a means of defending herself against the extreme vulnerabilities she felt, it no longer was a defense that she sought after he died. Emily's view of her father's pomposity was now turned to a picture of grace, as reverence grew to gross idealization, no longer displaced onto an image of a paternal god. She now eulogized her father's lonesome life as the grand life of a hero.

> Lay this Laurel on the One
> Too intrinsic for Renown—
> Laurel—vail your deathless tree—
> Him you chasten, that is He!
> (1393)

Whereas before she had highlighted the pathetic and tortured soul as the "oddest sort of foreigner" (66), now she memorialized her father, without mocking or pitying him.

## The "Nobodaddy"

Emily Dickinson's intensely frustrating relationship with her father, combined with the preoedipal intensity that she carried into the oedipal stage from earlier frustrations with a detached mother (Cody 1971), laid the internal-world blueprint for her relationships with all men, in life and in her poetry. Her inner blueprint led to compulsive reenactment. Separation from the internal mother-father person-ality could not take place. Thus, the internal father-mother remained a split-off constellation that was never adequately assimilated into the core self. The form of this internal object reflected the internal world of those in Melanie Klein's more punitive mental state, the paranoid-schizoid position. Its size was mammoth, and its idealized-god aspect was also reinforced by its huge and demonic counter-part. In this state of arrest, every god must turn demon, and every muse and mentor must take on the shapes of the god and demon. Personal hatred, unconsciously felt as badness, becomes so fused with the internal father and his actual inadequacy that one's self cannot be tolerated except as a pure, virginal spirit. Not to be pure is to be a witch.

The real father's actual personality imprints the masculinized primary moth-ering object. This actual personality becomes distorted by a daughter's uncon-scious or split-off aggression. Consequently, when Emily Dickinson's adoration of her father and her defensive distancing from him are combined, they are also intermingled with her own unacknowledged hate, developing a malignant blueprint for all of her other relations with men. Such a malignant blueprint can be conceptualized in terms of a perpetuated addiction to a malignant internal object that promotes the psychic paralysis of pathological mourning. Both Cody (1974) and Wolff (1986) refer to the pathological mourning seen in the poet's perpetuated reenactment of an internal-world blueprint. Cody speaks of Dickin-son's perpetual state of "bereavement" (494; 497); Wolff observes the static relationship between the poet and her father as reflected in repetitive enactments of the self and the paternal god in Dickinson's poetry. In these poetic reen-actments, we can see a father who appears godlike, because his stature is that of a man in relation to an infant.

Gilbert and Gubar use Blake's colorful neologism to describe the ratio between the mammoth father and the minuscule daughter. In *The Madwoman in the Attic*, they speak of the "Nobodaddy," punning on Dickinson's poem about being a "nobody" (no. 288):

> As many critics have observed, Dickinson began her poetic career by con-sciously enacting the part of a child—both by deliberately prolonging her own childhood and by inventing a new, alternative childhood for herself. At the same time, however, her child mask was inseparable from her even more famously self-defining role as the inoffensive and invisible soul of "I'm Nobody! Who are you?" (J. 288). In keeping with this early yet toughly enduring version of herself, Dickinson insistently described herself as a tiny person, a wren, a daisy, a mouse, a child, a modest little creature easily mastered by circumfer-ence and circumstance. Like Barrett Browning, whose poetry she much ad-mired, she seems at first to have assuaged the guilt verse-writing aroused by transforming Romantic poetic self-assertion into an aesthetic of female service

modeled on Victorian marriage. Certainly something like the relationship between a masterful husband and a self-abnegating wife appears to be at the heart
of much of her poetry, where it is also pictured, vicariously, as the encounter
of lover and mistress, king and queen. On closer examination, however, we
can see that—in keeping with this poet's persistent child poise—the male-
female relationship is really that of father and daughter, master and scholar,
slave, ferocious "man of noon" and vulnerable flower of dawn, reverent or
rebellious Nobody and (to borrow a useful neologism from William Blake)
"omnipotent omnipresent Nobodaddy. . . ."

(587)

Although Gilbert and Gubar write as literary critics, not psychoanalysts, they
see the difference between Emily Dickinson, a preoedipal-level character, and
Elizabeth Barrett Browning, who achieved an oedipal level of development. The
omnipotent "Nobodaddy" has quite another internal-object dimension than that
of the internalized Victorian male or husband. Dickinson is arrested in a state in
which the self has not yet been separated from that of the mother-infant dyad;
yet a turn toward father has been made, spurred on by the oedipal lust and longing
that all little girls have for their fathers. Thus, the self becomes merged with the
father in a symbiotic structure that is perpetuated in the internal world. The poet's
inner-world entanglement with her idealized father is thus reflected in an external-
world use of men as extensions of herself. The outer "self/object" men resonate
with the part object males within her.[7] Thus, the father and the males that follow
the father's imprint are sought as self-extensions along the lines of both mentors
and monstrous muses.

The mentors Emily chose were kept at the same distance as that she preserved
from her relationship with her father in her inner world. Colonel Higginson, the
reputed publisher who dismissed her work as "spasmodic" (Sewall 1974, 553)
and the poet herself as "my eccentric poetess" (566) who "drained his nerve
power," (563), is among the mentors whom she openly revered and secretly
rebelled against. Higginson had a distaste for her personal presence, telling his
wife, "I'm glad not to live near her." (567). He kept himself at a distance that
allowed the poet to alternately adore and despise him. Cody (1971) mentions
Dickinson's castrating slights toward Higginson. Whatever anger was behind
such slights was never openly acknowledged, and her anger did not allow her to
let go of him. She continued to correspond with him and to call him her preceptor
and master, even as her lifetime passed and he still dismissed her poetry as
inadequate for publication. Although Higginson too seemed slightly obsessed
with Emily, he continually failed truly to respond to her or her poetic missives.
He greatly supported and assisted another woman writer of the time, Helen Hunt,
who bent her will and literary style to his; nevertheless, he was adamantly beyond
encouraging the subtly rebellious and self-styled Dickinson. The latter cried in

her poetry that Higginson should use a microscope to see her poetry's worth (no. 185). Sewall believes that in this poem, Dickinson revealed a desperate wish to be published. However, Dickinson feared publication as much as she longed for it, and the provocative and indiscrete reactions that both Cody and Wolff have discovered in her letters to Colonel Higginson distanced her not only from him but from the world at large as well. Her relationship to a potential world of readers was as distant, fearful, and ambivalent as it was toward Higginson, who represented the world of male publishers. Both relationships could be modeled only from the same internal father-mother cloth. Through correspondence, Dickinson revered a number of men as mentors, including the law clerk Benjamin Newton, her school chum George Gould, the Reverend Watkins, and the editor of the Springfield Republican newspaper, Samuel Bowles. She contrived a distance from all those important to her. Her written correspondence could then serve as a transitional object—something between a separate other and a part of herself. Although she begged Samuel Bowles to visit, when he actually did so she refused to see him. Bowles also failed, however, to acknowledge her poetic talent and published only a handful of poems in his newspaper. All these men eluded her as her father did. Although Dickinson wrote "all men say What to me!" (Sewall 1974, 667), at the requisite distance they remained strangely attached to her as well.

Given all these mysterious male mentors in her life, there has been much speculation by Emily Dickinson's biographers and literary commentators as to the identity of the unnamed transferential figure that the poet calls "master" in her famous "master letters." It is in these letters that Dickinson most vividly displays the combination of reverent worship and tragic disappointment that echoes repeatedly throughout her love poetry (see Wolff 1986). The model of the internal father is seen again here, especially in the imagery of relative sizes and dimensions. In the third master letter, the poet shows abject despair at her master's rejection of a love that she revealed despite an overwhelming sense of shame. Her small size in relation to her master is emphasized here more than in the first two letters. In a related poem, in which she assumes the persona of "Daisy" as she had in her master letters, she is seen in relation to the gargantuan "Himmaleh":

> The Himmaleh was known to stoop—
> Unto the Daisy low—
>
> (481 [c. 1862])

Yet such size is always accompanied by the distance and the unavailability of the man; in keeping with her thematic mode of reenactment, the result is always profound rejection. The "master" has a wife, for the poet indulges in contemplation of being in the "queen's place," perhaps to breathe beside her master. Yet it is the queen's presence that protects her from the swelling ocean of sexual feeling, "the menacing sea" (Sewall 1974, 515), which she may have particularly feared because the persona of raw sexuality swims toward her chaotically, owing to her vulnerabilities sustained from preoedipal trauma. Her sexual feelings are not structured and seem dangerously out of control. She combines thoughts of sexual excitement and erotic longings with echoes of an insatiable sucking need: "[Y]ou know what a leech is, don't you—and [remember that] Daisy's arm is small-and you have felt the horizon hav'nt you—and did the sea-never come so close as to make you dance?" (quoted in Sewall, 515). Sexual thoughts turn to thoughts of reunion with her love, but she despairs of ever finding this on earth and seeks it instead in heaven. Even in heaven there is the "corporation" that might find them out; instead, the poet resorts to being a little girl and playing in the woods till dark, where "Sundown" cannot find them. A sense of secrecy, incest with a paternal figure, and hopes of oedipal triumph are all conflated. Yet ultimately they must meet in heaven as two bodiless angels, and she ends on a note of despair that he has failed to come to her in "white." Since sexual deprivation and virginity can be transformed into the pure ambrosia of love expressed through poetry, the poet can be consecrated into the role of the spiritual bride who comes to her lover through the "white election." "What would you do with me if I come 'in white'?" she challenges. (515). The faith behind this wish for a puritanical reunion in heaven rids the poet of fears of engulfment in erotic desires tinged with oral cravings. Although her lover may not have come to her in "white," the erotically desired paternal lover has now successfully been transmuted into a muse.[8] When we view the master letters, it becomes apparent that although the unavailability of the lover induces great suffering in the poet, from a psychological perspective this suffering can be seen as answering a profound unconscious need, i.e., the need to have an unavailable man to use as a muse. Her fear of sexuality is warded off to the extent that she succeeds in turning men into muses. Her longings are more tolerable when translated into poetry than sex. The poetry contains the rage aroused by her fear.

What happens, however, when the unavailable man becomes available? A late love in Emily Dickinson's life allows us to answer this question. Unlike the subject of the "master letters," who repeated the theme of unrequited love of Dickinson's internal-world blueprint from her incorporated father and father-daughter relations, the subject of her later love returns her passion and wishes even to marry her. How does the poet manage to turn this man into a muse?

Judge Otis Philip Lord was eighteen years older than Emily Dickinson. He had been a friend of the Dickinson family for many years. Both Otis Lord and Edward Dickinson were among the dwindling group of committed political conservatives who championed the traditional Whig Party. Both men were famous for their oratorical skills and were men of "action," committed to the causes of the public. They both had legal backgrounds, combining law and politics.

Emily Dickinson fell in love not only with the closest male affiliation of her father, but with a man who mirrored her father's rational, dominating, and dutiful way of life. During her later years (in her forties and fifties), the passionate—and sometimes erotic—adoration that Lord aroused in the poet may have been more possible than ever because of the literal absence of her father through death. Cody mentions the poem "Wild Nights—Wild Nights" (# 249) as testimony to the fact that she could feel erotic desires toward a man, although these desires had been greatly repressed.

Emily Dickinson had followed her inner imprint and turned her preoedipally structured father into a muse-god. This muse-god lived in her poetry, but he could also be seen in the image of a flesh-and-blood man, especially in a man who was such an obvious father substitute. The poet spoke of Judge Lord as "almost as omniscient as God" (Sewall 1974, 649), and languished on him an overflowing "idolatry that would crush us both" (655–56). Lord represented a supreme and kingly place in the world of affairs and common sense from which Emily had felt so totally cut off, particularly since the time of her father's death. In addition, Emily's "idolatry" was here for the first time requited. Although he may have seen none of her actual poetry, Lord spoke with great admiration of her occupation of "inertia" (653). From Lord, Emily could receive for the first time what she had sorely missed from her father: an open expression of admiration combined with affectionate love. Yet for Emily the affection and adoration could be transformed into the nurturing endeavor excitement of an oedipal-stage daughter who performs creatively with the fantasy of having captured a special position within her father's adoring eyes, the position of dancing "for his eyes only."

However, there were complications. Unlike Emily's earlier longing for a married man, as seen in her "master letters," Judge Lord's safe, married situation was altered by the death of his wife. At first, Emily felt released by Mrs. Lord's death (Sewall, 653). She guiltily confessed to the judge her elation at the removal of this rival. Yet as soon as the judge asked her to be his new wife, she replied that "No" is the most enticing word in the human language (655), emphatically declaring her philosophy of renunciation:

> Renunciation—is a piercing Virtue—
> The letting go
> A presence—for an Expectation—
> Not now—
>
> (Sewall, 656)

The poet tells Lord that he must forebear: "If you want the divine crust you must forego the daily bread" (Cody 1971, 44; 100). This daily bread obviously encompasses sexual relations. Although in "Wild Nights" Emily wrote of longing to be near Lord at night, what could emerge in poetic form was strongly repressed beyond daily consciousness. Dickinson wrote to Lord that if she was tempted by sexual desires she perhaps could not resist marrying him (100). Her reluctance to marry became an ultimate refusal through a series of excuses that delayed action until Lord died.

Despite the anguished suffering at unrequited love in her love poetry and master letters, Emily Dickinson turned down the opportunity she was offered. The critics suggest various explanations. Cody (1971, 101) cites incest guilt based on the intimate resemblance between Lord and her actual father. Her oedipal guilt at the time of Lord's wife's death has already been mentioned. Sewall and Wolff reduce the whole issue to a conscious and rational vocational choice on the poet's part. Wolff also speaks of the poet's wish to stay at home to care for her invalid mother, who had had a stroke during that period. Cody emphasizes the poet's general fears of her instincts, which would cause her to be too threatened by a sexual relationship. Wolff speaks of Dickinson's general need for distance. None of these explanations captures the whole story, which can be best viewed through studying the object relations within Emily Dickinson's internal world.

We know that that world was inhabited by mammoth "Himmaleh" god-daddies, all seemingly constructed out of an idealized primary object. This idealized object had been masculinized by the father's personality, just as it was imposed on that of the mother's. The father-mother object had been eroticized by oedipal-stage longings. Yet this idealization remained much more profound than the later eroticization. These condensations constrict the blueprint of the internal object that emerges through projections onto male father substitutes (as Blake's "Nobo-daddy" cited by Gilbert and Gubar). Judge Otis P. Lord was the last and perhaps the most revered "Nobodaddy." To turn the "Nobodaddy" into an idealized muse figure is the ultimate goal of the preoedipally arrested creative woman. Only by succeeding at this—by using the "Nobodaddy" muse for inspiration that allows self-expression through creative work—can the preoedipally arrested woman keep her self alive as a differentiated being. She cannot be kept emotionally alive by interpersonal relations, for they threaten self-loss and fragmentation through symbiotic mergence.

Marriage would have threatened to engulf Dickinson in the upheaval of sexual energies that remained chaotic and archaic because of preoedipal arrest. Such marriage would also threaten Dickinson with a submissive symbiotic merger with an overpowering male god figure, who once engaged would inevitably become a demon. She was in danger of repeating her mother's role in her marriage, in which enslaved submission and repeated abandonment both were perpetual conditions to be endured. Even more dangerous was the threat that marriage would bring demands for an interpersonal commitment that would choke off Dickinson's one primary mode of self-articulation, her daily self-expression through poetry. It was psychologically determined that her creative work had to be continually repeated. Her relief from it was temporary; no day could go by without it.

## The Dream King and the Yearning for a Positive Creative Force

Dickinson believed that to possess someone in fantasy is more desirable than to possess that person in reality. This applied particularly to her desire to have her father through a secret and incestuous incorporation of him and of all the masculine characteristics that he represented. John Cody (1971) writes of Dickinson:

> She expresses the idea that reality is unnecessary when one's fantasy is complete, vivid, and permanent: "What need of Day—/To those whose Dark— hath so—surpassing Sun—/It deem it be—Continually—/At the Meridian?" (poem no. 611). In these and many other instances Emily Dickinson equates love, fulfillment, and security with the possession of an abiding sun—the possession of a male lover patterned after her father or the establishment of his attributes within her own personality.

Dickinson connected the father, as well as the masculine personality that the poet sought to possess by means of dreams and fantasy, with creative strength and fecundity. These were seen as counteracting the maternal identification that she had all but repudiated through generally devaluing all that was feminine. In the middle of the night, Dickinson's unconscious often emerged with her internal father, whom she so craved to possess, believing him to be her only means to creative fulfillment. In her dreams, she would "peep in parlors shut by day," possessing and being possessed by her internal male father, who would drive her toward creative productivity, the bounty of a nurtured fantasy life. Dickinson called this internal father her dream king.

> Theodora Ward in *The Capsule of the Mind*, a somewhat Jungian interpretation of Emily Dickinson's psychology, cites a poem, "I have a King, who does not speak," and expresses the view that the poet here reveals her awareness of the degree to which her creative life is dominated by the masculine archetype— Jung's animus. On this point, I largely agree with Mrs. Ward, except that I read the poem as testifying to Emily's identification with the males in her family, which Emily to a degree welcomed, in contrast to feminine identification, which she repudiated. The poem tells of a "king" whose regular appearance in Emily's dreams causes her to wish the days away and to look forward eagerly to sleep, at which time, if she is fortunate, she may, by means of dreaming, "peep/In

parlors, shut by day" (no. 103). The poet says that when this occurs she awakens the following morning thrilling with an emotion of portentous triumph. On the other hand, when she does not have this dream the next day finds her unresponsive to the beauties of nature and feeling rebellious toward God. Mrs. Ward says of this poem: "The mysterious silence of the dream king and the happiness brought by a vision of him suggest that the figure is purely symbolic. Under his domination daily life becomes meaningful, but she can maintain contact with him only in the unconscious of sleep."

(Cody 1971, (121–22)

Dickinson's ability to make her dream king conscious, even if just for a day at a time, shows an ability to use her internal masculine object as a positive force for creation—albeit that a rape of her potential female identity can be the price. This ability in Dickinson to own her masculine object through unconscious fantasy brought to consciousness stands in contrast to Emily Brontë's loss of poetic voice every time that she attempts to engage the powers of her male muse in her poetry.[9] Perhaps there is a more developed sense of agency in Dickinson, despite a developmental arrest that will be seen in her inability ultimately to repair herself. On a day-to-day basis, her masculinity could energize her creativity and her creativity could allow her masculine identifications to live.

Dickinson's dream king arouses curiosity as to its origin. Cody disputes the Jungian view that an innate, a priori, male archetype is responsible for the emergence of the dream king. He prefers seeing real-object identifications or internalizations as the sole cause for Dickinson's dreams. Eugene Monick, like Ward, is a Jungian who might contradict this view. In *Phallos: Sacred Image of the Masculine* (1987) he writes

> What place, then, does phallus-animus have in the creative life of women without recourse to a man or masculine image on whom she can project her phallic qualities?
>
> Phallos can be a guide to a woman as he is to a man. His stirring, metaphorically, lets a woman know that creative action is on the horizon. . . . The stirring of phallos in a man shows his impending readiness to sow seed; in a woman, the positive aspect of animus manifests in impulses to establish herself creatively in the world.
>
> (123)

Another way to look at what Monick ascribes to the innate power of Phallos, however, involves the compounding of preoedipal- and oedipal-level relations and identifications with the father, which might be seen in the preoedipally arrested female in particular. When we learn of Emily Dickinson's preference for a dream king that she can meet only in the rich darkness of the night, as opposed to a real daytime father or of a real marriage with a man, it is certainly possible to read oedipal fantasies into the nightly rendezvous with the dream king. Dickinson's creativity was her baby born through her fantasy marriage to the idealized "king" father, whose idealization stemmed back to the god image of the early, preoedipal stages of life. As Lora Heims Tessman writes in her theories on oedipal-stage "endeavor excitement," the little girl doesn't just want to receive a baby from father, as Freud thought. She wants to "make a baby with father." What better model could there then be to describe the process of Emily Dickinson's creative work?

## The Oedipal Father in the Preoedipal-Level Woman

There has been much controversy over what role oedipal dynamics play in the preoedipal character. Is there an oedipal father for the preoedipally arrested daughter whose psychic structure is still somewhat merged with a mammoth primary parental object? Is it possible to have oedipal desires eroticize and intensify an earlier craving for the object as an idealized extension of the self, even if the triadic structure for a full-fledged oedipal conflict has not been adequately formed? Emily Dickinson's poetry suggests that this can be the case. Although John Cody's (1971) psychoanalytic study of Dickinson points out the dynamics of preoedipal fixation in her character, certain poems attest to the oedipal involvement that she did experience with her father, which could lead to much disappointment and shame. The following poem captures the essence of her oedipal longings and oedipal disappointment:

> The Sun—just touched the Morning—
> The Morning—Happy thing—
> Supposed that he had come to dwell—
> And Life would all be Spring!
>
> She felt herself supremer—
> A raised-Etherial Thing!
> Henceforth-for Her—What Holiday!
> Meanwhile—Her wheeling King—
> Trailed—slow—along the Orchards—
> His haughty-spangled hems—
> Leaving a new necessity!
> The want of Diadems!

The morning—fluttered—staggered—
Felt feebly—for her Crown—
Her unannointed forehead—
Henceforth—Her only One!

(1971, 232)

Cody comments on the oedipal daughter's experience in this poem:

> If one assumes that the unconscious meaning of "Sun" here is "Father," the hidden drama of the poem becomes amenable to analysis. The feminized "Morning," here of course representing the female child, mistakenly believing the Sun has claimed her as his own, is inflated with self-importance. Her happiness is short-lived, however, and after a brief period she makes the painful discovery that her possession by the Sun was illusory and that he has moved on (presumably to something more mature—possibly "Noon").

> (431)

Cody captures the sense of narcissistic deflation, which of course can be interpreted in terms of castration (the "want of Diadems!"). Yet the overriding theme is that of being dropped by the father; in Cody's interpretation, this involves an obvious queenly rival for the king's attention, "Noon." This poem can recall Emily Dickinson's eagerness to invent "an absence for mother" on the day that she chose to be at home with her father, a day that turned out to be the day before his death. It can recall the poet's wish to be in the "queen's place" that appears in the second master letter (Sewall 1974, 515). However, it can also recall the tragic ending to such a wish when the shame of paternal rejection extends to an earlier level of craving for affirmation of one's sense of self as the urge toward differentiation emerges. In the second master letter, the poet speaks of having revealed her love as Vesuvius erupting, and the consequent shame experienced following such exposure is encapsulated in the image of herself as Pompeii buried by her own explosion:

> Vesuvius dont talk—Etna—dont—[Thy] one of them—said a syllable—a thousand years ago, and Pompeii heard it, and hid forever—She couldn't look the world in the face, afterward—I suppose—Bashful Pompeii! "Tell you of the want."

> (quoted in Sewall, 515)

This passage foreshadows the denouement of the third master letter (518). In that letter, the poet is totally bereft, beyond shame, encased in total despair. She alludes casually to her pain as a "tomahawk in her side" and a continuous "stabbing" (supposedly in her heart) from her lover's lack of response, which resonates with another poem about a lover's desertion, where she refers to "staples" piercing her (Ferlazzo 1976, 71). Then she opts for the moral defense by claiming herself to be the guilty party. "Did I offend it?" is a question reiterated in various ways. She asks "Did my love for you kill you?"; the irony is that she is the one devastated by a love given, expressed, and exposed into a vacuum (see Fairbairn [1952] on schizoids' fear of their own love). She is here displayed as tiny, while her abandoning lover is gigantic, yet she makes her "crime of love" the force of reversal, defending against an exquisite vulnerability with the badge of guilt. In this way she protects the image of the internal parent, now displaced onto her "master." She attempts to retain an idealized view of the other in this way, refusing to consciously face her rage, while yet expressing it indirectly as a martyred victim. Like "Pompei," she turns in upon herself and hides forever.

## Conflation of Oedipal and Preoedipal Levels

As we see these dynamics played out, the oedipal and preoedipal fathers are conflated, and an obsession with rejection and loss emerges. We can recall the indifferent father figures of god and sun who jointly colluded in beheading an innocent spring flower (no. 1624). Certainly this hints at the oedipal dynamics of a father's chilly blindness to his daughter's emerging sexuality. However, when the king of the blatantly oedipal poem becomes God, we know that the preoedipal level of archaic idealization is operating as well.

The oedipal father is the father whose languid glance might shift abruptly in any direction, dropping his daughter from his imagined arms. The oedipal daughter imagines her father's longed-for touch as her father's glance falls casually on her, but then feels a terrible cut as his eyes move away. How much longed-for grace Emily must have imagined in her father's eyes, as she read them in an embrace, hoping that it would be conferred upon her through those eyes.

The exquisite vulnerability of the oedipal daughter stems back to an earlier time. When the father takes on the power of this earlier-level archaically idealized object as well, his godlike dimensions take on a demonic coloring as soon as indifference is felt. With a father as absent and emotionally distant as Emily Dickinson's "eclipse," it is no wonder that he is experienced as a demon lover or as a devil god. The following poem tells of this demon lover father that lived within her:

> He fumbles at you Soul
> As Players at the keys
> Before they drop full Music on—
> He stuns you by degrees—

Prepares your brittle Nature
For the Ethereal Blow
By fainter Hammers—further head—
Then nearer—then so slow
You Breath has time to straighten—
Your Brain—to bubble Cool—
Deals—One—imperial—Thunderbolt—
That scalps your naked Soul—

When Winds take Forests in their Paws—
The Universe—is still—

(315)

Dickinson exudes the torment of her exquisite vulnerability in relation to her father. This vulnerability colored her experiences with men she admired and longed to love, as well with her male editors. Ultimately, it colored her imagined experience of God, who had now explicitly turned demonic. Her imperial lord is the Himmaleh whom she matches up with an image of herself as a petite or even minute daisy. He is the editor (Higginson and Bowles) who subtly declines the core and soul of her poetry as he hastens to repair it into colloquial terms. He is the father who so intimidated her that she pretended she could tell time when she could not, just because her father had been the one to have instructed her to read a clock (Sewall 1974). This is the fantasy-enhanced father who held her fast through guilt to a lifetime secluded within his homestead. Locked away within his world, yet not feeling free to express any open criticism of him, Emily Dickinson's subversive reactions were confined to her poetry. As the internal world unfolds in poetic form, the erotic adoration of an oedipal father is intensified by the archaic idealization that persists from the preoedipal era owing to developmental arrest. In viewing the demon-god who scalps her naked soul, we can see a daughter's adoration, which turns to perennial tantalization within a state of torture. This turn seems dictated by the fusion of two psychic levels of need.

This last demon lover poem captures the torment with a subtle symbolic vividness so different from the more harshly graphic lines drawn by Sylvia Plath in her famous "Daddy" poem. When Dickinson writes, "Then so slow your breath has time to straighten—your brain—to bubble cool," we wait suspended between the threat of impending decimation and its actual occurrence. We see the anguish of a woman's erotic self, whose spiritual transformation is the "Soul at the white heat" (#365). This is the final yet subtle and rather casual blow that eradicates and fractures the inner soul. However, this demon-god also fascinates. He is a skilled artisan of torture.

### Fear of Male Sexuality

The power of indifference can quickly become the threatening power of lust when a father's tenderness is not felt and male sexuality begins to threaten. We see this transition in going from the malevolent god of indifferent torture to the an imperial snake god:

> A snake with mottles rare
> Surveyed my chamber floor
> In feature as the worm before
> But ringed with power.
>
> (#1670)

This fear of the snake's power is more strongly stated in the poem, "A narrow Fellow in the Grass" (no. 986), in which the poet experiences a sense of "zero at the bone" when she sees a snake. Ferlazzo (122) comments on the poet's fear of the slithering movements of the snake and of its fondness for "empty, unpleasant places," which lends to it connotations of evil related to those attributed to the snake in the Bible. All of this implies the dangers of male sexuality as well. Other poems make this fear even more explicit.

The sea is used as a metaphor for an ominous quality that the poet seems to associate with the threats of male sexuality:

> But no Man moved Me—till the Tide
> Went past my simple Shoe—
> And past my Apron—and my Belt
> And past my Bodice—too—
>
> And made as He would eat me up—
> As wholly as a Dew
> Upon a Dandelion's Sleeve
> And then—I started—too—
>
> And He—followed—close behind—
> I felt His Silver Heel
> Upon my Ancle—Then my Shoes
> Would overflow with Pearl—
>
> (#520)

It is obvious that a pervasive sense of engulfing forces in nature becomes related to a molesting-male instinct in this poem. In other poems about storms, these images of threatened violation become deadly, as when the poet refers to a storm as "Doom's electric moccasin" (Ferlazzo, 117). Such images transform sexual threats into threats from a demonic male god whose sexuality brings either actual or psychic death through the obliteration of self-identity. Male sexuality, as well as sex itself, is tainted with such fears when profound shame from a "Nobodaddy" rejection is mixed with expectations of self-fragmentation through object loss. Wolff (1986, 353) notes that Dickinson often combines metaphors of orgasmic delight and fatal loss in her poetry. As in the master letters, thoughts of sexual union can be frequently followed by thoughts of a reunion in heaven which turns sexual union into union through death.

From Emily Dickinson's letters, John Cody discovered some fantasies of rape that border on hallucination and delusion. He relates this preoccupation to a period of psychological breakdown in the poet's life, which he also believes to have directly overlapped with her most creative period. Her fears of male sexuality are heightened by the psychic form of the demon lover muse-god, which emerges with profound impact at this time of chaos and creation.

> The crashing through into consciousness of uprushing instinctual impulses that were formerly repressed is evident in the thinly veiled wish for sexual violation, which, from a conscious standpoint, her ego finds appalling. The "prowling bugger" against whom she guards with such desperation may invade the house if the front door slides open, but it is obviously not burglary she fears. The thought that clearly terrified her is that the imaginary intruder's real design is to seek out her person. Though any intruder would have the entire large house at his disposal, she nevertheless is concerned only with securing the windows of her little bedroom and bolting her door and keeping the gas lights burning so that she may see her attacker. To detect a realistic, rational basis for such fears is difficult indeed. She was, after all, a not very attractive, reclusive spinster whom her would-be rapist would scarcely have had occasion even to see, much less lust after, prior to his gaining her room. What one sees in this passage, therefore, is the emergence from the unconscious of her own previously suffocated sexual longings, now defensively disowned and projected to a threatening, fantasy male. It is of great interest and significance that this letter, which eloquently discloses the thought disorder, weakened impulse control, and inability of the ego to maintain repression—each a hallmark of the psychotic state—should have been written in the very middle of the three-year period that marks the climax of the poet's creative productivity.
>
> (Cody 1976, 288)

Although I agree with Cody that the poet was projecting fears of her own unconscious sexual desires, I think her profound anxiety needs to be seen in terms of her internal-object projections, not only in terms of projected drives or projected instinctual impulses. Since Emily Dickinson's internal father was such a mammoth figure and since reenactments of her relationship with him—as seen in her life and poetry—were so affectively colored by the humiliation and shame following profound seduction and rejection, her fantasies of rape might be better understood as projected reenactments than merely as disowned libidinal wishes. To desire a remote and indifferent god can provoke shame so severe that all sexual desire becomes the anticipation of an intrusive rape—not only because the desire cannot be consciously owned, but because one has psychically experienced such an overwhelming loss of one's sense of self that death is wished for and feared every time there is a sexual thought. When Emily Dickinson locked herself away for life, hiding herself from the world as well as harboring herself in her father's home, she was expressing an archaic form of enacted ambivalence. To have sexual desires toward an indifferent demon father is so intensely humiliating that one can wish to annihilate the image of one's own self. When such wishes are kept unconscious, thoughts of death can become a constant preoccupation. This is certainly true in the poet's expressions of her inner life in her poetry. Her biographers have all referred to her obsession with death and related questions about immortality as her "flood subject." She was flooded by thoughts of death; her heightened creativity brought out death obsessions along with a creative compulsion in which she ultimately envisioned her father-god demon lover as the personification of death itself.

## Death and the Demon-Lover Father

In the poem "The Frost of Death Was on the Pane" (no. 1136), death appears as a lustful snake god attacking a female victim whose friends fight to save her.

> The Frost of Death was on the Pane—
> "Secure your Flower" said he.
> Like Sailors fighting with a Leak
> We fought Mortality.
>
> Our passive Flower we held to Sea—
> To Mountain—To the Sun—
> Yet even on his Scarlet shelf
> To crawl the Frost begun—
>
> We pried him back
> Ourselves we wedged
> Himself and her between,
> Yet easy as the narrow Snake
> He forked his way along.

This conversion of a demon-lover father into an erotic persona of death is seen in many other preoedipally arrested woman poets, such as Sylvia Plath and Anne Sexton.[10] In Emily Brontë's novel *Wuthering Heights*, we have seen how the demon lover character Heathcliff led the heroine to death and then sought an erotic merger with her through his own death.

As with all demon lover figures, the demon is also a muse and a regal king. The following poem echoes Dickinson's poems on the husband's kingly role in marriage:

> Around this quiet Courtier
> Obsequious Angels wait!
> Full royal is his Retinue!
> Full purple is his state!
>
> (171)

The two best-known poems on death show the movement from a subtle demon lover theme to a more overt one. In the first poem, death enters as a courtly gentleman:

> Because I could not stop for Death—
> He kindly stopped for me—
> The Carriage held but just ourselves—
> And Immortality.
>
> We slowly drove—He knew no haste
> And had put away
> My labor and my leisure too,
> For His Civility—
>
> (712)

By the end of the poem, the heroine's gentleman friend has vanished, leaving her vanquished by isolation and by the cold facts of an inevitable fate:

> We paused before a House that seemed
> A swelling of the Ground—
> The Roof was scarcely visible—
> The Cornice—in the Ground—
>
> Since then—'tis Centuries—and yet
> Feels shorter than the Day
> I first surmised the Horses Heads
> Were toward Eternity—

Ferlazzo (1976) sees Dickinson's image of death in this poem as an ambivalent portrait of a courtly suitor and a fraudulent seducer (56). This ambivalence is the same ambivalence with which the poet experienced her father when she saw him as having a heart that was "pure and terrible" and also as being a revered hero. It is the ambivalence that she showed toward her father-god and toward her master-editor-preceptor when she sought to revere these male figures and ended up with mistrust and a sense of betrayal. Her original father was imprinted in her mind; now that imprint was being applied toward the ultimate male image in the world she inhabited, i.e., that of death.

In the following poem, death is more openly malicious. No longer is he a feigned gentleman. Now he appears as a seductive Satan, the "supple Suitor":

> Death is the supple Suitor
> That wins at last—
> It is a stealthy Wooing
> Conducted first
> By pallid innuendoes
> And dim approach
> But brave at last with Bugles
> And a bisected Coach
> It bears away in triumph
> To Troth unknown
> And Kindred as responsive
> As porcelain
>
> (1445)

We are reminded of the cold, dark, abyss within Dickinson herself, an abyss that she repeatedly falls into each time she reaches out her arms to an awesome and absent father. According to Ferlazzo:

This marriage is to Death, not to Christ; and the wedding bower is the family grave, not heaven. Eternity in this poem has a strong suggestion of being a mindless isolation—a condition of oblivion. She will be placed among kindred whose response are like porcelain, and porcelain figures are like corpses with cold, insensate stare.

(58)

It seems that the chill of a traumatically abrupt separation from her mother was the basic wound that Emily Dickinson carried with her, a wound which colored her religious views, her view of God, and her view of death. It is likely, as John Cody maintains in his book *After Great Pain*, that the maternal symbiosis was lacking in nurturance from the beginning; determining that separation would be an experience of being abandoned into an abyss. Dickinson's view of death would naturally therefore be influenced by this. However, the poet's oedipal experience with her father was a transitional stage that altered and harshly colored the structural dynamics of this earlier experience. Because of the lack of sufficient contact and bonding with the early mother to separate from her, the longing for the father seems to have been significantly intensified, and the pathological involvements with him as an internal object appear to have been greatly exacerbated. In the culminating image of death seen as a demon lover figure, at least three factors are synthesized: (i) a pathological-mourning tie with the father, in which the father retains omnipotent power as an archaic and split off internal object, a power transferred onto the father's image from the early internal mother; (ii) the eroticization of the internal-object tie from the oedipal phase; and (iii) the introject of a distant but also unconsciously seductive farther, who is the masculine form that is symbolized after being superimposed on an orally depriving, unavailable mother.

# 12

# Emily Dickinson's Breakdown:
# Renunciation and Reparation

Emily Dickinson never left her father's home again after returning from Mount Holyoke, following only one year of college. By age thirty she had terminated her last two forms of social engagement: going to church on Sundays and attending the yearly commencement reception of Amherst College, which took place in her own living room. She no longer visited friends, but only wrote letters. As Dickinson increasingly secluded herself from the world, she receded to the point of not going across the garden path to visit her brother's home next door. Often she locked herself within her own room at home and ate her meals there.

Hidden from the world and yet showing signs of herself through peculiar habits, Emily Dickinson became a strange ghost in Amherst. She was whispered and gossiped about. Contemporary literary and psychological critics dispute the nature and consequences of the poet's withdrawal from the world. Did this creative recluse undergo some form of breakdown as she left the world, or did leaving the world itself cause psychic breakdown?

Although Richard Sewall speaks of the degree to which Emily Dickinson retained the normality of her life even during the period of her deepest seclusion, other biographical commentators—such as Paul J. Ferlazzo, John Cody, Clark Griffith, and Henry Wells—have recognized the seclusive behavior as symptomatic of disabling mental disturbance. Cody (1971) in particular speaks of the tenuousness of the psychological precipice to which Dickinson clung, when catatonic numbness, dissociated detachment, and extreme depersonalization overwhelmed her. Cody has most explicitly declared the psychotic nature of the poet's breakdown. He writes of the psychological disruptions that precipitated a break with reality:

> The circumstances of Emily Dickinson's life pressed for a radical revision of personality. As she tried to grow fissures in the supporting framework of her attitudes and orientations kept appearing. From early adolescence through young adulthood, the forces of growth, under terrific pressure, groped vainly for a possible channel, until eventually the constituting and supporting husk

shattered. Before this occurred, though, the blocked energies, transformed by frustration into something dark and devious, had begun to create a strange psychic edifice of their own.

(261)

It is within Emily Dickinson's poetry itself that we can see the devastating inner reactions that she experienced during her years of deepening seclusion. Cody believes that the year 1857 to 1864 were decisive ones for her poetry, when her feelings of hopelessness and estrangement reached such severity that she suffered a psychotic episode. In the process of self-rehabilitation, which peaked during 1862, Dickinson's poetic outpourings reached their greatest level.

## Poetry of Madness

Sewall believes that Dickinson preferred to create her friends rather than actually to know them. By restricting her communication and contact to letter writing, she was able to create people through her imagination, forming transitional objects that must have reflected the dimensions of her internal objects. Although Emily Dickinson may have hoped to withdraw from a distracting external world into an interior life of personal design and internal relations, her interior world was unavoidably altered by the loss of contact with external objects. The poems of her most prolific creative period speak of isolation, loneliness, and psychic numbing. In one poem she writes

> I saw no Way—the Heavens were stitched—
> I felt the Columns close—
> The Earth reversed her Hemispheres—
> I touched the Universe—
>
> (378)

In another attempt to convey a state of psychic collapse, the poet highlights the impact of disappointment as opposed to the sense of isolation that can result from it. The following example also shows that the poet conceals her despair, creating her own isolation:

> A great Hope fell
> You heard no noise
> The ruin was within
> Oh cunning wreck that told no tale
> And let no Witness in
>
> (1123)

We can remember the disappointed love recorded by the poet in her "master letters" as well as the poet's wish to publish that met with editorial incomprehension.[1] The play *The Belle of Amherst* has Dickinson recite this poem just following Colonel Higginson's visit to her home. Of course, the disappointment with publication may have been only the last in a long line of disappointments, beginning with the preoedipal losses of which Cody writes in his psychobiography of Dickinson and followed by many losses of both homosexual and heterosexual love objects. All of these must have induced a form of despair and injury that could only fester until they caused an inner explosion as concealment and isolation took their toll.

In the following poem, we hear the tone of the unbalancing of mind, foreshadowing a more extensive mental collapse, analogous to the tenuous edge of a flat, pre-Copernican world:

> The mind was built for mighty Freight
> For dread occasion planned
> How often foundering at Sea
> Ostensibly, on land
>
> (1123)

After the collapse of hope and mind comes the blanketed condition of living death:

> A closing of the simple lid
> That opened to the Sun
> Until the tender Carpenter
> Perpetual nail it down—
>
> (1123)

Ferlazzo (1975) writes, "Several other poems give voice to this condition of life-in-death. Characteristically it is a feeling of paralysis, of being turned to stone, and of feeling extreme cold and numbness" (85). The following Dickinson poem imparts the bone-chilling feeling that the more recent female borderline poet, Sylvia Plath, has been so expert in creating:[2]

> I've dropped my Brain—My Soul is numb—
> The veins that used to run
> Stop palsied—'tis Paralysis
> done perfector on stone . . .
>
> (1046)

In the following poem, the paralysis of mind that goes beyond initial pain and despair proceeds one step further, to a catatonic state:[3]

It was not Death, for I stood up,
And all the Dead, lie down—
It was not Night, for all the Bells
Put out their Tongues, for Noon.

It was not Frost, for on my Flesh
I felt Siroccos—crawl—
Nor Fire—for just my Marble feel
Could keep a Chancel, cool—

And yet, it tasted, like them all,
The Figures I have seen
Set orderly, for Burial,
Reminded me, of mine—

As if my life were shaven,
And fitted to a frame,
And could not breath without a key,
And 'twas like Midnight, some—

When everything that ticked—has stopped—
And Space stares all around—
Or Bristly frosts—first Autumn morns,
Repeal the Beating Ground—

But, most, like Chaos—Stopless—cool—
Without a Chance, or Spar—
Or even a Report of Land—
To justify—Despair

(510)

The poet is not only beyond despair in this poem, she is also in a state of a soul without a subjective sense of self, being stretched so taut and breathless that there is no "key." The key can be only another live being, a person who could touch her from the outside so that interaction might transform her into affective body aliveness. Not to be touched is to have no key, and to have no key is to be unable to allow oneself to be touched. The sealed-off schizoid state is resonant since normal body sensation is lost.

In the poem that follows, Dickinson haunts the listener with the eery sensation of being in a state of nonbeing, of hearing one's inside nightmare as a funeral procession coming from without. Inside and outside become confused and merged, as diffusion of self-location symptomizes psychic breakdown:

I felt a Funeral, in my Brain,
And Mourners to and fro
Kept treading—treading—till it seemed
that sense was breaking through

And when they all were seated
A Service, like a Drum—
Kept beating—beating—till I thought
My mind was going numb—

And then I heard them lift a Box
and creak across my Soul
With those same Boots of Lead, again,
Then Space—began to toll,

As all the heavens were a Bell,
And Being, but an Ear,
And I, and Silence, some strange Race
Wrecked, solitary, here—

And then a Plank in Reason, broke,
And I dropped down, and down—
And hit a World, at every plunge,
And Finished knowing then—

(280 [c. 1861])

This is a poem that makes us feel par excellence the resonating inner phenomenon through the outward form of objective ritual. Three years later, Dickinson wrote a poem that nearly mirrors the rhythm and meaning of this one above. ("I Felt a Cleaving in my Mind") In it, we see the poet's sense of an inner breakdown in terms of a split in her psychic self structure, which she experiences as a split in her mind:

I felt a Cleaving in my Mind—
As if my Brain had split—
I tried to match it—Seam by Seam—
But could not make them fit.

The thought behind, I strove to join
Unto the thought before—
But sequence ravelled out of Sound
Like Balls—upon a Floor.

(937 [c. 1864])

This poem seems to recall Dickinson's state of breakdown from a much greater distance. It is probable that the severity of a psychic break did come some time around 1861 or shortly before that.[4] Through her poetry, Dickinson could express the inchoate emergence of strange sensation that she experienced, perhaps even at the time of the psychic break itself, and certainly in recollection afterward. Some of the poems that are most pervaded with catatonic self-absence and chilling psychic terror were composed around 1861.

Perhaps these are the poems of "raw agony" that Marian Woodman mentions in *Addiction to Perfection* (1982) when she speaks of Emily Dickinson's father obsession and of the related inner god projected into poetry. This god turns on her and becomes a malignant demon. Woodman speaks of a hidden incest wish that strangles the woman writer from within as she attempts to remain her father's spiritual bride and to keep the sexual wish in her body unconscious forever. Of course the unconscious incest wish reactivates the demon lover within, and an unconscious reenactment of the tie with the split-off dark side of her father, or with the split-off bad paternal object, takes place.

In other poems, Dickinson's depiction of madness as possession by a devil spells out the initial stages of mental breakdown and suggests the demon lover complex that Marian Woodman so aptly summarizes. In two such poems, Dickinson speaks of insanity as a possession from within.[5] Her images imply split off internal objects. Her nature poetry speaks of garden worms and spiders, which haunt like demons. Other poetry speaks of the unseen particle of "dirt" that threatens to transform into an overpowering internal demon. Such metamorphosis poisons the soul from within and creates madness:

> 'Tis first a Cobweb on the Soul
> A Cuticle of Dust
> A borer in the Axis
> And Elemental Rust—
>
> Ruin is formal—Devils work
> Consecutive and slow—
>
> > (997)
>
> And Something's odd—within—
> That person that I was—
> And this One—do not feel the same—
> could it be Madness—this?
>
> > (410)

## The Change in Self-Structure

Cynthia Griffin Wolff's extensive recent biography of Emily Dickinson (1985) describes a repetitive theme of battle between the poet and the Christian god whom she portrays. This god is seen as metallic, indifferent, or sadistically cruel. Wolff refers to Dickinson's perpetual battle with this demon-god.[6] A theme of battle and abandonment is repeated so often that it must strike us as reenactment due to unresolved psychic trauma. The obsessive and compulsive repetition reflects continual reenactment of a dynamic of internal-world self and object relations. The part objects involved suggest a preoedipal level of trauma. Cody, Wolff, and others have pointed to disruptions in early mother-infant bonding. Such early trauma suggests a sealing off of the primary or core self, determining that the story of this self can be told only in poetry. The one-note repetition in Dickinson's poetry before her breakdown would reflect the nature of her arrest. The poet's hostile, victimized, and combative relations with her father-god take on the form of a hostile symbiosis. A lack of adequate affect responsiveness from Dickinson's detached mother during her preoedipal years could have caused the ongoing reenactment of such a hostile symbiosis.

How was the poet's self-structure effected by the kind of breakdown depicted in her poetry? My theory of the change in Dickinson's self-structure is in part related to the theory of John Cody. The latter spent seven years researching Dickinson's letters and poems; he developed a reconstructive theory concerning her obvious depersonalization and self-fragmentation. Cody has written that during a period of such decompensation, which he diagnoses as psychosis, Dickinson's former self disorganized. He speaks of her self frame cracking, of "fissures in the supporting framework of her attitudes and orientations," and of a "supporting husk" that shattered (1971, 261). He obviously is referring to some general phenomenon of self-fragmentation and dissolution of her former identify. Through this fragmentation process, Cody believes that Dickinson became transformed from a "competent poet" into an "inspired one" (492–93; 350–51). Formerly unconscious impulses bypassed former defense barriers and became conscious. However, Cody also believes that a period of psychic chaos, as reflected in the breakdown poetry, was resolved into a new psychic self-formation. He attributes this new self to the poet's capacity to identity with her father's and brother's masculinity. Accordingly, Dickinson gained a borrowed sense of vitality that she could never have gained from her detached mother. Cody's postulation of a new self that is masculine points to some interesting concerns that he does not address.

My main concern is related to what happens to a female who takes on a masculine identification without having first formed an adequate autonomous and feminine self? Does she lose contact with an innately potential self, perhaps an innately feminine self? Does the new masculine identity, which is adopted without any adequate primary-self foundation, develop into a false self? In addition, can we attribute reparative value to Dickinson's poetry following her psychotic disorganization?

## Reparation: Renunciation and Compensation

Various commentators on Emily Dickinson, including Cody (1971), remark on the overlap between her most prolific period of creative inspiration and expression, which peaked in 1862, and the poet's psychological disturbance, which peaked around 1861. Writing in response to Henry Wells's belief that "grave abnormality" did in fact transform Emily Dickinson's life, Ferlazzo comments: "But, despite this view, Wells regards her madness as closely allied to her artistic genius; in fact, he believes that her madness was the fuel for her genius and that her artistic creations were the cure for her madness" (1976, 80). Wells's viewpoint has the advantage of not rationalizing Dickinson's withdrawal from the world as a clear artistic choice or as a self-protective stance in light of a vulnerable artistic disposition. His view acknowledges Dickinson's psychopathology and at the same the interaction of madness and creativity as artistically profitable. He proposes that this interaction of madness with creativity can lead to mental or psychological reparation. In my opinion, Wells is overly romantic in his optimism concerning psychological reparation through creativity, particularly in light of early preoedipal trauma causing psychic disorganization. Nevertheless, the interaction of creative inspiration and psychic trauma is a magnetically alluring one. Obviously, Dickinson's pathology had a major impact on her choice to seclude herself from the world during the height of her creative capabilities. The adaptive dimensions of this choice need to be considered seriously. Cody has suggested that psychic disturbance enhanced and even gave birth to a more profound form of creativity. However, it is a worthwhile question to ask as to whether the interaction between madness and creativity worked the other way around, effecting reparation as the inner psychic upheaval was expressed through poetry, with inchoate sensation becoming articulated representation. I will therefore discuss both the extent and limits of Dickinson's creative-process reparation, addressing compensatory adaptation as well as developmental self-repair.

## The Ability to Continue Functioning

Although Emily Dickinson's mother often withdrew into bed—resorting to invalidism—Emily herself withdrew only from interpersonal relations. She continued to communicate to many friends through letters, even as she secluded herself within her tiny bedroom. Although she called her poetry her "letter to the world that never wrote to me,"[7] it is clear that until her death she harbored thoughts of recognition that ultimately turned to hopes of publication after death. All of her biographers and critics comment on the careful manner in which Dickinson parceled her poetry into selected groupings and packets, preserving and organizing her work for the fortuitous event of discovery. Obviously, her belief in herself as a poet persisted in the face of horrendous psychic upheaval. Evidence of her strength is seen in her daily functioning as well. Although Dickinson appears to have undergone an acute psychotic trauma, she never ceased daily functioning. Also, she never relapsed into a second psychotic break.[8] Dickinson's poetry reveals her day-to-day endurance during psychological disturbance, suggesting that the poetry itself sustained her capacities to cope by adherence to ritual and function. In one poem, Dickinson writes:

> I tie my Hat—I crease my Shawl—
> Life's little duties do—precisely—
> As the very least
> Were infinite—to me—
>
> I put new blossoms in the Glass—
> And throw the old—away—
> I push a petal from my Gown
> That anchored there—I weigh
> The time 'twill be till six o'clock
> I have so much to do—
> And yet—Existence—some way back—
> Stopped-struck—my ticking—through—
> We cannot put Ourself away
> As a completed Man
> Or Woman—When the Errand's done
> We came to Flesh—upon—
> There may be—Miles on Miles of Nought—
> Of Action—sicker far—
> To stimulate—is stinging work—
> To cover what we are
> From Science—and from Surgery—
> Too Telescopic Eyes
> to bear on us unshaded—
> For their—sake—not for Ours—
> 'Twould start them—
> We—could tremble—
> But since we got a Bomb—
> And held it in our Bosom—
> Nay—hold it—it is calm—
> Therefore—we do life's labor—
> Through life's Reward—be done—
> With scrupulous exactness—
> To hold our Senses—on—
>
> (443)

Dickinson tells us of the "bomb in her bosom." She may be telling us of her destructive archaic rage, which she strains to hold within so as not to annihilate those without: "For their—sake—not for Ours—." She protects her family and friends by holding the bomb, "hold it—it is calm—." Only through the intense concentration on daily ritual and duty can the poet keep the calm, "With scrupulous exactness—/To hold our Senses—on—." The tasks divert her from the malignancy within, as well as protect others from an outward explosion. It is, however, the poetry about the tasks that allows her to contain the potential explosion within her.

The poet never revealed the dimensions of her psychosis to the family that surrounded her in her seclusion. To them, she must have appeared deadened and more withdrawn than ever. The loss of control and reason that she experienced inwardly was never revealed in outward form. The formal devil within her (no. 997), which could easily be likened to an internal obsessional father, always kept her minimally functioning. In 1862, when she actually wrote the poem, "I tie my Hat—crease my Shawl—," she was at the height of her creative powers. She may have been writing about surviving a psychotic episode that had occurred in the past,[9] or she may have been writing of surviving a psychosis in the present. Possibly, this poetry enabled her to prevent a second psychotic episode. In any case, the difference between an earlier period[10] and the present might be found not so much in the use of daily rituals to keep control, but rather in the compensatory or adaptive effect that expressing her struggle in poetry had. Since the "bomb in her bosom" was not just rage but also the father-mother within to whom she clung pathologically, Dickinson's need to obtain cathartic relief may have driven her to an intensely profuse form of creativity that achieved more than catharsis as it helped her contain and communicate the experience of her pain to her readers of a more benevolent future. Her psychic entanglement with an internal idealized and villainized father, as well as her newly forming identification with an external obsessional and aggressive father, may have simultaneously contributed to bringing her to the height of her creativity in 1862. Once so compelled—even though compulsion pushed her beyond any ordinary motivation—her prolific creative expression could serve compensatory functions that helped her survive daily existence.

The poet wrote many other poems in which she asserted that the formal functioning of work is a salvation from mental derangement or from total oblivion.[11] In the poem "As one does Sickness over" (no. 957), Dickinson compares her present efforts to revise her sickness "In convalescent Mind"—which can be interpreted to writing about her sickness in her poetry—to rewalking a precipice while whittling at a twig. The poet says that as she turns her sickness over in her convalescent mind she experiences the psychic precipice on which she totters and from which she might easily fall into "perdition"—madness—again. Speaking of herself in masculine form as she frequently does, Dickinson writes that being held from perdition while one balances on the precipice of sanity wholly depends on how one "whittles at the Twig":

> As One does Sickness over
> In convalescent Mind,
> His scrutiny of Chances
> By blessed Health obscured—
>
> As One rewalks a Precipice
> And whittles at the Twig
> That held Him from Perdition . . .
>
> (957)

Whittling on the twig appears to be a metaphor for the poet's daily chores; although mundane, they are dependable. Ritualistic work keeps her sane. However, this metaphor may also apply to the work of poetry. Piece by piece, she whittles into form and consequently maintains some balance on the "precipice." This poem appears to be written in retrospect, remembering a psychotic break to forestall a new one. However, the prior poem (956), on daily ritual, seems to have been written during the breakdown itself. It has a quality of experiencing the threat of breakdown within the intensity of a single moment. Does one poem seem more reparative than the other? If so, which is a more reparative mode—of immediate encounter or self-reflection? Is the ability to combine the two truly reparative? Cody's observations suggest that only an immediate encounter is taking place during Dickinson's mode of expression:

> At times, however, the emotion that she poured into poems seems to have been not merely a remembered feeling but the very one that gripped her at the moment of composition. Remarkable as it may appear, the poetry seems frequently to have served as a direct outlet, affording the kind of relief that in ordinary people is achieved by weeping, outbursts of rage, and fits of hysteria. That Emily Dickinson believed she wrote poetry for the direct emotional relief of many kinds of feelings is clear, and this explanation, which she repeated in many different contexts, was the one motive she acknowledged. . . . When Higginson criticized her unorthodox poems, calling her "gait" "spasmodic" and "uncontrolled," the excuse she gave for her metrical and rhythmic irregularities was: "I am in danger." It seems probable that the danger that would mold the structure of poetry might be an interior danger, a threatening pressure from one's own thoughts and impulses.
>
> (1971, 489)

Dickinson dealt with her psychic danger by expressing and possibly by expelling her feelings in a way that might be called cathartic. How much could she actually experience herself when compelled to express her feelings through the impinging anguish of the moment? Was this truly a self-encounter in which reflection as well as affective experience meet? Do Dickinson's erupting emotions show a potential for integrating experience through symbolizing it so that future reference might be made to a sense of self? Or was such expression merely a catharsis that led to no self-integrative awareness? There appear to be disruptions in capacities for self-reflection and affect awareness in Dickinson, although such capacities are combined in momentary flashes.

Emily Dickinson's own view of the creative process as reparative is worth noting. We hear the poet speak of how she used poetry to chase "awe" away.

> 'Tis so appalling—it exhilirates—
> So over Horror, it half Captivates—
> The Soul stares after it, secure—
> A sepulchre, fears frost, no more—
>
> To scan a Ghost, is faint—
> but grappling, conquers it—
>
> (281)

In response to this poetic statement of reparative motives, Richard Sewall (1974) writes "She can look back on the terror and the suspense of the action in the preceding poem and can now look it coldly in the face. She has even extricated a kind of exhilaration from the experience, suggesting an 'aesthetics of terror.' In the therapeutic view, she has come near mastering her affliction and is on the way to health" (503).

I agree that such mastery would be more than catharsis, but through affect and description does it allow any insight into the causes of the terror? Is there any insight into the internal world that has been so abruptly unleashed? Is there sustained reflection with sustained affective awareness? Cody writes:

> She herself explained that she "sang" because she was afraid, just as boys whistle when they pass cemeteries. Boys whistle in such circumstances, it can be assumed, for purposes of self-encouragement and to counteract the terrifying expectation of the resurrection of ghosts from graves. The cemetery Emily Dickinson was passing was the graveyard of the repressed that once again was stirring to life. The provocative effects of a fear of impending disorganization and loss of control appear to have brought about a defensive need to organize, contain, and channel the emerging images and emotions. One way she discovered to cope with these phantoms from the id was to subject them to rule—the rules of poetry.
>
> (488–89)

Whether they were phantoms of the id or split-off internal objects, these inner ghosts could be subject to reflection when they were externalized through the creative process. Was Emily Dickinson capable of this? Could she have been aware of experiencing inner phantoms that organized her view of the world so deeply that she was terrified of being a part of that world any longer? It is probable that she did not have this awareness.

Emily Dickinson survived through her creative work and was able to adore Judge Lord in her later years, but her compensation for her terror through a masculine identification seems to have blocked her from a more interpersonally engaged mode of loving. The compensatory vitality that she gained through identifications with her father and brother depended on the process of identification taking place through her creative work. She did not live out this masculine identification in life. She could never leave her work long enough to commit herself to Judge Lord. In addition, her compensatory identification was operating with defensive and pathological aspects that made poetry reflect a growing falseness or contrived, stilted attitude in her character. Also as Wolff notes (1986, 484), the continuity of her poetic themes could no longer be sustained, and the comprehensibility of her communications degenerated. Wolff writes: "It is perhaps a characteristic problem with this class of Dickinson's work that a poem may begin strongly and conclude weakly because a striking trope can neither be sustained nor brought to succinct and effective conclusion (484)."

It is my belief that the poet's compensatory identification could not promote growth since her inner self, no matter how momentarily expressive, was continually sealed off between eruptions of what appears to have been the reenactment of preoedipal psychic trauma. With time, her masculine compensation made her more schizoid, more constricted, and more shielded against contact. It seems that even her cathartic eruptions ultimately subsided. Consequently so did her creativity.

Dickinson's use of the creative process throughout her years of despair and mental disturbance allowed her to survive mentally and to reorganize a sense of self. However, in the end she could not leave her father's house and could not marry the only man who requited her love with equal adoration and genuine commitment. I believe that the true test of whether creative work is ultimately reparative is whether it can move its author toward a fuller and more-integrated interpersonal life that reflects an integrated intrapsychic life. In Emily Dickinson, we see no such movement, but instead only survival and an inspired creative development that goes hand and hand with a burgeoning creative compulsion. Dickinson's compulsive drive toward creativity was empowered with capacities to contain, symbolize, and articulate. We can attribute these capacities both to innate potential and to the unleashing of unconscious phenomena through psychosis. Dickinson's love for her internal father-mother appears to have perpetuated her creative output, despite whatever the degenerative effects ultimately seen in her creativity. Her passionate attachment to this internal parental object also promoted the compensatory functions of the creative process, not the least of which was the living out of a masculine identification through the "transitional world"[12] of creative imagination. The father who was formerly split into god and demon became a more-functional part of the self. However, I believe that this did not happen at the nuclear-self level at which self-integration could be promoted, because she was sealed off from actual affect contact in interpersonal relations. Instead, there was a narcissistic image fusion, in which she took on the image of her father's and brother's masculinity, as she perceived them in her envy, admiration and idealization of them.

## Manic versus True Reparation: Compensation versus Integration

To what degree can self-integration come about through the use of the creative process? We can try to answer this question by examining a Dickinson poem—one cited by Cody as a postpsychosis poem and as evidence of a newly formed, masculine-identified self. This poem has seemed obscure to many critics and even indecipherable to some. Like Cody, I see it as a postpsychosis poem. I believe it illustrates the degree of reparation the poet experienced after her seclusion from the world and after her mental disorganization.

> My Life had stood—a Loaded Gun—
> In Corners—till a Day
> The Owner passed—identified—
> And carried Me away—
>
> And now We roam in Sovereign Woods—
> And now We hunt the Doe—
> And every time I speak for Him—
> The Mountains straight reply—
>
> And do I smile, such cordial light
> Upon the Valley glow—
> It is as a Vesuvian face
> Had let it's pleasure through—
>
> And when at night—Our good Day done—
> I guard my Master's Head—
> 'Tis better than the Eider—Duck's
> Deep Pillow—to have shared—

To foe of His—I'm deadly foe—
None stir the second time—
On whom I long a Yellow Eye—
Or an emphatic thumb—

Though I than He—may longer live
He longer must—than I—
For I have but the power to kill,
Without—the power to die—

(754)

This poem was written in 1861, when Dickinson's creative powers, were ripening into the majestic period that climaxed in 1862. The creative urge at that time seemed to hold forth the promises of reparation. Cody stresses the masculine identification apparent in this poem: "The discharging gun suggests a masculine orgasm, the echo from the mountains a responsive orgasm from the female symbol." (408) He speaks of new masculine "sectors" of the personality becoming activated (414). He then relates the newly found incorporated masculine vitality to the poet's creative thrust, which had become so prolific and thus prominent at this time. He speaks of the exuberant release of "pent-up aggression" (403), Cody then points to the poet's words to justify his conclusion that the masculine aggression is intimately tied to the experience of creative generativity and productivity, if not to the experience of creative motivation itself. Citing the lines "'Tis better than the Eider—Duck's Deep Pillow—to have shared," he translates the poet's meaning: "I would rather nurse in solitude my frustrated sexual longings, my rage, and my aggression and cherish the creative faculties that afford these emotions expression than be physically close to the object of this mixed love and hate" (411). In other words, Cody interprets the "Eider—Duck's Deep Pillow" as the mother's breast. Since the breast has proved so unsatisfactory, the poet prefers to achieve a compensation through creativity that allows her the self-sufficiency of what she has formerly described as her "columnar self" (no. 789). According to Cody's line of thinking, by rejecting the breast and adopting the phallic power of the father's symbolic penis, the poet sees herself as avoiding a humiliating form of dependency on an inadequate mother, while gaining a form of phallic power that stimulates generative creativity in the form of symbolic self-expression. Cody credits this bias toward the incorporative identity of phallic masculine attributes as saving the poet's sanity. He stresses the reparative power of a compensatory masculine identification. It is significant, however, that he never addresses the issue of loss of a primary and/or feminine self:

The metaphorical essence of the lines consists probably in the poet's stressing the great value her masculinized, aggressive, creative self has for her. And

very understandably so—since it helped restore her to sanity. Thus any foe of
"His," that is any foe of her creative self, was a threat to her mental and
emotional life and would be dealt with emphatically. Her family to some extent
must have sensed this and left her to her solitary pursuits"

(412).

Cody stresses the threat of a psychotic state of decompensation in which
unregulated instinctual energies become destructive on account of a lack of
acceptable outlets for expression; he sees the creative faculties as mastering the
instinctual drives, all of which are dependent on masculine identification and the
creative possibilities this allows. However, Cody emphasizes the healthy ego
forms of control in interpreting the masculine aspect of creativity as a compensation for a missing feminine element. He fails to sufficiently deal with the defensive
and self-sabotaging aspects of such an adopted phallic force. He neglects to note
how the phallic identification perpetuates a pathologically self-constricting control
as long as the feminine aspect of the self is buried, blocked, arrested, or sealed
off. However, Cody does allude to these effects by acknowledging that as Dickinson's life continued after the creative climax in 1862, the poet became increasingly
schizoid. He acknowledges that the poet had arid periods when creativity failed,
while she also manifested progressively constricted behavior patterns.

Cody accurately notes positive developmental striving in Dickinson's use of
the creative process. Yet, despite such observations of her health, his findings
certainly contradict any conclusion that Emily Dickinson's creativity ultimately
led to reparation or that true self-integration had taken place for her, or even that
a self-split could have been healed in this particular poem. Even though Cody
points to the interaction of masculine orgasm and feminine mountain forms,
which he interprets as dancing together in constructive and sublimating harmony,
his female forms are phallic and lack feminine receptivity. Cody elsewhere speaks
of the hunted "doe" in the poem as a female symbol in an instinctually neutralized
relation to the masculine poetic character, who carries a gun and expresses power
with a phallic "emphatic thumb." Yet this could hardly be seen as an integration
of masculine and feminine elements within the self, even if Cody is right that to
"hunt" the doe softens and even sublimates the raw masculine aggression that
might in other cases merely shoot the doe (407). Although Cody's statements
tend toward a view of reparative creative symbolism in which masculine and
feminine forces are integrated, he himself is forced to speak of an "unstable
synthesis" of these elements, as opposed to curative self integration that takes
place at a primary level. He writes about a creatively profitable bisexualism:

> But in her creative states the opposing trends achieved an unstable synthesis in
> which both aspects of her personality—her need to be masculine and generative

and her feminine need to be receptive and gestative—combined in the production of poetry. A psychic bisexualism frequently marks the great artist, whose mind showers forth a multitude of ideas which subsequently must undergo an internal and often protracted incubation before the creative product can be delivered. It has frequently been asserted that the man who cannot accept the presence of feminine components in his personality cannot become a productive artist. The converse of this observation has received less attention. Yet it follows that a woman who cannot accept the assertive, penetrative, and fructifying masculine principle in herself remains forever unpregnant of her talents.

(398)

Cody's conclusions show his faith in the possibilities for creativity stemming from reorganization after psychosis. He also believes in the reparative potential of a masculine identification gained at a secondary level of identification, even for a woman who has a preoedipal disturbance. Yet his study fails to argue convincingly that the form of creativity developed through this masculine identification is truly bisexual, in terms of having an adequate female component interacting with a male self-structure component. He is unable to persuade us that Dickinson's bisexualism extends to actual integration of masculine- and feminine-self components so that overall integration and differentiation of the self would be promoted. He fails, therefore, to make a case for the achievement of true reparation within the life and work of Emily Dickinson. True reparation would involve the integration of internal male and female objects so that assimilation of self-structure could take place at a primary or nuclear-self level. Instead, we see that the male poetic voice and character in this postpsychosis poem have an affected quality created by a rigid manic-narcissistic aspect. The male voice could reflect a split-off internal object that is it does not express the resilient affect of an integrated phallic object internalization. The rigid tone of the masculine object highlights the rigid character of the entire poem, regardless of whether the enraged female "Vesuvian face" has found some phallic expulsive pleasure.

There is one key section in this poem that highlights the false-self quality of the postpsychosis resolution. It highlights the stilted quality of the masculine identification (or "incorporation") and its manic rather than true-self dynamic:

> Though I than He—may longer live
> He longer must—than I—
> For I have but the power to kill,
> Without—the power to die—
>
> (754)

I see the poet's statement here of her inability to die as a critical symptom of her resorting to a compensatory masculine identity in order to compensate for preoedipal developmental arrest. To say that she cannot die is to say that she does not have the feminine capacity to surrender, to yield, to merge. She cannot relinquish her self even for a moment so that psychic death could bring renewal of her psyche and self. She cannot let go to yield to the vulnerable affective process of mourning. The creative process thus inhibits her, through its reinforcement of an adopted masculine identity, rather than enables mourning to unfold. If mourning is perpetually aborted, so too are the potentially reparative powers fostered by the creative process. To say that she cannot die is to suggest that a state of pathological mourning persists within the internal world. The father, whose phallic masculinity is incorporated, becomes the focus of addictive cravings, and is reincorporated repeatedly. This must necessarily be the case since the more feminine affects of mournful sadness and loss are not available to promote an integration of the masculine element into the nuclear self. Even if a hostile symbiosis with the two-sided muse-demon father has been changed in its organization since psychosis, so that identification predominates over an oppositional battle with the object, the pathological form of attachment to the father remains. The masculine identification remains defensive as opposed to developmental. Self and other images—not bodies—merge. A narcissistic form of defense has merely been substituted for a borderline form of symbiotic merger.

The poet's declaration of her inability to die confronts us with how a masculinely imposed form of ego control stifles while it also defends a vulnerable primary female self that has been sealed off and arrested. By contrast, an authentic primary self, the spontaneous self labeled "true" by D. W. Winnicott, can die. The authentic self has the capacity to become integrated developmentally and to let go. An authentic self does not depend on a narcissistic form of image identification, since such an image identification is mentally split off from core affect. The self that cannot die is a false self, lacking the flexibility, resilience, and personal uniqueness that can emerge in lyric verse, as opposed to manifesting itself in stilted language. The self that cannot die is a grandiose self, which becomes manifest in manic modes of reparation, in which the mental self is above the innate self. The postpsychosis Dickinson seems to have been expressing the hope in poem no. 754 that her new phallic creative mode of pleasure could keep her from needing others, i.e., that it could keep her above the needy part of her infantile self that remained sealed off owing to early trauma. This hope resonates with her belief in a self-sufficient "columnar self," which is described in an earlier poem (no. 789). To be above the vulnerable, needy, and injured self, however, is to become increasingly inauthentic and constricted. Therefore, when Cody states that the poet gained control that could guide her "instinctual" energies into poetry, he also has to acknowledge that the control gained in this manner—no matter how creative—ultimately led to a constricted self structure.[13]

## The Disowning of Feminine Identity and Manic Defense

The female image in "My Life Had Stood a Loaded Gun" is that of a "doe." It is a devalued female image in that it is the image of an animal; it would be called a part object in Kleinian theory, as opposed to a whole object. This devaluation of the feminine seems significantly symptomatic of Dickinson's view of her mother, who was the main object available for female identification during the formative stages of her life. Cody speaks of Dickinson's attempt to identify with Susan Gilbert at a later date.[14] However, as Cody notes, this attempt to form a female identity during adolescence or adulthood could not succeed. The critical stage for such identity formation had passed. Still, Dickinson's wish for a female identity remained alive. Cody comments that when Susan Gilbert gave birth to a child, Emily Dickinson used metaphors of gestation and birth to describe her poetic process.

To develop a truly feminine self, Dickinson would have needed to open up the sealed-off self that was arrested and closed off by cumulative trauma in infancy. This would have required her to experience the kind of anguished abandonment depression mourning process to which those suffering from preoedipal developmental arrest are subject if they are to recover their potential true selves and to connect with the world from within. For Emily Dickinson to have experienced this on her own, merely through the medium of her creative work, seems impossible because of the intensity of archaic affect that she would have had to endure and to process.

I believe that if Dickinson had consciously identified with the feminine doe in her poem, she would have been threatened with the opening up of this archaic affect, as she was earlier when she could not face this experience and therefore disorganized into psychotic reactions. Instead of such feminine identification, the poet constructs females that take the form of phallic mountains, i.e., "the mountains [that] straight reply." She also represents the main female figure in subhuman form, as a "doe" (no. 754) that is reactive, lacking even the agency of reply that the mountains have. The doe's subjectivity is not developed. The doe remains an object to be hunted, to be acted upon, to react to aggressive threats from the gun that the poet as masculine subject carries. Although Cody refers to the release of masculine orgasms, the firing of the gun remains an act of assassination. The poet therefore assassinates her potential feminine force, externalized in the doe but coming from within. She appears to be reenacting a perpetual intrapsychic self-assassination, since her infantile self, as well as its female nature, has been sealed off, disempowered, and left in a passive-reactive, devalued form. This passive-reactive form can also be associated with her mother's personality and mirrors the mother's—as well as the poet's own—schizoid mode of withdrawal, fleeing from life as the doe flees from a world dominated by the masculine assassin.

Having disowned the female aspect of herself, the poet is free to identify consciously with her father's and brother's masculinity. She most fully emerges, then, in the masculine, aggressive, and phallic characterization of the poem, as the "loaded gun" with the "emphatic thumb." With such symbolic resolution, we cannot speak of a reparative integration of the masculine and feminine aspects of the self, or of the polar components of the self from which they are derived. Assuming a masculine identity that is not grounded in the primary and feminine self, we are looking at a female poet who is riding out a manic defense, keeping her mental identity and her masculine image of herself above her more vulnerable and more primary organic self. I define this as manic reparation as opposed to true reparation, in keeping with Melanie Klein's notion of manic reparation precluding awareness and mournful processing of loss. Manic reparation disguises and defends against the need for the other that must attend affective contact with the inner self. Such a manic stance also precludes shame, for the poet remains not only above the object of aggression and ambivalent desire but also above the inner self that is connected to the internal representation of this feminine object.

Throughout her life, Emily Dickinson wrote numerous poems about death. Cody (271) speaks of Dickinson's "death obsession," noting how she eagerly sought details about the scenes and experiences of others' deaths. Dickinson could never resolve her fears and wishes concerning the nature of death; she asked incessant questions about the prospect of immortality. She labeled her concerns with immortality the "flood subject" (Sewall 1974, 572–73). Yet her later concerns with death became more existential than transcendental. She imagines the minute vibrations of a fly buzzing in the room of a dying person, calling death an "insect" (no. 1716). Ultimately, she reduces her former hopes and curiosity about a form of transcendence to an obsessive detail that minimizes all meaning in relation to the transformation of death.

Dickinson also wrote many poems about grief (e.g., no. 252 and 561). Cody (272) cites the poem in which Dickinson speaks of her identity as a "mourner among the children" (no. 959). The poet ends up comparing grief to a mouse (no. 793), which "chooses wainscot in the breast." She infers that like a fly in the room of the dead, grief is like a mouse that fatally haunts the soul despite its trivial size. Her poems speak of failure to adequately respond to a developmental need to mourn, to grieve affectively, to internalize, and to die with hope that a spirit might survive within her by being transformed. Such disillusionment is further seen when she ceases to write about such questions as death and grief upon the assumption of her masculine identity. Unlike Cody, I believe that her functional use of an incorporated father as self-compensation was ultimately deleterious, even though its effects were degenerative over time.

## The Temporary Nature of Manic Reparation

Insofar as the compensatory masculine identity can exist only in symbolic form and only within the format of imaginative self-expression through the creative process, the poet could sustain neither an adequate sense of identity nor its related affective vitality. If her poetry had been published during her lifetime, perhaps it could have carried an identity based on the creative moment into the realm of interpersonal relations. As readers of poetry experience and respond to the poet's identity, they can sustain that identity. However, Emily Dickinson expressed an identity on paper that she failed to manifest in interpersonal relations. Her behavior with others was phobically inhibited. She became increasingly terrified of social and intimate relations that she could not control. It is likely that she wished to act out her aggressive strivings toward others, but when her aggression did emerge, it was manifested as the kind of contempt that she expressed in behavior toward Higginson, publisher of *The Atlantic Monthly*. Cody writes: "For years she adopted the pose of his 'pupil' and called him 'Master,' but whenever he took the trouble to point out the ways in which he thought her verse could be improved, she 'innocently' responded by sending him poems which utterly repudiated his every suggestion" (433).

Generally, her fears and defenses inhibited any direct expressions of aggression. Consequently, she expressed only her aggression in her creative work.[15] Sometimes it emerged as masochistic submission, as in the "master" letters, sometimes as an inverse bravado ("I'm nobody, Are you nobody too?"), and sometimes as a prideful (albeit defensive) autonomy ("On a Columnar Self"). Ultimately, her aggression showed itself—as in "My Life Stood a Loaded Gun"— as a combination of suppressed rage and phallic strivings. Tragically, however, when creative inspiration dried up, Dickinson's aggression, as well as the masculine radiance that enlivened it, died as well. The poet depended on a continual flow of creative inspiration to be in contact with her masculine form of aliveness; therefore, she was compelled, not merely motivated, to seek the active creative process of her poetry. The highly energizing aspect of this creative process involved the entrance into consciousness of a masculine internal object (the "dream king") that expressed its generative powers through a dream image that could be secondarily converted into poetry. Dickinson's masculinity could live by day only through her poetry; she had to find her internal father in the unconscious night world ("entering parlors shut by day") so that she might make a critical transition to life by day in poetry. This mode of compensatory aliveness could be reparative only to a relative degree. The magic of her phallic mania could last only temporarily. Because her self-foundation remained impaired by the female potential within her, her compensatory identity was brief. We can see Dickinson's image of perpetually "whittling at a twig" in relation to her self-construction through creativity. Her daily reconstruction of herself through poetry was a perpetual task.

Such was the hardship of her mode of existence. Since the poet's constructed self depended on the fertile juices of creative expression for its daily resurrection. I suggest that the same convalescent restructuring of personality that saved Dickinson from the threat of renewed psychosis not only failed to cure her but left her with much structural impairment and psychic imbalance. According to Cody

> [t]he emergence of the masculine elements, and with them previously repressed bisexual impulses, appears to have prevented the re-establishment of the degree of integrity characteristic of the poet's personality prior to her breakdown. Her convalescent personality, though enlarged and deepened, always remained to some degree disturbed. She seems never afterward to have functioned in a completely intact manner, and she was beset with many inner conflicts and irrational fears
>
> (414)

The imbalance in Dickinson's convalescent masculine personality turned in a schizoid direction with age and declining creativity. Cody mentions a late-life constriction of self: "Another, almost equally oppressive, alternative to the creative state (an alternative not mentioned in the poem) is the repudiation and stifling of all instinctual gratification in a kind of living death. The latter course is the one the poet seems to have taken" (413).

This personality constriction can be seen in the drying up of the poet's creative process. In 1867 (Cody 415), Dickinson only produced 10 poems, as compared to the 366 poems she wrote in 1862, at the height of her post-breakdown productivity. Also, the content of the poetry of Dickinson's later life hardly resembled the inflammatory creative inferno of her postbreakdown creative peak, when the poet defied the world to see "a soul at its white heat" (no. 365). Age brought many new losses of family and friends, the most poignant of which was the death of her nephew, Gilbert. Although she might express the pain of regret in her poetry, speaking of her poor "birds" dying,[16] her capacity to mourn through the creative process was limited by the arrest of her primary self. Thus, increasing internal aridity could be her only fate, as long as her masculine-narcissistic defense system prevented the total disorganization of psychosis. Countering such a regressive trend was the poet's ability to love, or at least to be profoundly infatuated with a paternal figure. When the late romance with Judge Lord occurred, Dickinson renounced marriage and sex but poured newfound emotional force into her poetry. This resulted in a late-life creative period. The male touch from without awakened the poet's creative inner life, even if she could not respond to a full interpersonal engagement. Her compensatory masculine vitality could once more come to fruition through the external male who resonated with the incorporated internal male. Even in her most sexual love poem, she reverses the genders of her subjects, so that she is in the masculine role, speaking of herself as subject "mooring tonight in thee." She is the phallic subject who enters the receptive other. (#249) The line in poem 249 is, in "Wild Nights—Wild Nights!" poem "might I but moor—Tonight—In Thee!"

When the poet's mother had a stroke and became permanently ill and bedridden, Emily cared for her. Cody believes that Dickinson acquired a deeply craved nurturance through her own nurturance of her mother. Again, he fails to note the manic aspects of the poet's emotional position. Although Dickinson may have found soothing contact in the role of physical caretaker, she remained in the role of the giver, and thus above the closed-off needy part of herself. She remained in control.

Emily Dickinson's constriction over time is, therefore, not surprising. Still, we can remember her as the "soul at its white heat." Through a creative-process mode of compensatory reparation, Dickinson was able to come alive with a symbolic masculine aggression. As long as her creativity was at its peak, with each new creative spurt, she could pour her masculine incorporations into an emotive form of expression; in this way, she could prevent self-strangulation or rape by the masculine forces that lived so precariously within her. Creativity became the poet's emergency stop-gap measure against psychosis or possible suicide. It was also her path to the vitality of an imagined communication.

As her creativity died, so did the poet. Instead of being a transitional mode to a renewed interpersonal life—owing to the lack of true reparative self-integration in her work—Dickinson's creativity could take her only so far. It conferred on her an immortal existence in the minds of generations of poetry readers. Her hope for an immortal existence has in some sense come true. Tragically, Dickinson will never be able to sense—through an alive body and its interpersonal connections—her own life. Her life, therefore, remains a postdated existence.

Emily Dickinson's work achieves a symbolic linkage between the immediate and the universal. She appears to reflect continually on self-loss that is experienced as a state of inner void. When she writes "I felt a funeral in my brain" or "It was not Death for I stood up and all the dead lie down," we hear and feel her, and yet we are conveyed beyond any individual sense of self by experiencing a whole symbolic environment of the "no-self." Can we simply call this externalization? It is both immediate and conceptually generalized. Are we given the interpretation of a reflective subject? In contrast with Charlotte Brontë's *Villette*, there appears to be no observing ego. Instead, we encounter something intangible, yet "almost" tangible, that is always eluding us, as the sparrow eludes the poet in her nature poetry. This effect seems related to the psychic dynamics of the paranoid-schizoid position (see Ogden, 1986). There is an obvious lack of the object integration and intrapsychic dialogue and conflict seen in Charlotte Brontë. There is no self with its own sense of agency in Dickinson.

Analogously, we see no psychic progress in terms of developmental mourning. There is only the mournful tone of perpetual bereavement. Narcissistic rage remains frozen, and depersonalization leads not to sadness but to despair. Yet there is a powerful compensatory dynamic that is carried through the vehicle of the creative process, prior to its diminishment through the stifling of manic defense. The creative process allows a protosymbolic, and sometimes a truly symbolic, mode of being through descriptions of "non-being" that compensate for a blocked-in, cut-off state of despair. When the poetry is based on protosymbols, we see descriptions of states of sensation, without any symbolic representations of a subjective self's affect experience. In Ogden's words (1986), there seems to be no interpreting subject, no self that is separate from that symbolized (often a self state) and from the symbol employed. In Cody's view (414) the unconscious is being expressed in the poetry without any mediating ego (Ogden's interpreting subject). In some of Dickinson's poetry, a plea is made to the object indirectly, even though catharsis and enactment predominate over encounter with the other. The visceral authenticity of Dickinson's "nonbeing" is conveyed in symbolic form, through conceptual words and images. Still, there is no developmental progress due to the lack of achievement of a self as an interpreting subject using symbols to express affects and interpersonal, or even intrapsychic relations.

The result of unconscious experience being symbolized through the opening up characteristic of a psychotic breakdown (see Cody 1971) is not self-integration. Rather, we see a phase before manic defense seals the self off again. When Dickinson's self becomes sealed off once more, she comes to exist behind a split-off masculine facade that can appear as an artificial, false, or grandiose masculine self. We can speculate about the developmental predisposition for such a phenomenon. The father identification seems to have taken place after the primary feminine self and its identification with the mother had already been arrested.

## Symbolization in Dickinson

Symbolization is not enough for self-integrative reparation, or what has traditionally been called sublimation. In Dickinson's poetry, symbols often depict archaic part objects rather than representations of an integrated self or the others it subjectively experiences. Such symbols, sometimes called "protosymbols," are developmentally transitional in nature and present rather than "represent" a meaning.[17] They are commonly produced by those who have not achieved differentiated self and object representations,[18] i.e., those who have not achieved whole object integration. Such protosymbols do not represent a differentiated self or object; therefore, they cannot be looked upon as evidence of the capacity for mourning and self-integration. The intrapsychic dialogue for such mourning and self-integration is missing.

With such arrest in psychic structuralization, the sealed-off internal self must be opened to object contact so that a mourning and self-integration process can unfold. Both internal-object experience and dialogue, as well as external-object experience, might lead to these developmental processes for most persons. However, in the case of the preoedipally arrested person, an attuned form of relatedness[19] must be provided so as to facilitate the reparative opening up of the sealed and split-off areas of the self. Once there has been a failure of internal-object assimilation at a primary level, this can be found only in a psychotherapeutic relationship, since such failure prohibits an ongoing intrapsychic dialogue, as well as the vicissitudes of its ongoing developmental process. Without a therapeutic contact that provides both attunement and containing, there is no sustained self-encounter that can promote the affective process of mourning within the creative work expression. Instead of seeking such requisite contact with external objects, Emily Dickinson continued to isolate herself. Perhaps her late-life care for her sick mother was one exception to this, as Cody suggests. However, the poet's overall trend was toward withdrawal and isolated seclusion. In fact, even the care for her mother did not involve direct contact with the vulnerable area within her inner self. In being the caregiver, Dickinson could maintain a stance of manic defense in being a giver rather than a person with exposed needs. This stance precludes healing contact with the inner self; thus Dickinson's inner self would have remained sealed off. Her shame, rage, guilt, and need could still be kept from consciousness. Such evasion prevents whole object integration, observing-ego formation, and overall self-integration.

Neither whole object character symbolization nor the conscious self-observation of the process of such symbolization, appears within the work of Emily Dickinson. It likewise fails to appear in either the work of Emily Brontë or, as will be seen, in that of Edith Sitwell. Instead, in the work of these last two women writers, we see a fusion of signified and signifier, with no intermediary agent of an observing self.[20] This can be likened to the regressive cognition of the "symbolic equation" described by Hanna Segal (1981) and Thomas Ogden (1986), in which preoedipally arrested individuals who react from the Kleinian paranoid-schizoid position fail to experience any psychic reality that they themselves create. Those whose psychic functioning evidences the "symbolic equation" are unaware of interpreting their own thoughts and feelings. In fact, they have no awareness that thoughts and feelings are thoughts and feelings, not actualities. In such cases of psychic arrest, the symbol is experienced not as representing an inner psychic experience but as "the thing in itself" (Segal 1981). Segal contrasts the neurotic and the psychotic along these lines. She indicates that for the neurotic, a violin can be seen to be like a penis, i.e., as a representational symbolic form known through associational thinking. For the psychotic, on the other hand, the violin is experienced as actually being a penis and is thus phobically avoided. This is like a borderline patient who experiences the analyst as his or her actual mother rather than as merely like the mother.

The psychotic's pseudosymbolism is symptomatic of the psychic fusion that can persist from the preoedipal period because of developmental arrest, since the self and other have failed to become clearly differentiated. The self of the past, as object (e.g., in Dickinson's "breakdown" poetry), and the self in the present, as the subject writing about the prior breakdown experience, appear to merge within the psychic perspective of her poetic work. Therefore, only defensive compensation—not inner self-integration—can consolidate the self after its encounter with itself. Experiential awareness of the past self as other is lacking. Compensation is accomplished through manic defense, and thus manic dynamics ultimately lead to greater defense and to self-constriction rather than to a sustained equilibrium. Consequently, the creative act must be performed again and again, in an attempt to counteract psychic deterioration.

Manic defense prevents interpersonal contact as well as its internal-world parallel, whole object encounter. Without such forms of encounter, there can be no true self-transformation, or what Melanie Klein has termed "true reparation." The transforming encounter involves the capacity to mourn and thus to relinquish the old internal object and internalize the new form of the other. The work of an oedipal-level woman such as Charlotte Brontë illustrates that the developmental mourning process leads to ever new themes of creative resolutions. In Emily Dickinson's work, by contrast, we see the same thematic antiresolution again and again. All mourning and potential interaction are aborted. Any beginning theme of mutuality, as seen in Dickinson's love poetry (see Wolff 1986), regresses into a repetitive motif of cut-off relations, which is symptomatic of abandonment trauma and its unresolved loss. The cutoff of potential interpersonal relations is ever present, as can also be seen in the creative work of the suicidal Sylvia Plath. Even the poem noted by Cody (1971) for its compensatory structure of masculine identification ends in such a cutoff: "For I have but the power to kill,/Without— the power to die" (no. 754). My interpretation is that the poet cannot yield, surrender, or merge with another. There is no freedom to merge if there is no capacity for separation; there is no capacity for separation if differentiated self and object representations have failed to form. For Dickinson, to merge would mean to lose her self.

Also symptomatic of a developmental arrest is the inability to sustain object ties, whether these object ties are expressed in interpersonal relations or in creative work. For Emily Dickinson, it is the creative work that tells the story of such failed object connection. Despite her brilliance, her eloquence, and her novelty, as she grew older and reparation failed to be more than temporary relief, the poet could not finish out a thought. Wolff (1986) writes of Dickinson's later work: "a poem may begin strongly and conclude weakly because a striking trope can neither be sustained nor brought to succinct and effective conclusion" (484). The follow through, or what from a psychological view can be seen as the working through, does not emerge naturally. This would be true particularly if the poet psychologically regresses after a psychotic mode of opening up leads only to compensation. The trend of Dickinson's work reveals an inability to sustain affective veracity that belies the inability to sustain object ties: "The tone is mysterious, quiet viscidity is dissipated into a cloying cuteness" (Wolff, 484). Wolff also notes that Dickinson declined into a self-consciousness that interfered with the "integrity of the scene" (483). This seems to have been a consequence of her feeling failing her. Whereas she shows more mastery in her earlier nature poems (no. 1302), later—as in "There came a Wind like Bugle—/It quivered through the Grass" (no. 1593)—Dickinson lapsed into contrived "artistry" (Wolff, 483). Like Cody (1971), Wolff too observes the increasingly schizoid constriction that affected Dickinson as her secluded life continued.

## The Use of the "Word" in Attempting To Integrate Shifting Self-States within the Paranoid-Schizoid Position

When there is a significant absence of the separation-stage mother in an artist's childhood, that artist may use words and symbols not only as vehicles to the object[21] but also as links between self-fragments and self-states and between internal part objects that constitute aspects of unintegrated self-experience.[22] The symbol can be used as a link between psyche and soma, between inner and outer reality, and between proprioceptive and exteroceptive sensory awareness. Whenever a schizoid barrier is formed because of preoedipal arrest in infancy, an outside link between these self-states is sought, just as a transitional object can be sought in infancy prior to full self-consolidation as the mother herself is relinquished for periods of time. The symbol becomes the mental link, imbued with affective experience, which the artist uses to cross a gap or barrier from inside to the other outside, as well as from one self-state to another. Yet when a schizoid barrier within the self and its internal work exists, as it does for the paranoid schizoid artist, the mental symbol is not organically felt and affectively processed. The symbol, therefore, is primitive in its function, as it remains split off in mental abstraction, or in an isolated sensation. The splitoff, or isolated quality of the symbol, is related to the failure of an inner locus of subjectivity to be available for the processing of developmental mourning.

In the case of Edith Sitwell, we will see her view her creative work as a "tightrope over the abyss." Her attempt to bridge the inner void with mental concepts, words, and poetic images results in a prominent air of abstraction. In Emily Dickinson, we see a poet using dashes to indicate her inner voids—voids that were perhaps actually felt in relation to gaps in early mother-infant contact. Such voids are presumably much more than metaphorical gaps in emotional bonding. By making the void explicit with a dash, Dickinson takes some control over her internal state, particularly when it becomes a state of numbness (which seems to recreate her self-state during a traumatic separation-individuation period). She articulates it and thus psychically owns it, naming an absence of name and of communication in both its nonverbal and its verbal forms. The words around Dickinson's dashes become punctuated with the gaps in her internal world, and so the gaps become links between her moments of self-experience. They come to highlight meaning rather than to detract from it, even through feeling is still largely numbed, since such symbolic links cannot provide containment for the affective mourning process. Mental symbols cannot replace the response of interpersonal affect contact. Further, when the linking process is largely unconscious, there is no insight to bridge the gap between mental thought and the interpersonal touch of the inner self.

McNeil (1981) writes of how Dickinson searched for a boundary with her poetic words where none was felt between her and her objects. Her dashes are fragmentary boundaries, and her words give vent to the expression of frustrated needs and desires for early parental contact. Holding, sensing, seeing, crying, and orgasmic rhythms become body articulations through the vehicle of symbols in words. Wolff (1986) writes of Dickinson's orgasmic rhythms expressed in the rhythm of words, illustrating how the poet's sense of archaic loss is associated with intense erotic reactions. Cody (1971, 489) writes of how Dickinson cried and screamed through her poetry, cathartically expressing the more hysterical affects that stem from pent-up emotion. As in the definition of "protosymbols," such emotional meaning is "presented" rather than represented.

Yet even more extreme than the case of Dickinson is that of Edith Sitwell, a poet who appears to lack all body sense as she records the fragments of her self-experience in mythic character symbolization. Edith Sitwell's manic defense exists as a more pervasive narcissistic character structure than that which imprisons and envelops Dickinson. Perhaps, as Cody suggests, psychosis actually opened Dickinson up to unconscious sensory perception. She could be personal in her communication of self-deterioration as she could in her anguish over unrequited love; her sensory perception was present, even when evidencing fragmentation.

# 13

# Edith Sitwell I: The Demon Lover, Poetry and Writer's Block

Edith Louisa Sitwell was born in 1887, the daughter of George Sitwell, a baronet, and Ida Denison Londesborough, the seventeen-year-old granddaughter of a duke. Two younger brothers, Osbert and Sacheverell, followed Edith.

At twenty-six Edith made a longed-for escape from her family. Having just published her first poems in the London *Daily Mirror,* she and her loyal friend and governess, Helen Rootman, moved to a boarding-house in London's modest Bayswater district. Edith had lived for poetry from early in her life. She schooled herself, became enamored with Yates, and ritualistically began to compose her own pieces. Her notebooks of poems also led to one theater production performed with her two brothers. Entitled "Facade," it was a major attempt to seek publicity, as Edith became obsessed with promoting her creative work.

Edith Sitwell's early poetry was replete with atirical characterization. Her major early groups of poetic works were "Sleeping Beauty" and "Troy Park." Unable to write poetry for periods of time, she also attempted a novel and several biographies. Her one novel was entitled, *I Was Born Under a Black Sun.* Her best biography was of Queen Victoria, and it gave her her greatest commercial success. A later biography, *Fanfare for Elizabeth,* attracted attention in Hollywood and was almost adapted for the screen.

During the 1930s, Edith suffered through a decade of writer's block that affected her ability to write poetry. Instead, she dabbled in journalism and wrote a good deal of commentary on poetry, ultimately putting together an anthology of prominent modern poets. Then during the 1940s, she reemerged as a war poet and developed a reputation as a prophet for the future era. In the late 1940s and 50s, she toured America and presented her poetry in New York, where she was much acclaimed.

Back in England, Edith Sitwell was recognized during these years as a major English poet. She was awarded honorary doctoral degrees by Oxford and Cambridge universities. When Queen Elizabeth II made her dame of the British Empire, the poet became officially addressed as Dame Edith Sitwell, having formerly been addressed as Doctor. Many literary societies recognized Sitwell as a major literary figure. During her last years she was made an English Companion of Literature.

Edith remained single and celibate. Her one ongoing love affair was with the homosexual painter Pavlick Tchelitchew. In later years, she converted to Catholicism, and an ideal of Christ made its impact on her poetry.

Edith lived with Helen Rootman, her former governess, until Rootman died of cancer. In her later years, unable to care for herself and no longer welcome at the Sesame Club where she had often lived when in London, she was fortunate to find a secretary, Elizabeth Saltar, who organized a household for her, cared for her, and acted as a nurse. Yet the poet entered a period of increasing emotional isolation. Edith Sitwell died in 1964.

The marriage linking the Sitwells and the Londesboroughs took place in November 1886. A few days following the wedding, Lady Ida "scampered from her marriage-bed in horror" (Pearson 1978, 29), running home to her mother. She was sent back to the twenty-six-year-old Sir George immediately. Nine months later, Edith Sitwell was born, first child of such auspicious beginnings. In her autobiography (*Taken Care Of*), Sitwell attempts to comprehend her mother's continuous wrath toward her by recalling this incident.

The man Edith Sitwell's mother married had his own peculiarities, but they were characterized by design more than by reaction. John Pearson comments on his approach to marriage, indicating his general attitude toward life:

> Instead, as he embarked on his romance, he was concerned with those essentially non-human rules that he employed in garden architecture and in tracing pedigrees—symmetry, a fine effect, and the baroque splendour of a noble name. Love he apparently ignored—or possibly just took for granted, as he would naturally assume his shrubs would grow when planted in some great design. But then, he always was convinced that he knew best, so why should love be any different?
>
> (25)

This introductory portrait of Edith's father helps set the scene into which Edith was born. Her father practiced the same contrived approach to gardening and architecture that he applied to the art of marriage, since sustained genetic superiority was his ultimate goal. As a student of genealogy, Sir George Sitwell searched for the perfect formula that would provide him with a golden lineage with which he might impress the world. Always behind his plotting was the image of his own greatness which he hoped would someday be his legacy. Designing gardens of architectural splendor at his Renishaw estate in England, and later at the Italian palace he purchased, Montegufuoni, the Baronet imagined himself to be following his destined avenue to greatness. In truth, as Pearson documents, his role in the world had been a rather ineffectual one, and by the time he planned to marry, he was setting all his new hopes for magnificence on plans for a royal lineage. To accomplish his goal he sought to marry a lady of the most highborn birth possible. Pearson writes:

> The young lady finally selected by Sir George for his exercise in dynastic architecture was ravishingly beautiful—and barely seventeen—though it is doubtful whether either fact appealed to him as much as that she was the daughter of a famous peer and grand-daughter of a duke, and so would bring the maximum enhancement of the Sitwell name. But had he paused for just a moment to regard her as a human being rather than as an entry on a family tree, he must have noticed also that she was hardly suited as the life companion of a person of his tastes and temperament. Behind her great brown eyes and Burne-Jones profile, young Ida Denison possessed a nature that was uncontrolled, unformed and virtually uneducated. Indeed, this high-born school girl lacked the faintest interest in those tastes and rarefied pursuits he lived for. Where he was serious, she was frivolous; where he was mean she was unthinkingly extravagant; where he appeared the coldest of cold fish, she was a passionate young woman with a fiery temperament.
>
> (26)

Yet it appears that Sir George did not want to see Ida as a human being, for he had bigger things in mind. Further, to see her as human would have forced him to see himself in that cast, which would have made him less than exceptional in his own eyes, for it would have meant acknowledging his desires, needs, longings, and real capacities. This he could not and would not do. He had a golden image of himself to sketch anew with each new plot and plan. Getting married to Ida seemed to be the perfect plan for the artifice of the perfect image.

The plan for the perfect heir was considered a dud, however, when Edith was born. Sir George had not accounted for the possibility of a daughter, which seems to have led to Edith's later essay in her autobiography entitled "In Disgrace for Being Female." Osbert Sitwell later satirized Sir George's reaction to Edith's birth in his autobiographical work, *Left Hand, Right Hand* (1977).

> Often he used to deplore the strange chance by which, having taken so much trouble to get intelligent children, his whole early life having been modelled, apparently, on a sort of Nietzschean-Darwinian uplift scheme towards that goal, we three had been sent down—or up—to him . . . It was really very unfair, most disappointing. . . . And that the Life Force should have shovelled my sister on to him was even more patently unjust than that It should have allocated to him my brother or myself. Birth, no less than marriage was plainly,

a lottery: but whereas he had gone in for it to obtain for the next generation a straight nose and charm, he had drawn a booby-prize, an aquiline nose and a body inhabited by an alien and fiery spirit. . . . It was difficult to know, really, where to begin the list of just complaints.

(Vol. 3, 44)

Osbert's irony shields us from the actual impact that this kind of father had on his sister, Edith. More poignantly, Edith's own memory depicts this impact, which borders on Gothic horror: "Edith used to tell of how as a girl she was once sitting in a railway compartment, opposite her father who was reading The Times. Suddenly he lowered the paper, shuddered visibly, then raised The Times again so that he would not have to see her—all this without a word spoken" (Pearson 1978, 35). Edith's feeling of being ugly and undesirable as a woman could easily be traced back to her father's reaction to her, and it seems to be a feeling engraved upon an earlier black void created from maternal rejection, compounding fears of self nihilation and self mortification. Like her father, she defended herself with the grandiose defense. It seems that her pain was not felt but rather turned into drama. According to Victoria Glendinning, Virginia Woolf recalled Edith reciting the spectacle of her childhood victimization as an anecdote at a party. Edith was noted for describing the "bastille" that she had been physically imprisoned in at the request of her father. The bastille was a contraption prescribed by doctors of the time, which symbolized her psychological imprisonment, an imprisonment with her father as jailor. Glendinning quotes Edith herself in her biography (1981):

The imprisonment began under my arms, preventing me from resting them on my sides. My legs were also imprisoned down to my ankles, and at night-time these, and the soles of my feet, were locked up in an excruciating contraption. Even my nose did not escape this gentleman's efficiency, and a band of elastic surrounded my forehead, from which two pieces of steel (regulated by a lock and key system) descended on each side of the organ in question, with thick upholstered pads at the nostrils, turning my nose very firmly to the opposite way which Nature had intended, and blocking one nostril, so that breathing was difficult.

(27)

John Pearson (1978) writes of Edith's later reactions: "During the bitter years of her extreme old age she would tell friends and interviewing journalists of how Sir George had 'mocked' her nose, her looks, the curvature of her back" (36). As Glendinning comments, Sitwell came to disown her body. Although through-out her life Sitwell built a facade of dress that suited her and her desired image, she chose a male homosexual as the one man she loved, a man who explicitly rejected her body and any physical connection to her. In doing so she reproduced her paternal rejection.

Yet Edith's rejection by her father extended beyond a rejection of her looks. He had designs for her that were totally contrary to her nature. He had no concern for her real needs or talents. He harped on what he considered to be her defects, even citing her in her entirety as a defect. She became a blot on his mental portrait of his perfect family. Osbert recalls Sir George's abusive nagging, a bullying preoccupation that haunted Edith's daily life as long as she lived with her parents, until her mid-twenties.

Osbert also describes in his memoirs the public humiliations that Edith suffered at the hands of their mother. He writes that their mother mocked and attacked Edith before her perpetual crowd of "friends" and admirers. Edith herself speaks of her mother's black rages as repeated outbursts vented on her since her early childhood (*Taken Care Of*). This maternal attack as well as a corresponding detachment must have contributed to Edith's sense of having a black void within her, a void which compelled her to speak of "walking a tightrope over an abyss" and haunted her with a fear of an "engulfing boredom" (see Glendenning 1981). Yet her later demons appear in masculine form; e.g., in the poems; "The miser Foscue" (S and H, 228), "The envious ghost" (238) and "The naked Knight in the coat of mail" (Salter and Harper, 1976, 239). These are all seen in her 1940s war-period poetry. One "sun" or many "suns" generally appear in this poetry, which can be seen as symbolic of the paternal rejections and the ever hoped-for paternal love that she abstracts into a universal form.[1] Tigers and lions also appear repeatedly, suggesting her masculine preoccupations and her masculine-colored internal objects. From whom would such masculine objects, or part objects, be derived if not at their root from her father? Imprints from a later male love would only further color the forms.

## Her Father's Narcissistic Character

How are the masculinized part objects of muse and demon derived? Osbert Sitwell's descriptions of their father show the paternal imprint on the original maternal introject. They characterize the demonic force that dominated Edith in her childhood and took its toll in her internal world, as illustrated in her life and poetry. In *Left Hand, Right Hand*, Edith's brother depicts the seeds of intense narcissistic mortification:

> And, if anything, my father's inclination to nag at her on the one hand, my mother's, to fall into ungovernable, singularly terrifying rages with her, on the other, because of her non-conformity, seemed stronger when there were people,

as here, to feed the fires of their discontent, and other children to set a standard by which to measure her attainments. "Dearest, you ought to make her like killing rabbits," one could hear the fun brigade urging on my mother. But while my father was angry with his daughter for failing to comply with another standard—his own—, for not having a du Maurier profile, a liking for "lawn-tennis," or being able to sing or play the zither after dinner . . . he was also disappointed on another score. She seemed far less interested than I was—or even Sacherell who was only six or seven—in his stories about the Black Death (a subject he had been "reading up" in the British Museum), and she seemed to have no natural feeling for John Stuart Mill's Principles of Political Economy. . . . "

(*The Scarlet Tree*, 182).

This illustrates to what extent Edith's parents, and particularly her father, expected her to mirror him perfectly, to be the perfect image of the daughter, and to be an ear for everything he had to say, regardless of her inner response or of her own need to speak.

The passage above shows the controllingness of her father's narcissistic personality.[2] The following passage illustrates his contempt and omnipotent grandiosity (Kernberg, 1975).

Never did my father permit anyone to argue with him, or to state views that were contrary to his own. That there could be such, he would not allow himself to perceive. Nobody had argued with him, nobody had contradicted him now for several decades, perhaps for nearly half a century. If anyone ventured to dispute any opinion he held—as sometimes we children did—or to combat any particularly extravagant statement about, for example, some friend one knew much better than he did, he would omnisciently reply, with an air of final and absolute authority, and without deeming it necessary to offer proof or divulge the source of such no doubt, mystical awareness, "We happen to know."

(Sitwell 1977, vol. 3, 49)

Edith's own portraits of her father can be seen in both her prose and her poetry, but it is in her prose that she, like Osbert, uses satire to dull her ache and sharpen his blow. Edith's satirical picture of Sir George as Sir Henry Rothderham in her one novel, *I Live Under a Black Sun*, is quoted by Glendinning:[3]

Edith portrayed him . . . in the guise of Sir Henry Rothderham. She described how he paced up and down in front of the house, or along the passages, slowly, sometimes pausing at a doorway to listen to voices, not because he was interested in what was going on but because he was enabled in this way to touch, for a moment, the world in which others moved, thought, acted, without being obliged to become a part of it, and thus made him feel real to himself, real in his isolation. . . .

(25)

She wrote "my father" over a passage in her novel fragment which describes "Mr. Londersfield," another paternal portrait quoted by Glendinning:

> He spoke, always, as if his mouth was full of dust; and this he did in order that he might accuse others, when they were unable to hear him, of being inattentive, and because, too, he was aware that the fact of his mumbling had a strange effect on those whom he engaged in conversation. It produced in them the half-unconscious impression that he must be deaf as well as dumb, and they would, insensibly, speak above their usual tones, which gave Mr. Londesfield the opportunity to drop the mumbling and say sharply, "Don't shout." And coming from his lips the sudden burst of sound had a disconcerting effect, as though a hidden door had been opened and an unexpected scene had revealed itself.
>
> (25)

Glendinning adds: "There is irony in these knife-sharp notations of his alienation, but there is also understanding, however dispassionate; it is as if Edith included her father among those who are 'a little outside life,' like herself" (25).

## Horrors of Childhood

When plagued by bluebottle insects at Wood End (her grandmother's house), Edith was made to kill them by herself, despite being locked into her bastille while in bed at night. Later she recounted these horrors at social gatherings, as reported by Virginia Woolf in her diaries (see Glendinning 1981, 111). The future poet was forced to learn poetry she didn't like and had to hide the reading of the poetry that she had chosen. When she wished to play the piano, her father insisted she play the cello.

Fortunately, Edith did have a nurse, Davis, to whom she grew attached in the midst of her parental abandonment and intrusion. Yet when Davis had a disagreement with Sir George and impulsively handed in her resignation, all the pleas and cries of Edith and her siblings would not budge her father to reemploy the nurse. Sir George's preoccupation with his own false, narcissistic pride—with consequent lack of empathy for his children—is apparent in this incident, as in many others.

Osbert wrote that his father believed that the best thing for his children was to be forced to do the opposite of what they wanted, i.e., that which ran totally contrary to one's nature (Glendinning 1981, 210). Edith later said that she could write knowingly of a mother's grief over a lost child despite her own childless state because she had experienced the blotting out of her own instinctual nature. Her father had contrived plots to dictate not only her manners, but her entire mode of being, and he tried to construct her like a jigsaw puzzle, even though the pieces did not fall willingly into his design.

Behind her own facade of satire, both different from and similar to her brother's, Edith could portray the father who had made her feel ugly and detached from her body. Satire built her a wall of protection, as did the general narcissistic defense of contempt. Her early writing did not show the inner horrors of her fusion with her demonic father. Instead, she used satire to conceal and display at the same time, describing her father's offending self-absorption. In fact, in the 1920s Edith and her brothers performed a piece entitled "*Facade*," a string of poems set to impressionistic music and recited on stage. These poetic pieces were dramatically enhanced in volume and aura by use of a microphone.

The title "Facade" is eminently suited to the poet's style of defense. It also suits the male caricatures that she derived from her inner imprints of Sir George and related masculine figures. Poems like "Sir Beelzbub" (S & H, 148) and "Colonel Fantock" (S & H, 14–15, 19–22) mocked the arrogant masculine character. Yet sometimes she want past the mockery to some empathic insight into the reason for the "facade" that he and she shared as a defense. In "Colonel Fantock" she writes:

> And so for ever through his braggart voice,
> Through all that martial trumpet's sound, his soul
> Wept with a little sound so pitiful,
> Knowing that he is outside life for ever
> With no one that will warm or comfort him. . . .
> He is not even dead, but Death's buffoon
> On a bare stage, a shrunken pantaloon.
> His military banner never fell,
>
> (Salter and Harper 1976, 20)

Perhaps the glimpse of the soul which she managed to spy in the model for Colonel Fantock (a male employee of her father) was something she could never see in its full exposure when it came to her real father. Perhaps only through viewing a similar, yet different, male could the poet attempt a glimpse at the father who lived behind the mask.[4]

When she wrote satire directly about her father, there was no glimpse of the inner self. Instead, we see a behavioral portrait of detachment, of narcissistic preoccupation, and of a marginal, schizoid attempt to preserve a sense of self. Her father's symptomatic behavior was all that she could grasp in her prose. In her description of Sir Henry Rotherham in *I Live Under a Black Sun*, she writes tellingly, although satirically, of her father.

> He would, too, spread various objects belonging to himself all over the house, in the many rooms—his hat in one room, his stick in another, his spectacle case in a third, because when he came face to face, once more, in the course of his wanderings, with these records of his own personality, he was reminded of himself, which was pleasant, and because it enabled him to stake his claim on every room in the house as sole inhabitant. Should another person enter one of the rooms in question, Sir Henry would follow him there, and, conveying suddenly the impression of great age, would make it clear by his manner that he had intended to rest there, and had hoped that he would not be disturbed; then, having by this means routed the intruder and put him to flight, he would continue his walk.
>
> (Salter and Harper 1976, 37)

## Poetry

Upon entering her poetry, we view Sitwell in relation to her father, and satire yields to nightmare. The level of terror she felt in relation to her father is seen in her poetry, whereas in her prose her father is merely an odd and eccentric creature. Sitwell's internal world, as seen in her poetry is a cold one, and her father is the chief demon who imprisons her.[5] If, as Ronald Fairbairn (1952) believed, dreams are analogous representations of the internal world rather than just symbolic disguises for wish fulfillments or drive enactments, poetry can be seen as such as analogous representation as well. Sitwell's poetry elaborates the themes of her father and of her own narcissistic personality dynamics that appear at least partially derived from her identification with him.

### Early Poetry

In the early poetry, such as in the 1920s classics, "Troy Park" and "Sleeping Beauty," Edith Sitwell's affect themes are still disguised in both satire and nursery rhyme. She masks the horrors in idealized forms and lyricism, turning anguish into elegance with the characteristic manic-grandiose defense of the narcissist. Yet the grandeur exudes the stale air of decadence, and the message lingers despite lyric and rhyme. It is the message of inner isolation, agitated emptiness, and alienated paranoia. It is the message of the father's bad qualities swallowed whole, when true internalization through integration cannot take place. Edith Sitwell is the princess abandoned, never kissed; oedipal strains become distorted into black contents. The poet makes the tragedy beautiful, but we feel the chill. Her pain is seen and never touched, for it remains encased in a glass cocoon and hidden behind an elegantly contoured mask. The wound is not opened. The barrier remains, and is fortified by manic magic.

In "Sleeping Beauty" (1924), Edith Sitwell writes of living in the palace of a mad king. This king is encased in his own delusional dream of greatness, just as Sitwell's father was. We can easily associate this poem with Sir George's obsessions with becoming "immortal." We can also see the father who was more involved with his palaces than with his children.[6] The mad king is the dotty father who spent so much time in preoccupations with his medieval ancestry in Nottingham. All this is suggested in the following lines from "Sleeping Beauty":

> My life is like this.
> And drifts into nothinness! . . .
> .........................................
> The King bows and mutters . . .
> His eyelids seem shutters
> Of a palace pavilion
> Deserted a million
>
> Echoing years ago.
> Oh, but the rain falls slow.
>                    (Salter and Harper, 1981, 29)

Here the king's eyelids seem shutters. Later, Sitwell writes of a knight who uses the cold of the world as a coat of mail. In both cases, the poet seems to describe her father's cold and persistent barrier against her as if his awareness of her would be too tremendous an intrusion. In "Sleeping Beauty," Edith's father ("the King") echoes "years ago." He does not provide a mirroring echo for his daughter's actuality—her being. He echoes a fantasy domain from historic texts of the past. We are told of his barrier and also about the grandeur in which this barrier is encased. The barrier becomes a "palace," an adequate symbol for the grandiose self.

The themes are preoedipal. Although the internal bad object displayed is of a masculine cast that seems like the sculptured form of her father's manifest personality, we can perceive also the original imprint of the mother on the masculinized internal-object form. This is seen more clearly in the later poems. Also, in lines like "Oh, but the rain falls slow," we see a state of perpetuated depressive gloom, characteristic of blocked mourning, or of a pathological mourning state, in which the bad object cannot be surrendered. In a later poem, "Still Falls the Rain," an internal state of perpetual bereavement, without relief or resolution, is seen even more clearly.

There is a ten year gap between Edith Sitwell's early poems and her later poetry of the war years (W.W. II). During these ten years, Sitwell, who had written poetry all her life, ceased to write all poetry. She wrote only prose. Significantly, her "writer's block," in relation to poetry, came after she wrote the poem, "Gold Coast Customs," in which the pain of her childhood seems to rise to the surface in its most vivid form. In images of the horrors of the skid row derelicts that she saw in a California slum, Sitwell seems to expose the raw agony of her own internal world, and of the childhood trauma with which it is stamped:

> What is that wimpering like a child
> That this mad ghost beats e drum in the air?
> The heart of Sal
> That once was a girl
> And now is a calico thing to loll
> Over the easy steps of the slum
> Waiting for something dead to come . . .
> (Salter and Harper, 158–159)

> Perhaps if I too lie down in the mud,
> Beneath tumbrils rolling
> And mad skulls galloping
> Far from their bunches of nerves that dance
> And caper among these slums, and prance,
> Beneath the nose of the hell that rolls
> I shall forget the shrunken souls,
> The eyeless mud squealing 'God is dead,'
> Starved men (bags of wind) and the harlo's tread,
> The heaven turned into monkey-hide
> by Lady Bamburghers dancing fleas,
> Her rotting parties and death-slak ease,
> And the dead men drunken
> (The only tide)
> Blown up and down
> And tossed through the town
> Over the half of my heart that lies
> Deep down, in this meaner Death, with cries.
> (Salter and Harper, 160–161)

After writing this poem, Edith Sitwell had to earn money through journalism and prose biography, because she was blocked as a poet. This block extended through the decade of the 1930s. I think it is extremely significant that just after she wrote the poem that brings her closest to her own pain, she could not go on writing poetry. She shut down. She could not face her pain on her own. She could not contain it and mourn it. She didn't have a psychotherapist to help her contain her pain and mourn the childhood traumas and losses that it represented. Like many artists, Sitwell might have feared that a therapist would incarnate a persecutory object who would intrude on and diminish her creativity. In actuality, a therapist could have helped her contain the intense archaic affects lying behind the images in her poetry. Without the reparative psychotherapy process, she retained the sado-masochistic dynamics of her internal world that became manifest again in her later war-time poetry, in the 1940s.

## Later Poems

In "The Song of the Cold," the demon lover theme emerges through the oedipal erotic coloration. As the poet portrays the cold kiss of the narcissistic oedipal father, we sense the early cold chill of the preoedipal mother. The "Knight of mail" symbolizes this father who attempts to convince the female subject of the poem that she is exclusively his. Then he rejects her:

> The naked Knight in the coat of mail
> Shreiked like a bird that flies through the leaves—
> The dark bird proud as the Prince of the Air—
> I am the world's last love . . .
> Beware—
>
> Young girl, you press your lips to lips
> That are already cold—
>
> (Salter and Harper 1976, 239)

This seems like a young oedipal girl's reaction to a narcissistic father, who would seemingly promise only a cold kiss. The knight has not only cold lips and a barrier of mail, but envious eyes that are reminiscent of the preoedipal level.

We can compare this poetry to that of Emily Dickinson, who also had a father evidencing narcissistic dynamics. Dickinson writes of "haughty spangles" on her father's gown. Yet, the narcissism of Dickinson's father seems more like the characteristic contempt of a severe obsessional character than the essence of the character type. Dickinson's father, unlike Sitwell's, appears to have felt love for his daughter in spite of his narcissistic mode of defense. Consequently, it seems that Dickinson's oedipal experience was not as cloaked in falsehood and coldness as was that of Sitwell. Emily may have felt humiliated by the haughty air of her father, particularly as she might have perceived it during the oedipal period. Also, her father may have unconsciously conveyed to her that he wished exclusively to possess her love. Yet, if her father had true feeling for her, both his contempt and possessiveness would have been more like those of a parent who wishes to have his child reflect his own self, rather than of a parent who wants reflection for a pathological grandiose self (see Kernberg 1975). In contrast, Edith Sitwell's father appears through biographical description,[7] and through the poetic portrayals of his own daughter to be the kind of hard-core narcissistic character described in Kernberg's diagnostic and clinical descriptions of narcissistic personalities with severely paranoid qualities.

In his autobiographical memoirs, Osbert Sitwell quotes their father as saying, with all seriousness, that it would be dangerous for his children to lose touch with him for even one day, because "You never know when you may not need the benefit of my experience and advice" (*Left Hand, Right Hand*, vol. 1, 132–133). From such real-life anecdotes we can sense the father's grandiose self that is depicted through metaphors and symbolic imagery in Edith's poetry. The air of perfection and superiority that Sir George displayed can be seen as a massive narcissistic structure used to militate against any awareness of emotional need, particularly any need that would suggest loneliness or the wish for interpersonal contact. It shielded him from awareness that he was clinging to his children in response to his own need, not theirs.

Edith's father was a singularly isolated human being. He was truly a sort of alien, and Edith's incorporation of him appears to have compelled her to write of tyranical and possessive men who are inwardly dead. The demon lover thus emerges in her poetry as a sterile death force in masculine form. This demon lover blocks out the spring, i.e., nature's birth; instead, he breeds decay and violence. Sitwell's poetry reveals that the demon lover takes certain shapes in the poet's inner world. He is a knight in a coat of mail, a ghost of envy, and a miserly spider who feeds upon himself. He breeds "doom in the egg" and leaves a trail of mourning women who are frozen in a state of perpetual bereavement. In her poems from the mid and late 1940s, such as "The Song of the Cold" and "Green Song," Edith Sitwell's internal father can be seen most vividly.

In "Green Song," Sitwell expresses the fantasy that she might be rid of her guilt by getting rid of the internalized demon-lover father—her inner attacking father—whom she describes as an "accusing light." He is the knight in mail who uses the world's cold as a wall against contact, against love, against spring. As will be seen later, he is reminiscent of the miser in "The Song of the Cold," who turns love into possession (Salter and Harper 1976, 228). In "Green Song," the poet plays out the fantasy of rescue that she never had from her attacking, possessive, cold, and miserly father. By making herself the rescuing fairy god-mother, Sitwell is able to split off from the vulnerable young girl, who is the captive of the demon-lover father. She comes "as poverty," which is anathema to the envious and miserly ghost. Poverty seems to connote some form of purity as well, perhaps the purity of Sitwell risking her own financial impoverishment at the time when she chose to risk leaving her father's palace so that a truth apart from his truth might be sought. Disguised as a young girl, the poet (or her personna) receives the "serpent's kiss" from the male death force (the masculinized bad object). In this way, she scares the male demon away, and saves nature itself, i.e., saving the feminine force that is seen in spring (Salter and Harper 1976, 239).* The salvation of spring explains the poem's title:

> And hearing that, the poor ghost fled like the winter rain—
> Sank into greenish dust like the fallen moon
> Or the sweet green dust of the lime-flowers that will be blossoming soon.
> And spring grew warm again—
>
> (240)
>
> No more the accusing light, revealing the rankness of Nature . . .
>
> (240)
>
> Singing how winter's dark was overcome,
>
> (240)
>
> ...................................................
> And Death the pain of earth turning to spring again
> When lovers meet after the winter rain.
>
> (240)

We can see a fantasy here of freeing the self by expelling the bad object. It is also a fantasy of rebirth, of repeatedly starting all over, so characteristic of the paranoid-schizoid-position thinking process (see Ogden 1986). These fantasies of bad-object exorcism and of rebirth are seen in the work of all the preoedipal- or paranoid-schizoid-position women of the present book. Sitwell's fantasies echo the work of Sylvia Plath in particular. In the work of Emily Brontë and Emily Dickinson, we also see fantasies of death leading to a rebirth and merger with the idealized male muse, while the demonic male is rebelled against and exorcised. Anne Sexton is another female poet who repeatedly illustrates these themes of the paranoid-schizoid position.[8] Such themes in the work of these women reflect both addictive cycles within the use of the creative process and cycles of phallocentric or internal-male-object addiction.

On the basis of Sitwell's biography, the demon lover in her poetry appears to be her father, colored by the actual characteristics she viewed in him but seemingly also colored by the earlier incorporated mother. In "Green Song," Sitwell's "Knight of mail" is full of the death that she felt in her cold, distant, and internally

---

*The quotes from Edith Sitwell's poetry are taken from Salter and Harper volume, *Fire of the Mind*, 1976.

dead father. He is also a "ghost of Envy," which relates back to the early oral Kleinian level of envy. Both the father and the mother exist in part object form, as bad objects, fused together. The poetic themes that reenact their impact must be endlessly repeated because of the malevolent form of these part objects that prevents integrative internalization. Neither mourning nor resolution proceeds.

In "Green Song," Sitwell writes of the demon-lover ghost's bravado. This male ghost brags, "My frosts despoils the days' young darling." (Salter and Harper 1976, 239). How easily this can remind us of Emily Dickinson's indifferent god, who haphazardly beheaded fresh spring flowers with his winter frost. However, there is one significant difference. By having the male ghost speak in the first person, Edith Sitwell conveys the ghost's grandiose bravado. He is not merely indifferent; he is seen as narcissistically malicious. Sitwell's male demon has been colored by her father's unique character structure, just as the male demons of other female artists were colored by their particular fathers.

Three of Sitwell's poems from the years between 1942 and 1947 are most evocative in telling of her grief and its connection to her incorporated father. Unlike the mythological and nursery-rhyme disguises of her earlier poems, such as "Sleeping Beauty," these poems bring the internal world out into the light of day. Their metaphors seem open to translation once one knows the poet's biography and has read her own satirical descriptions of her father. The phrases most resonant with the internalized father are seen in the first poem, "The Song of the Cold." The theme of coldness itself was common to her work, but it was never so crystallized as in these later poems. Her inner world was cold, apparently because good-object internalization had been blocked.

Having viewed with awe and dismay the skid row derelects in California, the poet writes of the cold, sexless, and lone souls, who starve in the "famine of the heart." The poet obviously identified with such isolated and starving beings. They are subject to masculine malevolence just as she felt herself to be. However, it is in her view of the god who betrayed these lost souls that the reader can catch a glimpse of the poet's internal father. He is:

> The miser Foscue,
> Weaving his own death and sinking like a spider
> To vaults and depths that held his gold, that sun
>
> ..................................................
>
> Deserted by the god of this world, a Gold Man like a terrible Sun,
> A Mummy with a Lion's mane,
> He sits in this desert where no sound of wave shall come,
> And Time's sands are of gold, filling his ears and eyes;
> And he who has grown the talons of the Lion
> Has devoured the flesh of his own hands and heart in his pain.
>
> (Salter and Harper 1976, 228)

The theme of the miser cannot help but remind us of the poet's father, who niggardly counted each penny he gave his children, without considering any of their real needs. Edith's brother Osbert writes much about his father's nigardly attitudes toward money. Edith suffered the most severe impact of her father's reluctance to give. First, as a daughter, she was the child from whom he withheld most. She never had either the allowance or the prospects of inheritance that Osbert had. When she left her parents' home in her midtwenties, her father gave her no money. During Edith's entire life she lived in dread of the financial debts that she incurred, haunted by the fear that she would ultimately wind up like her extravagant mother—on trial and imprisoned for debts that Edith's father refused to pay. However, the worst blow came when Sir George died. Edith discovered how he had converted his will so as to not leave her more than a pittance. He reduced her share of his fortune from the originally promised one thousand pounds to sixty pounds. Edith obviously felt written off in more ways than one. She was so overcome with rage upon her father's death that she could not write, and her perennial headaches and back pains became acute (see Glendenning 1981). Also, her paranoia escalated, so that she and Osbert actually conjured up a tale of murder to explain the changes in her father's will. This must have served to help Edith deny the degree of rejection that she would have to face if she were to confront her father's behavior toward her. Yet her body registered the severity of this paternal rejection, which she expressed in her poetry by declaring her father a miser.

Edith's picture of the "miser Foscue" hoarding his gold while the bereft "lone souls" starve and freeze, is that of an internal world in which she exists as her father's starved victim. She was starved of emotional warmth and of empathic concern as others are starved of food. Only the poet's grand facade, contrived through theatrically Gothic dress and through a display of exhibitionistic performance, hid the "lone soul" of the childhood starvation that she had never mourned.

Another aspect of her internal father is seen in the phrase "a Mummy with a Lion's mane." This image perhaps captures Sitwell's experience of her father as a mummy, an outer case holding only death and emptiness within. The "Lion's mane" may also represent her father's bush red beard.

In essence, Sitwell seems to be illustrating how split her father is between an outward persona of a lion's pride and his inner deadness, i.e., his internal emotional void. It is this same mummy with a lion's mane who sits in a desert "where no sound of wave shall come." The poet paints her father's isolated state, going beyond the grandiose facade and into the void she had always felt was inside. This is the void her herself had derived through incorporation of her father.

The poet goes further and speaks of how her incorporated male father feeds on his own pain. He has "devoured the flesh of his own hands and heart in his pain."

This perhaps presents us with another part of her father as she perceived him. In fact, this could be a portrayal of the Sir George who became an invalid, exploiting whatever claims to ill health he could make to escape his responsibilities. Edith's portrait of a male cariacature feeding on his own pain reflects John Pearson's history of Sir George as a confirmed and self-serving invalid (1978, 42). Was this the father that Edith saw as devouring his own flesh?

When Edith then also refers to her "miser" as a man, we observe the father experienced at the level of the early primary mother "who spins but for herself" (Salter and Harper 1976, 229). From this phrase, we can reflect back to an earlier line of the poem, where the poet writes: "And love is but masked murder, the lust for possession" (228). The miser, the spider, the mummy all declare the maliganant state of the internalized father and prepare us for the demon lover themes to come. Sitwell writes:

> Soon comes the Night when those who were never loved
> Shall know the small immortal serpent's kiss
> And turn to dust as lover turns to lover . . .
>
> (229)

The "immortal serpent's kiss" is the kiss of death spelled out in demonic form. As seen in the work of the suicidal poets Sylvia Plath and Anne Sexton, the demon-lover bad-object half becomes associated with death.

The poem "The Song of the Cold" shows a shift. Although the demon lover's power turns to the blackness of death, the poet steps into the role of an age-old savior, with prophetic powers and purifying inflammatory rage. Generally, Sitwell's poetic persona is always one of commentator or savior, rather than of the experience of the abandoned ones, such as the "rag-picker," (229), who she calls "small babe," (230). In this way, she avoids any affective awareness of her own internal state and of the profound intensity of her childhood pain. Here, however, the poet discovers that she can be saved from deadness by rage. Her rage is alive. In "Song of the Cold," the poet's rage is used as a counterforce to the demon lover's coldness. She ends the poem in triumph, and declares:

> But the great sins and fires break out of me
> Like the terrible leaves from the bough in the violent spring . . .
> I am a walking fire, I am all leaves—
> I will cry to the Spring to give me the birds' and the serpents' speech
> That I may weep for those who die of the cold—
> The ultimate cold within the heart of Man
>
> (230)

These themes of fire and ice, of an icy hell and a smoldering rage, are the affective aspect of the arrested stage in development in which internal objects remain split. They show the split bad- and good-self states still merged with the split bad- and good-object states. This borderline split-image system is revealed in Edith Sitwell's poetry; it is expressed in relation to her internal-male demon lover.

In "Eurydice"—written during the same period as "Song of the Cold"—a theme of bereavement appears. Sitwell's work displays perpetual bereavement, which is accompanied by perpetual rage and obsession with death. These themes never get resolved into an active emotional process of mourning. Sometimes the splitting reappears as a theme of contrasting the grandeur of death and its persona with the spontaneity and warmth of nature.

In "Eurydice," this grandeur of death is likened to the falseness of miserly greed and to the worship of mammon. The poet expresses a yearning to return to the smallness of natural things and to the personal, to a more intimate way of life. In her own life, Edith Sitwell could never actually do this. According to her chief biographer, Glendinning, Sitwell could not lose herself at all in any intimate moments of life; she could not simply be. As for all who are imprisoned in a narcissistic character structure, doing is compulsive and becomes a defense against being.[9] Sitwell was possessed by her persona and by her own carefully constructed elegant facade. Without it, as Pearson remarks, she was merely an aging spinster living with her brother (1978, 373).[10]

In "Eurydice," we are teased into thinking that a theme of mourning actually does lead to a rebirth of the natural soul (or self), or to a rebirth of a natural life. Yet in the end we are left only with a return to the grandiose defense of seeking the idealized object as an antidote to a cold death and its related bad-object force. Thus, the manic-narcissistic defense state of pathological mourning persists, and the theme of mourning brings illusion rather than actual rebirth. The theme of Orpheus and Eurydice is used to display the perpetuation of an idealized love.

The theme of mourning appears but is aborted by an image of death:

> In the lateness of the season, I wish the golden feet
> That had walked in the fields of Death, now walk again
> The dark fields where the sowers scatter grain
> Like tears, or the constellations that weep for the lateness of the season—
> Where the women walk like mourners, like the Afternoon ripened,[11]
>    with their bent heads;
> Their golden eyelids, like the drifts of the narcissus
> In spring, are wet with their tears. They mourn for a young wife who had
>    walked these fields—
> So young, not yet had Proserpina tied up her golden hair
> In a knot like the branched corn . . . So good was she—
> With a voice like the sweet swallow. She lies in the silent Tomb.

(Salter and Harper 1976, 236)

Then follows the theme of rebirth:

> We are heavy with Death, as a woman is heavy with child,
> As the corn-husk holds its ripeness, the gold comb
> Its weight of summer . . . But as if a lump of gold had changed to corn,
> So did my Life rise from my Death. I cast the grandeur of Death away
> And homeward came to the small things of Love,
> the building of the hearth, the kneading of daily bread
> The cries of birth, and all the weight of light.
>
> (237)

The conclusion is idealized love, the fantasy of union with the god Orpheus:[12]

> With one who had come glittering like the wind
> To meet me—Orpheus with the golden mouth,
> You—like Adonis born from the young myrrh-tree,
> you, the vine-branch
> Broken by the wind of Love . . . I turned to greet you—
> And when I touched your mouth, it was the Sun.
>
> (237)

## Edith Sitwell and Pavlik Tchelitchew: Early Relationship

Edith Sitwell was introduced to her one life-long love during a stay in Paris in the 1930s, when she was forty years old. Gertrude Stein then reigned as queen in the Paris salon world of artists. She introduced the poet to the painter.

Pavlik Tchelitchew was at least ten years younger than Edith. He was a confirmed homosexual who lived with his male lover (then Allen Tanner) and his sickly sister, Chora. In the midst of her friendship with Pablo Picasso and other painters, Gertrude Stein briefly adopted Pavlik Tchelitchew as a favorite. She exhibited his paintings in her drawing rooms and became the painter's sybil. During this brief period, Stein introduced Tchelitchew to Edith Sitwell, and a flame of idealizing images and passions were immediately ignited. Tchelitchew painted a series of portraits of Edith—preferring to view her rather than to touch her but adoring the image of her that he could create in his own paintings. Stein quickly dropped Tchelitchew from favor, which left Tchelitchew to choose Edith as his new sybil.

Edith spent one very happy Christmas in Paris living with Pavlik, Allen Tanner, and Chora. She became very friendly with both Allen and Chora, and she continued her relationships through correspondence when she left Paris.

In these early days, Edith and Pavlik laughed, joked, and played together like many lovers. They each had found an idealized image in the other to reflect their own idealized selves. Each mirrored the artistic ideals of the other, but Pavlik kept his emotional distance. He never allowed himself to be alone in a room with Edith because he feared what he perceived as the threat of her devouring femininity. He maintained paranoid vigilence against Edith's potential sexual desires, even though she never showed any awareness of them herself. At first, however, they managed to get on through simply adoring each other. Edith denied all sexual impulses and suppressed any part of her personality that she thought could be a threat to Pavlik. She also sacrificed much time, effort, and inspiration toward the enhancement of Pavlik's career, putting her own career aside. She even enlisted both her brothers in the construction of large painting exhibitions to publicize Pavlik's work and searched out buyers for his paintings.

After Edith returned to England, she corresponded with Pavlik, who kept wooing her back to Paris. He spoke of his loneliness and promised total devotion should she return to live. These were words of charm, seduction, and charisma— promises easily broken when the time actually came. Edith did return to live in Paris and spent many miserable, lonely, and poverty-stricken years there. During these years her friend, roommate, and former governess, Helen Rootman, died torturously and slowly from cancer.

Edith did not feel free to leave Paris until Helen died. This gave Pavlik a chance to abandon her in many years of anguish. As Edith wrote, "P. left me to it . . . " (Glendinning 1981, 219). For long periods of time, Pavlik, who was known for frequent temper tantrums (as reported by Wyndham Lewis) and all kinds of erratic behavior, would absolutely refuse to see Edith, who was now living so near him. A friend of Edith's reported an incident to Glendinning (183) in which Edith came to call on Pavlik, who refused to let her in. The friend was overcome by the humiliation and pain that Edith allowed herself to endure.

Even though Edith seemed compelled to protect her idealized picture of Pavlik—who reflected her own idealized self-image—her bitterness broke through first in a letter to a friend, and then in her writing, but was still kept split off from her interpersonal relations with this male muse-god. She wrote a friend on her return to England that Pavlik, who had left her to her isolation, poverty, and poetic sterility while in Paris, was now apt to claim kinship with her on his tour of London, where her "name held some glamor" (Glendinning, 214).

During her disillusioned stay in Paris in the 1930s, Sitwell wrote her only novel, *I Live under a Black Sun*, which presents a macabre portrait of her affair with Pavlik Tchelitchew.

# 14

# Edith Sitwell II: The Aging Narcissist

## The War Years and Later 1940s

Edith suffered and endured. She would not willingly give up the idealized male love of her life. During the war years, when Pavlik Tchelitchew resumed an enthusiastic correspondence with her, Edith quickly warmed to reciprocation. Pavlik's charming words still worked on her; he now began to promise her everything as long as she was at a distance. Through letters, the two artists renewed the flame of their passion for each other. They each needed a muse and chose one from the feared but idealized opposite sex. For ten years, they could commiserate with one another through their letter writing, lending each other support and admiration.

Glendinning writes: "An idealized Edith had written weekly to an idealized Pavlik, as he to her; apart, they had met in an area without conflict, speaking directly to that part of the other which each needed. It was fantasy, but only in the sense that reality for both of them was infinitely more complex and cluttered" (274).

In this way, they could have a narcissistic alliance against the world which seemed alien and intrusive. Pavlik shared all of his ideas with her, e.g., about the mystic function of anatomy. He gave Edith the assurance of her exclusive value to him, devaluing his new sexual relationship with Charles Henri Ford as "a kind of madness, contrary to love." He told her, "I have no friends besides you, no real friends." Glendinning writes:

> Edith, with an ocean between them, became once more Pavlik's "spiritual confidante." There was a renewed rapport, so intense as in the earliest days of their friendship. For her, it was a miracle. She was again his Delphic Oracle, his Dame Blanche, the Sibyl of his 1937 portrait of her, the "bee-priestess"— honey is liquid gold. He wrote about himself, and his moods. He said he dreamed about her, wrote about his work, and his ill health. He gave her the reassurance she needed; "No no my dear, don't be childish, you are my greatest friend of heart and brain. And Edith my dearest friend you are like an enormous heart who is also an ear and an eye to read through my madman's [sic] thoughts."
>
> (222)

In 1945, Edith Sitwell published a poem entitled "The Two Loves" in *New Writing and Daylight*, dedicated "To Pavel Tchelitchew and his work in progress," (242). In this poem, Sitwell writes of her understanding of Pavlik's fear of the female:

> And the lover seeing in Women the rankness of Nature,—
> A Monstrous Life-force, the need of procreation
> Devouring all other life . . . or Gravity's force
> Drawing him down to the centre of his earth.
>
> (242)

The male's fear in this poem corresponds to Edith Sitwell's own fear of the male, as shown in her theme of the "ghost of Envy." Who is the father glaring at her with accusatory looks; "no more the accusing light revealing the rankness of nature " ("Green Song"). It seems that she felt that the rankness of nature was always seen in her by a male—first by her father and now by his transferential derivative, Pavlik Tchelitchew. Both men provided the inner imprints for Sitwell's "ghost of envy." In a wish—during the 1940s fantasy of reunion—to restore Tchelitchew to his idealized, unadulterated form, the poet accepts his view of her. To appease his fear of her, she sublimates her love and becomes a sacrificial Christ, thus removing herself as a threat. She molds herself to the sublimated form he desires through the following lines in "The Two Loves":

> I see Christ's wounds weep in the Rose on the Wall.
> Then I who nursed in my earth the dark red seeds of Fire—
> The pomegranate grandeur, the dark seeds of Death,
> Felt them change to the light and fire in the heart of their rose . . .
>
> (242–43)

## The Intrapsychic Object World of the Two Pavlik Tchelitchews

Many creative women have their muse. Often they have a man in their life who serves the function of the idealized part object. The fantasy of union with this man activates a "reunion fantasy" (see Masterson 1976), i.e., a fantasy of rejoining the early symbiotic mother of infancy. If the separation period in development is traumatic, the reunion fantasy will be particularly intense. Consequently, the idealized person, who resonates with the fantasy of the internal object world, can have the power of almost unendurably seductive charm. When a man is in the position of a woman's muse (a part object derivative from the symbiotic merger in infancy), his attraction has the trenchant force of resonating with the whole internal grandiose self-structure.[1]

In Edith Sitwell's poetry, we see a cold preoedipal mother fused with a cold oedipal father, as seen in the images of the knight of mail and the ghost of envy. It is interesting that even though Edith Sitwell never felt conscious yearnings for an erotic relationship until very late in her life,[2] probably owing to developmental arrest prior to the oedipal stage, she selected a man to be her idealized love object. Initially, she saw in Pavlik Tchelitchew a fresh energetic child (Glendinning 1981, 330); he became her muse. It seems that he mirrored the oppressed and warded off child-self within her. Her child-self was imprisoned within and remained outside interpersonal relationships. This child-self showed its reflection only in the poet's creative work, where victimized beings were tempered with the poetic pen. In essence, her creativity allowed some expression of this part of her, but as Edith made plain when speaking of her ability to write about a mother's anguish at the loss of a child, her understanding of this event stemmed from the early experience of having her natural instincts crushed out of her by her parents' attitudes (Glendinning, 210).

The poet yearned for the spontaneity and resilience of a lively body; this can only come from an inner world of lively objects. As Glendinning records, in actual fact her body was dead to her—she never even took walks. Any physical exercise was painful, never pleasurable (317). Not only her erotic life, but her very essence, her potential for natural affect and vitality were deadened. The poet operated in a hall of mirrors, coming to life only through reflection in the eyes of others. Consequently her life was a continual performance; even as she aged and the effort became an excruciating strain, she had to obey when the audience called. As Glendinning notes (317), only in her writing did feeling, thinking, mind, and body, all come together. Perhaps this was the only domain for expression that had been free of the intrusive father-mother. To protect it, the poet kept it separate from interpersonal relationships. Yet this inevitably perpetuated her internal split.

Ironically, Edith Sitwell's theory of poetry was a physical one, a theory of physical dynamics based on the concept that rhythm and meter were seen as akin to muscle form and structure. Nevertheless, the affect life that she experienced in her poetry was more spiritual than erotic, loving, or aggressive. It had the quality of the collective-unconscious archetypes that the Jungians describe, or of the a priori internal objects that Melanie Klein wrote about. Its metaphors are symbolic, universal, and broad in intellectual concept—especially in Sitwell's later writings. Her physical theory had to yield to a spiritual talent, one more disembodied than embodied. However, in Pavlik Tchelitchew, Edith Sitwell could see and desire the lost physical part of her being.

Tchelitchew was not only an external reflection of Sitwell's stunted inner child-self. He was also the idealized father who repeated her disappointment with her original father. In addition, he was the demon-lover counterpart.

With the intuitive striving of the unconscious toward reenactment, Tchelitchew was increasingly revealed to be the demonic real father cloaked in the facade of the romantic ideal. Even in the beginning, when he worshipped Edith, he did so through painting portraits of her rather than though lovemaking. This appears reminiscent of her father's character. In the poet's autobiographical essays (*Taken Care Of*), Edith tells us of how her father lived as if always in a photograph. Rather than relate to his daughter as a child, Sir George would suddenly react to a fantasy image in his mind and would seize upon her to force her to conform to the image. For example, when she was quite young, he would picture himself and her in a photograph as the prosaic "father and daughter." Then, in his compulsion to contrive the portrait germinating in his mind, he would, according to Sitwell, "bowl me over with a cushion, pinning my forehead to the iron fender" (16). The poet adds, "I have referred already to the fact that my father saw himself always as the centre of a photograph" (18). The use of the daughter as an extension of the father's grandiose image-self is obvious in his indifferent manipulation of Edith into place.

Similarly, in Sitwell's adult life, Tchelitchew would view rather than touch her. From far away he could adore her as he imagined her to be what he wished, flattering his image of himself. However, he was terrified of her sexuality; although she never imposed it on him (she herself not being conscious of it), he continued to have a paranoid dread of her femininity. He would accuse Edith both of being devouringly feminine and of not being feminine enough. How similar this was to her father's attitude toward her during her oedipal phase we can only imagine. Her poetry in any case suggests that her father was frigid to her approaches, and seemingly to those of her mother as well.[3] In "Green Song," in particular, the "ghost of Envy" is a cold and malevolent lover, and the "Knight of mail" rebuffs all kisses. Even more tellingly, in "Song of the Cold" the "Serpent's Kiss" brings death.

In what other ways does Pavlik Tchelitchew reveal himself to be like the internalized father? Similarly to Sir George, he holds on to Edith while he simultaneously pushes her away. He wishes to possess her. Yet he will respond to none of her needs, particularly to her feminine needs. As already mentioned, during the era in Paris, Tchelitchew turns out to be as emotionally abusive of her as her father had been.

During her Paris years (1937–1939), when Edith Sitwell wrote her one novel, *I Live under a Black Sun*, she used her experience with Pavlik Tchelitchew to spell out her demonic themes. In the guise of writing about Jonathan Swift and his female lovers, Edith slipped in her own story as the split-off victimized part of her felt it. According to Glendinning:

Edith's Stella/Anna figure is the woman who sacrifices herself for love. She has devoted "my whole life, the whole of my existence, all my thoughts to Jonathan, for years now. . . . My life has been given up to helping him make his life." She is growing older: There are "little lines round the corner of her mouth" now; there are "depths of hollow darkness about her, behind the vast black blaring shadow of her eyes," and in the "large beast-furred male near her lips, that belied the tiptoeing life that she had led for so many years." For Jonathan has told her the truth: "There are certain things for which most women hope—things that mean nearly everything in life to nearly every woman, that you must give up forever, for they will never to yours—hopes, wishes, which belong to one side of your nature. In return for this sacrifice, "I will give you everything I have it in my nature to give. You will be the only woman in my life whom I will call my friend."

(209)

Although Pavlik Tchelitchew probably betrayed her more than anyone else, Sitwell—who would impulsively accuse almost anyone else of betrayal—never said more to Pavlik than that he should be ashamed of his behavior toward her. Even that she did in a letter that she never sent to him. After his death and until her own, Sitwell protected her image of Tchelitchew, the man whom she had chosen as her idealized muse. She protected him most from her own wrath, never acknowledging his defects. Thus, she never integrated her own inner world in which she kept her demonic father isolated from his idealized counterpart.

## Period in America

Edith Sitwell's first tour of America was a sensation. She became the recipient of all the applause of which she had ever dreamed. However, freedom from her British critics did not sustain the poet beyond the initial glamor of fresh applause. There is a devastation that narcissists experience in the inner world once the "glitter" has worn off (see Kernberg 1975). In actuality, the glitter wears off pretty quickly. After the performance comes inner restlessness, boredom, and a sense of empty vapidity. For someone with a paranoid mode of self-esteem regulation, such as Edith Sitwell, there must be a battle to fight to forestall the inner state, which threatens to enter into awareness as soon as the drug of applause and adulation wears thin.

In America, Edith Sitwell did not have her tried and true enemies, such as Wyndham Lewis, F. R. Leavis, and Gregory Grigson, to battle with. George Pearson (1978) writes that during her stay at the Hotel St. Regis in New York, Edith said to the novelist Glenway Wescott: "Oh, how I just wish somebody would put his head in my mouth so I could bite it off!" "Anyone in particular,

Edith?" "No, almost anyone would do" (403). She was obviously feeling desperate without her enemies, yet she wouldn't bite Pavlik Tchelitchew's head off, however much he may have contributed to her sense of ugliness. He was her idealized object and could not be tampered with.

In her biography, Glendinning attributes Sitwell's growing despair to Pavlik's rejection of her. It was at this time that Edith and Pavlik were to rendezvous after ten years apart. For a decade, they had been faithful correspondents. Their relationship had never been as smooth as during this ten-year separation.

Pavlik nearly evaded their meeting at the pier. When Edith's transatlantic steamship pulled into the pier in New York, it was only because of the intervention of his lover Charles Henry Ford that Pavlik didn't abscond. The painter was edgy from the beginning; on seeing the aging Edith, he was unable to refrain from incessant criticism. He hardly attempted to conceal his overwhelming sense of disappointment. Her looks, her dress, and its design—all seemed to offend his sensibilities. She could not fit into his view of his "sibyl" or "muse." This produced nothing less than disaster. The death blow to their fantasied reunion came at the moment when Edith stood before Pavlik's painting "Hide and Seek" at the Museum of Modern Art. Pavlik had described to Edith every thought and aspiration he had during the process of painting it (Glendinning 1981, 274). Now he omnipotently expected immediate rapture from Edith as his masterpiece stood in front of her. The tremendous yet silent pressure to respond just as he wished, and upon cue, must have stunned Edith. The following day she wrote a long letter full of the ecstatic praise that she could not produce on cue the day before. However, the rapport between them would never be restored.

On Edith's last night in New York, Pavlik, who had silently withdrawn until that time, burst forth with his narcissistic rage at her farewell dinner party. Glendinning describes it:

> A farewell dinner was given for Edith and Osbert at Voisin's. Pavel Tchelitchew and Charles Henry Ford were there, and Auden, Kirk Shew, Lincoln Kirstein, and David Horner. For once Pavlik did not hog the conversation; on the contrary, he seemed very subdued. Then towards the end he silenced everyone, exploding into a loud, hectoring monologue of complaint and criticism against Edith—he made a scene "of intentional humiliation," accusing her of preferring her rich vulgar new friends to her old friends, of being self-obsessed, of betraying the poet who had been, of every sort of unworthy and cheap and disloyal behavior. All between them was now over. Edith, ashen-faced and shattered, said nothing at all. Nor did anyone else make any more than calming noises; no one, not even Osbert, counterattacked, and when the storm was over, the dinner drew to a close in a thinly disguised icy awkwardness—one of Edith's hells of Cold. In this way they parted.

> (278–279)

Glendinning obviously relates Edith's feeling of ugliness to Pavlik Tchelitchew's rejection of her at this time. Looking at Pearson's portrait, it is clear that Edith was devastated by Pavlik and that Pearson attributes Edith's restless boredom in America to her rage. When he writes of Edith's comment on needing somebody's head to bite off, Pearson conveys to us that Edith could not tolerate being away from her critics. The glamour and the glitter were not enough. Also, they wore off quickly. Edith had lost Pavlik as her muse, although she struggled to resurrect him despite everything. Her view of herself as reflected in his demonically disapproving eyes was an ugly one. As with her literary critics, she seems to have found in Pavlik's response to her, the negative mirror reflected in her father's eyes. Yet, Edith was compelled to deny her experience. To protect her image of Pavlik as her muse, Edith denied Pavlik's malign intent as much as she could. Suppressing her reactions, she never mailed the letter in which she attempted to confront him (Glendinning, p. 280, and Pearson, p. 405).

Then she received a vicious letter from Pavlik, blasting her again. According to her biographers, Edith Sitwell had had a recurring nightmare, throughout her life, that she would be confronted with an "impertinence" and would not be able to slap down the hostile offender. Yet, this never happened in actuality, as long as the injurious insults could be seen as impertinences from plebians whom she believed she outranked in aristocratic and artistic supremacy. She was ready to retaliate against critics, artists, or nobility alike. However, she met her nemesis in the person of Pavlik Tchelitchew. Here, the nightmare came true. His vicious attacks on her went far beyond the more shielded hostility of her father's nauseous disdain. One minute he could be the cold and disdainful father, but the next he was assaulting her with the vehement narcissistic rage more characteristic of her mother's form of hysteria, while being more woundingly articulate still. Edith was paralyzed in response, turned ashen with suppressed pain, and failed to "slap down" the soul of impertinence.

She even arranged to see Pavlik again, inviting him as her houseguest at the family's Renishaw palace. She returned to worrying about his health and his financial condition. When Pavlik arrived, sickly and looking old, Edith made herself into the essence of compliance. The poet molded herself into the image that didn't offend. In sum, she silenced herself completely. With suicidal tact, Edith attempted to be feminine according to Tchelitchew's ideal by not allowing herself any self-expression. She listened attentively, played the hostess, and inquired anxiously about his state of health. Although she tells us in her autobiography that being good had nearly driven her crazy with inner tension as a child, at this significantly later date she attempted to conform to her "god-daddy's" definition of "good" posture. Narcissistic depletion would result if she didn't express her narcissistic rage. However, now Edith Sitwell was back in England and could foment fights with her literary critics, creating enemies that allowed her an avenue to express her narcissistic rage, through a paranoid mode of operation.

Sitwell had a hard time leaving the admiration that she encountered in America. Yet it seems that she had a harder time staying in America without her critics. Because of her paranoid form of regulating self-esteem, it was safer for her to bury herself in compliance to Pavlik in England than it would have been during her generously received stay in America, where Pavlik's abusive insults repeated the negative mirroring of her father. In such a vulnerable state, Edith could not forestall a descent into an abyss of misery. All of the acclaim, fame, and celebration of her poetic grandeur could not allay these affects. Perhaps we cannot clearly delineate which contributed more to her state of self-depletion: her rejection by Pavlik or her loss of her familiar enemies when she came to America. It is clear in any case that the admiration she yearned for her whole life wore thin within minutes. Nowhere had she received a purer dose of it than in America. Yet like any drug, it wore off, leaving her with only more craving. The primitive aggression that resulted from this was manifested in body symptoms, as well as in a paranoid-schizoid form of depression (depletion as opposed to neurotic guilt depression). Admiration was only a substitute for the empathic understanding, recognition, and support that she had not received during critical childhood periods. Without mourning the actual loss of that earlier time, her craving for this drug could lead only to narcissistic rage at her critics; they were blamed for the fact that her wish for admiration was insatiable. Without her critics, Edith Sitwell sank into a sense of ugliness and into the "cold slum in hell" so vividly residing behind the contrived image-self in her novel *I Live under a Black Sun*. Once more, the black sun of her father's negative mirroring had arisen, in the external form of Pavlik Tchelitchew; it resonated with her inner ghost, her internal demon lover.

## "His Blood Colours My Cheek"

After Tchelitchew's death, Edith chose another idealized part object. Her new muse-god was not a living man, but a man in spiritual form: Jesus Christ. Edith converted to Catholicism, and her yearning to believe in Christ as her savior emerged in her poetry. In the poem "His Blood Colours My Cheek," she seems to feel compelled to articulate the newly idealized counterpart to her internal male demon. Here is a new form of the wish for a compensatory object, perhaps a wish for what Bollas (1987) would call a "transformational object." However, the fantasy of such union with a "transformational object" (Bollas 1987), or of reunion (Masterson 1976) with an original symbiotic object is only an attempt to deny the original childhood trauma and the need to open oneself to consciously experiencing it so that it can be understood and worked through. In adulthood it is too late to receive that missing in critical periods of childhood for an outside object, because the inner self and its wound are sealed off. Sitwell did not have a real transitional object in the form of a therapist to provide a consistently containing and empathic presence so that the pain and fear behind the darkness might be entered, and the defenses against contact might be brought into awareness. Compensation through the illusion of rescue from an idealized object can lead only to renewed disappointment. Sitwell defended against the anguish of traumatic disappointment with narcissism and withdrawal. She ultimately disconnected herself from the Catholic Church (Glendinning 1981, 320).

Opening and closing with the line "His Blood colours my cheek," she ends the poem as follows:

> His Blood colours by cheek;—
> No more eroded by the seas of the world's passions and greeds, I rise
> As if I never had been Ape, to look in the compassionate,
>     the all-seeing eyes.
>
> (Salter and Harper 1976, 296)

The poet looks to her new muse-god to protect her and to be her "tight-rope over an abyss." Here, the poet uses the phrase as a seemingly double entendre—i.e., to suffer blind faith in worldly demons, as well as to lead to a thread of faith in her god:

> Building a new Babel for the weak
> Who walk with the certainty of the somnambulist
> Upon the tight-rope stretched over nothingness—
>
> (295)

Here, she blends the blind somnambulist, so reminiscent of her detached schizoid father, with her tight-rope over the abyss." She seeks to neutralize her demon father with the power of her new god. Yet, her god can only be a "tight-rope" over the abyss, the abyss remains. The black void of unconscious and split remnants of childhood abandonment trauma, which continues to haunt her and to demand a constant drug-like antidote, when the compensation of faith fails.

### The Shadow of Cain

While on a train during a poetry-reading tour, Edith and her brother Osbert saw a picture of the mushroom cloud from the Hiroshima atomic bomb explosion on the front page of a newspaper. Startled and dismayed, Edith likened the shape of the mushroom cloud to the shape of the totem, a symbol of fertility and of life. She was aware of the black irony in such a shape bringing devastation and death to millions. From her reaction, she wrote the poem "The Shadow of Cain":

> Under great yellow flags and banners of the ancient Cold
> Began the huge migrations
> From some primeval disaster in the heart of Man.
>
> There were great oscillations
> Of temperature . . . You knew there had once been warmth;
> But the Cold is the highest mathematical Idea . . . the Cold is Zero—
>
> (264–65)

Is this a portrait of the poet's inner cold or a picture of an inner primal disaster that occurred when she was deserted by her father's heart, which may have felt as cold as zero? Is it the loss of warmth from a symbiotic mother, as separation reveals the mother's cold abandonment that leaves her with an internal, black abyss? What seems interesting here is that a mushroom cloud is not only the inverse of destruction and alienation, when it is seen as a totem pole, but that it is also a symbol of phallic fertility. Perhaps in thinking of a totem pole, Sitwell's subliminal consciousness had conjured up the image of a phallus, only then to sublimate it into a symbolic and ritualized form. Such was the manner in which Sitwell was apt to deal with all blunt, bodily things. Drawn to a symbol of phallic power, she seems captivated by observing how the symbol of the phallus could be inverted into a malignant form of power. Her sensitivity to such a masculine image of inverted power could relate to her own experience of having a father whose emotional abuse and deprivation were incorporated as a split-off demonic object.

Moreover, perhaps in thinking of the myth of Cain after seeing the mushroom cloud, she could be reflecting on her own inner split and inner severance, since they resulted from the masculinized bad object's malevolent effects. It is in this poem that the poet depicts an image of severance, perhaps reflective of her own inner state as it persists into her later life:

> The Earth had cloven in two in that primal disaster.
> ....................................................
> Between Man and his brother Man—
> Although their speech
> Was alien, each from each,
> As the Bird's from the Tiger's,
>    born from the needs of our opposing famines.

...................................................

The gulf that was torn across the world seemed as of the beds of all the Oceans
Were emptied . . . Naked, and gaping at what once had been the Sun.

(267)

This poem makes vivid the state of perpetual bereavement characteristic of the pathological mourning state. It evokes the sense of being internally torn in half by perpetual splitting processes and by perpetual cold rage. The poet's inner coldness is externalized; we sense the pathological fixation related to addiction to the paternal object, the lost "Sun."[4]

In the poet's life, one sees the results of this internal state: failed reparation, failed mourning, and failed internalization over and over again. External part objects are continually needed like drugs; when the supply dries up, the inner self becomes dead.

A critical example of this can be seen in Sitwell's later life, following the writing of the "Shadow of Cain." In February 1948, Edith Sitwell wrote to Jack Lindsay (a literary critic favorable to her): "I have been finding it almost impossible to work, and have been feeling a strange bereavement—" (Glendinning 1981, 263). Symptomatically, she turns the bereavement into blame and devaluation, which arrests the grief. The poet's next line in her letter to Lindsay is "—I suppose owing to the increasing menace and stupidity of the world" (263). Lindsay's praise and reassurance allowed her to sooth away her "black" feelings temporarily, but then she was compelled to externalize blame once more—and the vicious cycle of splitting was renewed. Coldness could sometimes yield to an active grief, but not for long. Edith Sitwell could feel tears for the war dead (Pearson 1978, 380); perhaps this shows that her inner grief was briefly available. Yet the lake of grief inside her, [mixed with her internal wound,] quickly froze over as externalization and splitting won out. Narcissistic devaluation, and paranoid fantasies of persecutory objects, became her only friends as she withdrew further from the world.

## The Aging Narcissist

In *Borderline Conditions and Pathological Narcissism* (1975), Otto Kernberg speaks of the narcissistic character's incapacity for "in-depth empathy." Having the privilege of looking at an entire lifetime of experience, in terms of both the outer and the inner life as revealed through the combination of biography and creative work in Edith Sitwell, we can most vividly see how the consequences of this incapacity seem to become greater in impact with age.

Kernberg writes that a most poignant area for this failure is in the aging narcissist's inability to empathize with his or her own children, or with the younger generation in general. As the occupational life becomes curtailed with the aging process, the lack of ability to empathize with the younger generation becomes critical. There is no sense of self-renewal through empathic identification for the narcissistic character as her own life diminishes. Although Edith Sitwell never had children, we are presented with certain biographical extensions of her preoedipal condition that indicate that she might have failed to experience their subjective reality even if she had had them.

Sylvia Plath chose to act out her suicidal demise while her children were asleep upstairs. Some of Plath's biographers (Wagner-Martin [1987] and Anne Stevenson [1989]) write of how Plath feared for her children when she contemplated their loss of a father following her marital separation. Perhaps, she could fear for them in that regard because their loss mirrored a major loss of her own—her father's death when she was young. It nevertheless seems odd that Plath apparently never contemplated the impact on her children that loss of their mother would bring directly following loss of their father. This oddity reflects the failings in basic empathic capacity that all narcissistic characters show and highlights the similarities between Plath's and Sitwell's lives.

Edith Sitwell expressed longings for a child, but her lack of empathic capacity made poetry her only home, for she could not truly care for others. What limited caring she could feel could not be sustained. Her biographer Glendinning relates this to a basic failing in "being," which is so resonant with D. W. Winnicott's (1971) emphasis on the empathy within the parent-child bond. Glendinning comments:

> In her own life, she had no way other than through her poetry (which was drying up) of transcending herself. Most people find a way to flow out of themselves; most know the nonphysical realities that are reached through physical love, or through caring for a child. [Edith could not even lose herself in making a garden, a home, a cake.]
>
> (317)

Edith Sitwell lived in her poetry, and since her poetry too was so contaminated with her haunted inner world, she could not encounter herself through it in any sustained, self-reflective manner. Although her inner tragedies were perpetually restated and symbolized, they existed in the space of her creative work as if in a cocoon. She shielded herself in her role as prophet or narrator. Her damaged inner self appeared as a self-contained victim. Although an atmosphere of grief appears in the poem "Still Falls the Rain" (1940), this atmosphere exists in an externalized form in which mourning remains perpetual. Her grief comes from the outside as she shows through the symbolism of rain. The poet's subjective self does not exist within it. Consequently, there is no movement through developmental mourning and self-integration. The inner world reechoes itself, but it does not change. We must conclude that the creative process could not be used.[5] If Sitwell could not use it because she failed to encounter her inner self, she could not internalize her creative work to build psychic structure. Her self remained sealed off, perpetually engaged with its internal masculinized object. She projected this enactment into all of her interpersonal relations. Thus, although the poet expressed regrets that she could not have a child,[6] she failed to sustain her attempted nurturance of young poets.

The most poignant example of this failure is found in her relationship with Quentin Stevenson, a young poet she chose as her protege. The aging Edith assumed he would adopt her ideals and values. She may have even thought that he would continue for her the chosen lines of her own craft. At first she was embarrassingly admiring of Stevenson for poetry that others thought needed much improvement. Her unrealistic assessment of him made the young male poet quite uncomfortable. His betrayal of her was inevitable, set up by the blueprint of her expectation of what he was to be as an extension of herself. She could allow no autonomy—just as her father had allowed none for her. Even Stevenson suspected his betrayal was inevitable. As soon as he asserted his autonomy, Edith turned quickly away.

Stevenson's first violation was to choose to embark on a trip. He was inspired by ideals foreign to Sitwell. Not long afterward, Quentin took a career turn to acting. Edith had no sympathy whatsoever with such an experiment. She abruptly wrote him off not only as a lost cause, but as another blackguard who had shown no gratitude or trust. She could never see her own need to control those she signified as her chosen ones. Typical of those with narcissistic character disorders, Sitwell identified with the aggressor in her internal world and reenacted the same controlling behavior that her parents had acted out toward her. Further, like them, she based her behavior on a grandiose presumption of having the ultimate and final vision.

Glendinning indicates the pain that was barely shielded by Sitwell's indignation (332–33). According to Glendinning, the poet's inability to come to terms with her vanity and with her need to dominate simply repeated the pattern that made Sitwell feel that "love had failed again." Glendinning (333) makes us aware that in *Fanfare for Elizabeth*, Sitwell writes of the queen's mourning for her own childless state, suggesting her own state of feeling. However, Sitwell's mourning was pathologically arrested and thus was perpetual. She writes of Queen Elizabeth as she generally wrote of others—as reflections of her own self: "The lonely queen, constantly mourning secretly for her childless state . . . " (Glendinning, 333).

The poet's attempt to support another was continually contaminated by the prevalent need to control that person. When Quentin Stevenson had predilections contrary to her own blueprint for him (332), he immediately became a traitor in Sitwell's eyes; there was no forgiveness.[7] When neither subtle nor overt coercion worked to modify this young male protege's straying tendencies, Sitwell canceled the bond between them with cold rage that shielded anguished disappointment:

> Quentin Stevenson was writing less and less; he wanted now to act, which Edith refused to take seriously. . . . Edith dedicated a poem to him. . . . Quentin thought it was not a good poem, so said nothing, and did not even thank her for the dedication. She was very hurt, and wrote to Father Caraman: He has not written to thank me. He makes a great mistake from his own point of view by being so appallingly bad-mannered having got exactly what he wanted from me i.e. he has been introduced to everybody who could be of use to him. He now never writes to me unless he wants something. . . . She removed his name from the poem, and rededicated it to Alberto de Lacerda.
>
> (332–33)

## The Last Performance

Despite sensational acclaim at her last performance, Sitwell took it as a death knell because she knew there would be no other. Her humor turned macabre, revealing the bitterness within. With morbidity, she tells the tale in *Taken Care Of* of her enfeebled entry into the celebration being held for her (1965, 355–56). She embellishes her description of the bulk of her dependent and cumbersome weight, as she recollected her secretary and her nurse conveying her to the stage from her wheelchair, exuding obvious self-disgust. All joy in fame and adulation is lost. Not being able to retain an autonomous internal sense of herself, i.e., a view which could ultimately extend beyond the audience's view of her—she finally gets it all and cannot keep it. She cannot keep it beyond the stage or beyond the grave. The poet then broadcasts the message that none of it was worth it. In the end, the performance and its applause can be viewed as an addictive mode of reassurance that failed to substitute for the recognition of an individuating self that Sitwell missed during critical stages in early development.

At the end of her life, Edith Sitwell's paranoia lost the ego-controlled quality that she had maintained as she battled in court, or in newspapers and interviews. There was no more clearly articulated retort to the "philistines' " impertinences. In the end, she was reduced to quivering terror.

In an interview with Robert Muller for *The Daily Mail* of September 10, (1959) she lost control and gave way to her fears. "You will be kind to me, won't you?" she begged him, "Because people hate me so very much" (Glendinning 1981,

340). Prior to this reaction, Sitwell had responded to members of an audience who said they could not hear her in a presentation with a prompt acidic flash: "Then get a hearing aid" (340 see also Salter 1967). This was an embittered version of her usual style of defensive repartee. Although often self-defeating, it was at times quite successful, at least when she could create the necessary awe. When successful, intimidation was turned to adulation. Sitwell enacted the narcissistic style of retaliation, which wards off an extreme self-vulnerability. However, at this late age, her warier facade was breaking down. In a *Daily Mirror* interview, she is seen to have lost her sting. Her internal anxiety explodes into open exposure. She reveals a haunting fear of being hated. Given the decline of her writing, as well as of the admiration that it brought her, as well as the loss of Pavlik Tchelitchew's idealization of her, Edith Sitwell no longer could keep up her guard; she could no longer shield herself from her inner world in which she felt herself hated. To combat this decline in her "designed" self, she drank heavily. At the end, she was alone, except for her new and reliable secretary, Elizabeth Salter, and for the nurse whom she also paid to take care of her. Her brothers, particularly Osbert, were declining in their own ways.

This picture of aging might made us heed Otto Kernberg's comments on the aging narcissist (1975). He reminds us of the need to treat those with narcissistic disorders through psychoanalysis whenever possible, because even when external success gives them a sense of inflated well-being, as the glitter wears off, a hungry, raging, and paranoid skeleton remains. He also recommends seeing narcissistic characters for briefer treatment of crisis when they are too successful in the world to sustain long term treatment. When their success is lost later in life, those treated on this brief basis, might be more likely to return for treatment.

## Failed Reparation

Edith Sitwell remained imprisoned within her closed internal system. Due to the splitting processes of the narcissist, the paranoid defense, and the schizoid sealing off of affect, the creative process could not help her to mourn. She failed to process and integrate the losses of her past.

Sitwell seems to have written her poetry when her grandiose self and its manic-defense system were in effect. When she got reassurance from a supportive figure, such as Jack Lindsay, her arid state would yield to a feeling of impending creative revival. This reassurance provided relief and regenerated a sense of inner aliveness. Since this temporary inner aliveness apparently did not result from emotional contact, but rather from the rekindling of an idealized self-image seen in the inner world, it was merely like a drug. In essence, the psychic system remained closed. No new psychic internalization could take place with the narcissistic defense system intact. To the degree that Edith Sitwell's poetry supported such a narcissistic defense system, her writing failed to expose the preoedipal wound, or "basic fault" (Balint 1979), in her—an inner psychophysical wound that needed exposure in order to heal.

Unlike Dostoyevsky, who apparently could expose both humiliation and guilt in the creative process (Breger 1989), allowing grieving and insight to take place, Sitwell never wrote when consciously wounded. Her narcissistic defenses worked too quickly and securely. According to Dostoyevsky's psychoanalytic biographer, Louis Breger, the novelist would sit down to write just at the point of having lost all his money at gambling, when he had been thoroughly humiliated in every way and was in an acute state of shame and loss. Probably because of a borderline psychic structure, he was able to bleed out his remorse, shame, and grief. He used the creative process to expose himself rather than to hide. He did not place himself above the pain as did Edith Sitwell.[8]

Glendinning speaks of the "indignation" (101; 144) that Sitwell used to shield herself, throughout her life, from both humiliation and grief. According to Glendinning, "Edith found some satisfaction in picking her scabs. She could never let a hurt heal of its own accord, still less in silence" (101). Such narcissistic defense prevented the healing of the split in her self-structure. Without an open wound, there can be no healing. The paranoid defense also remained to regulate self-esteem, but in her later years, as she withdrew from public life, the opportunity and strength for "biting" the other guy's "head off" largely diminished. The alternative form of regulation of self-esteem, i.e. winning admiration for her idealized self through the poised persona, the perfect performance, the grand exhibition, also extinguished its candle. What remained were many empty hours when the emptiness inside was felt in the form of boredom and restlessness.

Edith Sitwell had sought to evade the twin symptoms of boredom and restlessness all her life. In the end, they entrapped her. She fought back now only with alcohol, subliminally refueling her grandiose image-self. Encroaching isolation, even beyond the professional isolation she had always known, brought increasing escape into drink. Over the last decade of her life, there were other signs of deterioration that also highlighted the fragmenting-self consequences of a personality based on a false grandiose self. In addition to the many psychosomatic symptoms that Edith had been experiencing all her life (e.g., constant back pains and headaches), there were now also the "falls." Late in life, Edith had been named a Dame by Queen Victoria. Now, time after time, the great Dame Edith took spills on large palace floors at Renishaw and Montegufuoni, her family's ancestral homes. Falling on stone steps and marble floors, she took a bad bruising. Shaky, split off from her body, unconnected to the affective center inside of her, Edith Sitwell was at the mercy of the fates as she aged. In her later years, she paid the biggest price for the lack of failure to connect with her internal self.

Without the compensatory, albeit addictive, mirroring provided by a literary audience, her poetic output dissipated; even the prose writing and journalism that had sustained her when her poetic inspiration had dried up came to a halt. The poet drew deeper and deeper into a state of isolation. To avoid the cold hell she held within her, she continued to drink. She even stopped eating and substituted a milk-laced champagne brandy for food, showing regression to an early infantile state. This refueling from alcohol was regressive.

Even if the poetic flow from within her could once serve as catharsis from her rage and as stimulation for the grandiose self established so prominently in her intellect, it now failed her. The creative work that had served as a compensatory structure itself—through mirroring her own visions and thoughts back to her and through presenting an idealized view of her to the world—had now dried up. For people such as Sitwell, the end of creativity can mean the end of life. Her creative powers no longer provided the compensation and catharsis that she needed. There was no mourning, although perpetual themes of bereavement reflected the pathologically arrested mourning state. Her late suicide was not acute but gradual. Without internal healing, the alcohol as well as the imprisoned rage within her body took their toll.

## Pathological Mourning and Its Psychic and Creative Arrests

According to her own description of her creative work process, Sitwell reenacts her psyche in a mechanical way, hardly conscious of what her psyche filters through her hands and onto the written page. As Glendinning points out, Sitwell never observes and consolidates what she spews forth. She never engages in any reflective mode of encounter with her work. We can see this within the work itself, as her prophet persona fails to reflect, fails to encounter, fails to promote dialogue, and ultimately fails at all interaction.

We see many manifestations of psychic arrest in Edith Sitwell. Most pertinent to affect experience and its developmental process, we see that the poet is unable to mourn. There is a poem by Sitwell, called "Still Falls the Rain" (1940), which particularly highlights this. This poem—written and read during the continuing air raids in World War II—uses a repeated litany of the funeral dirge "Still falls the Rain—", while depicting horrors of wounded and bleeding victimized saints.

> Still fall the Rain—
> Dark as the world of man, black as our loss—
> Blind as the nineteen hundred and forty nails
> Upon the Cross.

Still falls the Rain
With a sound like the pulse of the heart that is changed to the hammer-beat
In the Potter's Field, and the sound of the impious feet
On the Tomb;
   Still Falls the Rain
In the Field of Blood where the small hopes breed and the human brain
Nurtures its greed, that worm with the brow of Cain.

Still falls the Rain . . .

(Salter and Harper 1976, 217)

Sitwell's bereaved description of rain that never ceases to fall can be easily likened to an externalized flow of tears that can never cease because they can never be cried from the internal locus whence they need truly to come. The rain seems to be the symbolic form of perpetual bereavement that is symptomatic of the pathological mourning state, in which the psychic structure for tolerating and processing grief has not been adequately developed. The externalized reenactment continues as the inner self remains sealed off and the organic experiences of childhood injury, loss, and guilt, as well as the painful sadness of disillusionment, are all evaded. When potentially reparative crying is never felt and expressed, because tears are perceived as falling outside like rain, it becomes natural to fear that if own should begin to cry the crying would be endless.

Like Sitwell, other narcissistic characters generally fear crying. They spit out their curses at the therapists who point out that they are blocking their pain and tears. "What good does it do to cry?" they ask both petulantly and incredulously, "It doesn't do anything!" Then, they might reveal their fear, as one narcissistic patient did to me, that if they were ever to begin to cry, they would cry forever. The pain sealed off for so long, which keeps the inner self from connecting with the world and growing, seems ominous and thus endless. Such people fear that they will cry forever because they fear that nobody will come to comfort them, to be with them. The predominant connection to this fixed, current belief is the early childhood experience in which nobody did come to comfort them. In the spontaneity of childhood, they were often humiliated for crying out their pain, for revealing their inner hurt through their tears. Their parents shamed them through either unconscious or conscious messages. Consequently, if their needs showed they felt flawed and damaged.

In their resistance to tears, such narcissists can never appreciate a basic psychic truth, i.e., that mourning does indeed do something. Mourning moves the whole developmental process forward and allows the inner self to take on its own individuated personality and vision as it connects with others in the world outside who do have the capacity to be with them. In "Still Falls the Rain," Sitwell reveals that she never learned this truth and never gained the key that could release her from her imprisoned state of victimization, and from the eternal litany of that victimization, as she raged against her demon-lover father-god.

This poet did not seem to have an insight into the evident connection between the rain in her poem and her own unshed tears. She connected her rain only with bombs falling from the skies in the violence of a world war. She knew of her rage as it attacked her from without, or as her demon-father males attacked her female-child victims or starved the needy beggars, but her grief remained almost fully a mystery to her. With no psychotherapist to be with her in her grief, and with no one to help her face the despair of not having a self, we see in her writing the lack of a defined subjective sense of self. We also see the lack of an embodied sense of self and an extreme alienation from her body. The poet could not tolerate, let alone work through, an understanding of her feelings. The abstractions characterizing her poetry are symptomatic of this. Potential feelings are enacted in a perpetual rage and paranoia. With a reactive rather than an experiencing self, the end of her life left Sitwell no depth meaning for her interpersonal experience. Potential encounter, both with her outer life and within the transitional world of her creativity, became a one note drama of reenactment. With no experience of the early trauma, no unique feminine self could be formed. In my view, the endless repetitions in "Still Falls the Rain" mirror the endless repetitions of a developmentally arrested self and its split-off psyche, which can be seen in all schizoid-narcissistic characters.

Related to Sitwell's incapacity for mourning is an arrest in both intrapsychic and creative-process potential for dialogue, reflecting parallel arrests in the capacities for interpersonal interaction, empathy and mutuality and for internal world dialogue. Victoria Glendinning (1981, 210) comments: "Edith had no gift for dialogue whatsoever. As soon as two characters strike up a conversation they become stilted and unreal."

Related to the failure to write dialogue is another failure, i.e., the failure to modify archaic aggression through self-integration so that an observing ego can be constituted. Therefore, the poet could not have an observing-ego dialogue with her own work. For example, in writing her novel, *I Live under a Black Sun*, Sitwell failed to bring any objective reflection to a first draft, which appeared to burst forth from her psyche in what she herself describes as a rather mechanical form. The result was a mixture of confusion along with moments of sharp psychological insights. There was no sense of place in her novel. According to Glendinning, "Everything that is not in a slum in the suburbs of hell seems to take place in a pleasantly wooded area of the moon" (210). Glendinning comments that the poet was handicapped by her inability to look objectively at her work and to make editorial decisions (210). Sitwell never allowed time after the initial writing for revisions. According to Glendinning (210), she never let the dust settle," She sent it off to the publisher without sorting out the quagmire of emotional moments and elements. Sitwell's inability to write dialogue might be seen to correspond to her inability to have an editorial dialogue with her work—the kind of dialogue which might have resulted in discriminating integration and differentiating "cutting."

As we look at Sitwell's poetry, we see split part objects or flat two-dimensional figures that seem like fragments of an unintegrated self. When we see that her part objects never "talked" to each other in her work or responded to each other in any interactive form, it is not surprising that there was no developmental process within her creative work that could bring her self-fragments together. This lack of dialogue among her poetic characters and her other literary characters also appears to reflect the lack of an internal dialectic between an internal object and a self, between an ego and a self, or between a superego and a self. Without such internal dialectic, both intrapsychic conflict and affective mourning fail to unfold. Splitting is perpetuated. Healing fails and repression and intrapsychic conflict cannot be tolerated. Self-fragmentation then results from the perpetual splitting; only part objects appear within the internal world. The part object of obsessive fixation is the masculine demon lover, the failed form of the yearned-for muse-god. Sitwell, like all preoedipally arrested characters, cannot internalize the muse-god's power, the particular phallic power that such characters may look to for inspiration when their borderline nature has robbed them of their core femininity. When the muse-god's power cannot be internalized, it remains external and is felt as persecutory. The poet's yearnings for phallic power impel her toward death, and she is enveloped in images of the black god-father, the demon lover.

## Conclusions

From the study of Edith Sitwell, we can draw conclusions highlighting why this literary artist significantly failed to repair herself and her internal world through her creative work. We can also understand why this female artist remained pathologically addicted to a demon lover both within her internal world, as shown through her creative work, and without in the external world of her interpersonal life.

Sitwell symbolizes herself within her poetry as an abstract prophet or a satirical narrator. As readers, we see her stand above an injured, needy, and vulnerable part of her own self. Images of emaciated beggars and helpless victims imply to us the starvation of a sealed-off, traumatized inner self. Figures in the creative work—such as the greedy Midas, the ghost of envy, the father as a black sun, and the malignant archaic phallus in the form of a mushroom cloud—seem to capture a father-god aggressor who devastates a female-child victim. Yet the poet herself is in a constant defensive stance of being above the damaged internal victim, above the enraged and injured child within. Perhaps Sitwell senses a child within that she dare not wake for fear that she would feel traumatized by her own injuries. Since this manic-defense stance does not yield to an active and affective struggle that can bring psychic integration through psychic dialogue, however, little psychic growth can result.

Sitwell's work also presents us with the black abyss or void. This nightmarish void to which allusion is often made becomes filled with the mental images of part objects, which appear in the form of victim and aggressor personae. These personae often connote themes of hostile father-daughter relations. Maternal archetypes, such as greedy spiders, also illustrate how the paternal object often fades into the primary maternal-object form, demonstrating the psychic fusion characteristic of developmental arrest. Still, the tone of masculine power pervades even the more-maternal shapes.

Sitwell portrays herself neither as the aggressor nor as the victim. Her figure of conscious identification does not have a body. The poet paints herself with allusions. She takes on a spiritual and otherworldly air. By remaining so disembodied, the psychological sense of emotional void becomes ever more threatening, for no interpersonal relations bind or ground her. Essentially, Sitwell as a poet does not internalize and assimilate the split-off victim and aggressor parts of her psyche but merely watches from above as her psyche reenacts a screen play.

Sitwell's writing demonstrates psychic arrest through creative-process arrest. This arrest does not curtail the novelty of theme, image, or symbol in the work, but it does impede development toward subjective meaning and toward intrapsychic and interpersonal conflict resolution.[9] For Sitwell, as subjective truth and meaning fail to evolve, growth into the developmental achievement of symbolization also fails, so that whole object representation is never achieved. The poet's object forms are mythic. They are not personal or related in any way to separate objects. They are therefore devoid of interaction and mutuality.

## The Demon Lover

The figures in Sitwell's poetry reflect the Jungian archetype of the demon lover, as well as the demonic erotic object that Ronald Fairbairn (1952) called the "tantalizing and rejecting object." Melanie Klein's bad persecutory object also resonates in Sitwell's dark and demonic phallic figures.

He is a figure who reflects the universal image of the demon father found in the writings of other paranoid-schizoid women such as Emily Dickinson, Emily Brontë, and Sylvia Plath. At the same time, he has a unique form taken from

Sitwell's own father's personality. For example, whereas Dickinson's father demon is indifferent as well as seductive, Sitwell's father demon is pompous and greedy. He is an aristocrat, a rich phoney with a prominent face, symbolized by his coat of mail. Behind this image, we can see the man who lived immured in huge palaces, perpetually preoccupied with the design of his exterior image. We can also see the man who withheld his entire fortune from his daughter during both his life and his death, leaving her with nothing but piercing headaches of suppressed rage as her legacy (see Pearson and Glendinning). This father is also calculating—like a spider spinning his web. Sitwell presents spider imagery that encapsulates her psychic view of the greedy midas.

Yet despite these idiosyncratic features, Sitwell's mythic Black Sun father is omnipotent, resembling the omnipotence of Emily Dickinson's paternal god and of Sylvia Plath's god-daddy figure. He reminds us of the omnipotence of Emily Brontë's deserting muse-god as well. Sitwell's father is similar in additional ways to these other poet's fathers, in contrast to the father figure lovers that develop in the work of Charlotte Brontë. Edith Sitwell's demon is a flat, two-dimensional figure, with no virtuous traits that could highlight blemishes and with no ambivalent reactions that could give him a whole object human form, or an individuated identity. He cannot be engaged in a mutual interaction. He cannot be spoken to and never yields or changes. There is no encounter between him and his female victims. Consequently, he cannot be transformed. Neither he nor his victims experience the other empathically, i.e., in terms of attunement from within to the other's subjective sense of self.

The father as "sun" is an archetypal symbolic image, as opposed to a subjectively defined symbolic image. Therefore, the same symbol can be seen in Emily Dickinson and in other poets. This archetypal sun could bring the light of a differentiated self as opposed to a "moon" mother who remains too much in the dark because of her merger with her child. Yet Sitwell's sun is black. His powers of differentiation are obviated since he is revealed as a fake. This negating of the father's "sun" functions, i.e., the negating of the father figure as a differentiated other to promote interaction, seems clearly represented by his being black and is symptomatic of the developmental arrest of the poet, which keeps the father image negated in any developmentally functional form, just as the absence of good takes on the blackness of evil. Yet the absence of good is not sufficient to create evil. It is the instinctual aspects of the father who cannot be adequately internalized that cause the father to take on the evil tone of black. The black sun tells us of the father who fails as a developmentally facilitative transitional object. The failed transitional object has its own archetypical themes, which are apparent since many authors who psychically live in the paranoid-schizoid split reflect common themes. In this case, the shared and diagnostic theme is that of the demon lover. For instance, although the father sun in the poetry of Emily Dickinson, is not painted black, he is a "metallic god" who threatens to drop his female victim into a black "abyss" or void if she cannot contain him as he "drills his welcome in" (no. 286). For Sitwell, as for Dickinson, the failed father is not a psychically individuated father. The female poet's own lack of adequate mournful separation has resulted in failure to define her internal male object. He remains an archetype of universal psychic dynamics. Only an individuated father can be a transitional object, for he must, in Winnicott's terms, "survive" the omnipotent gesture of his child. He must be able to sustain his own autonomy in the face of his child's autonomous and aggressive strivings, rather than either submit or compulsively retaliate. The failure of Sitwell's father to be such a transitional object[10] reflects his own failed separation and ultimately his own failed identity formation. His daughter's failure in the development of healthy object relations reflects his own failure. This failure is evident in Sitwell's work and life.

## Failed Authenticity

Of all the women in this study, Edith Sitwell appears the most lacking in authenticity. This is demonstrated through a mode of creative expression that displays abstract mental images rather than the spontaneous emergence of an inner life. Unlike the work of Emily Brontë and Sylvia Plath, which reveals borderline alternations between moments of experiential immediacy (related to inner affect contact) and moments of abstraction in which the inner self is overpowered by an intrusive object or by its own detachment, in Edith Sitwell we see a well-defended consistency of abstracted image perception. The images in Sitwell's poetry are archaic and archetypic in form, expressing universal symbolism that has a stereotypic quality. The spontaneous impulse appears to be missing. As D. W. Winnicott has so emphasized in his essays on self-development, this absence of spontaneity is the chief diagnostic criterion for the absence of true self-developmental evolution. In Winnicott's terms (1965), Sitwell represents a schizoid person who operates through the impinging images of her own unconscious, as opposed to coming from any subjective connection with impulse and affect. Infant and innate archetypical images that she expels or exorcises in her work seem to impinge on the poet. Early preoedipal trauma can be read into these images, but their mythic, religious, or universal quality also betrays an alienation from any subjective-self experience of the original traumas that formed the images and their associated abstract themes. These images are static in nature.

The injured child self, as portrayed in Sitwell's poetry, is not affectively alive. We can see this lack of affective aliveness as images are etched before us in a decorative vein that indicates contrived artfulness. The creative process itself seems to be contrived, for it is used defensively, perhaps with the unconscious intention of keeping the victim selves split off from one another. As such, these self-fragments are like part objects that can never be encountered and mourned. If the childhood pain behind these split-off elements within the internal representational world cannot be felt as part of the self, then the self cannot be repaired. If reparation were to take place, it would mean reexperiencing the childhood injuries that lie as latent psychic content behind the manifest part object victims. Without the affective link to these early experiences, the potential self-parts, represented in part objects, cannot be truly internalized through integration into the inner self.

Sitwell also cannot tolerate disillusionment, as she cannot tolerate guilt. There is no evidence in her work of an integrated parental object to sustain the sense of self during trials of either disillusionment or guilt. Although demonic and ugly in form, the idealized father lurks behind the devalued male images, resonating with early breast-mother idealization. To risk disillusionment would be to feel the narcissistically devastating loss of this early mother. Instead, the poet attempts to preserve this image of the idealized mother-father by externalizing it. She does this through projection onto a male figure in her life, Pavlik Tchelitchew, which counterbalances the projection of the demonic father-mother onto male figures in her creative work. This is a delicate balance, as when a borderline psychotherapy patient defends against the projection of the "bad mother" onto the analyst by projecting an idealized counterpart onto a lover. Because of the precariousness of such primitive defense, the tie to Pavlik has to be maintained at all costs. Pavlik becomes not only the externalized breast-mother, whose symbiosis is fundamental to any preliminary sense of self, but the idealized father in both his erotic and grandiose aspects. The two levels of mother and father resonate with and reinforce one another, both within the internal world and in the external world. In this mediating "transitional world" of art as well (Winnicott 1971), fantasy forms and image innuendos capture the fusion of the psychic levels.

## The Grandiose Self

Identified with the prophet and with the elegant form that she gives her frightening figures, Sitwell appears to use the creative process for the magical refueling of a grandiose self. This is a self sealed off with its idealized primitive parents. Melanie Klein ([1957] 1975)[11] has described this as manic-narcissistic defense. More recently, Kernberg (1975) has stipulated that such a grandiose self is a split-off image self, which needs audience applause to be continually reinflated. The craving for such audience applause is extremely addictive, because the applause is used as mirroring for a false and pathological image-self, still fused with its primitive or part object parents. The inflation of this image self defends against psychic pain. The narcissistic "glow" derived from the mirroring audience must be attained repeatedly, since its elusive power wears off quickly. Thus, use of the creative process as a vehicle for such mirroring becomes manifest in a highly compulsive need to create.

Such a compulsive cycle of failed attempts to repair the self through creative work can be seen to operate in Dickinson and in Emily Brontë as well as in Sitwell. However, it is in Sitwell's work in particular that we see how persistently mirroring of an idealized self is sought, as is apparent in the roles of prophet, seer, and satirist. When this image-self substitutes for a potential true self that is sealed off, the creative process does not lead to the self-encounter and self-integration necessary for the creative process to be reparative (see also Plath). Instead, we see that late in her life Sitwell could no longer compensate for her inner depletion with the ideal image conjured up by applause, and she regressively turned to alcohol to seek reinflation of the grandiose image-self. As with the earlier addictive use of the creative process, in which the process itself replaced intimate interpersonal life, alcohol became the heir to addiction to the creative process as Sitwell used it for manic reparation, (see Segal ([1964] 1975). This manic reparation induces a feeling of restored well-being without going through the necessary and painful process of true reparation. (true reparation requires facing ones fears and traumas).

We have seen images of splitting in Sitwell's work. Beneath the surface identification with an idealized male father-god, symbolized as Orpheus or Christ, the primary sealed-off self remains fundamentally split. The splitting becomes a degenerative process. Turning to an audience or to the delusion of an audience that can be promoted with alcohol are ways of preserving an ideal view of the self as an extension of an idealized father-mother. Such an ideal is continually assaulted by reality. It is eroded away as new injuries resonate unconsciously with early trauma. Consequently, the addictive pull toward the audience's reflection will be perpetuated, as an alcoholic takes "just one more sip."

Without normal developmental disillusionment with her father, which would allow a selective internalization of real paternal features, Edith Sitwell appears to have incorporated her father's defensive grandiosity as an extension of herself. This adopted grandiosity appears on the level of the internal self in manic form as the image of the prophet and on the level of the internal object as a mythic god-father. It prevents Sitwell's cry in the darkness from being heard and responded to with compassion.[12] Such an incorporated grandiose self precludes the element of emotional touch that could promote responsive concern. Furthermore, such a grandiose self remains split off from organic self-development, unlike an oedipal-level ego ideal that is more easily psychically integrated. Probably because of an earlier preoedipal failure of adequate mother internalization, the incorporated grandiose father remained split off from Sitwell's core self and was experienced as malignantly intrusive, as manifested by the demon lover theme that emerged in her creative work. In her writing, Edith Sitwell continually devalued her father, seemingly unable to tolerate disillusionment. While devaluing him, she projected the grandiose ideal image of his character onto another man in her life, Pavlik Tchelitchew. With these defensive dynamics, Sitwell avoided relinquishment of her father ideal and remained psychically unchanged.

## Arrest

Edith Sitwell displays an arrest in all of the psychic functions of integration and internalization, so that neither developmental deficit resolution nor psychic conflict resolution could be achieved through her creative work. Her identification with her father takes on the form of a merger with her father's false or grandiose self-structure, and this becomes a narcissistic defense of characterological proportions. In this way, all affect experience is short-circuited.

Sitwell's perpetual and voracious emotional hunger, symbolized by flat, two-dimensional, beggar victims in her poetry, remains sealed off from interpersonal contact, and thus fails to be modified by interpersonal nurturance. This hungry victim or child-self then appears next to other self-fragments, such as the father parts of the self. These fragments cannot be assimilated into Sitwell's more-external consciousness self, so that her external self lacks the internal contact necessary for sustained and genuine interpersonal relations. Her external self is emptied of affect, since so much of her internal life is split off from it. Fairbairn (1952) has described this external self as the central ego, which can become empty and lifeless in the more schizoid character, although narcissistic mirroring can lend it a sense of false vitality. The combination of this eviscerated central ego and its split-off self-fragments creates the personality diffusion described as diagnostic by Kernberg (1975). Such personality diffusion reflects borderline-level splitting within the sealed-off world for the narcissistic character. Personality diffusion indicates the pathology of a borderline narcissist.[13]

A look at Sitwell's poetry reveals a split-off and intrusive father-mother part object. This malevolent part object appears as the demon lover figure in her poetry. Something akin to a father archetype seems heavily to influence this perseverated and unresolved image, which at first is manifested in fragments and allusions but which eventually becomes distinct part object masculine images. The weak patriarchal image of Midas turns to the more explicit symbolic form of the mushroom cloud. In her later years, Sitwell is still psychically dominated by this malignant perversion of the universal phallus, i.e., the image of the phallus turned to demonic patriarchy. This symbolic patriarch, like the Egyptian god of death, lacks the life-giving masculine thrust of phallus. He seems to be all power without energy, all control without internally motivated vitality. He is the "mummy" of the tomb to which Sitwell refers and the Midas whose touch destroys life in the pursuit of gold. The individual father, or the father figure's personality, is much less in evidence at this poet's developmental level of creative expression than it would be in the work of a developmentally higher-level poet. Still, the universal deadness of the individual father's narcissistic character is captured by Sitwell.

## Phallic Father and Archaic Mother

It is not the father's narcissistic grandiosity alone that causes Sitwell to be unable to use the creative process to integrate the self, but also the phallic-erotic attributes that accompany this grandiosity and its idealized image. In their split-off form, these attributes create a malignant impact on the psyche.

To understand this split-off malignancy of the father, we must return to the mother. The poet apparently suffered parental rejection right from birth. The mother's hatred for her husband, as well as her generally inadequate personality, suggests that she was impatient and therefore lacking in attunement to her infant. However, prior to phases of separation, the mother may have liked to hold her baby, perhaps as one would enjoy clinging to a doll. It would presumably then be during the separation phases of Sitwell's preoedipal development that the more severe lack of attunement would begin. Creative abilities can germinate from the early symbiotic phases, even when trauma follows.

Overall, however, the attuned mother described by the pediatrician and psychoanalyst D. W. Winnicott would be notably lacking in Edith Sitwell's history. Such an attuned mother would hypothetically continue affective contact with her infant throughout all the preoedipal phases, so that a cohesive sense of "going-on-being" (Winnicott, 1971) could consolidate a psychic self. In the absence of such an attuned mother, psychic trauma evokes the persecutory dynamics of Melanie Klein's paranoid-schizoid position. No sustained subjective sense of self is formed in this position. An absence of a subjective sense of self, or what Thomas Ogden (1986) has called an "interpreting subject," can then lead to a constant sense of malignant intrusion from without.[14] As seen in Sitwell's creative work, black hells of contactless despair and perpetuated and stifled tones of bereavement accompany this persecutory intrusion. To avoid the "unthinkable anxieties" (Winnicott (1965), 1971) related to a deteriorating stage of void or fragmentation, we well to ward off the projected persecution with which paranoid narcissists fill their inner void, the narcissistic character turns to manic defense, or alternatively to paranoid rage, with its accompanying modes of self-annihilating devaluation and spoiling. However, these defensive strategies simply perpetuate the barriers against contact with the other, with the inner self, and with mournful affect. The necessary experience of depressive despair is evaded.

If the primary mothering was never sufficiently integrated into Sitwell's primary self, there would be no tolerance for mourning, and integrating self-differentiation must therefore have failed. In this case, self and object, as well as father and mother, remain fused together within the split-off, internal-object world. The father as substitute becomes a target for the displaced primary mother. Yet the precocious turn to the father for mothering mandates that he be perceived in a grossly idealized form. If he is then externalized through representational form within the creative process, he is symbolized as a god-muse and as a devalued demon lover. As Sitwell projects the demon lover counterpart of the idealized Pavlick Tchelitchew onto her work, this demon figure becomes the antihero of her novel *I Live under a Black Sun*, in which a sadomasochistic form of love experienced with Tchelitchew is displayed. However, Sitwell also projects the masculine demon onto any critics in the external world, and the idealized counterpart originally projected onto Pavlick later enters her work in the forms of Christ and Orpheus figures.

The story to be told by a preoedipally arrested woman such as Edith Sitwell overlaps with that of other preoedipally arrested women who are transfixed in relation to their fathers. There is less individual variance of their fathers' forms than of those in the creative work of higher-level women. A monolithic, archetypal symbolism can be seen continually to reappear in the work of these psychically arrested women. Sitwell's ghost of envy carries a primordial kiss of death, just as the mushroom cloud carried a foreboding of world annihilation. The demon lover leads to the personification of death in Edith Sitwell just as it does in the poetry of Dickinson, in which a demonic god becomes death as "the supple suitor who wins at last." Similarly, Sylvia Plath's god-daddy becomes the impenetrable specter of death; Emily Brontë's muse turns into Heathcliff who drives his own object of love—Catherine—to suicidal death. In Sitwell, the muse-god-father is abstract and can be replaced. Pavlick or Orpheus easily convert to Christ. The manic-defense function of the idealized part object is switched from one phantom to another.

Such easy switching or "displacement" illustrates that Sitwell's archaic father is a stereotypic fantasy father. This is the fantasy father of a borderline's delusional transference, which Jungians, such as Nathan Schwartz-Salont (1982), see as a real patriarchal spirit. Such a fantasy father can appear through various archetypes, including those of the muse and the demon lover. These archetypal forms seem to correspond to Melanie Klein's a priori predispositions to specific psychic fantasies.

As mentioned, the god-father is only minimally defined by any actual human male personality. As in the creative work of the other paranoid-schizoid women studied, we see in Sitwell's writing that the repetition of the psychic theme is endless. It is a mythic one note that is never basically transformed. Sitwell is entangled with an archaic fantasy father, not with a real flesh-and-blood father figure whom she might assimilate into an intrapsychic image. This demonic fantasy father is partially fused with the self so that primitive forms of splitting and projective identification prevail over neurotic modes of defense. Such a dynamic sharply contrasts with Charlotte Brontë's psychic mechanisms, whose neurotic modes of displacement onto a human, whole object male are easily seen in her novel *Villette*.

Also in contrast to Charlotte Brontë, Edith Sitwell's internal world, as revealed in her work, lacks a sense of authentic encounter between self and other. Sitwell appears to use her work as a cocoon or container for various split-off self-parts or part objects. It is never the scene for visceral and affective immediacy. The characterizations and symbols are abstract. Their flat forms, which lack the multiple dimensions of a human dynamic, are analogous to religious iconography, royal banners, or aristocratic emblems. Consequently, the poet uses myths as opposed to subjective-self phenomena to express her internal world within her creative work. There is no organic movement from an emergent internal process as there would be in a less-mechanistic form of creativity. This seems related to the lack of self-to-self encounter and of self-and-other encounter within the creative work. This lack seems symptomatic of Sitwell's inability to experience others as separate and truly external to her inner world.[15] She fails to view people as having individual needs, perceptions, and affects.

However, an even greater impairment is seen in Sitwell's inability to present a dialogue of experiential encounter through images, let alone through spoken language. None of her characters seem embodied; we are told about their perceptions indirectly, through an abstract narrator. This abstract narrator, who seems to be in the prominent position in which the poet places her consciously identified self, assumes the attitude of one above it all, who approves as prophet and seer and who observes and omnipotently rescues. This is true in her later poems in particular, whereas in her earlier satires her own victimization is more obvious.[16]

It should not surprise us that Sitwell was so detached. As Glendinning has shown, Sitwell always remained barred from affective contact with her body. Following from this, Sitwell's split-off mental mode of abstraction was hyperconscious, when not paranoid, and it exhibited the perpetual hypervigilance of the paranoid type. Her images are detached. Although they are violently ominous, they are abstracted. The poet does not seem to have sustained a genuine internalization of another person, and her sense of self is thus flat as well, appearing reactive, imposed on, and sometimes preoccupied with an idealistic delusion.

Throughout, there is a quality of stasis. Sitwell's poetry demonstrates a shallowness with words even as we are promised intensity. Her words seem haunted with a need to escape, to exorcize, and to merge. Yet there is no felt intensity; therefore the poems seem to become decorative wall-hangings with painted on demons, rather than live terrors. Charlotte Brontë's evocative terror is certainly not felt here in the world of Sitwell; even Emily Dickinson's more abstract "awe" is lacking. A potential cry from the darkness seems to be continually short-circuited by manic defense.

We find that even the premonition of tears is abstracted, coming from a locus outside the body and its sense. In "Still Falls the Rain," Sitwell paints a motif of perpetual grief; yet the grief is not viscerally felt, and one suspects that this is why it is perpetual. Sitwell read this poem aloud during World War II air raids, ignoring the sirens, focusing on what went beyond the momentary fate of life or death to the eternal purgatory of her own pathological mourning state.

After reviewing the women authors of this book, it appears that the creative process cannot transcend developmental limitations. The author as artist may use the creative process as a transitional object if development fails to achieve separate self and object relations, but the process itself is limited by the artist's psyche, as defined by the object relations within that artist's internal world. This appears in contrast to the developmental potential of the creative process when used by an artist of oedipal-stage developmental achievements, someone equipped with the psychic-structure capacities characteristic of Melanie Klein's depressive position. Differentiation of self and object of differentiation is possible when an artist's psyche is operating with depressive-position capacities. Self-reparative integration takes place at this psychic level. Such self-integration is experienced through affective encounter with others in the form of mutuality in the interpersonal realm, and of affective mourning experience in the intrapsychic realm. The marked contrasts between the oedipal-level Charlotte Brontë and the preoedipally arrested Emily Dickinson, Emily Brontë, and Edith Sitwell illustrate this developmental contingency.

# 15

# The Turn to Psychoanalytic Psychotherapy

Suppose that Edith Sitwell, Emily Dickinson, and Emily Brontë had been able to enter psychoanalytic psychotherapy. Suppose that they had been treated according to today's understanding of the object relations factors in self-development and reparation. We can speculate whether their fates would have been different. Could they have lived more fulfilled lives, in terms of relationships and in terms of the development, fruition, and reception of their creative work? As a way of addressing such issues, I present the case of a patient of mine, a dancer and choreographer who exhibited the psychic arrest seen in Sitwell, Dickinson, and Emily Brontë. Not only did my patient possess an internal demon lover, but she manifested the compulsive splitting and projective identification of the paranoid-schizoid position.

## The Case of Ms. A.

Ms. A., a thirty-year-old single woman, entered psychotherapy three years ago. Tall and slender, with long brown hair and dark eyes, she has the physique of a dancer. Her carriage greatly affects her appearance. In the beginning of therapy, Ms. A. seemed to be perpetually bent over, often weeping, sometimes twisting her hair into a ponytail above her head as she straightened her long neck to look at me. She often suddenly darted her neck and head forward as she vented her anger. In these early stages of treatment, she appeared awkward despite her ability suddenly to straighten up and look like a posed dancer. Over time, her appearance changed. As she showed progressively greater natural inner strength, she permanently straightened her bent posture, revealing more signs of inner grace and beauty. Over time she was able to smile, laugh, and sustain the genuine interest and engagement of eye contact in a way that formerly was blocked out or avoided.

Ms. A. entered psychotherapeutic treatment when she was overwhelmed with the pain of loneliness. This pain was raw and open, although she also suffered additionally from many psychosomatic symptoms, since her rage was too great for her to contain. She presented herself as a love addict, that is, a woman desperately clinging to a relationship with one man, believing that she would be empty and have no meaningful existence if he left her. Yet she experienced difficulties being only with this one man,[1] projecting her own impulses to escape the relationship onto him. Despite her continuing difficulties in staying with Jim, Ms. A. felt he was truly special. Jim was the first man she had been with for any sustained period of time and the first to whom she had fully formed an emotional attachment. Formerly, she had experienced many short-lived relationships with men, by whom she felt used and exploited, especially sexually. Even now, she did not enjoy sex, but gave her body in exchange for the holding and nurturance that she sought. Her career as a dancer-choreographer had sustained her through-out the breakup of previous relationships. In contrast to these affairs, she felt that she deeply loved Jim, who appreciated her talents and supported her artistic endeavors.

Our first year of therapy had focused a great deal around her anger at Jim and her fears of losing him. During this phase of treatment, very little work could be done concerning Ms. A's defensive distancing from contact with me and the transference dynamics related to it. While she had distanced herself from direct contact, Ms. A. also clung to me as someone who could rescue her from her pain, fears of abandonment, and suicidal obsessions. Employing our sessions cathartically to unburden herself of her anguish, she generally released a good deal of affect, displaying powerful abandonment depression affects of rage and loss (Masterson 1976). She was not yet ready to address conflicts over guilt and shame, since she would attack herself with blame for her reactions rather than reflect at all dispassionately on her experience or her interpretation of it.

Ms. A. also had creative problems. Although the creative process was her salvation in allowing her to reveal aspects of herself that she could not reveal in interpersonal relationships, it was also a vehicle for the expression of highly defended and fragmented parts of herself. It had not helped Ms. A. to integrate herself psychically and to do the mourning that she now began during this first year in our psychotherapy sessions. The creative process did allow her to express her rage, but this fury came out in a veiled form of sarcasm that did not touch its source: the internal parents to whom she still was tied. The connections between Ms. A.'s reactions and her internal parents became conscious only as our work moved into the transference. The avenue to the transference first had to be opened. The following incident during the second year of treatment illustrates this transition.

After a successful performance and unable to wait for our next session, Ms. A. telephoned me. During our conversation, she urgently attempted to convey to me the internal void that she felt to be swallowing her up. She related agonized feelings of total emptiness, expressing a wish for a quick and painless form of suicide, "to get rid of the pain." In her performance, she had succeeded in exhibiting major parts of her inner life. The display however did not emotionally touch her because the dances she had choreographed and performed were split-off enactments of self and object constellations from her inner world that remained unintegrated into her conscious and interpersonally related self. The audience's applause, therefore, fell flat. It did not ease her overwhelming loneliness, made even greater by her recent breakup with Jim. In his absence, she had no one special person with whom to share the performance. Without such sharing, her experience within it seemed limited. She did not feel or even know how these dances defined her own identity. Her anguish after a warm audience reception could be conceptualized as a borderline psychopathology dynamic in which success threatens to break the bond with the symbiotic mother. Such a mother rewards regression by merger and punishes self-individuation with abandonment, rather than by staying present to share the individuation experience (See Masterson, 1976). Indeed, Ms. A.'s postperformance loneliness and desperation were related to the unconscious triggering of early abandonment trauma.[2] Ms. A. consciously responded as though she had been abandoned after this performance. Because of the recent breakup with Jim, success meant nothing. Her reactions resembled those of a traumatized toddler at rapprochement, returning from practicing-stage self-expansion to find no related mother with whom to share experiences (see Mahler, 1975). Yet several months later, after Ms. A. and her boyfriend had reunited, she failed emotionally to be with him, paralleling her failure to be emotionally with me in the treatment room. Just as she could not feel the success of her performance, my patient could not feel her boyfriend when he was there. She rationalized this by saying that when she was with him she had to do her creative work. Ms. A.'s creative work, then, showed the compulsive quality of a disconnected state. Her creative-process dynamics, on the one hand, were similar to her love addiction: she longed to be with her creative work, obsessed about losing it by being blocked, and still had difficulty actually being with it when she had the opportunity. On the other hand, she resented doing anything else—spending time with others or working to earn an income—because of her wish to be with her creative work. Ms. A.'s dynamics in relation to her creative work may be called creative addiction, in analogy to love addiction; alternatively, we may call it creative compulsion or the compulsion to create. To a significant extent, Ms. A. could not genuinely connect to the parts of herself that she split off in the dance characters of her choreographic scripts. She was similarly unable to be within the creative process of her work so that she could mourn and gain insight and self-integration. Nor was she able to be fully within the process of the performance of her creative work. Unlike the narcissist whose idealized or grandiose self is mirrored by the audience's applause, Ms. A. did not even have the illusion of a mirrored image-self to ease the loneliness of her disconnected state.

What does Ms. A.'s dilemma demonstrate about her capacity to employ the creative process reparatively? Was it possible to use the psychotherapy process reparatively when the creative process had failed her? Could the reparative process in psychotherapy enable her to employ the creative process reparatively? The following description of the case and process involving Ms. A shows that she was able through psychotherapy to mourn and integrate herself so that self-individuation and its concomitant mode of object-related capacity could develop. For such patients, the therapist's awareness of object relations issues is critical. As Ms. A.'s psychoanalytic psychotherapist, I used myself as an auxiliary ego, a holding and containing object. I functioned as an interpreter of the defensive maneuvers she employed to avoid the necessary contact with her affective (or inner) self within the interpersonal context of object internalization. Only through such intervention could Ms. A. tolerate and process the painful abandonment depression affect experience, promoted by early and continually repeated trauma, that she needed to endure to become whole and related. Only in this way could she begin to internalize a good enough object rather than kill off such potential internalization with her rage. Prior to treatment, this rage perpetuated her splitting and its bad-object mode of incorporation as she destroyed the good in the object and in herself. Helping Ms. A. own what she projected outward because of shame and guilt, formed a critical part of the work that enabled her to digest the split-off parts into her central core self (Fairbairn's "central ego").

## Psychoanalytic Psychotherapy

Ms. A. protected herself from knowledge of her internal persecutory objects by projecting all attacks as coming from others. The patient's father had continuously attacked her in a hostile and accusatory manner throughout her childhood and adolescence. As an adult, she generally expected hostility from men and focused her attention on such perceived attacks, usually interpreting them as threats of abandonment. Preparing herself for them often became a total preoccupation. During one session, she recounted the latest attack from Jim. Less consciously, she seemed to be expecting a similar aggression from me. She expected critical judgments and subliminally projected them onto me. This was only revealed when I asked her what she believed I was thinking. By focusing on a male demon, someone outside the room and the moment, Ms. A. warded off any direct contact with me. As I interpreted Ms. A.'s defenses and made contact with her, she became increasingly conscious of the fantasies through which she perceived me and everyone else in her life. These fantasies depicted the horrors of her internal world, where male dictators and female judges triumphed over her. As both fused together they were felt as abusive—a demon lover image that was compulsively projected. Only when she began to realize that she experienced these internal demon's threats as accusatory attacks from me, not just from Jim, could Ms. A. feel the inner rage and terror that accompanied being so psychically under siege.

In choreographing and performing her own dances, Ms. A. assumed the personae of her own inner persecutors. She expressed the attitudes of her internal male chauvinist dictators and her contemptuous female judges. Acting out the persecutory personalities within her however did not help Ms. A. integrate these inner phantoms or their emotional meanings into a conscious sense of self. The judgmental parts of herself, which potentially could facilitate observing-ego and self-reflective capacities, remained as split-off internal persecutors. That is, they were internal part objects or split-off parts of the self. Ms. A. frequently exhibited these personalities without achieving any sustained alteration either in her inter-personal relations or in her self structure. Neither creative work itself nor sharing it with others through performance affectively penetrated into her sealed-off inner core. Therefore, prior to psychotherapeutic engagement, she remained isolated from others, in a state of perpetual loneliness.

Although Ms. A. could use her mode of creativity to enact a cynical shrew or a seductive nymph, these unintegrated parts of herself functioned like external skins shed after each dance performance. By herself, Ms. A. was unable to feel and connect to the dissociated instinctual impulses or to the object-related yearnings that perpetuated her characterizations of self and objects. Thus, she employed her talent to reenact the perpetual drama of her internal world. This drama would never change as long as she remained isolated from affective contact with others, because her internal personalities remained split off. Ms. A.'s father had been continually abusive toward her, punishing any display of anger or self-assertion with threats to beat her. She also saw him belittle her mother. Now, she expected similar abuse from others and fixated her rage on male indifference and exploitation.

While Ms. A. recounted the abuses from men in her life, a chorus of female advisors simultaneously enacted a persecutory play in her mind. This chorus reflected psychically incorporated female friends and the internalized voices of her sisters and mother. Their persecution consisted of taunting criticisms about how Ms. A. was living her life. For example, they scolded her for being a wimp or idiot for staying with her boyfriend. Ms. A. usually introduced her internal chorus to me by saying that "all her friends" thought or said such and such. She did this particularly when she was in conflict and couldn't think for herself. There was no sense of hallucinations, only of internal objects. Ms. A. did not hear voices; she reacted to obsessively haunting "opinions" that often related to ones she couldn't own herself.

I believe that critical elements that were present in Ms. A.'s psychotherapeutic process were missing from her creative process. In the second year of treatment, an important opening to contact occurred. It followed the expression of much pain, during the course of which I had empathized with her anguish. It also followed many preliminary interpretations of Ms. A's resistance to connecting her own thoughts to the affects of rage and loss that she spewed out abundantly. In the midst of these tortured reactions to her internal chorus, Ms. A. suddenly turned to me and asked, "What do you think?" More insistently, she added, "I wish you would tell me what you think!" When I turned her question back to her, saying "What do you think I'm thinking?" she relinquished her coercive demands for my reassurance, thus letting go of her defensive diversion from the aversive aspects of her internal world. For the first time, she truly took me in, digested my question, and responded by initiating a dialogue between the two parts of herself. She began to express the critical part of herself, which she generally projected onto me, in relation to the victim part of herself, which generally was the intimidated reactor to her persecutory critic's attacks. I asked Ms. A. to spell out in her dialogue what her victim and aggressor parts of her could say to one another. She had imagined that I was thinking that she was a fool for staying with a boyfriend whom she saw as so cruel and mean toward her. As she began speaking for the parts of herself, she realized that it was the judgmental element that was belittling and ridiculing her, saying she was weak for remaining in the relationship. Then she let the victim part of her respond, realizing that it was crying, "But I love him! He's in my soul! I can't leave him! I'll never leave him!" She screamed this at the interior persecutory judge who held her in contempt for following her own heart. The more the victim part of Ms. A. felt held in contempt, the more she wailed like a punished, tortured, humiliated, and abandoned child in response. This exchange reinforced her sense of weakness and fears of judgment from me and others, which in turn occasioned an urgent need for reassurance. The cycle was endless, performed within a closed system of victim and aggressor, sadist and masochist, self-preoccupation and projective identification, which prohibited interaction with others. As Ms. A. permitted an interactive dialogue between the two split-off parts of herself—in contrast to the perennial and reflexive reacting of the victim to the aggressor (and visa versa)—she was transformed, within and without. She gradually realized that she could stay with Jim if she could set limits with him rather than allow him to manipulate her. This realization calmed her and caused her to lessen her clinging behavior with me. Ms. A. saw that she could diminish her desperate demands for reassurance. This gradual realization granted her the psychic and analytic space actually to feel my presence. By experiencing me, she also felt her inner self and slowly permitted the pain, rage, and loss related to her years in emotional isolation to emerge. From this session, a developmental mourning process began. Each time that I subsequently interpreted her projections—actually projective identifications[3]—

Ms. A. heard me with increasing clarity. This was possible because she had experienced that something significant could happen if she stopped playing out her old defensive maneuvers and allowed herself to feel my presence in addition to her own.

Feeling my presence, Ms. A. could experience the pain of her own long-frustrated hunger for contact. Such intense loneliness had left her with a perpetual sense of being wounded. In missing the other, she felt as if she was missing a part of herself. Her self-accusations were heightened because of the sense of injury caused by this isolation. But with my presence, Ms. A. felt secure enough to experience the pain that had perpetuated the enactment of being a wounded victim or child. This conscious sense of pain enabled Ms. A. to experience more clearly her need for me, her boyfriend, and her creative work for what they were. With this increasing sense of reality, her internal confusion and sense of being our prisoner lessened. Moreover, Ms. A.'s interpersonal relationships improved, and her creative work expanded and deepened. She was now more directly connected to the deeper parts of herself and therefore more consciously to the personalities in her dance performances. Now, for the first time, she experienced these personalities as parts of herself. This evolution obviously did not occur overnight or with one self-dialogue. It unfolded slowly as Ms. A allowed herself to feel and respond to my presence, thereby opening up an overall reparative mourning process. Having never sufficiently internalized such a presence in her early life, she needed my external presence to reopen the channels to developmental mourning as well as to the creative work that could come from it. In internalizing me and integrating our relations into her core sense of self, she connected with her creative work so that it offered an avenue for her mourning process.

## The Cyclical Process of Mourning

The following three-session treatment process with Ms. A. (during her third year of treatment) shows the developmental growth promoted through the analyst's object relations engagement with the patient. James Masterson (1976) describes the psychodynamics of the borderline triad. The confrontation of defenses against abandonment depression feelings, he argues, can lead to the tolerance of abandonment depression mourning in borderline patients (beginning to allow work in the depressive position) and then to steps in separation-individuation. In retrospect, I can observe that such a triad of the developmental and clinical process is evident in these three sessions. Another way of discussing the defenses against abandonment depression affects is to describe defenses against contact and relatedness within the "therapeutic object relationship" (Grunes 1984) as well as within the transference. As indicated, Ms. A.'s distancing defenses consisted of splitting and projective identification. She split off the guilt-ridden part of herself, projecting it onto the therapist. She then attempted to coerce me into owning her own split-off "badness" even as she still identified with it. These coercive tactics were highlighted by accusatory rage. Such feelings represented an attempt to ward off not only Ms. A.'s guilt, but also the shame of experiencing herself as an abandoned child who desperately needed a "bad" transferential mother, whose autonomy (the mother's) was experienced as indifference. In her accusatory rage, Ms. A. also attempted to project onto the therapist and thus ward off her own sense of loss in having to relinquish a symbiotically related mother and to accept instead a more separate mother, whom she interpreted as being cold and rigid. Within our psychotherapy, Ms. A.'s accusatory rage—normally experienced by others as abusive—was accepted during this period of separation-individuation as a first step in the mourning process. As her therapist, my acceptance or, in Winnicott's terms, my "survival" of this rage involved containing my own reactions to it, without withdrawing or retaliating with counterattack. Over time, such survival meant interpreting the fear and the frustrated need that perpetually generated the rage. Such a response by the therapist encourages certain psychological functions that had been inhibited by the mother of the separation-individuation stage to develop. In Klein's (as opposed to Mahler's and Masterson's) terminology, patients so engaged are aided in transversing the paranoid-schizoid-position vicious cycle of projective identification. They are consequently enabled to enter the self-integrative healing stage of the depressive position. In the depressive position, dysphoric affects can be tolerated so that a sealed-off self may open to object contact and thus to growth. In this process, parts of the self that have been disowned are reowned and assimilated through mourning. Winnicott probably would add that healthy parts of the therapist are also internalized as object contact is promoted. Michael Balint, another British object relations theorist, has described such a mourning process as the healing of the "basic fault," referring to the preoedipal trauma. It should be noted that lower-level borderline patients, who evidence schizoid withdrawal, may need more emotional holding before they can tolerate surrendering rage to the experience of guilt, shame, and loss. This holding partly involves an empathic attunement to the subjective consciousness of the patient.

## Ms. A.'s Three-Session Process

Ms. A. evidenced cycles of blocked mourning. In the first phase of the cycle, she defended against her aggression by splitting self and object experience. Splitting was then reinforced by projection and projective identification. In the second phase, her expression of aggression led to a self-reflective dialogue. This dialogue revealed the freeing up of observing-ego capacities and the consequent demonstration of an ability to own and experience psychic and interpersonal conflict. In the third phase, such contact led to the intense experience of loss, echoing extreme abandonment trauma from the preoedipal past. These three phases can be seen in the following sequence.

In the first session, Ms. A. entered my office and commented about the bad smell. The odor, she remarked, came from my last patient and made her nauseous. She then said, "While in the waiting room, I thought that you were doing a role-play with the last patient." The very idea of this was disgusting. The other patient, Ms. A. added, had left her shawl in the waiting room. Seeing this shawl also was "disgusting." It made Ms. A. think that her predecessor was a nauseatingly vulnerable and frail thing.

I suggested to Ms. A. that she was jealous. "No," she declared, "I feel nauseous."

"You would rather feel nauseous than jealous," I responded. "It feels humiliating to admit jealousy of my other patient. Moreover, it's especially humiliating to admit it to me."

Ms. A. then became angrily defiant and seemingly defensive, saying that her previous therapists (there had been three) had also imagined that she was jealous. "Perhaps we all saw the jealousy you display," I said. "Not long ago," I reminded her, "you went into a jealous rage about Jim seeing an old girlfriend for dinner. In your rage, you pulled everything out of the medicine chest and smashed things on the floor."

After I said this, Ms. A. remained indignant. "This isn't what I wanted to talk about. You're wasting my session. I really want to talk about my relationship with Barbara."

"What we are talking about may be related to your difficulties with Barbara," I suggested.

Ms. A. retorted, "All therapists say that." I interpreted back to her that she always said that she needed Barbara to help her focus on her creative work. It seemed to me that the difficulty she experienced in focusing on her creative work by herself was related to her disowning her feelings so that she felt blocked and disorganized. "If you could own your jealous feelings," I continued, "you wouldn't be out of touch with a part of yourself, and might be more focused."

Ms. A. responded by shouting that she hated everyone. "Barbara would think I'm horrible if she knew that I hated blacks, whites, women, children, Southerners, Northerners, everyone!"

This outburst apparently relieved Ms. A. I interpreted her reaction: "You're relieved because you thought I would hate you for saying these things, but since you feel that I don't, this helps to relieve you of your tremendous guilt about your hatred. Being able to express your hatred, rather than blocking and defending against it," I added, "could help you be in touch with yourself so that you may focus on your own without Barbara's help. You seem receptive to me at this moment," I observed, "and seem able to let me be with you for the first time during the session." My words had a calming effect. Her eyes became open and serene.

When Ms. A. came to the second session, two days later, she was relaxed and poised. Her body posture also differed markedly. Now, instead of being hunched over, she entered graceful and erect. She talked to me about her awareness that she was holding onto illusions. "I kept believing that Barbara was supportive of me, even when she wasn't at all, she said pensively."[4] Then, Ms. A. told me that she had phoned Jim's female friend and had told the woman that she didn't want to make her feel uncomfortable about having dinner with him anymore. In describing this conversation, Ms. A.'s manner of speaking was related and receptive. She allowed me to be with her and to engage in an amiable dialogue. Ms. A. observed that she felt more able to do her work on her own. She was considering how she could earn enough money to continue her twice-weekly therapy sessions while still doing her creative work. Following this session, she phoned to say that she had terminated her working relationship with Barbara. The separation was "very hard." She sounded mournful.

During the third session, Ms. A. warded off her developing sadness by provocations and projections. "My insurance is going to run out next month," she said. "I won't be able to continue twice a week during the next month." (This preceded my summer vacation.) "I expect you to give me a big argument," she added. "I know you're going to tell me I can get money from my parents or work a hundred hours a week to pay for therapy without insurance."

I remarked to her that it was she who wanted to create an argument, because she didn't want to feel her sadness about having less time with me. At this point, Ms. A. started crying, saying that she was scared that one session a week wouldn't be enough. "I'm finally picking up momentum in the therapy. You're different twice a week than once a week."

"I can see that you're scared," I observed, verbally reaching out to her as she became more vulnerable.

She then said, "I wanted you to reassure me that it was all right, that once a week is enough." When I did not, she accused me of making her feel guilty by asking her not to put paper cups in the bathroom wastebasket. Ms. A. said that she thought she was the only one to whom I told this and added, "You make me feel like I'm dirty."

"You're the one who thinks that you're dirty and bad," I responded. "Perhaps you're projecting onto a practical situation a whole drama about yourself being the 'black sheep' in the family.[5] Maybe you want to provoke an argument with me again, because the prospect of having to cut back to once a week is haunting you. Do you think that you might be fighting me to ward off your intense feelings of sorrow?"

Ms. A. responded with more tears, grieving that she wanted me to reassure her so that it wouldn't feel that she was losing anything. "You're trying to avoid the harsh reality that once a week is not enough contact with me," I said. "You want me to participate in creating another illusion with you by reassuring you."

She cried some more, observing, "Jim faces reality better than I do." Tears of anguish streamed down her face. "Facing reality is really hard for me," she said in a low voice.

We agreed that in the future she might be able to work at another job that had insurance for psychotherapy, even though she feared that such work would interfere with her creative projects.

## The Overall Mourning Process

This cycle of psychotherapeutic process shows how Ms. A.'s rage increasingly yielded to sadness and a deep sense of her longings. Such mournful self-awareness comes with the self-contact that sadness from interpersonal attunement can provide. As Ms. A. integrated from within, she became both more differentiated and more separate. This increasing autonomy caused Jim to feel less threatened by her demands and eventually led to his gradually offering more commitment to her.

There is one fundamental affective link in this process that needs to be reemphasized. The awareness of guilt within a context of interpersonal contact evokes deep sadness. Ms. A.'s sadness surfaced as she began to reflect on her own part in her difficulties, especially with her boyfriend. Witnessing her pain motivating her to go beyond her resentment toward him, whereas formerly she had denied these feelings. She was also beginning to understand that her manner of giving created resentment because of its compulsive element. Her compulsion to give involved her demanding that Jim reciprocate in ways that were impossible for him. This continuous cycle of compulsive and overextended giving, and then demanding but not receiving reciprocation led to increasing levels of frustration and resentment.

She complained, "I was there for him when he needed me, but he can't do one little thing for me. Even if he tries he's so inept I end up doing it for him!" Now, although Ms. A. still complained that she gave so much to Jim and that he failed to reciprocate, she began to admit that a great deal of her behavior represented a compulsive attempt to control him by "taking care of him."

"It seems that you're compelled to give to him," I suggested, "because of your guilt about wanting to control him, so that he fits into your blueprint of life, your blueprint that dictates, 'I give to you and then you give back in the way I want you to!' You think you're bad," I added, "so you give to him in order to prove that you're good. But who are you really trying to prove it to?" She acknowledged my interpretation, saying "I think you're right. I want to prove it to myself or to the female judges inside of me."

Ms. A.'s compulsive giving also appeared to be a way of denying anger toward her mother. It was an enactment of her identification with a material figure who had always avoided any confrontation with her own hostility or wish to control by performing the role of saintly and martyred giver. By becoming her mother, Ms. A. "identified with the aggressor" and provoked guilt in her boyfriend as her mother provoked guilt in her. Then, Ms. A. self-righteously claimed that she was being betrayed and victimized by Jim's lack of reciprocal giving. When Ms. A. began to reflect on her responsibility for provoking her boyfriend with her compulsive giving, she was able to separate more from him. Additionally, she was able to relinquish a bit of her confining identification with her mother. Ms. A.'s new awareness helped turn her guilt, which had formerly led to defensiveness and countering accusations, into the softer sadness of empathic caring. She began to notice her boyfriend's vulnerability and feel compassion for her own entrapment in identifications from the past.

Becoming aware of how she participated in her plight, Ms. A. also realized that she had a conscious choice: to feel no longer like a victim. This recognition allowed Ms. A. to feel freer, and, consequently, express compassion for her mother as well as for herself. These new attitudes were experienced through the emotional experience of mournful sadness. Ms. A. now saw that although her mother had genuinely given her a great deal, she also had used compulsive giving as a method of control. Her mother's "selflessness" without boundaries was abusive in that it provoked terrible guilt and also induced an identification with this model of martyred or masochistic love. A child whose mother gives without limits is overwhelmed with guilt related to his or her wishes for infinite emotional supplies. Identifying with the martyred mother serves as a defense against the guilt. Such an identification can also function as a defense against the loneliness that comes with the lack of separation from the early symbiotic tie.

Ms. A. reacted by trying to give herself an identity through the role of the "giving mother" because she was fighting against a deep sense of loneliness within herself. Such loneliness was a necessary consequence of her inability to differentiate from a symbiotic fantasy relation with her internal mother so that she might relate with others who were separate from her. Becoming like her mother allowed her to stay connected to her internal mother, and, therefore, to create the illusion of not being alone. Yet her psychic clinging to her mother, and to the father-boyfriend who was fused with this mother, was exactly what kept her perpetually alone in reality. Ms. A.'s awareness came full circle as she felt grief for her mother in grieving for herself. This grief further encouraged the separation process. She no longer excused her mother but could view her mother's faults more objectively (formerly she had transferred her anger against her mother onto Jim, herself, and myself). The recognition of these weaknesses permitted her first to differentiate herself from her mother and then to forgive her.

Only Ms. A.'s feelings of true grief and conscious and acknowledged anger could lead her to forgiveness. In owning her anger, she could stop displacing it onto herself, Jim, and me. Now that she could face her anger at another woman, such as Barbara, she was able to separate from her. Barbara became less idealized for Ms. A., and Ms. A. modified her idealization of her own mother. In turn, the demonic form of her father became modified, since her internal father (or father-god) had always been the dynamic counterpart to the idealized mother (or mother-god at the preoedipal level). She began to become friends with her father.

As guilt is acknowledged, buried love emerges, carrying with it the grief of loss. There is loss within love and love within loss. To mourn those we love is to begin to possess them internally, through conscious psychic images and available memory. Feelings of loss accompany the grief of relinquishing early relations that have become pseudorelations because they block new modes of current relatedness and their internalizations.

In these three sessions, Ms. A. started to let go of Barbara, who represented a malignant internal object, a combination of the negative characteristics of her parents. This internal object obtained its psychic dynamic from the primitive identificatory fusion of a split-off part of herself with the object representations of two malignant aspects of her parents (part objects). Barbara resembled Ms. A.'s father by continually attacking Ms. A; and resembled her mother by being judgmental. My patient's internal demon lover, so frequently projected onto Jim, had been a displaced form of the bad father and the bad mother—the part object construction of mother inside father. Ms. A. was previously unable to relinquish the "bad" internal father-mother that had become her demon lover. One reason was that Barbara possessed some good characteristics associated with Ms. A.'s idealized mother. Even more importantly, Ms. A. refused to let go of Barbara until she allowed herself to internalize the therapist as a better object. Mourning was opened up by the dialogue created by consciousness of the therapist as an external object. This mourning then encouraged an internal dialectic that permitted me to appear as a more-benign internal object than Ms. A.'s parents and parent figures. In becoming a more-benign internal object, I also became a better-integrated object whose representational form was more like that of a whole object. I became a more differentiated object, one no longer fused into the self through identification.

In my capacity as therapist, I contained my patient's harsh affects and assisted her in understanding the shame, guilt, and fear of loss behind her intense rage. I interpreted Ms. A.'s attempts to turn me into the disowned "bad" part of herself. By showing that she was trying to do to me what her parents had done to her, I was helping her see the pattern perpetually reenacted in the split-off part of her internal world,[6] prior to psychotherapeutic intervention.

## The Therapist's Embodied Presence

We grieve for unfulfilled fantasies and wishes, as well as for that which we truly encountered in the past. This process allows us to open up to and to explore new and better connections in the present. Only my physical and emotional presence diminished Ms. A.'s intense and wrenching pain as she experienced her grief. My presence helped change an acute anguish into a quieter and gentler sobbing associated with felt loss and acknowledged, rather than disowned, need. Ms. A. had been unable to reach such a point on her own. Attuned to her distancing maneuvers, I was with her through her withdrawal, rage, tentative movements toward contact, distrust, and agonized cries of despair.

In my role as Ms. A.'s witness and reflector, I helped her to contain the overwhelming intensity of her rage and grief so that the softer sadness of mournful contact could follow. My responsive presence enabled Ms. A. to contain the archaic affects that someone who is developmentally arrested must endure on the road to mourning and interpersonal connection. As Ms. A.'s tolerance to feel loss[7] increased, so did her ability to feel tender love and concern. Her mourning could then transform into an ongoing capacity to be emotionally touched by another. Her sadness grew more subtle. It became the sadness of interpersonal touch, of feeling the other, of opening herself to the inner resources of love. Ms. A. began to learn that grief may be experienced throughout life. To the extent that each of us tolerates the affective mourning processing of grief, we continue to deepen and expand our psychic life and its related sense of self.

Ms. A. came to observe herself with an objective perspective that brought her into simultaneous contact with her inner feelings and me.[8] This form of objective self-observation significantly differs from a split-off or dissociated form of self-critical judgment, which at the borderline level becomes profoundly intense and persecutory.

Since self-integration requires authentic mournful suffering, the evolution of mourning through psychotherapy is of primary concern. I clearly distinguish such mournful suffering from masochistic suffering. When her inner self was still largely sealed off, Ms. A. expressed masochistic suffering in her complaints of abuse. She felt tortured because she had been imprisoned in her own closed system. Closed to feeling the genuine affects of her pain, she was also closed to being interpersonally touched by another. Masochistic crying, in contrast to mournful crying, does not originate in an alive awareness of the object in its responsive and good interactive form. Nor are masochistic tears derived from an awareness of another's pain, whether a mother's or a father's. For these reasons, such crying cannot heal.

Within the transference, Ms. A. moved from masochistic crying, and an accompanying somatization, to the intensity of grief characteristic of individuals suffering from preoedipal trauma who must endure the abandonment depression mourning process. At the end of every session, Ms. A. experienced extreme loss. Before the mourning process unfolded in treatment and strengthened Ms. A.'s autonomy, she frequently was unable to bear remaining without telephone contact between sessions. On becoming more capable of expressing her feelings to me, she experienced a transition from rageful, tantrumlike affect to sadness. Her sadness was filled with longings for love, care, and nurturance. She experienced profound shame and guilt about her longings that needed to be analyzed to be understood. But simultaneously, Ms. A.'s guilt was being transformed into yearnings to give to others, as she had always wished to be able to give to her mother. Her compulsive form of giving, so dominated by guilt and its identification with her mother, became modified into genuine giving. In treatment this was shown by Ms. A. revealing both more of her own fear and her love for me. She expressed concerns for my welfare for the first time. Her true interest in her boyfriend emerged, as she sensed his loneliness and worried about his feelings when they had to be apart for some time. She feared Jim would be lonely, and this turned out to be not only a projection of her own loneliness, but also a compassionate longing to ease the loneliness of her internal father-mother, whom he transferentially represented. When Ms. A. began to feel for others, getting beyond herself, her self-image improved. The shame over her neediness subsequently lessened.

Ms. A.'s sadness also permitted her to be aware of her own envy, which when projected had caused her to be the agent and subject of self-sabotage. Such projection provoked much fear of others' envy. Ms. A. began to understand how projecting this envy onto others interfered with her ability to own and sustain what she did possess. She also needed to discover the unconscious parental envy that was inside her since childhood. Sadness encouraged awareness of how she used the envy of her internal father-mother to spoil all the good that she had with me and others, as well as with her internal objects experienced through creative work. Ms. A. realized how, in clinging to her internal accusers, she turned all good experience into bad, creating an ugly, shame-ridden view of herself.

Especially in the third year of treatment, Ms. A. demonstrated her envy via bitter protests about the success of other dancers and choreographers. The usual scenario consisted of her parading before me a list of the latest leaps to stardom of other choreographers. "It's not fair!" she exclaimed. "I'm more talented than most of them, and as good as the best of them. They just know how to make contacts, or sell themselves out, or do stuff simply to make it commercially. I'm not good at selling myself! I'm not self-absorbed enough!" These expressions of envy toward other artists disguised the displaced envy Ms. A. covertly felt toward me. Sometimes, she expressed this envy toward me more directly, as when she burst out, "You have a skill you can use. You're more integrated. You never have to deal with the insecurities I face!"

Ms. A.'s attacks on people she envied were also manifested in attacks on herself, since she had incorporated them in distorted form. These "stars" never had to suffer like she did. Ms. A. continually disowned her own success, killing off the good in her and recreating a view of herself corresponding with an early-fixated one of a starving, clumsy, and inept child. She canceled out any success by claiming that it was nothing compared with the achievements of "famous" dancers and choreographers. In disowning her own accomplishments, she saw herself as a starving child, thereby repeatedly recreating her sense of internal starvation. Yet because she was still so identified with her primary objects, her self-destructive attacks were manifestations of attacks on the incorporated others. Internalized in a primitive oral way, they were undigested—the internal persecutors psychically formed in her preoedipal years, to whom she had remained addictively attached. By attacking herself, she attacked those others whom she imagined as laughing and triumphing over her. This was shown one day when she came into a session unaware that part of her dress was hitched up in back. On noticing it, she accused me of having relished the spectacle of seeing her underwear showing. "Why didn't you say anything?" she asked. "You were probably getting off on seeing me look ridiculous!" She imagined me laughing at her and gloating with sadistic pleasure. I was contemptuously triumphing over her just as Jim did and just as her father had. I wondered with her why she viewed me in this way. It emerged that she experienced some perverse enjoyment in finding herself in this victimized position, for she projectively identified with the hostile and ridiculing criticism that she imagined emanating from me, her boyfriend, and rival dancers and choreographers. She imagined us all reveling in our triumph over her.

Ms. A.'s envy could be traced back to the feelings she had toward a martyred, compulsively "all-giving" mother. She envied her mother for being so "good." Yet she also wished to knock the mother down, to expose her flaws so that they would be on a more equal level. Guilt toward her mother prevented Ms. A. from consciously being aware of her destructive wishes. They were generally displaced onto her two sisters,[9] members of her own internal critical chorus, whom she could more openly ridicule with sarcasm. She attempted to spoil their "image" just as she turned her ridiculing envy into contempt against herself and spoiled her own success.

Ms. A.'s envy of stars not only related to her envy of her mother as she had been incorporated. It also originated in the mother's unconscious envy of her daughter. Ms. A.'s virtually blanket denial of her own successes and her devaluation of all her work because she didn't see herself as a star suggested clearly that being a star held a very special meaning. For Ms. A., stardom not only had the conscious connotation of having her talent and industry recognized, it signified the fulfillment of her mother's dreams; to fulfill these was to save her victim mother from her demon father. Throughout Ms. A.'s childhood and adolescence, her mother was her main support, applauding all her daughter's artistic efforts. The mother encouraged and admired the daughter. She pushed her daughter so that Ms. A. would not pull back from being the star she was obviously "destined" to be. After Ms. A. left home at 16 to join a dance company and found the separation intolerable, her mother told her that she had to stick to it, since she was meant to be a dancer. Although Ms. A. somatized her pain, developing terrible stomach problems, she "toughed" out the separation and became the company's star dancer. Separation was encouraged by her mother as long as it was in the service of fulfilling her own narcissistic desires—as long as Ms. A. lived up to being the embodiment of her mother's own narcissistic images.

This scenario suggests that Ms. A. felt compelled to fulfill her mother's frustrated ambitions. Her mother remained an elegant housewife who failed to achieve a place in the spotlight in the outside world. The mother's conscious encouragement was most probably accompanied by an unconscious envy toward the daughter who was to have the fame and recognition that she had never earned. Certainly the daughter's unconscious, fused with her internal mother, registered the maternal envy. Did it also register the mother's demand that the daughter serve as her narcissistic extension? Ms. A.'s transference to me reflected not only incorporated envy, but defensive narcissistic idealization. By serving as an idealized extension of her mother, she warded off conscious awareness of the older woman's envy.

Ms. A.'s father too suffered from frustrated ambition. Although an attorney, he continually felt that he had failed financially and socially to live up to his professional goals. Therefore, whenever Ms. A. did not live up to the image of what she imagined both her parents wanted her to be, her own envy toward those who had apparently achieved success was overwhelming. A frustrated internal father-mother haunted her, and her own frustrated desires became fused with the power of this muse figure.

Ms. A.'s transference to me reflected this incorporated envy and its defensive narcissistic idealization. One day, she expressed her emphatic belief that I would like her much more if she were a star. I asked why she assumed this, suggesting that it was one of the illusions that trapped her in self-hatred. She could not yet face that she was addicted to identifying with her parents' ideal of her. This ideal continued to elude her, no matter how much she achieved. Seeing me as having "skills" seemed to be part of a father transference. Her father-demon had money and accomplishments that she envied, just as she envied the money and career accomplishments of her boyfriend.

Ms. A. was in a bind. On the one hand, the envy of her incorporated demon parents made her fear that her real parents would hate her if she achieved success. On the other hand, if Ms. A. did not "make it," she earned her parents' hatred for not fulfilling their own idealized image of themselves. Ms. A. wished for success, but the unconscious pressure from her internal father-mother made her deny this goal.

The only way out of this dilemma was through mourning. When Ms. A. finally felt the grief of her own hatred toward her parents, and the loss created both by her hatred and by the need to separate, she viewed them more objectively. Ms. A. then had to see that in clinging to her internal accusers, she held on to an inverted hatred that deflected her aggression away from her mother and toward herself and anyone who represented her father, such as Jim. This clinging was, she slowly realized, a way of preserving her idealized mother. When she gradually began to mourn, by feeling and expressing her disappointments with me (her transference mother), she faced for the first time the wishes behind this idealization. Relinquishing her idealized mother bit by bit, she didn't need to devalue herself so much, and could accept more readily the good things in herself and her mother more readily. Now Ms. A. could view her mother's real defects more objectively and tolerate the anger she felt toward her without turning it against herself in the form of self-accusations of failure and guilt. As she increasingly understood the meaning of her feelings, Ms. A. could grow in self-value. In recognizing her envy as a sign of devaluing herself, she felt the sadness of the losses she kept creating. The beginning of self-compassion caused her to sustain a sense of her own real accomplishments. By valuing herself she felt less starved and desperate, which then allowed her envy to decrease. It also increased her consciousness of the origins of her envy.

As Ms. A. owned, and thus understood, all of her feelings, her mode of interpersonal relations began to change. Whereas formerly masochistic cries for help disguised her feelings of love and hate,[10] she now related by direct communication. For example, previously she expressed her feelings of jealousy by becoming nauseous. In fact, Ms. A. had formerly somatized feelings or felt an emptiness. Her cries for help came from real terror, but they were masochistic because she kept herself in the position of a helpless child, compulsively disowning her aggression and the love behind it as she split off parts of herself. The hatred Ms. A. expressed by putting everyone else in a superior and envied position relative to herself became conscious as she experienced the idealized and contemptuous part of herself—also a part of her internal father-mother that she put into others (projective identification). Ms. A. started to grieve over her hatred, experiencing a mournful sadness that allowed her to take interpersonal steps toward relieving her guilt. I saw this when she showed love for me after expressing the most accusatory hatred, and gratitude for my acceptance of her hatred without retaliation, which brought sad tears to her eyes. For example, during one session she revealed the sadness of grief after accusing me of secretly sneering at her.

Ms. A.'s somatic symptoms gradually subsided. This came about with her increasing capacity to tolerate sadness and to process cognitively the meaning of her feelings in the context of our relationship. She now was increasingly connecting her feelings with reactions in her body that signaled anxiety about her wishes toward me and her fears of closeness with me. When the body symptoms appeared and reappeared, they now had a meaning that could be discussed. Since Ms. A. understood this meaning in the context of our relationship, she could also understand what was frightening in her other relationships, such as the one with Jim. Her anger and fear in relation to sexual activity with Jim could now be addressed in terms of her defensive behavior in sessions with me and her body reactions in response to fears of me emotionally penetrating her. Ms. A. wanted to be held, but resisted my addressing the defensive behaviors that she used to avoid an emotional penetration that would make this possible.[11] As she mourned, however, she began to develop an observing ego that allowed her to reflect on herself and to open up to analysis of her self-sabotaging defenses.

In watching and empathically experiencing Ms. A.'s growth process, it seemed obvious to me that feelings of mournful sadness are full of inner and interpersonal contact. Masochistic wailing, in contrast, emanates from behind a wall of blocked grief. Such walls are constructed by defenses against guilt and shame.

Ms. A. defended against grief with masochistic submission to others onto whom her self-tormenters were projected. She thus repulsed the intense pain of grief and of early, unmourned loss. She also warded off the love of the internalized other capable of giving her true power. By opening up her grief, she separated by experiencing loss. She was then able to let me and others in her life into her confidence. With this, she experienced her ability to connect through her love, tenderness, and anger, rather than through clinging to others like a helpless child. This recognition diminished her shame at ambitions that always outreached her accomplishments.[12] Severe shame had been a symptom of how Ms. A. devalued herself in order to disown the power of her own aggression, which she continually projected onto others. Along with disowning the aggression that made her feel so guilty, Ms. A. disowned her sexuality and her hunger for creative success. Both her success and sexuality had been denied, undone, and devalued. Allowing herself to re-own good parts of herself, along with her internal object, made it possible for Ms. A. to gradually relinquish the persecutory internal demon and to let go of the hostility she induced in others as she projected persecutory aspects of herself onto them. In opening up her grieving process, she was able to feel love for others and for herself. This allowed her to better sustain a good internal object. As she sustained this goodness, her sense of shame became modified and guilt lessened.

Mourning within treatment not only enabled Ms. A. to improve her interpersonal relations. Her creative process changed too. She reowned the parts of herself that she had previously split off into part object characters in her dance and into her psychoanalyst and boyfriend through projective identification. In reowning these parts, she had to experience her own belief that she was bad, instead of seeing herself simply as the victim of others. This painful perception allowed her to feel her aggression, something she needed to do in order not to feel overwhelmed by shame and envy.

Her creative work reflected this reowning process. She choreographed a dance about a woman starved for fame, who after receiving an award could not surrender it the following year to the next recipient. In choreographing this scenario, Ms. A. had to admit her own aggression, which she bestowed upon her character. She could no longer split off her reaction and exorcise it by cathartic performance. Through the awareness facilitated by mourning, Ms. A. had begun to confront her aggression and the self-perpetuated starvation behind it. Now she consciously identified with her dance character and learned from this identification, rather than creating caricatures for enactment, that she could put on like a glove but from whom she remained emotionally detached. More specifically, she acknowledged her identification with this character who desperately sought to be the center of attention to avoid an internal emptiness. She had learned that her own emptiness was related to a self-created emotional isolation from others, and she used this understanding in her choreography. With this self-awareness, Ms. A. connected to the creative process of writing and performing her work and therefore was not, as formerly, swallowed up by a void after a performance. The overall change in the nature of her creativity requires some more commentary.

## Resolving Compulsion

### Changes in Creativity

Ms. A. previously had been compelled to create compulsively because she had to exorcise the split-off parts of herself that she disowned. This exorcism set up the same pathological-mourning reenactment that appears in the work of the preoedipally arrested women writers I have discussed. As mourning freed Ms. A. from the pressure of projective identification, however, her creative work started to express an active internal process of psychic dialectic. She showed the psychic conflict and the realistic consequences behind her character's actions, suggesting her own whole object development.

Her reaction to the patient in my waiting room may be seen as one indication of how Ms. A.'s earlier form of creativity was changed as she confronted her defenses and acknowledged her previously disowned feelings. Ms. A. expressed her hostility toward this other patient somatically and verbally. The woman smelled and seemed disgustingly fragile. Ms. A.'s reaction implied contempt for the patient's vulnerability. In the past Ms. A. might have incorporated this woman into her creative work to defend against these jealous feelings, her shame about them and her own vulnerability. She might have created a dance presenting a part object caricature of this woman. This patient whom she spied coming out of my office would probably have become another semiabsurd character in her comical dance scripts. Ms. A. would then have disowned her reactions and split off the part of herself she felt ashamed of, using a created character as a receptacle for her projective identification. But unlike a therapist, a character in a dance or play cannot detoxify the projection and return it in a more digestible form (i.e., as when I conceptualized Ms. A.'s jealousy and vulnerability within the context of a relationship).

If Ms. A. had made her female competitor into a dance character, she would not have experienced her own inner affect life. Instead, she would have constricted rather than developed her self-structure and consequently would have continued to feel empty, lonely, and inferior. With the sealing off of her affect, she would have split off the object representing a part of herself, since it was not yet fully differentiated from her and thus could be neither owned nor digested within her internal world.

While I interpreted Ms. A.'s disowned feelings and the splitting off of the internal-object relation attached to them, I encouraged her to express the rage related to her guilt, as when she became jealous of my other patient. She then connected her reactions to objects in her interpersonal and internal worlds. By making the connections and understanding them, she contained her internal objects, continuing to integrate instead of splitting them off. Feeling greater inner connectedness, she became more independent and therefore more separate from others. Ms. A. revealed this self-development, and its object-related capacity, by informing me of the amends that she had made to another woman of whom she had been jealous: Jim's female friend. Similarly, in owning her jealousy of the other patient, Ms. A. created a "rapprochement" and took a further step toward self and object differentiation and its related self-individuation. This rapprochement demonstrated not only the insight that she had acquired through owning her jealousy, but also her capacity to modify her jealousy by owning the vulnerability that she had psychically discarded onto this other female patient. Because she felt for her boyfriend's female friend, Ms. A. developed an empathic capacity, which by furthering a sense of self-pride diminished her shame. More-over, her growing empathy allowed love for the object, which in turn promoted more internal openness to self-integration. Loving feelings open up inner space, just as angry feelings diminish it. When anger is in the form of intense rage it can feel like suffocation.

The change in Ms. A.'s internal-object relations, then, transformed her creative work. In moving beyond her part object perception of "the other woman," based on a split-off self-part, she perceived the other woman as a subject whose vulnerability could affect her. This awareness of subjectivity in another enhanced Ms. A.'s ability to develop differentiated and whole characters in her choreography, such as the star who relinquished her award. This new dance character represented a creative advance, for she was not, unlike previous creations, a caricature with a flat attitude. Instead, the character possessed the ambivalence characteristic of a whole person who lives with psychic conflict. The character feared the loss of her narcissistic "star" image. Because of her inability to let go, she lapsed into a disenfranchised state that forced her to confront her shame, jealousy, and guilt. Ms. A.'s star attempted to avoid any conflict over guilt for her narcissistic desires[13] by acting them out. She hoped by this to avoid the loss attendant on the acceptance of reality's limits. "It's really hard for me to face reality!" Ms. A. had exclaimed in our session. Yet through her star character, she discovered that facing loss and accepting limits were preferable to holding onto an illusion of surpassing all needs for others with an image. No image, Ms. A. realized, could save her from feeling empty and alone. The image of stardom held only the illusion of rejoining an idealized mother or father-mother. Ms. A. learned that facing her true feelings enlightened her about the real world—a place where others existed and where overcoming loneliness involves sharing with other competitors, whether they be her therapist's other patients, her boyfriend's other friends, or her fellow artists who sought the same awards. Her mourning within the therapy—a mourning that allowed good-object internalization—en-abled Ms. A. to use her creative work to discover herself and her internal others, just as she had discovered herself and the realities of the interpersonal world within psychotherapy. Mourning within the treatment encouraged her increasingly to surrender to mourning within creative work—gaining empathy and relatedness. Ms. A.'s loneliness was diminished by this painful lesson, and by its products—empathy and relatedness. Her characters could now develop the mutual dialogue of object relatedness.

### Changes in Ms. A.'s Life

Ms. A.'s personal life changed as she mourned within her psychoanalytic psychotherapy (the prescribed treatment for borderline pathology, Kernberg

1975). The retaliatory nature of her internal-world objects determined that each positive change—one offering the possibility of opening up to new and healthier relations that supported her desires and ambitions—brought a backlash reaction. With each regression came a new sense of despair, related to the repetition of early object loss and its intimately related sense of self-inferiority. This process had to be experienced, understood, and worked through. Confronted with the tenacious repetition of her identification with her bad internal object,[14] Ms. A. learned how her backlash self-sabotage fueled the despair that she experienced. She could learn this only in the consistent holding environment atmosphere of the psychotherapeutic clinical situation. Each time Ms. A. cancelled out her life gains, I was there in my capacity as a therapist to renew hope by pointing out how her fear of changing her identity promoted the backlash through which she clung to past pathological and incorporative modes of identification.

For example, as treatment progressed, Ms. A. moved forward in her life by asserting herself with others. By being clear about her anger and needs, she prevented the accretion of secret resentments along with their capacities to destroy relationships. She gained grants for her work and negotiated more successfully with theaters and with Jim. She and Jim began living together. Yet while all this was happening, Ms. A. tore up a choreographic script, claimed that she was getting nowhere, and reverted to provoking fights at home. As she mourned the losses in the present, which resonated with her losses from the past, she nevertheless let me be with her. I became important for this function, and she subsequently allowed me to interpret the fears motivating her, such as those behind her angry self-sabotaging reactions. As she opened to these fears, I could say, "You're scared now of not making progress, but you need to see how you stop your progress, because of your fear of change." Although Ms. A. feared being stuck and going backwards, progress and success were even more frightening. Not only would her success arouse the envy of other women she feared, but it threatened to change her sense of herself. I helped her see that she clung to her old "inadequate and bad self" because she feared change which made her lose her old and familiar identity. Through my attempts to contact her in this manner, holding her with my presence and aiding her to gain understanding through my interpretations, the pattern of her backlash reactions became clearer to her. With this understanding her despair decreased and her hope rekindled.

Despite her regressions, Ms. A.'s ability to grieve within her despair significantly enlarged her capacity to become her true self. She began consciously to create and live her life. Ms. A.'s, as noted, became capable for the first time of living with a man. When she provoked violent fights at home, I indicated how she was attempting to do the same with me in therapy. Rather quickly, she stopped provoking the fights at home with her boyfriend.[15] Such interventions had to be repeated with our cycles of work.

As we worked on Ms. A.'s resistances to allowing herself truly to be with me in the treatment room, she began to understand how she similarly resisted being with her boyfriend. She then yielded more readily to real contact. This allowed her gradually to gain the internalizations of good-object experience that she had always sought. Because such internalization allowed her to feel better within, her sessions with me allowed her to decrease the degree to which she would overreact at home to every minor deprivation or gesture of hostility in her relationship with Jim. She became more appreciative of the good things she could have with Jim, and this motivated her to tolerate his failings.

During treatment, Ms. A. also separated from two female friends with whom she had perpetuated self-destructive relationships. One of these women was Barbara, whom she used as an auxiliary ego to help her focus on her work. Ms. A. began to become more discriminating about whom she came to depend on and whom she created friendships with.

Ms. A.'s difficulties with female friends related to intense envy and to wishes to regress to an infantile state at times. She resisted mature relations with friends, wishing to turn them into mothers. Her relations with her actual mother had become strained too. She still longed to please her but was now more conscious of the erratic nature of her mother's behavior toward her. Periodic visits home gave Ms. A. the opportunity to observe her mother more objectively than she had in the past when she was blinded by a powerful idealizing love, which had been used defensively.

Ms. A. had idealized her mother and turned her father into a demon, hiding her mother's aggression from herself, placing it within the image of her father, which as an integral object had become a demon lover in her internal world. For most of her life, her rage at her father's punitive and intimidating control was used to block out any awareness of her anger toward her mother. Behind the idealized mother, however, was the real mother who was simultaneously critical and indulgently, seductively nurturant. Also behind the idealized mother was the mother who used her daughter as a narcissistic extension of herself so that Ms. A. was constantly overwhelmed with her own ambitions to be a star. In confronting her real internal mother, rather than turning her into a chorus of female judges defended against by projection and idealization. Ms. A. faced the nature of her connections with women. She saw that what she held onto with some women, such as Barbara, was an idealized fantasy about her relationship with them.

Thus, Ms. A. had kept holding onto Barbara, thinking that her friend would be supportive, would publicize her work, and so forth. In reality, Barbara gave her none of these things, and the assistance she did offer came at the price of much hostile verbal abuse, which turned her into the demon-lover father in Ms. A.'s mind.

The emerging consciousness of her own anger caused Ms. A. to confront the anger toward her mother. She had previously defended against these feelings with a maternal idealization, the counterpart of the villainization of her father and victimization of herself. Having less need of such a defense, she began honestly to deal with the areas of her denial. This process helped her to understand the connection between holding on to women such as Barbara and holding on to her internal mother, the negative mother she had incorporated behind the idealization.

Ms. A. improved in every area of her life. She became more developed in her creative work and even changed the conditions around it. A greater trust in her own abilities showed her that she could work either solo or with others. She became more open to earning money while pursuing her creative work. The driven and yet blocked character of her creative process eased as interpersonal areas of her life expanded. Now she discovered the gratification of becoming herself in ways other than through her creativity. Her compulsion to create became a freer motivation either to create through self-expression or to create herself through interpersonal relations, both complementary modes of object relationship. Significantly, her compulsion to create and her love addiction were parallel modes of psychodynamic psychopathology.

As her capacity for object relatedness developed through the mourning and object relations work in psychoanalytic psychotherapy, Ms. A. resolved the analogous problems of creative compulsion and love addiction. Whereas formerly she had employed her creativity compulsively to defend against overwhelming and painful interpersonal relations, with time, as she mourned and resolved her pain, she found interpersonal relations more rewarding. This allowed her to feel free to surrender her work for periods of time and then return to it more easily, refreshed by the nurturing dialectic interchange of interpersonal relations. These changes also contributed to her ability to tone down the integrity of her craving to be a star so that she could enjoy more of her life offstage. As the nature of her interpersonal relations altered, her creativity did as well, because the basic internal-object relations which motivated her in both areas were changing. Mourning her primary objects, she separated from them. She was able to develop whole object relations within her internal world and to internalize others as whole objects. Having whole self and object relations within her creative work enabled her to connect to others whom she loved, and to differentiate character traits within herself. Today, her creative process is moving her toward people rather than away from them. She has even begun to choreograph dance pieces based on the intimate relationships in her life. Unlike before, others do not simply constitute an audience, but are becoming people with whom she can genuinely share both her work and her life; therefore she can recreate more realistic aspects of these people within her work. Slowly, Ms. A. is learning that she can choose individuals with whom this is truly possible.

## Conclusion

### *Ms. A.*

Ms. A.'s treatment continues after the three-year process presented here. Her abilities to integrate the split-off parts of herself—by owning dissociated feelings and impulses—continue to grow. This ongoing development is based on Ms. A.'s increasing awareness of her defenses against such self-integration, which she has learned about within the context of the therapeutic object relationship. With increasing internalization of the therapeutic object relationship, Ms. A. has enlarged this integration process on her own, through other intimate relationships and her connection with herself through the process of creative work. As Ms. A. expresses her feelings and yearnings, she has become aware of her fantasies about being nurtured by a caretaking figure. Other fantasies have also become conscious, such as that of murdering off an abusive father whose eroticism toward her is expressed through beatings, and that of murdering a mother who either abandons her if she is autonomous or attacks her with guilt-provoking rage when she fails to live up to the maternal image of her. Growing awareness of such fantasies, along with understanding of how these interact with her own feelings of loss, murderous rage, guilt, shame, and envy, can further help Ms. A. to solidify an individuated self-structure. As Ms. A. becomes more autonomous in this way, she can mourn her attachment to me. Mourning of the therapeutic object relationship serves to help someone with early difficulties in separation to differentiate the internal-object parent (mother-father) from the external object. When the external object is the psychotherapist, he or she can functionally serve as a transitional object (Winnicott 1971) that can be relinquished when interpersonal relations outside the treatment situation become adequate.

Although some patients do not follow this process through these later stages, many do. I have worked with a significant number of patients with difficulties similar to those of Ms. A. who remain in treatment long enough to connect emerging fantasies in the therapeutic object relationship to their childhood relations, thereby beginning to comprehend the compulsive pressure to reenact early traumas that operates within them. Such patients become analysands as they analyze the dynamics of their intrapsychic lives. They experience a process of grief as they gradually separate from the psychotherapist-analyst, so that termination involves their clear distinction of the psychotherapist from the original parent figures.

### *Women Writers*

How would the distinguished women writers discussed in this book have fared in an object relations-oriented psychotherapeutic treatment? Someone as severely traumatized as Emily Dickinson would have probably needed many years of therapy, but I believe that an object relations-oriented treatment could have provided a holding environment in which a sealed-off schizoid self-state might have opened to interpersonal connections over time. Such connections, initiated through a psychotherapeutic object relationship—which unfortunately Dickinson didn't enjoy—would have allowed her to sustain an integrated state that might have been first formed through the expression of her feelings within the creative process. The therapist would have to tolerate Dickinson's tremendous rage as the poet emerged from her cocoon, the kind of rage that she implies metaphorically in her descriptions of her demon-lover god. The ability to form an external-object relationship through the mourning process would have depended on the ability of Dickinson's therapist to survive her patient's rage and to help her see the demon lover figure with which she projectively identified in the context of the psychotherapeutic relationship.

Emily Brontë's hypothetical treatment would probably have been quite similar to that of Emily Dickinson, since in each case the seclusive schizoid character structure dominates. Edith Sitwell, in contrast, may have been an even more difficult candidate for psychotherapeutic treatment. Her rigid narcissistic defenses, associated with a pathological grandiose self-structure, would have required ongoing confrontation before an empathic approach could be usefully established. Sarcasm and contempt probably would characterize the distancing armamentarium she employed in warding off any dependency on the psychotherapist. I imagine that through these means she would have attempted to maintain a manic-defense stance of being above her potentially highly vulnerable and needy self.

I speculate, however, that if Sitwell became despondent enough to remain in treatment, her failure to ward off her inner sense of emptiness despite ongoing applause would conceivably have resulted in persistent withdrawal from affect contact, manic-defense resistance, and hostile sarcasm used as a distancing maneuver to ward off conscious dependency. She could have eventually yielded to an empathic holding environment; but her rage would have been fierce. That is, Sitwell's constant backlash reactions of paranoid projective identification and other forms of distancing maneuvers would have exploded into rages. Yet she may have eventually seen the relation of such responses to her intense fears of vulnerability, as well as to a profound shame that was still too inchoate to conceptualize.

As Sitwell's rage gradually yielded to powerful grief reactions, her inner despair, and the internal relations from which such despair stems, could have become communicable. In the one-on-one interpersonal therapeutic environment, such communication could have helped transform the malignant images of demon persecutors in her poetry into a more subjective anguish. The therapist's ability to understand Sitwell's anguish and to contain it by remaining empathically in touch with the patient's pain as she felt it could have allowed the therapeutic object relationship necessary to permit the necessary transition to sustained interpersonal contact. Such sustained contact also would have created a more profound subjective experience within the creative process, allowing mourning and self-integration to become increasingly possible within it.

Charlotte Brontë too may have benefited from psychotherapy. Unlike the other writers discussed, she was capable of sharing highly affective experiences from a subjective locus that also allowed for experiencing the other with whom she shared them. Yet treatment may have enhanced, elaborated, and more fully sustained her mourning process. More-dissociated aspects of her personality, therefore, could have become integrated.

Like Ms. A., all of the women writers discussed in this study may have emerged from psychotherapy less-compulsively engaged with the creative process. Freer to immerse themselves in it by naturally alternating between interpersonal contact and the contact with one's internal objects within the creative process, they would have probably discovered their creative process to be less blocked by defenses against the affects of mourning, and to be increasingly sustained and self-integrative. They could have then become less isolated personally, since their fears of interpersonal contact would have decreased. Had this occurred, they could have used the creative process to deepen their interpersonal relations, while using their interpersonal relations to deepen an awareness necessary to enhance and nurture the reparative aspects of their creativity.

# Notes

## 1. Compulsion versus Reparation

1. See *Lives, Events and Other Players* (Coltrera 1981, 33).

2. One merges with the idealized object as it is projected outside of the self, i.e., as it is externalized through the avenue of the creative work.

3. D. W. Winnicott (1965) defines the holding environment in terms of the therapeutic functions that the therapist, like the preoedipal mother, provides. These functions involve containing, soothing, validating mirroring, and empathically interpreting the patient's feelings, as well as providing limits and affective nonretaliatory responsiveness. Modell (1976) follows up on Winnicott's descriptions by speaking of the holding environment as the mode of therapeutic action within the framework of psychoanalysis. More recent uses of the term also refer to the atmosphere that allows patients to build their self-structures by internalizing ongoing transactions of self and other (see Grunes 1984), on the permeability of the analyst as an extension of Winnicott's function of "holding.").

4. Stern (1985) distinguishes among parental engagement that is validating of parts of the self, parental uninvolvement, and overt parental rejection through withdrawal that taints areas of the self with a sense of shame.

5. This doesn't preclude that creative process work can have "selfobject" functions in the sense of self-validation through the experience of self-articulation of all parts of the self (even those denied by the parents) being reflected back through the work. In my view, using the creative work successfully in this way, in terms of sustaining such validation, depends on an oedipal level of psychic structuralization. Failures to sustain such validation within the interpersonal world will be seen in several preoedipal-level women writers to be presented.

6. Many who appreciate Kohut's clinical contributions have made statements indicating that they do not accept this particular theoretical premise of his.

7. See Silverman and Will 1986 ("The Failure of Emotional Self-Repair Through Poetry"). Sylvia Plath is viewed by the authors as withdrawing from interpersonal relations during her last and greatest creative work. Her withdrawal, they suggest, was a major factor in her despair and suicide.

8. See Stone 1934 (*Lust for Life*).

9. Jeffrey Meyers 1978; Antony Alpers 1980; Claire Tomalin 1988.

10. They refer to the dual unity in terms of states of projective identification within the paranoid-schizoid position. The infant fuses with the idealized part object other. As this occurs within the internal world with the internal ideal mother, a projective identification process occurs with the external mother, in which good parts of the self are put into her for safe-keeping as well as for merger. This is how Segal, and later Kleinians, come close to Winnicott's idea of a mother-infant "matrix" (Ogden, 1986) and dual unity.

11. This developmental process is referred to in terms of the "depressive position."

12. Stern (1985) also cites examples from mother-infant research of such intrusiveness, which at a verbal level can create a false self.

13. In Donald Stern's reports of his infant research, he speaks of dynamically interactive self and other "rigs" (1985).

14. I use Melanie Klein's term "part object." The part object is an object that is not perceived as a human being who has both good and bad qualities. Instead it is perceived as all bad or all good. The term can also imply that a person is perceived in an unconsciously infantile way as a breast or a penis, providing functions of nurturance or penetrating arousal that are dissociated from the constellation of the whole personality who is providing such functions.

15. Following Klein, Guntrip refers to this level as the paranoid level.

16. Guntrip refers to this as the schizoid level, separating Klein's paranoid-schizoid position into two levels.

17. This is the essence of the "true self" as defined by D. W. Winnicott.

18. While an archaic idealized self must be relinquished, remnants of it remain in unconscious fantasy and also become part of the ego ideal.

19. As Stern (1985) points out, the mother's capacity for intersubjective modes of relatedness at this time can be crucial in determining whether there is continuing healthy development.

20. This comes with the beginning of Klein's depressive position, which will be discussed in a later chapter. It is a developmental stage as well as a psychic state that one enters throughout life.

21. See the case of Ms. A. which is discussed in chapter 15.

22. D. W. Winnicott has conceptualized the roles of the therapist as container and as object of affect as the "environment mother" and the "object mother." See *The Maturational Processes and the Facilitating Environment* (1965).

23. A detailed example of this will be given in the last chapter.

24. Called internal objects by Klein and Fairbairn.

25. As Otto Kernberg's (1975) clinical examples show, the patient may enact the role of the child or of the parent, projecting the other half of the internal relationship onto the therapist. If the patient plays out the mother, he or she tries to induce the child role in the therapist, and vice versa.

26. *Playing and Reality* (1971).

27. Stern (1985) writes about the intensity of affect-influencing memory, i.e., influencing the recording of the object. Stern believes that we need much more research on this issue.

28. Fairbairn speaks of a primitive mode of primary identification. I use the term "incorporation" because I think it is more appropriate to the primitive-level early infant experience.

29. As in the case of the photographer Diane Arbus (see Kavaler 1988b).

## 2. From Mother to Father

1. This can be related to the proprioceptive and motoric dimensions of representations as reported by Beebe and Lachmann 1988.

2. The Kleinians use the British spelling "phantasy," in keeping with their origins.

3. Donald Stern (1985) has objected to Mahler's use of the concept of "symbiosis." In his observations of mothers and infants, he emphasizes the degree to which infants are differentiated from earliest life. However, he addresses differentiation in terms of perceptual and proprioceptive functions, not in terms of psychic fantasy and the formation of cognitive representations that allows for a form of separation beyond perceptual differentiation. Melanie Klein's conceptualization of the paranoid-schizoid position, and its mechanism of projective identification, accounts for what Mahler's empirical observation noted to be symbiotic in behavior.

4. See the study of Charlotte Brontë (chapters 7 & 8).

5. Kohut has never acknowledged Winnicott for the origins of this concept.

6. I will be using the male pronoun to distinguish the paradigmatic child spoken of from the mother. To write he or she continually is ponderous. Of course, all being said about the hypothetical male child applies to the female, who is the subject of this book's studies of women writers.

7. I refer here not just to physical needs, but to the infant's ongoing needs for stimulation by interpersonal response.

8. This can be seen to be repeated in the artist's propulsion into creative activity following object loss. See S. A. Kavaler 1985; 1986; 1988; 1989a; and 1989b.

9. Ronald Fairbairn (1952) used both the terms "internal saboteur" and "antilibidinal ego" to describe the intrapsychic structure related to internal bad objects. Melanie Klein ([1940] 1975) spoke of "bad objects" in a more diffuse way, speaking of them as internal within the psychic self, but not giving them any technical terms as psychic structure.

10. The order of the passages has been rearranged.

11. He can be seen as a part object malignant phallus, symbolizing his grandiose bad-object dimensions. See the study of Edith Sitwell.

## 3. Mourning and Creative-Process Reparation

1. Later, we will see this omnipotent part object become manifested as the muse-god of psychically arrested creative women.

2. The tantalizing and rejecting object of Ronald Fairbairn (1952) is also perceptually split into an erotically arousing part object and demonic object that allies itself with the "anti-libidinal ego" or "internal saboteur."

3. In Margaret Mahler's model, the idealized other is derived from the symbiotic primary unity in infancy.

4. In Kleinian theory, both part objects are labeled in terms of the infant's perspective as breasts: the good breast and the bad breast.

5. See Ogden (1986) on the "interpreting subject" as a phenomenon that grows with depressive-position dynamics.

6. Fairbairn's theory emphasizes this primitive identification by speaking of the holding on to the bad early parental object. The fusion of self and object after splitting makes clear that there is no integrated identification, but rather the formation of an incorporation or introject.

7. In Margaret Mahler's schema, this is attained at rapprochement, which occurs at eighteen to thirty-six months.

8. I see this depressive-position dynamic first occurring during the toddler years, rather than during early infancy. The "terrible twos" express the new struggle of ambivalence.

9. Klein did not specifically deal with shame.

10. Winnicott speaks of a maturing capacity to tolerate dependence that is determined by the mother's capacity to allow a long-enough infant state of "absolute dependence," a time when the infant can be dependent without any awareness of its dependent state. Without this primary state of unconscious absolute dependence, the realization of conscious dependence becomes traumatic. Fairbairn, as well as Winnicott, emphasizes the mother's role in such growth from "immature" to "matures" dependence.

11. These processes, in relation to a primitive stage of self-development, have been called "pre-stages of defense" by Stolorow and Lachmann 1980.

12. One's own need for the other is threatening.

## 4. Creative Women and the Internal Father

1. These papers in progress were received in personal correspondence in 1987, then they appeared in a chapter of Father and their Families, (1989).

2. D. W. Winnicott tried to speak about excitement as a self phenomenon beyond the instinctual in his paper on "The Capacity to be Alone" in which he speaks of the "ego orgasm." See *The Maturational Processes and the Facilitating Environment* (1965, 35).

3. See Fairbairn (1952) on dynamic structure.

4. Pleasure and pain are perceived as "Mommy is good" or "Mommy is bad."

5. See Ogden 1986 for a discussion of the derivation of the psychic dynanism of the internal object.

6. The "ego ideal" could be renamed the "self ideal," since the term self is used in a broad sense, just as the term ego has been used.

7. For a poignant illustration of these dynamics, see the case of Sylvia Plath in "Lord of the Mirrors and the Demon Lover" (Kavaler, described 1986).

8. The separation between the idealized and demonic father is illusory. There is a split in a woman's mind that gives her the delusional belief that they are separate figures.

## 5. The Demon Lover Theme as Literary Myth and Psychodynamic Complex

1. I.e., Freud's oral stage and Margaret Mahler's symbiotic stage.

2. I.e. James Masterson's reunion fantasy.

3. I.e. Fairbairn's exciting and rejecting object and Klein's omnipotently idealized part object, in a masculine form.

4. It was only after I had studied these women writers myself that I came across Marian Woodman's description of the demon lover complex in relation to the specific women that I had chosen.

5. D. W. Winnicott (1953) originated the term "transitional space" to refer to an area of psychic engagement that is between engagements with external others and absorption within the realm of the self. The area for creative work and its representations is designated as transitional in

that it is a space for the expression of the self in its engagement with objects that are not yet fully external objects, but like the child's teddy bear are one-step removed from the core omnipotent self.

6. See Kavaler on Sylvia Plath (1986), Diane Arbus (1988b), and Anne Sexton (1989a).

7. There may be some relative difference depending on the personality of the real father, but if the self is sealed off from contact, mourning of the trauma with the early mother must be done to allow contact with the actual father, so that he is not just incorporated as a projected form of the idealized or bad part object mother. The external father's ability to relate may affect the situation to the extent that the daughter has part of herself still affectively engaged with others in the outer world. If the father is significantly narcissistic, his inability to relate will compound an already atrophied psychic situation.

8. D. W. Winnicott first coined the term "good enough" mother, also called "good enough" object, in his papers collected in *The Maturational Processes and the Facilitating Environment* (1965).

## 6. Portraits of Two Kinds of Creative Women

1. See Kavaler (1985; 1989); see also Anai's Nin's *A Spy in the House of Love*.

2. See *A Spy in the House of Love*.

3. See Plath's poems in *Ariel*; see also Kavaler 1985 ("Mirror, Mirror on the Wall . . .").

4. See Silverman and Will on Plath's withdrawal from other artists when she wished to create the emotional intensity of *Ariel*.

5. Plath's view of her mother can be seen in her poetry, her journals, and in her *Letters Home to Mother*, published as a book by her mother. She can be seen to be most false in her correspondence to her mother, in which she attempts to fit into a perfect image.

6. See Fairbairn 1952 on "exorcism" of the bad object.

7. These are the borderline cycles described by Klein and Kernberg as cycles of "projective identification."

8. The depression underlying self-fragmentation is never tolerated.

9. D. W. Winnicott was the originator of the term "good enough mother," which can be found in his papers collected in his book *The Maturational Processes and the Facilitating Environment* (1965).

10. Emily Brontë and, later, Katherine Mansfield fatally incorporated the disease of tuberculosis.

11. The containing function of the psychoanalyst (or of the original mother) implies survival of aggressive attacks and seductions so that retaliatory and abandoning part object forms can be modified or transformed. The survival of the psychoanalyst means an understanding of the attacks, allowing restraint against retaliation or submission, and an interpretative mode of communication that allows the patient to understand the motivations for his or her own attacks. The behavior of the psychoanalyst is internalized, and to the degree that it is assimilated into the central self (or ego), the internal part objects become transformed into more benign whole object forms that are reminiscent of the psychoanalyst, who serves as a better object than the original parental object as originally incorporated.

## 7. Charlotte Brontë: Biography and *Jane Eyre*

1. In my discussion of Charlotte Brontë I am indebted to Margot Peters for many of her acute observations.

2. Charlotte Brontë's childhood tales were published in 1933 as *Legends of Angria* in an edition by Fannie E. Ratchford and William Clyde De Vane.

3. Wise and Symington 1932, 157–58.

4. He was immortalized as Graham Bretton in *Villette*.

## 8. Villette

1. Peters describes the agonies that Brontë suffered merely in trying to break free from her father long enough to take a vacation by the sea with her girlfriend, Ellen.

2. At one point Lucy becomes so anxious from the professor's intimidations that she breaks his glasses. Her anxiety is obviously mingled with her unconscious retaliatory aggression.

3. The placidity in question is overt. For example, she tries to persist in correcting papers rather than respond to his insults.

4. These despotic behaviors of the professor resemble those of Charlotte Brontë's father.

5. Note her last name ("Snowe").

6. Ironically, he originally exhorted Lucy to be a nun.

7. Charlotte Brontë never received such affirmation from her father. Her portrayal of M. Paul Emanuel suggests that M. Héger's response to her did encourage her to enter the world and that she was repairing her later disappointment with him by creating the character of M. Paul, who even more fully and directly aided her.

8. This resuppression by Lucy can be seen in her acting scene or in a scene in which she vents her critical thoughts about Graham and then apologetically withdraws them.

9. Madame Beck controlled Lucy as her employer.

10. Peters (170) offers this explanation for the professor's cruel indifference to Charlotte's pleas: he needed to deny his own secret knowledge of Charlotte Brontë's passion, a knowledge that she knew he possessed, as demonstrated in her fiction.

11. This contrasts with Rochester from *Jane Eyre* who is an entirely fictive character. Gilbert and Gubar (1979) note this purely fictional character of Rochester. The realistic comparisons between M. Héger of Brussels and *Villette*'s M. Paul Emanuel have also been generally noted by critics and biographers.

12. Here I've borrowed Tanner's phrase (1985, 14).

13. This theme appears also in the characterization of Madame Beck as the machinelike embodiment of domestic concern.

14. She is abandoned by Graham, by Madame Beck, and eventually by M. Paul as he leaves her and fails to return.

15. See Tanner 1985, 30.

16. Tanner writes: "There is, as it were, an unconscious conspiracy on the part of her surroundings to make her turn herself into a non-person" (1985, 20).

17. As in "My outward sense is gone, my inner essence feels."

18. She feels distrust on learning that the professor is spying and intruding on others.

19. This includes integration of polar male-female, tender-aggressive, and loving-hating aspects of her self.

20. During this internal dialogue, Lucy remarks: "Reason is vindictive as a devil: for me, she was always envenomed as a step-mother. If I have obeyed her it has chiefly been with the obedience of fear, not of love" (307–8). This unkind stepmother is most readily labeled as Fairbairn's (1952) "internal saboteur" or "anti-libidinal ego."

21. See Cohen 1988.

22. See Margaret Mahler et al. 1975. (*The Psychological Birth of the Human Infant*), in which Mahler discusses psychic individuation as opposed to mere psychical separation, psychological "hatching" (53–54).

23. " 'Dog in the manger!' I said; for I knew she secretly wanted him, and had always wanted him. She called him 'insupportable;' she railed at him for a 'devot'; she did not love, but she wanted to marry, that she might bind him to her interest. Deep into some of Madame's secrets I had entered—I know not how; by an intuition or an inspiration which came to me—I know not whence. In the course of living with her, too, I had slowly learned, that unless with an inferior, she must ever be a rival. She was my rival, heart and soul, though secretly . . . " (544).

24. At the time of Charlotte Brontë's oedipal stage, her father was grieving over the death of his wife.

25. As in Tessman's (1987) fathers, who allow "permeability of boundaries."

26. See Tessman 1987, on ego ideal formation in women.

27. See Fairbairn 1952 and Winnicott 1965 on the transitional stage.

28. See Margaret Mahler et al. 1975 on rapprochement.

29. See Stern 1985 on the intersubjective dynamics of mothers and infants.

30. The mother of separation has also been called a transitional object (Winnicott 1965), in terms of the supportive functions provided for the transition from the "dual unity" or "symbiosis" to the stage of separation.

## 9. Emily Brontë I: The Messenger of Hope and the Demon in the Nightwind

1. Ronald Fairbairn speaks of the "tantalizing and rejecting object" in the schizoid personality. Emily Brontë's muse-gods can be seen as reflecting the early internal objects spoken of by Fairbairn. As tantalization turns to torment, to rejection through abandonment, and to the consequent death of the preoedipally dependent self, the muse-god always turns demonic.

2. As seen in chapter 2, Sylvia Plath's poetry reveals a similar theme of being imprisoned in a hall of mirrors as she is created through the images of men. Her rage at the symbolic male who incarcerates her in his image system is expressed in the poem "Death and Co." from *Ariel* ("Bastard masturbating a glitter. . .").

3. In Daniel Stern's theory, the failure of self-agency goes back to the first few months of life,

when the core sense of self is forming. Whatever forms at this time, however, then needs to be allowed its autonomy and development during separation-individuation.

## 10. Emily Brontë II: *Wuthering Heights* and the Demon Lover

1. See Kohut 1971 (*Analysis of the Self*).

2. In Klein's terms, they are part objects, while for Fairbairn they would be seen just as internal bad objects.

3. The idealized and demonic objects of Melanie Klein can also be related to the tantalizing and rejecting bad objects of Ronald Fairbairn.

4. The holding environment of D. W. Winnicott has also been called the "maternal matrix" or the "dual unity."

5. Emily Brontë's relationship to her father is similar to that of Emily Dickinson. Both daughters became special through doing special tasks for their fathers. One main task was baking the father's bread. Perhaps the common symbolism of dough rising in relation to pregnancy and wishes for pregnancy is significant here.

6. See also Kavaler 1988b; 1989a.

7. Metaphorically expressed in the poem about being a prisoner ("Silent Is the House") as well as in other poetry and in *Wuthering Heights*.

## 11. Emily Dickinson: Muse and Demon

1. See Winnicott 1965 and Ogden 1986.

2. See Wolff's commentary on the psychological meaning of the dashes in Dickinson's poetry (1986 52).

3. The Emily Dickinson poems are quoted from collected poems entitled *Complete Poems* (1960), as edited by Thomas H. Johnson.

4. Her brother also presented this image of intellect, which the females in Dickinson's family, e.g., her mother and sister, seemed so totally to lack.

5. "Play" could also be interpreted here in D. W. Winnicott's sense (1965) of lacking a flexibility of dialectical consciousness that could allow the fruitful and enjoyable experience of internal space.

6. See Jessica Benjamin's (1988) writings on the yearning for recognition displayed by women in relation to men, and Kavaler (1985; 1986) on the eroticized striving for mirroring recognition by their fathers as shown by women authors.

7. The term "self/object" later called "selfobject," was invented by Heinz Kohut, following D. W. Winnicott's use of the term "subjective object" (see Winnicott 1965).

8. The term "subjective object" was first used by D. W. Winnicott and can be applied to the functional use of the muse for self-inspiration and thus for self-enlivening.

9.  See the chapters on Emily Brontë.

10. See Kavaler 1986; 1989a.

## 12. Emily Dickinson's Breakdown: Renunciation and Reparation

1.  The publishers Higginson and Bowles both failed to encourage her.

2.  See Plath's *Ariel* poems.

3.  See Ferlazzo 1976 and Cody 1971.

4.  Cody 1971 suggests the mid-1850s.

5.  See Ferlazzo 1976, 83.

6.  Wolff speaks of the battle between the poet and her demon-god as an imitation of the biblical wrestling between Jacob and the Lord.

7.  Quoted in *The Belle of Amherst*, as well as by her biographers (see Sewall).

8.  See Cody 1971.

9.  *Ibid.*

10. Cody cites the mid-1850s as the time of an acute psychosis.

11. See Ferlazzo 1976.

12. See Winnicott 1971.

13. This is because of the lack of object contact in an already preoedipally arrested individual.

14. Susan Gilbert had been her schoolmate and became her brother's wife.

15. Cody points out (433) the death wishes the poet expressed toward her father in her poetry, using the symbol of the sun.

16. See final chapter of Wolff 1986.

17. See Grolnick and Baskin 1978, 546.

18. See Loewald 1988.

19. Attuned contact involves a continuing, containing, and empathically responsive presence.

20. Ogden (1986) believes that symbolic expression includes three psychic perspectives: the thing signified, the symbol used as a signifier, and the self observing its own mode of signification.

21. See Susan Derin's writing on the symbol as the link between the self and the object in Grolnick and Baskin 1978.

22. See Sheldon Bach 1985 on self-state splits in the narcissistic patient.

## 13. Edith Sitwell I: The Demon Lover, Poetry, and Writer's Block

1.  See Cody 1971 on Dickinson's sun imagery as paternal symbolism (e.g., p. 433).

2.  See also *The Scarlet Tree* (Osbert Sitwell 1975, 157 and 283).

3.  See also Salter and Harper 1976, p. 37.

4.  Bromberg 1985 writes of the narcissistic character as living behind a mask.

5. In terms of endopsychic structure, the role the poet's father plays in her mind can be seen as that of Fairbairn's internal sabateur or antilibidinal ego.

6. George Sitwell was obsessed with plans to rebuild the family palace in England (Renishaw) as well as with his reconstruction of his Italian purchase, the mammoth and decayed castle of Montegufoni (see Pearson and Glendinning).

7. See Pearson and Glendinning.

8. See Sexton 1981 (*The Complete Poems*) and McClatchy 1978.

9. See Schwartz-Salant, 1982.

10. She was living with her brother Osbert at Renishaw at the time of writing her later poems.

11. Pine (1985) has written of how borderline children continually express images of fiery heat and frigid coldness, images which never get assimilated and integrated.

12. See the reunion fantasy described by Masterson 1976.

## 14. Edith Sitwell II: The Aging Narcissist

1. The defensive use of the idealized part object—here called the male muse—was originally commented on by Fairbairn and Klein. Fairbairn sees the developmentally arrested person as defending against inner bad-object experience by attempting to merge with an external idealized object. Melanie Klein speaks of idealization of an external object as a defense against strong aggressive instincts, particularly in relation to envy and greed.

2. See *The Indigo Blanket* by Elizabeth Salter.

3. Her parents' marriage was a cold one (see Pearson). The father and mother lived separate lives, the father studying in libraries, while the mother entertained guests perpetually in their homes. The father abandoned his wife to a court trial, and to imprisonment where she ran up debts.

4. Sun imagery is an archetypical symbol for the father and his paternal power. It is seen in Emily Dickinson's poetry as well.

5. I refer to "usage" in Winnicott's (1968) sense of the use of the object and to his discussion of all transitional phenomena.

6. She expressed such regrets in her portrayal of Queen Elizabeth I in a biography (see Glendinning).

7. See Kernberg (1975) on the "unrelenting" devaluation of the narcissist.

8. See Edmund Bergler ([1899] 1950) for a description of the use of the grandiose defense in the writer.

9. In his studies of creativity, Stanley Stark (1968) highlights the distinction between objective creativity and subjective creative expression by contrasting "novelty creativity" with what he calls "meaning creativity."

10. Or a "selfobject" in the language of self psychology.

11. See Klein's ([1937] 1975) *Love, Guilt, and Reparation* and Hanna Segal ([1964] 1975).

12. Glendinning speaks of this cry from the darkness in describing one literary critic's response to the "horror" experienced when reading Sitwell's novel *I Live under A Black Sun*.

13.  As opposed to a neurotic or "rapprochement narcissist." See S. Johnson 1987 on the rapprochement narcissist.

14.  D. W. Winnicott (1965) refers to such intrusion as "impingement."

15.  This aspect of psychic arrest is seen by D. W. Winnicott as stemming from the failed separateness of the mother, which he refers to as the mother's "survival" in the face of infant aggression and autonomous strivings.

16.  An example of such satire is that of "Jane, Jane, Tall as a crane . . . " from "Aubade" (c. 1913) (Salter and Harper 1976, 79–80).

## 15.  The Turn to Psychoanalytic Psychotherapy

1.  The belief of the female love addict that there is only one man who can give her life is a sign of the unconscious fantasy of the "god-daddy" or of the demon-lover father-god, discussed here in relation to female writers with father obsessions.

2.  Such postperformance depression could be compared to postpartum depression.

3.  Her projections are really more accurately called projective identifications in that she remained partially merged with me and others in her fantasies. What she imagined was coming from me was a part of her (such as her opinions) with which she also identified with. She could not get rid of what she emotionally and psychically put into me. Thus, her projective mechanisms differed from neurotic projection, in which there is a more intrapsychic separation between self and other. Also, she displayed the controlling coercion of projective identification by trying to force me to be what she imagined me to be, or by attempting to force me to think what she imagined me to think.

4.  Ms. A. had been talking about Barbara's abusive behavior toward her for several years, but prior to this session she had been unable to terminate their relationship.

5.  Ms. A. used the term "black sheep" within this session and often described herself as her family's scapegoat. Earlier, during the session, she had noted that being on her own in the world was too complicated and that she would like to go back to the days when "mothers were mothers, fathers were fathers, and black sheeps were black sheeps, rather than bragging rebels."

6.  The split-off part of the internal world is sealed off and acts on the consciously owned self as a dissociated self-part. The self that is split and therefore sealed off is fused with the malevolent part object, that is, with the unintegrated demon aspect of the parent (mother-father).

7.  Generally seen as the losses of the past.

8.  Daniel Stern (1985, 131) distinguishes between the capacity in infants to sense how to elicit a response from the other and a capacity to do so with self-awareness.

9.  Ms. A. had two older sisters, one successful in her chosen career and the other totally preoccupied with being a mother.

10.  These cries for help were expressed indirectly through Ms. A.'s sickness, obsessions about suicide, and anguished expressions of pain. Her need to be indirect seems symptomatic of her shame about the infantile nature of her needs and especially about needing my help in particular.

11.  Winnicott's ideas on "holding" need to be understood in terms of how new, benign psychological internalizations can be formed only if emotional contact is achieved. If Ms. A. were still in a cocoon in which she shielded herself from affective contact in the moment, she could experience

holding only as a fantasy, not as an actual emotional penetration that can promote internalization of new modes of relationship. Mourning allowed affective contact to come about.

12. The negative ego ideal (also Fairbairn's "internal sub ") that she had incorporated from her mother was continually persecuting her with demands that she do more. Her internal chorus of female judges reflected this negative ego ideal, which induced unrelieved shame.

13. Her erotic desires were also displaced into these image modes of narcissistic goals.

14. Ronald Fairbairn (1952) was the first to emphasize the self-destructive, tenacious tie to the bad object, following Freud's description of the melancholic's pathological mourning in "Mourning and Melancholia" (1917). Fairbairn spoke about "holding on" to the bad object in the cases of preoedipal characters, whom he generally classified as schizoid.

15. Ms. A.'s boyfriend was also in treatment with a colleague of mine to whom I had referred him. He was in an extensive psychoanalysis and was making progress; this modified his aggression toward Ms. A. over time. Ms. A. could only appreciate that he was changing, as she began to acknowledge rather than disown her own aggression.

# References

Abrams, M. H., Donaldson, E. T., Smith, H., Adams, R. M., Monk, S. H., Fod, G. H., and Daiches, D. eds. 1962. *The Norton anthology of English literature*. New York: Norton.

Alpers, A. 1980. *The life of Katherine Mansfield*. New York: New Directions.

Alvarez, A. 1970. *The savage god*. New York: Bantam.

Appleton, W. S. 1981. *Fathers and daughters*. New York: Doubleday.

Bach, S. 1985. *Narcissistic states and the therapeutic process*. New York: Jason Aronson.

Balint, M. 1965. *Primary love and psychoanalytic technique*. London: Butler and Tanner.

———. 1979. *The basic fault*. New York: Brunner/Mazel.

Bassin, D. 1982. Woman's images of inner space; data towards expanded interpretive categories. *Int. Rev. Psycho-Anal.*, 9: 191–203.

Beebe, B., and F. M. Lachman 1988. The contribution of mother-infant mutual influence to the origins of self and object representations. *Psychoanalytic Psychology* 5 (4): 305–38.

Bell, Q. 1972. *Virginia Woolf: A Biography*. New York: Harcourt Brace Jovanovich.

Benjamin, J. 1988. *Bonds of love*. New York: Pantheon.

Bennet, P. 1990. *My life a loaded gun . . . Dickinson, Plath, Rich, and female creativity*. Urbana: Univ. of Illinois Press.

Bergler, Edmund. [1899] 1950. *The writer and psychoanalysis*. New York: Doubleday.

Bergman, M. 1987. *The anatomy of loving*. New York: Columbia Univ. Press.

Bond, A. 1989. *Who killed Virginia Woolf?* New York: Human Sciences.

Bollas, C. 1987. *The shadow of the object: psychoanalysis of the unthought known*. London.

Boswell, P. 1984. *Diane Arbus: A biography*. New York: Knopf.

Bowlby, 1969. *Attachment,* New York: Basic Books.

———. 1980. *Attachment and loss*. vol. 1 of *Attachment and Loss* New York: Basic Books.

Bradley, S., Beatty, R. C., and Long, E. H., et al., eds. 1962. *The American tradition in literature*. New York: Norton.

Breger, Louis. 1989. *The author as a psychoanalyst*. New York: New York Univ. Press.

Brent, L., and R. C. Resch. 1987. A paradigm of infant-mother reciprocity: A reexamination of emotional refueling. *Psychoanalytic Psychology* 4 (1): 15–31.

Bromberg, P. M. 1985. The mirror and the mask: On narcissism and psychoanalytic growth. *Contemporary Psychoanalysis* 19: 359–87.

Brontë, Charlotte. 1985. *Jane Eyre*. In *The Norton anthology of literature by women*, edited by S. M. Gilbert and S. Gubar. New York: Norton. 347–734.

———. 1933. *Legends of Angria*. Edited by Fannie E. Ratchford and William Clyde De Vane. New Haven: Yale Univ. Press.

———. 1985. *Villette*. Edited by Tanner, T. New York: Penguin.

Brontë, Emily. 1941. *The complete poems of Emily Jane Brontë*. Edited from the manuscripts by C. W. Hatfield. New York: Columbia Univ. Press.

———. 1965. *Wuthering Heights*. Edited by Daiche, D. and Hamondsworth, Middlesex, England and New York: Penguin Books.

Butscher, E. 1976. *Sylvia Plath: Method and madness*. New York: Simon & Schuster.

Caper, R. 1988. *Immaterial facts*. New York: Jason Aronson.

Chicago, J. 1977. *Through a flower*. New York: Bantam.

Cody, J. 1971. *After great pain: The inner life of Emily Dickinson*. Cambridge: Harvard Univ. Press.

Cohen, R. O. 1988. Psychoanalytic aspects of pregnancy. In *Critical psychophysical passages in a life of a women*, edited by J. Zuckerberg, 103–20. New York: Plenum.

Coltrera, J. T., ed. 1981. *Lives, events and other players*. New York: Jason Aronson.

Daiche, D. 1965. *Introduction to Wuthering Heights*. New York and Hamondsworth, England, Penguin Books.

Dickinson, E. 1960. The complete poems of Emily Dickinson. Edited by T. M. Johnson. Boston: Little, Brown.

Ellenberger, H. F. 1972. The story of "Anna O." A critical review with new data. *Journal of the History of Behavioral Sciences*, 8: 267–79.

Fairbairn, R. D. 1952. *Psychoanalytic studies of the personality*. London: Routledge.

Ferlazzo, P. J. 1976. *Emily Dickinson*. Boston: Twayne.

Frank, Katharine. 1990. *A chainless soul: A life of Emily Brontë*. Boston: Houghton Mifflin.

Fraser, R. 1988. *The Brontës: Charlotte Brontë and her family*. New York: Fawcett Columbine.

Freud, S. 1914. On narcissism: an Introduction, in *Collected Papers*, Vol. IV, 30–59.

———. 1917. Mourning and melancholia, in *Collected Papers*, Vol. IV, 30–59.

Gaskell, E. [1857] 1983. *The life of Charlotte Brontë*. Edited by Alan Shelston. New York: Penguin.

Gedo, J. 1983. *Portraits of the artist*. New York: Guilford.

———. 1989. A Psychoanalysts response (133–152) collected in *Michelangelo's sistine chapel* (1989), by Jerome D. Oremland.

Gerin, W. 1971. *Emily Brontë*. New York: Oxford Univ. Press.

Gilbert, S. M., and S. Gubar. 1979. *Mad woman in the attic*. New Haven: Yale Univ. Press.

———. 1985. *The Norton Anthology of Literature By Women*. New York: Norton.

Glendinning, V. 1981. *Edith Sitwell. A unicorn among lions*. New York: Knopf.

Gorkin, M. 1984. Narcissistic personality disorder and pathological mourning. *Contemporary Psychoanalysis* 20 (3): ..–. . .

Greenacre, P. 1960. Woman as artist. In *Emotional growth II*, 575–91. Madison, Connecticut: International Univ. Press.

Grolnick, S. A., and L. Baskin. 1978. *Between reality and fantasy*. New York: Jason Aronson.

Grosskurth, P. 1986. *Melanie Klein, her world and her work*. New York: Knopf.

Grotstein, J. S. 1987. eds. Milman, D. and Goldman, G. An object relations perspective on resistance in narcissistic patients. In *Techniques of working with resistance*, 317–338. New York: Jason Aronson.

Grunes, M. 1984. The therapeutic object relationship. *Psychoanalytic Review* 71 (1): 123–43.

Guntrip, H. 1976. *Schizoid phenomena, object relations, and the self*. New York: International Univ. Press.

Hatfield, C. W. 1941. *The complete poems of Emily Jane Brontë*. Edited from the manuscripts by C. W. Hatfield. New York: Columbia Univ. Press.

Heiman, P. 1942. A contribution to the problem of sublimation, and its relation to processes of internalization. Paper given at the British-Psychoanalytic Society. *International Journal of Psycho-Analysis*, 22, 8–17.

Higgins, D. 1967. *Portrait of Emily Dickinson*. New Brunswick, N.J.: Rutgers Univ. Press.

Hintz, J. 1973. *The mirror and the garden*. New York: Harcourt Brace Jovanovich.

Hinz, E. J. 1973. The mirror and the garden. New York: Harcourt Brace Jovanovich.

Homans, M. 1980. *Women writers and poetic identity*. Princeton: Princeton Univ. Press.

Horner, A. 1984. *Object relations and the developing ego in psychotherapy*. New York: Jason Aronson.

———. 1988. *The wish for power and the fear of having it*. New York: Jason Aronson.

Horney, K. 1967. *Feminine psychology*. New York: Norton.

Hyman, Virginia. 1983. The autobiographical present in "a sketch of the past." *Psychoanalytic Review* 70 (19): 24–32.

Hymer, S. 1983. The therapeutic nature of art in self reparation. *Psychoanalytic Review* 70 (1): 57–98.

Inhelder, B. and Jean Piaget 1958. The growth of logical thinking. New York: Basic Books.

Jacobson, E. 1954. The self and the object world. *The Psychoanalytic Study of the Child* 9:75–127.

———. 1964. *The self and the object world*. Madison, Conn.: International Univ. Press.

Joffe, W. G., and J. Sandler 1965. Notes on pain, depression and individuation. *The Psychoanalytic Study of the Child* 20: 394–424.

Johnson, S. 1987. *The humanizing of the narcissistic style*. New York: Jason Aronson.

Johnson, T. H. 1960. *The complete poems of Emily Dickinson*. Boston: Little, Brown.

Kavaler, S. 1987. *The nightmare: Psychological and biological foundations*. New York: Columbia Univ. Press.

Kavaler, S. A. 1985. Mirror, mirror on the wall . . . *Journal of Comprehensive Psychotherapy* 5: 1–38.

———. 1986. Lord of the mirrors and the demon lover. *American Journal of Psychoanalysis* 46 (4): 336–44.

———. 1988a. The father's role in the self development of his daughter. In *Critical psychophysical passages in the life of women*, edited by J. Zuckerberg, . . .–. . . New York: Plenum, 49–65.

————. 1988b. Diane Arbus and the demon lover. *American Journal of Psychoanalysis* 48 (4): 366–70.

————. 1989a. Anne Sexton and the demonic lover. *American Journal of Psychoanalysis* 49 (2): 105–14.

————. 1990. Charlotte Brontë and the feminine self. *American Journal of Psychoanalysis*. 50(1), 37–43.

Kavaler-Adler, S. 1991a. Emily Dickinson and the subject of seclusion. *American Journal of Psychoanalysis* 51 (1): 21–38.

————. 1991b. Object relations insights concerning the female as artist. In *Psychoanalytic Perspectives on Women,* edited by Elaine Segal. Monograph no. 4 in *Current issues in psychoanalytic practice.* New York: Brunner/Mazel, 100–120.

————. 1991c. A theory of creative process reparation and its mode of failure: The case of Katherine Mansfield. *Psychoanalysis and Psychotherapy* 9 (2): 134–50.

————. 1992a. Anaïs Nin and the developmental use of the creative process. *Psychoanalytic Review* 79 (1): 73–88.

————. 1992b. The aging decline of two untreated borderline geniuses: Virginia Woolf and Edith Sitwell. *Psychoanalysis and Psychotherapy* 10 (1): 77–100.

————. 1992c. The process and conflict theory of Melanie Klein. *American Journal of Psychoanalysis.* In press.

————. 1992d. Mourning and erotic transference. *International Journal of Psychoanalysis,* vol. 73 (3), 527–539.

Kernberg, O. 1975. *Borderline conditions and pathological narcissism.* Newvale, New Jersey: Jason Aronson.

————. 1980. *Internal world and external reality.* Newvale, NJ: Jason Aronson.

————. 1988. Object relations theory in clinical practice. *The Psychoanalytic Quarterly* 42 (4): 481–504.

Khan, M. 1974. *The privacy of the self.* New York: International Univ. Press.

Klein, M. [1930] 1975. The importance of symbol-formation in the development of the ego. In *Love, guilt and reparation and other works—1921–1945.* London: Hogarth.

————. [1936] 1975. Weaning. In *Love, guilt and reparation and other works—1921–1945.* London: Hogarth. 219–232.

————. [1937] 1975. Love, guilt and reparation. In *Love, guilt and reparation and other works—1921–1945.* London: Hogarth, 306–343.

————. [1940] 1975. Mourning and its relation to manic-depressive states. In *Love, guilt and reparation and other works—1921–1945.* London: Hogarth. 344–369.

————. [1946] 1975. Notes on some schizoid mechanisms. In *Envy and gratitude and other works—1946–1963.* London: Hogarth. 1–24.

————. [1957] 1975. Envy and gratitude. In *Envy and gratitude and other works—1946–1963.* London: Hogarth. 176–235.

Kligerman, C. 1980. Art and the self of the artist. *Advances in self psychology,* edited by A. Goldberg. New York: International Univ. Press. 383–396.

Knapp, B. 1978. *Anaïs Nin.* New York: Frederick Ungar.

Knies, E. A. 1969. The art of Charlotte Brontë. Athens: University of Ohio Press.

Kohut, H. 1971. *Analysis of the self*. Madison, Connecticut. International Univ. Press.

———. 1977. *The restoration of the self*. Madison, Connecticut: International Univ. Press.

———. 1978. Creativeness, Charisma, Group Psychology. *Search for the self*, volume II, 793–844. Madison, Connecticut. International Univ. Press.

Kohut, H. 1984. *How does analysis cure?* Chicago: Univ. of Chicago Press.

Kris, E. 1956. On some vicissitudes of insight in psychoanalysis. *International Journal of Psychoanalysis* 37: 445–55.

Kubie, L. 1958. *The neurotic distortion of the creative process*. New York: Farrar, Straus & Giroux.

Leonard, L. S. 1984. *The father-daughter wound*. Boston: Shambhala Press.

———. 1986. The demon lover. In *On the way to the wedding*. Boston: Shambhala Press.

Loewald, H. 1962. Internalization, separation, mourning, and the superego. *Psychoanalytic Quarterly* 31: 484–504.

———. 1979. The waning of the Oedipus complex. In *Papers on psychoanalysis* (1980). New Haven: Yale Univ. Press.

———. 1988. *Sublimation*. New Haven: Yale Univ. Press.

Mahler, M. S., F. Pine, A. Bergmen 1975. *The psychological birth of the human infant*. New York: Jason Aronson.

Mansfield, K. 1956. *Stories*. Selected and with an introduction by Elizabeth Bowen. New York: Knopf.

Masterson, J. 1976. *Psychotherapy of the borderline adult: A developmental approach*. New York: Brunner/Mazel.

———. 1981. *Narcissistic and borderline disorders*. New York: Brunner/Mazel.

———. 1985. *The real self*. New York: Brunner/Mazel.

McClatchy, J. D., ed. 1978. *Anne Sexton: The artist and her critics*. Bloomington: Indiana Univ. Press.

McDougall, J. 1980. *A plea for a measure of abnormality*. Madison, Conn.: International Univ. Press.

McNeil, H. 1981. *Emily Dickinson*. New York: Virago.

Mendell, D. 1988. Early female development from birth through latency. In *Critical psychophysical passages in the life of women*, edited by J. Zuckerberg. New York: Plenum. 17–36.

Meyers, J. 1978. *Katherine Mansfield*. New York: New Directions.

Mitchell, S. 1988. *Relational concepts in psychoanalysis*. Cambridge: Harvard Univ. Press.

Miller, A. 1979. Depression and grandiosity as related forms of narcissistic disturbances. *International Journal of Psychoanalysis* 6: 61–76.

———. 1986. *Prisoners of childhood*. New York: Basic Books.

Modell, A. 1975. A narcissistic defense against effects and the illusion of self-sufficiency. *International Journal of Psychoanalysis* 56: 275–82.

———. 1976. "The holding environment" and the therapeutic action of psychoanalysis. *Journal of the American Psychoanalytic Association* 24: 285–308.

Monick, E. 1987. *Phallos: sacred image of the masculine*. Toronto: Inner City Books.

Newman, C., ed. 1971. *The art of Sylvia Plath*. Bloomington: Indiana Univ. Press.

Nin, A. 1986. *Diary, 1903–1977*. Chicago: Swallow.

———. 1958. *House of incest*. Chicago: Swallow.

———. 1958. *Solar Bauque*. Edwards Brothers New York.

———. 1959. *Children of the albatross*. Chicago: Swallow.

———. 1959. *Ladders to fire*. Chicago: Swallow.

———. 1959. *Under a glass bell*. Chicago: Swallow.

———. 1961. *Winter of artifice*. Chicago: Swallow.

———. 1964. *Collages*. Chicago: Swallow.

———. 1966. *In favor of the sensitive man and other essays*. New York: Harcourt Brace Jovanovich.

———. 1966. *Four chambered heart*. Chicago: Swallow Press.

———. 1968. *The novel of the future*. New York: Macmillan.

———. 1973. *Seduction of the minotaur*. Chicago: Swallow.

———. 1974. *A spy in the house of love*. New York: British Book Centre, 1954.

Ogden, T. H. 1986. *The matrix of the mind*. Newvale, New Jersey: Jason Aronson.

———. 1989. *The primitive edge of experience*. Newvale, New Jersey: Jason Aronson.

Onhelder, B. and Jean Piaget. 1958. The growth of logical thinking. New York: Basic Books.

Oremland, J. D. 1989. *Michelangelo's Sistine ceiling: a psychoanalytic study of creativity*. Madison, Conn.: International Univ. Press.

Orgel, S. 1981. Fusion with the victim: A study of Sylvia Plath. In *Lives, events and other players*, edited by J. T. Coltrera. New York: Jason Aronson, 123–172.

Panken, S. 1983. Working through and the novel. *The Psychoanalytic Review* 70 (1): 4–23.

———. 1987. *Virginia Woolf and the lust of creation: A psychoanalytic exploration*. Albany: State Univ. of New York Press.

Pearson, J. 1978. *The Sitwells*. New York: Harcourt Brace Jovanovich.

Peters, M. 1986. *Unquiet soul: A biography of Charlotte Brontë*. New York: Atheneum.

Pieget, J. 1954. The construction of reality in the child. New York: Basic Books.

———. 1969. *The psychology of the child*. New York: Basic.

Pine, F. 1985. *Developmental theory and clinical process*. New Haven: Yale Univ. Press.

Plath S. 1961. *Ariel*. New York: Harper & Row.

———. 1968. *The colossus*. New York: Vintage.

———. 1970. *The savage god*. New York: Bantam.

———. 1971. *Crossing the water*. New York: Harper and Row.

———. 1972. *The bell jar*. New York: Bantam.

———. 1977. *Letters home*. New York: Bantam.

———. 1982. *The journals of Sylvia Plath*. New York: Dial.

Pollock, G. K. 1975. Mourning and memoralization through music. *Annual of Psychoanalysis* 5: 423–36.

————. 1977a. The mourning process and creative organizational change. *Journal of the American Psychoanalytic Association* 25: 3–34.

————. 1982. The mourning-liberation process and creativity: The case of Kathe Kollwitz. *Annual of Psychoanalysis* 10: 333–52.

————. 1987. *Psychoanalytic studies of biography*. Madison, Conn.: International Univ. Press.

Quinn, S. 1987. *A mind of her own: The life of Karen Horney*. New York: Summit.

Reich, A. 1940. A contribution to the psychoanalysis of extreme submissiveness in women. In *Psychoanalytic contributions 1973*. Madison, Connecticut: International Univ. Press.

————. 1953. Narcissistic object choice in women. In *Psychoanalytic contributions 1973*. Madison, Connecticut: International Univ. Press.

Salter, E. 1967. *The last years of a rebel: A memoir of Edith Sitwell*. Boston: Houghton Mifflin.

Salter, E., and A. Harper. eds. 1976. Collection of Edith Sitwell's poetry, *Edith Sitwell: Fire of the mind*. New York: Vanguard.

Sandler, J., and W. G. Joffe. 1969. Towards a basic psychoanalytic model. *International Journal of Psychoanalysis*, 50: 79–90.

Schwartz-Salant, N. 1982. *Narcissism and character transformation: The psychology of narcissistic character disorders*. Toronto: Inner City Books.

Segal, H. 1952. A psychoanalytic approach to aesthetics. *International Journal of Psychoanalysis* 33: 196–207.

————. [1964] 1975. *Introduction to the work of Melanie Klein*. London: Hogarth.

————. 1986. The work of Hanna Segal. Edited by Jason Aronson. Newvale, New Jersey.

————. 1985. *The work of Hanna Segal*. New York: Jason Aronson.

Sewall, R. 1974. *The life of Emily Dickinson*. New York: Farrar, Straus & Giroux.

Sexton, Anne. 1981. *The complete poems*. Boston: Houghton Mifflin.

Silverman, M. A., and N. P. Will. 1986. The failure of emotional self-repair through poetry. *Psychoanalytic Quarterly* 55 (11): . . .–. . .

Sitwell, Edith 1965. *Taken care of*. New York: Atheneum.

Sitwell, Osbert. 1977, original 1948. *Left hand, right hand*. 4 vols. London: Quartet Books.

Sitwell, O. 1977, original 1944. *The Cruel Month*, vol. 1 of *Left hand, right hand*, London: Quartet Books.

————. 1977. *The scarlet trees*. Vol. 2 of *Left hand, right hand*. London: Quartet Books.

————. 1977. *Great morning*. Vol. 3 of *Left hand, right hand*. London: Quartet Books.

————. 1977. *Laughter in the next room*. Vol. 4 of *Left hand, right hand*. London: Quartet Books.

Spencer, S. 1977. *Collage dreams: The writings of Anaïs Nin*. New York: Harcourt Brace Jovanovich.

Spieler, S. 1984. Preoedipal girls need fathers. *Psychoanalytic Review:* 71 (1), 63–79.

Spitz, R. A. 1983. *Dialogues from infancy—Selected papers*. Edited by R. N. Emde. New York: International Univ. Press.

Stark, S. 1968. On the confounding of creativity contexts: Maslow's psychology of science. *Psychological Reports* 23: 88–90.

Stern, D. 1985. *The interpersonal world of the infant*. New York: Jason Aronson.

————. Fall 1989. The world of the infant. Lecture given at the New York Academy of Medicine, by the Association for the Advancement of Psychoanalysis.

Stevenson, Anne. 1989. *Bitter fame*. Boston: Houghton, Mifflin.

Stolorow, R., and F. Lachmann 1980. *Psychoanalysis of developmental arrests*. New York: International Univ. Press.

Stone, I. 1934. *Lust for life*. New York: New American.

Tanner, T. 1985. Introduction to Villette. New York: Penguin.

Tessman, L. H. 1978. *Children of parting parents*. New York: Classics Jason Aronson.

————. 1982. A note on the father's contribution to the daughter's ways of loving and working. In *Father and child: developmental and clinical perspectives*. Boston: Little, Brown. Editors are Coth, S. H. Gurrivitt, A. & Gunsberg, L.

————. 1989. Early Tones, Later Echoes. In *Fathers and Their Families*, ed. by Cath, S. H. et al. Hillsdale, New Jersey. Here & London: The Analytic Press.

Tomalin, C. 1988. *Katherine Mansfield: A secret life*. New York: Knopf.

Wagner-Martin, L. W. 1987. *Sylvia Plath*. New York: Simon & Schuster.

Winnicott, D. W. 1953. Transitional objects and transitional phenomena. Collected in *Playing and reality* (1971). Middlesex, England: Penguin.

————. 1965. *The maturational processes and the facilitating environment*. New York: International Univ. Press.

————. 1967. Mirror-role of Mother and Family in Child Development, collected in *Playing and reality* (1971). Middlesex, England: Penguin Books.

————. 1968. Interrelating in terms of cross identifications. Collected in *Playing and reality* (1971). Middlesex, England: Penguin.

Winnicott, D. W. (1969). "The use of the object and reality through identifications," collected in *Playing and Reality,* 1971. Middlesex, England: Penguin Books.

————. 1971. *Playing and reality*. Middlesex, England: Penguin.

Wisdom, J. O. 1961. A methodological approach to the problem of hysteria. *International Journal of Psychoanalysis,* 42: 224–37.

Wise, T. J. and Symington, J. A., eds. (1932). The Brontës: their lives, friendships, and correspondence, 4 vols. Oxford: Shakespeare Head Press.

Wolfenstein, M. 1966. How is mourning possible? *The Psychoanalytic Study of the Child* 21: 93–123.

————. 1968. Loss, rage, and repetition. *The Psychoanalytic Study of the Child* 24: 432–60.

Wolff, C. G. 1986. *Emily Dickinson*. New York: Knopf.

Woodman, M. 1982. *Addiction to perfection: The still unravished bride*. Toronto: Inner City Books.

————. 1985. *The pregnant virgin: A process of psychological transformation*. Toronto: Inner City Books.

Zaller, R. ed. 1974. *A casebook of Anaïs Nin*. New York: Signet.

Zucherberg, J. ed. 1988. *Critical psychophysical passages in the life of a woman*. New York: Pleneum Press.

# Index

Abandonment depression, 17–18
Acting-out, 179–180
*Addiction to Perfection: The Still Unravished Bride* (Woodman), 77–78, 226
*After Great Pain* (Cody), 219
Agency, mourning and, 45–46
Alvarez, A., 100
*The Anatomy of Loving* (Bergman), 9
Anorexia, 190
Antiheroes, 164
Appleton, W., 63–64
A priori psychology, 66
"As one does Sickness over" (Dickinson), 230–231
Authenticity, creative expression and, 291–292
"Aye, There It Is" (E. Brontë), 166

Bad objects, concept of, 13–14
Balint, Michael, 9, 22, 26, 306
Beckett, Samuel, 136
Beebe, B., 24–25
Bell, Quentin, 32
*The Belle of Amherst* (play), 223
*The Bell Jar* (Plath), 83, 101
Benjamin, Jessica, 28, 62, 334n.6
Bergman, Martin, 9, 10
Bond, Alma, 3
*Borderline Conditions and Pathological Narcissism* (Kernberg), 279–280
Borderline complex, 185, 189, 305–306, 336n.11
Bowles, Samuel, 205
Breger, Louis, 284
Brontë, Anne, 110
Brontë, Branwell, 109–110
Brontë, Charlotte

Emily Brontë compared to, 172
creative process and interpersonal relations, 103
creative work and level of psychological development, 38
Dickinson compared to, 243–244
life of and *Jane Eyre*, 105–120
object relations-oriented psychotherapeutic treatment, 326
psychoanalytic interpretation of *Villette*, 121–153
publication of childhood tales, 332n.2
relationship with father, 182–183, 332n.1, 7
Sitwell compared to, 297
Brontë, Emily
critical response to *Wuthering Heights*, 111
death of and Charlotte Brontë, 110
demon lover as literary theme, 23, 168–191, 218
Dickinson compared to, 210, 334n.5
male muse and demon lover, 156–167
muse-gods and internal objects, 333n.1
object relations-oriented psychotherapeutic treatment, 325–326
Plath compared to, 102–104
psychic development compared to Charlotte Brontë, 142, 148, 172
publication of poetry and life of, 111, 154–156
whole object character symbolization, 245
*Wuthering Heights* and demon lover, 168–191, 218
Browning, Elizabeth Barrett, 204
Butscher, E., 101

Catholicism, Sitwell and, 276–277
*Children of the Albatross* (Nin), 94
Chomsky, Noam, 66
Cody, John, biography of Dickinson, 192–248, 335n.15
Coleridge, Samuel Taylor, 77
*Collage Dreams* (Spencer), 92–93, 95, 96
"Colonel Fantock" (Sitwell), 256
"Colossus" (Plath), 98
Creative process
    and Charlotte Brontë's level of psychic development, 149, 151, 152–153
    case study in psychoanalytic psychotherapy, 299–324
    Dickinson and reparation, 228–238, 241–244
    father's role in female, 61–69
    as mother, 35
    mourning and reparation through, 52–58
    objective and subjective creative expression, 336n.9
    pathological mourning and developmental arrest, 285–288
    preoedipal arrest and trauma in adult artists, 20
    psychoanalytic studies of in women, 59–61
    psychological uses of, 4–5
    self psychology versus object relations theory, 5–11
    self-validation and, 327n.5
    Sitwell and developmental arrest, 288–289
    women authors and developmental limitations, 298

"Daddy" (Plath), 98–99, 103
Daiche, David, 174, 176
Death. *See also* Suicide
    creative women and demon lover theme, 82–83
    fantasies of in works of preoedipal- or paranoid-schizoid position women, 262

images of in literary works of Emily Brontë, 155–156, 166, 187, 191
images of in poetry of Dickinson, 201–202, 217–220, 240
Sitwell and demon lover theme, 265
"Death and Co." (Plath), 333n.2
Demonic object, 41–42
Demon lover
    in Charlotte Brontë's *Villette*, 126–127, 149
    in Emily Brontë's poetry and prose, 156–167, 168–191
    case study in psychoanalytic psychotherapy, 299–324
    creative women and muse, 75
    Dickinson's poetry and, 213–214, 217–220
    and father-mother object, 35–39
    female love addict and father-god, 337n.1
    internal father as source of literary theme of, 23
    myth of, 76–77
    object relations theorists on, 86–87
    Plath and developmental arrest, 101–102
    as psychodynamic complex, 77–84
    reparative motif in theme of, 58
    Sitwell's poetry and theme of, 260, 261, 262–263, 265, 288, 289–291, 293–294
    and Sitwell's relationship with Tchelitchew, 272
    symptomatic literary theme of, 84–85
    and work of Annie Reich, 85–86
Depressive position
    Charlotte Brontë's *Villette* and, 142–145, 149
    Kleinian theory of, 43–53
Deutsch, Helene, 60
Development, psychological
    Charlotte Brontë's level of, 145–152
    of Charlotte and Emily Brontë compared, 142
    creative motivation in women and father-daughter relationship, 63–64
    summary of issues concerning female growth, 69–74

Developmental arrest. *See also* Preoedipal arrest
Emily Brontë and *Wuthering Heights*,
179, 186–187
case study in psychoanalytic psychotherapy, 299–324
concept of, 25–26
Dickinson and creative work, 246–247
father and female creativity, 67–69
internal father and preoedipal-level
women, 74
mothers role in, 337n.15
oedipal-level women and, 73–74
pathological mourning and creative
work process, 285–288
Plath and other psychically arrested creative women, 101–104
Sitwell and creative process, 288–289,
294–295
Dialogue, Sitwell and creative process,
287, 288
Dickinson, Emily
change in self-structure, 226–227
Emily Brontë compared to, 158, 184,
185, 334n.5
life of and relationship with father,
192–220
manic defense and feminine identity,
239–240
object relations-oriented psychotherapeutic treatment, 325–326
paranoid-schizoid position and creative
works of, 247–248
Plath compared to, 102–104
reparation and creative process, 228–
238, 241–244
sadomasochism and internal mother-father, 36–37
seclusion and psychic breakdown,
221–226
Sitwell's poetry compared to that of,
260, 290–291
symbolization in poetry of, 244–247
themes of death in works of, 82, 83
Differentiation, self and object, 11–12
Dominance, male. *See also* Patriarchy;
Sexism
and poetry of Emily Brontë, 163

symbols of in Charlotte Brontës *Villette*, 132–133
Dostoyevsky, Fyodor Mikhaylovich, 284
Dream king, Dickinson's images of,
209–211

"Edge" (Plath), 101
Education, of Charlotte Brontë, 107–108,
109
Ego
creative motivation in women and father-daughter relationship, 63–64,
67–69
negative ideal, 338n.12
observing-ego development, 20–21
use of terms, 330n.6
Eliot, George, 121
Emerson, Ralph Waldo, 162
"Eurydice" (Sitwell), 266–267

Fairbairn, Ronald
defensive use of idealized part object,
336n.1
demon lover theme, 80, 84, 86–87
mourning and object survival, 30
narcissism and self, 294
pathological mourning, 19
primitive mode of primary identification, 328n.28
psychic structure and internal bad objects, 329, 334n.2, 3
self-destructive tie to bad object,
338n.14
self and object differentiation, 11
tantalizing and rejecting object in schizoid personality, 333n.1
whole object internalization, 13, 24
*Fanfare for Elizabeth* (Sitwell), 249, 281
Father
ability of external to relate, 331n.7
Charlotte Brontë's relationship with,
112–116, 122, 126–130, 134,
147–149, 332n.1, 7
Emily Brontë's relationship with, 160,
181–185, 189–190
demon lover and, 23, 35–39, 78, 80–
81, 82
Dickinson's relationship with, 192–220

idealized and demonic, 330n.8
internal in preoedipal-level women, 74
intersubjective matrix and, 32–35
Nin's relationship with, 88, 89–96
object survival and, 30
Plath as creative woman, 97–100
role in female creativity, 61–69
Sitwell's relationship with, 250–268,
    272, 290–291, 292, 293, 295–298
Feminist theory. *See also* Gilbert, S. M.;
    Gubar, S.
importance of mother in psychic devel-
    opment, 34
language and male power in Victorian
    era, 160
Ferlazzo, P. J., 215, 218–219, 223, 228
*Four Chambered Heart* (Nin), 94
Frank, Katharine, 165, 170
Freud, Sigmund
    affective process and structure of psy-
        che and self, 46
    demon lover theme, 87
    description of melancholic's pathologi-
        cal mourning, 338n.14
    feminine turn from mother to father,
        175
    ideas about inner representational
        world, 4
    influence of negative views of women,
        59
    theory of triadic psychic structure, 31
"The Frost of Death Was on the Pane"
    (Dickinson), 217


Gaskell, Elizabeth, 106, 112, 113–114
Gedo, John, 7–9, 61, 62
Gerin, Winnifred, biography of Emily
    Brontë, 76, 154, 155, 156, 181–
    182, 188
Gilbert, S. M.
    feminist analysis of Dickinson's life
        and works, 203–204
    feminist critique of *Jane Eyre*, 117
    feminist critique of *Wuthering Heights*,
        170, 178, 185
    George Eliot on *Villette*, 121
    *Jane Eyre* compared to *Villette*,
        332n.11

Glendinning, Victoria, biography of Sit-
    well, 252–288, 336n.12
God. *See also* Religion
    Charlotte Brontë's view of in *Villette*,
        144
    Dickinson's poetry and images of, 195,
        197–198, 226–227
    and male muse in Emily Brontë's po-
        etry, 161
"Gold Coast Customs" (Sitwell), 259
Gorkin, M., 15
Greenacre, Phyllis, 59–60, 61–63
"Green Song" (Sitwell), 261–263, 272
Gubar, S.
    feminist analysis of Dickinson's life
        and works, 203–204
    feminist critique of *Jane Eyre*, 117
    feminist critique of *Wuthering Heights*,
        170, 178, 185
    George Eliot on *Villette*, 121
    *Jane Eyre* compared to *Villette*,
        332n.11
Guntrip, Harry, 14, 22


Heroes, Emily Brontë's romantic, 164
"He Saw My Heart's Woe" (C. Brontë),
    144
Higginson, Colonel, 204–205, 241
Homans, Margaret, on Emily Brontë,
    156, 158–159, 160, 164–165, 175,
    186, 190
Horner, Althea, 56–57
Horney, Karen, 59–61
*House of Incest* (Nin), 93–94


Identity, Dickinson and feminine, 239–
    240
"I Felt a Cleaving in my Mind" (Dickin-
    son), 225
*I Live Under a Black Sun* (Sitwell), 254–
    255, 257, 272, 287, 336n.12
"To Imagination" (E. Brontë), 156–158
Incorporation, use of term, 328n.28
Inhelder, B., 66
Internalization, mourning and, 46–47
Internal object, 24–25
Intersubjective matrix, 32–35
*I Was Born Under a Black Sun* (Sitwell),
    249

Jacobson, Edith, 24, 56
*Jane Eyre* (C. Brontë)
  and Charlotte Brontë's level of psychic development, 146–147
  effect on Charlotte Brontë's literary reputation, 105
  life of Charlotte Brontë and analysis of, 106–120
  *Villette* compared to, 121, 332n.11
Joffe, W. G., 16
"Julian M. and A. G. Rochelle" (E. Brontë), 161–165, 169

Kavaler, S. A., 334n.6
Kernberg, Otto
  father-mother figure, 34
  on grandiose self, 292
  roles of therapist and patient, 328n.25
  Sitwell and narcissism, 279–280, 283, 294
Khan, M., 22
"Kindness" (Plath), 100
Klein, Melanie
  defensive use of idealized part object, 336n.1
  demon lover theme, 84, 86–87
  depressive position, 43–53
  developmental mourning, 17, 40
  innate a priori phantasies, 66, 296
  malevolent internal part object, 13, 328n.14, 334n.2, 3
  manic-narcissistic defense, 292
  mothering and internal object, 24
  paranoid-schizoid position, 41, 42–43, 329n.3
  preoedipal development, 69–70
  psychic structure and bad objects, 329n.9
  psychic structure theory, 31
  self and object differentiation, 11
Kligerman, C., 7, 35
Knies, Earl, 125, 128, 140
Kohut, Heinz
  child's identification with second parent, 38
  healing powers of creative process, 6–10
  on preoedipal mothering, 26
  selfobject and internal self, 48

Kubie, Lawrence, 5, 20
"Kubla Khan" (Coleridge), 77

Lachmann, F. M., 24–25
*Ladders to Fire* (Nin), 94
"Lady Lazarus" (Plath), 97–98
Language, Emily Brontë and, 160–161. *See also* Voice
"Last Words" (Plath), 100
*Left Hand, Right Hand* (O. Sitwell), 251–252, 253–254
*Legends of Angria* (C. Brontë), 332n.2
Leonard, Linda Schierse, 77
Lindsay, Jack, 279
Loewald, Hans, 55
Lord, Judge Otis Philip, 206–208, 233

McDougall, Joyce, 188
McNeil, Helen, 195, 248
*The Madwoman in the Attic* (Gilbert & Gubar), 203–204
Mahler, Margaret
  creative process and mourning, 54
  developmental arrest, 25
  developmental mourning, 17
  father in mother and mother in father, 33
  internal object and object relations theory, 24
  preoedipal development, 69–70
  preoedipal mothering, 26, 27, 28
  psychic individuation and psychical separation, 333n.22
  psychic structure theory, 31
  self and object differentiation, 11, 12
  on symbiotic mother, 9
Manic defenses
  in Emily Brontë's poetry and prose, 180, 186
  depressive position and, 47–51
  Dickinson and feminine identity, 239–240, 246
Mansfield, Katherine, 10
Marriage
  Charlotte Brontë and psychic development, 112, 114–115, 131, 134, 153
  Dickinson and rejection of, 194, 208–209

Masterson, J.
 abandonment depression, 83
 developmental arrest and failure of ego
  ideal formation, 68
 external mothering object, 13
 father as preoedipal mother, 34
 manic defense, 48
 preoedipal mothering, 27
 psychic coloring of parental object, 22
 psychodynamics of borderline triad,
  305
*Michelangelo's Sistine Ceiling: A Psycho-
 analytic Study of Creativity* (Gedo),
 8
Miller, Alice, 7
*The Mirror and the Garden* (Nin), 93
Mirroring, 7, 28
Modell, A., 327n.3
Monick, Eugene, 65–66, 210
Mothers and mothering
 Charlotte Brontë's level of psychic development, 146, 150–151
 Emily Brontë's relationship with, 168
 creative process as, 35
 demon lover complex and creative
  women, 79–80
 Dickinson's relationship with, 192–
  193, 194, 219–220, 227, 243
 external object and role of, 12–13
 Nin's relationship with, 88–89
 paranoid-schizoid position and role of,
  42–43
 Plath and role of, 101, 331n.5
 preoedipal development and, 26–32
 of separation as transitional object,
  333n.30
 Sitwell's relationship with, 253, 295–
  298
Mourning, developmental. *See also*
  Mourning, pathological
 arrested in Charlotte Brontë's *Villette*,
  134–142
 case study in psychoanalytic psychotherapy, 305–318
 comparative dynamics of reparation,
  51–52
 creative women and developmental arrest, 103–104, 285–288

depressive position and internalization,
  46–47
 manic versus true reparation, 49–51
 and object relations theory, 15–17, 18–
  20
 object survival, 30
 process of, 40
 reparation through creative process,
  52–58
 self-reflection and, 21
 use of term, 3
Mourning, pathological. *See also* Mourning, developmental
 Emily Brontë's literary work and, 186–
  187
 Dickinson's relationships with men
  and, 203
 Freud's description of, 338n.14
 Sitwell and, 279, 285–288
Muse
 creative women and demon lover, 75
 defensive use of idealized part object,
  336n.1
 Emily Brontë and male, 155–167
 Sitwell's relationship with Tchelitchew,
  270–273
"My Life Had Stood a Loaded Gun"
  (Dickinson), 239–240

Narcissism, Edith Sitwell and, 279–298
"A Narrow Fellow in the Grass" (Dickinson), 215
Nature
 Dickinson's poetry and images of,
  196–197
 in Emily Brontë's life and literary
  works, 165, 173
 in life and creative works of Charlotte
  Brontë, 106
*Neurotic Distortion of the Creative Pro-
 cess* (Kubie), 5
Nicholls, Arthur, 112, 114–115
Nin, Anais
 Charlotte Brontë compared to, 148–
  149
 creative process and interpersonal relations, 103

demon lover theme and creative work of, 38
Plath compared to, 98, 101
portrait of as creative woman, 88–96
"No Coward Soul Is Mine" (E. Brontë), 186

Object relations theory. *See also* specific concepts
demon lover theme and, 86–87
Emily Brontë and language, 160–161
Plath and creative work, 101–102
psychological use of creative process, 4–5
self psychology and, 5–11
separation-individuation period, 11–23
Object survival, 29–30
Observing-ego development, 20–21
Oedipal-level women, developmental arrest and, 73–74
Ogden, Thomas H., 11–12, 34, 66, 245, 335n.20
*On The Way to the Wedding* (Leonard), 77
Oremland, J. D., 8
Orgel, Shelley, 101

Panken, Shirley, 3
*Papers on Metapsychology* (Freud), 4
Paranoid-schizoid position
Charlotte Brontë compared to other women writers, 151–152
Emily Brontë's literary works, 155, 177–181, 187
case study in psychoanalytic psychotherapy, 299–324
Dickinson's poetry and indications of, 247–248
phenomenological stasis of, 41–42
projective identification process, 327n.10
role of real mother in, 42–43
Sitwell's creative work and relationship with father, 296–297
Parents and parenting, 21–23. *See also* Father; Mothers and mothering
Patriarchy, 178. *See also* Dominance, male; Sexism

Pearson, George, 273, 275
Pearson, John, 250, 252
Peters, Margot, biography of Charlotte Brontë, 105–106, 108, 112–115, 125, 139, 332n.1
Phallocentrism, 60
*Phallos: Sacred Image of the Masculine* (Monick), 210
Piaget, J., 64, 66, 180
Pine, F., 336n.11
Plath, Sylvia
Emily Brontë's vision of death compared to, 187, 190
demon lover as literary theme, 23
Dickinson's demon lover poems compared to, 214
father and developmental arrest, 69
imprisonment theme in poetry, 333n.2
portrait of as creative woman, 97–104
sadomasochism and internal father-mother, 37
Sitwell compared to, 280
themes of death in works of, 82, 83
view of mother in works of, 331n.5
withdrawal from interpersonal relations, 327n.7
*A Plea for a Measure of Abnormality* (McDougall), 188
Poetry
Emily Brontë and psychic arrest, 154–167, 174
Dickinson's psychic breakdown and, 222–226
Edith Sitwell and narcissism, 249, 257–267, 271
Pollock, George, 53–54, 57
*Portraits of the Artist* (Gedo), 7, 62
Possession, literary myth of masculine, 159–160
*The Pregnant Virgin: A Process of Psychological Transformation* (Woodman), 78–79
Preoedipal arrest. *See also* Developmental arrest
adult artists and creative work, 20
Charlotte Brontë's level of psychic development, 146
Sitwell and narcissism, 288, 296

summary of theoretical issues, 71–72
Preoedipal development, summary of is-
    sues, 69–72
Preoedipal-level women
    Charlotte Brontë's level of psychic de-
        velopment, 152
    internal father and developmental ar-
        rest, 74
    oedipal father in, 211–214
Preoedipal mothering, 26–32
*The Professor* (C. Brontë), 105, 144
Projective identification, 14, 337n.3
Proust, Marcel, 52
Psychic arrest. *See* Developmental arrest;
    Preoedipal arrest
Psychic structure, dialectic of, 30–32
*Psychoanalytic Contributions* (Reich), 86
Psychoanalysis, case study in psychother-
    apy, 299–324
Psychobiography, 3–4

Reich, Annie, 85–86
Religion, Sitwell and Catholicism, 276–
    277. *See also* God
Reparation
    in Charlotte Brontë's *Villette*, 142–
        145, 151
    in Emily Brontë's *Wuthering Heights*,
        176–181
    comparative dynamics of, 51–52
    Dickinson and creative process, 228–
        238, 241–244
    manic versus true, 49–51
    primary criteria of true, 58
    Sitwell and failed, 283–285
    through creative process, 52–58
*Restoration of the Self* (Kohut), 6, 8

Sandler, J., 16
Satire, Sitwell's use of, 256–257
*The Savage God* (Alvarez), 100
Schwartz-Salont, Nathan, 296
*Seduction of the Minotaur* (Nin), 94
Segal, Hanna
    artist and depressive fantasies, 172
    comparative dynamics of reparation,
        51–52
    creative process and reparation, 52–53

father-mother in developmental se-
    quence, 34
manic versus true reparation, 49
regressive cognition of symbolic equa-
    tion, 245–246
self and object differentiation, 12
Self. *See also* specific concepts
    mothering and internal object, 24
    sealing off of, 14–15, 17–18
    Sitwell and grandiose, 292–294
    use of terms, 330n.6
    *Wuthering Heights* and Emily Brontë's
        subjective sense of, 180–181, 189
Self-integration, 12
Selfobject, 6–10
*The Self and the Object World* (Jacob-
    son), 56
Self psychology, 5–11
Self-reflection, 21
Self-structure, 226–227
Self-sufficiency, 8–9
Self-validation, 327n.5
Separation-individuation period, 11–23,
    141
Sewall, Richard, biography of Dickinson,
    194, 199, 200, 205, 208, 221, 222
Sexism. *See also* Dominance, male
    male chauvinism in *Villette*, 125, 126
    psychoanalytic studies of women and
        creativity, 60
Sexton, Anne, 102–104
Sexuality
    Charlotte Brontë and *Villette*, 131
    Dickinson and fear of, 206, 215–217
    demon lover as psychodynamic com-
        plex, 81
    "The Shadow of Cain" (Sitwell), 277–
        279
*Shirley* (C. Brontë), 105, 111
Sitwell, Edith
    critique of The Shadow of Cain, 277–
        279
    Dickinson's psychosis compared to,
        248
    narcissism in later life of, 279–298
    object relations-oriented psychothera-
        peutic treatment, 325–326
    Plath compared to, 102–104
    relationship with father, 250–268

relationship with Pavlik Tchelitchew, 267–268, 269–273
religion and muse-god, 276–277
summary of life, 249–250
tour of America, 273–276
whole object character symbolization, 245
Sitwell, Osbert, 251–252, 253–254, 261, 264
"Sleeping Beauty" (Sitwell), 249, 258
Smith, George, 131, 132
*Solar Barque* (Nin), 94
"The Song of the Cold" (Sitwell), 260, 261, 263–266, 272
Southey, Lord Robert, 109
Spencer, Sharon, 92–93, 95, 96
*A Spy in the House of Love* (Nin), 89, 94–95
Stark, Stanley, 336n.9
Stein, Gertrude, 267
Stern, Daniel
 affect-influencing memory, 328n.27
 developmental mourning, 16
 failure of self-agency, 333–334n.3
 infants and self-awareness, 337n.8
 Mahler's use of concept symbiosis, 329n.3
 mother-infant research, 328n.12, 13, 19
 parental engagement and self, 327n.4
 preoedipal mothering, 26, 27
 roles of father and mother in intersubjective matrix, 33
 self and object differentiation, 11–12
Stevenson, Quentin, 281, 282
"Still Falls the Rain" (Sitwell), 258, 280, 285–287, 298
Stone, Irving, 10
Subjective object, use of term, 334n.8
Suicide. *See also* Death
 Emily Brontë and *Wuthering Heights*, 190
 women writers and demon lover complex, 82, 166
Symbolization, poetry of Dickinson, 244–247

*Taken Care Of* (Sitwell), 250, 253, 282
Tanner, Tony, 131, 134, 136, 141

Taylor, Mary, 114
Tchelitchew, Pavlik, relationship with Sitwell, 267–268, 269–273, 274–275, 292
Tessman, Lora Heims, 62–65, 67, 68, 211
Thackeray, William Makepiece, 107
Transcendentalism, 162
Trauma
 creative process and preoedipal arrest, 20
 Dickinson and preoedipal, 195–196, 219–220
 Emily Brontë and *Wuthering Heights*, 171, 188
"Troy Park" (Sitwell), 249
"The Two Loves" (Sitwell), 270

van Gogh, Vincent, 7, 10
*Villette* (C. Brontë)
 Charlotte Brontë's relationship with father, 105
 compared to *Jane Eyre*, 116, 117, 118–119, 332n.11
 Dickinson's works compared to, 243–244
 life of Charlotte Brontë and, 111–112
 psychoanalytic interpretation of, 121–153
Voice. *See also* Language
 Charlotte Brontë's struggle for own, 141
 extinguishing of female in *Wuthering Heights*, 169, 170

Wagner-Martin, L. W., 101
Wells, Henry, 228
"Wild Nights—Wild Nights" (Dickinson), 207–208, 243
Winnicott, D. W.
 authenticity and self-development, 291
 depressive position and mothering, 43, 44, 47
 external mothering object, 13
 holding environment, 327n.3, 337n.11
 malevolent internal part object, 14
 mother-infant relationship, 13, 24, 26, 27, 29, 330n.10, 337n.15

object relations theory and creative process, 10–11
psychic coloring of parental object, 22
on role of therapist, 328n.22
self and object differentiation, 11
term transitional space, 330–331n.5
use of term mirroring, 7
use of term play, 334n.5
*Winter of Artifice* (Nin), 89, 90, 93
*The Wish for Power and the Fear of Having It* (Horner), 56–57
Wolfenstein, M., 54
Wolff, Cynthia Griffin, biography of Dickinson, 192, 193, 195, 208, 226–227, 233, 247, 248, 335n.6
Women writers
creative process and developmental limitations, 298
father's role in creativity, 61–69
as focus of study, 2

object relations-oriented psychotherapeutic treatment of, 324–326
psychoanalytic studies of creativity in, 59–61
Woodman, Marian, 77–79, 81–83, 226
Woolf, Virginia, 252, 255
Writers, women
Charlotte Brontë compared to paranoid-schizoid, 151–152
Charlotte Brontë and male literary world, 139, 140
creative process and developmental limitations, 298
as focus of study, 2–3
object relations-related psychotherapeutic treatment of, 324–326
*Wuthering Heights* (E. Brontë)
critical response to, 111
psychodynamics of demon lover theme, 168–191, 218